PRAISE ⌐∩□
CIVIL WAI

"Guy Saperstein's autobiography—*Civi*
Rights Attorney—is more than a Horat
and with realism litigation as it played ⌐
the last three decades. It takes the reader on the roller-coaster career of
an idealistic, anti-establishment activist through his student days at
Berkeley into public interest law, ending as the most successful private
civil rights lawyer in the country, measured by the extraordinary
recoveries obtained for his clients.

The trial strategy he describes—meticulous preparation, dedication
to your case, understand the position of your opponent, and be
yourself in court—is applicable to any type of trial work. Guy has
always been himself. He has never copied or followed anyone. He
describes in detail his non-conventional career as he saw and lived it.
He does not mince words or fail to identify those whom he felt were
wrong or whom he did not respect. While his achievements have been
phenomenal, the real interest in and significance of this book are in the
lessons it outlines—lessons for everyone, lawyer and non-lawyer alike.
Be yourself, do not be afraid to take risks; when you take on a task,
commit yourself, do it to the best of your ability. But above all—never
neglect your family, for they are the ones who are your life and give it
the value and meaning it has, no matter what you ultimately may do.

A very readable story—with its infectious zeal for life. It can inspire
others to strike out on their own, in accordance with their convictions,
with the confidence that it is the quality of their efforts that are a vital
part of their goal."
—Former United States District Judge Charles B. Renfrew

"This excellent book is a celebration of what can happen when a really
smart guy puts his talents and passion to work for the public good.
Civil Warrior offers an inspiration especially for young people as a path
to doing right and making a difference."
—Ben Cohen, Co-founder of Ben & Jerry's

"I've had the pleasure of watching Guy Saperstein in action as a lawyer, and
always knew I was seeing a master craftsman at work. This book makes
clear why. In today's line-your-pockets-quickly business culture, how often
do we get to see major corporations wriggle and squirm uncomfortably in
court, and ultimately go down to legal defeat? Saperstein has spent his life
defending the powerless against the powerful and, amazingly, winning. He

tells these stories here, he tells them well, and I hope tomorrow's idealistic young lawyers follow his lead."

— Adam Hochschild, Author, publisher of *Mother Jones* magazine

"Mr. Saperstein has written a compelling, high-energy story reminiscent of *A Civil Action* that provides proof positive that a dedicated civil rights lawyer can do good and at the same time do well. Mr. Saperstein's journey takes him from an under-achieving young rebel to the most successful employment discrimination attorney in the country. Law students and aspiring public interest attorneys in particular will find both inspiration and lessons to be learned in this highly memorable memoir."

— United States District Judge Thelton E. Henderson

"A wonderful book demonstrating that courage, commitment and clarity of purpose can overcome powerful special interest to eradicate social injustice. Guy's remarkable balance of his personal and professional life is a road map for all lawyers seeking to have both. His extraordinary success during the difficult and challenging times of the 70's, 80's and 90's is the stuff of legends. This book is a must read for all lawyers trying to find a way to fight for the less fortunate without taking a vow of poverty."

—John Burris, Oakland civil rights lawyer and author of *Blue vs. Black: Let's End the Conflict Between Cops and Minorities*

"Guy's story is a fascinating one which will inspire many. The story of how he surrendered to a spiritual force in order to find his way in the material world should persuade us all to rethink how we make our way in this perplexing yet beautiful world."

— Eva Paterson, Lawyers' Committee for Civil Rights

"With wit, humor, and decades of personal experiences, Guy Saperstein recounts how he practiced law as a 'whole life' experience. Few lawyers could sue a company for millions of dollars, as Guy did with State Farm Insurance, then be offered a job by the same company as their general counsel. *Civil Warrior* is fascinating reading."

—Jerry Brown, Mayor of Oakland

"A fascinating story, full of commitment and great truth. A classic American tale, and every page pulsates with life."

—Lawrence Ferlinghetti, Poet, founder of City Lights Bookstore

To Jeanine, my partner in all things

WITHDRAWN

CIVIL WARRIOR
Guy T. Saperstein

Memoirs of a
Civil Rights
Attorney

BHB
Berkeley Hills Books
Berkeley, California

Published by Berkeley Hills Books, Berkeley CA

Distributed by Publishers Group West

Library of Congress Cataloging-in-Publication Data

Saperstein, Guy T.
  Civil warrior : memoirs of a civil rights attorney / Guy T. Saperstein.
    p. cm.
  ISBN 1-893163-47-4 (alk. paper)
  1. Saperstein, Guy T. 2. Lawyers—United States—Biography. 3. Civil rights workers—United States.—Biography. I. Title.

KF373.S28 A3 2002
340'.092—dc21

                    2002014140

CONTENTS

photographs after page 204

Introduction

"Go confidently in the direction of your dreams.
Live the life you have imagined."
— Henry David Thoreau

During the late 1980s and early 1990s, my law firm won a series of precedent-setting, $100 million-plus civil rights cases that broke all prior records for sex, race and age discrimination litigation, and I received substantial attention from the media. Soon thereafter, a number of literary agents and publishers contacted me about publishing my memoirs, but I declined each offer. I was in the thick of my legal career, I was regularly being asked to tell the story of my success to newspapers, magazines and audiences of attorneys at law conferences, and I had no interest in writing a book.

Later, after I had decided to retire from practicing law, I began to get calls from young men and women—architects, journalists, photographers, filmmakers, authors, actors, entrepreneurs, psychologists, as well as law students and lawyers—seeking my advice about their careers and the life choices they faced. Many of these people I didn't even know, but they had heard about me and sought me out. When I had been a young attorney learning my profession, I had received advice from attorneys I sought out and who generously gave me their time, so it was only fair that I did the same. In doing so, I found that I had something to say to these young people, that my experiences and advice could help provide direction and give them encouragement to take chances with their careers, and not simply travel conventional career paths. One story is illustrative.

A young attorney from Los Angeles called me one day a few years ago. She didn't know me, and I didn't know her, but she had heard about me and my career from a mutual friend. She told me she was in a career crisis and wondered if I would be willing to speak with her for an hour. I said fine, and within a few days she was in my Oakland office telling me about herself and her career. She had graduated law school four years earlier with a good academic record and had been working for a well-respected Los Angeles law firm doing environmental litigation. Unfortunately, she was on the defense side of environmental issues, defending corporations and government agencies against environmental cases brought mainly by citizens and environmental groups. She loved the work, particularly the scientific and technical aspects of the cases, but was bothered by the fact that she felt she was on the wrong side most of the time. She wanted to continue to do environmental litigation, but on the side of the environment, not polluters.

Her instincts were good, but her fears were substantial. Jobs with public interest organizations paid significantly less than jobs with corporate law firms, there were very few public interest law jobs available at any price, and when they were available they were highly competitive. She was married and didn't want to have to move out of Los Angeles to find a job more to her liking. She wanted to explore her options in the public interest field, but didn't want her current employer to know she was less than 100% happy and, given her busy law practice, had little time to look for a public interest job in any case.

I asked her about her personal circumstances and needs. She told me she lived a comfortable, but relatively non-consumptive life, that her husband made a decent salary and that he supported her interest in public law. If she wanted to make a career move, even at risk of making less money, he would support her. I asked her how she saw herself making the transition to a public interest job, and she said, "That's where I'm blocked. I don't want my boss to know I want to look for another job and, given the responsibilities in my current job, I don't have time to look for public interest jobs, make phone calls, or go to interviews."

I told her that her problem was that she had one foot in one camp, and the other in another camp. She liked the security of her current job, but her heart was elsewhere. "The way for you to re-solve your dilemma is to stop trying to go in two directions at once. You know what you want to do, and now you have to do it. It is going to take you time to find a public interest job where you can work to protect the environment, but those jobs do exist and you need to begin taking time to look for those kind of jobs, network with people about potential opportunities, distribute your resume, and appear at job interviews. Looking for your new career is a full-time job and is not compatible with working 60+ hours a week at your current job. You have to take some risks in life and this is not such a great risk, because if you cannot find a public interest job, you can always go back to working for corporate America. You need to give your firm fair notice that you will be quitting to seek em-ployment with a public interest law firm, then begin working full time finding the job you really want."

The next day, I received a call from this young woman. "You won't believe what happened. I told my boss this morning that I had decided to quit the firm and begin looking for a job in a public interest law firm. I expected him to be angry with me, as I have a lot of work on my desk that he was depending on me to finish, but he wasn't angry at all. In fact, he was happy and excited for me. He told me that twenty years ago he had thought of doing the same thing, but he vacillated and delayed, and, in the end, never did it. He said he has always looked back to his moment of indecision and fear and wondered, 'What would have happened if I had fol-lowed my instincts and had the courage to do what I wanted?' Fur-thermore, he told me he had just heard that the Center for Law in the Public Interest (CLIPI) was looking to hire an attorney with some environmental law experience, and got on the phone right in front of me, called them, and asked if they were still taking applications. They are and I'm working on mine right now."

Three weeks later, she called back again to tell me she had interviewed for the job at CLIPI—perhaps the finest public interest law firm in Southern California—and had been offered a job that morning!

Perhaps things worked out for her more quickly and easily than most, but nothing positive would have even been possible if she had not confronted her fears and taken concrete and immediate steps in the direction of the career she really wanted.

That's why I wrote this book—to provide information about, and an example of, a career marked by taking risks and succeeding. The greatest obstacle to achieving dreams is fear. People are tracked into conventional careers by fear of the unknown, fear of choosing independent paths, and belief that employment in the corporate world is the only place they will find security. So they take conventional jobs, make big starting salaries, and think they can pursue their ideals in their spare time. But the big salaries are predicated on big hours too, often spent on unsatisfying work. The money is good, but the price is high and job satisfaction low. And, as corporate mergers and down-sizing have shown, security is never obtained. Risk and chance can't be removed from the equation, so why not choose to spend your career doing something you really believe in? Everyone I know who has done this has lived lives of sufficient income to be comfortable—some even have become wealthy, as I did—and all have had meaningful careers and satisfying lives.

I had a rocky start in life and it took me quite a while to figure things out. But I did and now I want to share my story with you so you will be encouraged to follow your essence and pursue your ideals. Don't obsess about what could go wrong, just believe in yourself, follow your best instincts, and get moving in a new direction—your own.

1

Growing Up in Chicago and North Hollywood

"Experience is the name everyone gives to their mistakes."
— *Oscar Wilde*

M Y DAD, HARRY, a soldier in the U. S. Army infantry, was off fighting the Germans in Italy, Austria and Germany when I was born on June 20, 1943, and I lived with my mother, Florence, and my grandmother, Cecelia, in a four-story apartment building in Chicago for the first two years of my life. A floor below lived my mother's good friend, Lillian Brinn, and her daughter, Lynda, whose father Harvey also was fighting the Germans. I was surrounded by women. My mother told me that by the time I was one, I was controlling everyone. That situation changed abruptly, however, when dad returned home from the war. My mother said his return began with his immediate assertion of authority and the beginning of conflict with me that would continue until I left for Berkeley to attend the University of California, sixteen years later.

My mother told me that when I was two months old, Dr. Hammond, who had delivered me, told her, "Florence, this little boy is a very strong-willed child. He will need strong guidance. Never break his will, but guide it." My mother also told me that when I was four years old, playing in the park, a stranger approached her and asked for my birthdate. After making calculations on a piece of paper, the woman said, "I am a practicing psychic and I've been watching your son closely. This boy has the capacity for great success, but also for causing a lot of trouble. You have the responsibility of providing good guidance so that his talent will not be used in negative ways." My mother didn't understand how this woman got such information and thought it was odd for a total stranger to be offering such pointed advice, but she paid attention to it, remembering the event even fifty years later.

In 1947, my mother, dad, grandmother and I packed our belongings into a 1940 Plymouth and headed to California. Relying on the GI Bill, my parents bought a house in North Hollywood—just over the hill from Hollywood in the San Fernando Valley. It had two bedrooms, one bathroom, no landscaping and no garage, a total of 850 square feet, and cost $9,000. Soon, my sister Tina was born and the five of us—mom, dad, granny, Tina and I shared the small house. My dad built a garage, and several years later, a 250-square-foot addition, which doubled as a family room and my parents' bedroom. The five of us lived in that house until I left for college.

Growing up, I was given a lot of chores. I washed or dried dishes each night, vacuumed the house, cleaned my room, and began shopping for my mother at the local grocery store when I was five years old. This required that I cross busy Vineland Avenue—four lanes wide—without a traffic signal. It also was my responsibility to mow and edge the lawns in front and back, weed all the flower beds, rake and sweep the yards, prune the box hedges and our many bushes, and help my mother whenever she worked in the yard on her roses and flower beds. I also had to wash and wax the family car and be on-call to help my dad with his many repair projects around our house, and jobs he did on weekends for others. I painted fences, our garage, and the exterior of the house, and I helped my dad lay a brick patio. Most of my friends had similar responsibilities.

My earliest memory of our house in North Hollywood is of working with my mother in the yard. I spent many days working and talking with my mother there, which made the work more enjoyable than my other chores. Our house had been built in the middle of a wide sandy wash. The soil was miserable—all sand and rocks, not a bit of top soil. For years, when I got into trouble with my dad, he would lock me in the bathroom or send me out to the yard, telling me to fill a couple of coffee cans with small stones from the yard. But, in time, with fertilizer and extensive plantings—plus my removal of thousands of stones—we had a nice yard. Our neighborhood was full of kids—someone once counted twenty-seven within a block and a half—and most of us hung out together as a pack. I was the youngest, but I was accepted into the group. One of the oldest and most popular neighborhood kids, Jack Robertson, took a liking to me and made sure I was included in all neighborhood activities. Jack became a role model for me, as I saw in him someone who treated everyone fairly, regardless of age or status. And he saved my life one day, grabbing me as I was about to try to cross a railroad track on my bike in front of a high-speed train.

One of the girls in the neighborhood, Patty Bassler, two years older than me, had been born missing most of her fingers. She was very self-conscious about this condition, seeking to cover up her hands whenever possible and her self-consciousness seemed to have been enhanced by her comparisons with her older, prettier, sister. Patty compensated by becoming intensely competitive in everything, particularly sports. She joined the boys in all neighborhood street sports—stickball, dodge ball, basketball, tether ball, kickball, and handball played against garage doors—and just had to win at everything. I remember playing her one-on-one for hours and having her get real angry at me if my parents called me home for dinner while I was ahead in a game. I've never met a more fierce competitor. We accepted her as one of the boys, but her athletic prowess, her tomboy attitude, and her self-consciousness about her hands alienated her from the prettier, more feminine girls in the neighborhood. Patty had a tough adolescence and I hope her adulthood was easier.

The neighborhood had its share of delinquents, and I seemed to include each of them as my friends. Red-headed Joe Bill, son of a musician and freckled head-to-toe, got into the most trouble, playing drums at all hours of the night, shooting out many windows in the neighborhood when his father made the mistake of giving him a BB gun for Christmas, stealing equipment from parked cars, robbing a gas station. He eventually spent time in jail, but last I heard he had rehabilitated himself and become a fine musician and a responsible person.

Joe Bill was a prankster and a delinquent, but he was not malicious. Steve, a big guy with greasy black hair, was malicious. Steve could be a mean bully and violent when it was least expected. Once, while playing in the playhouse we had built in his backyard, he decided to create "an electric chair." We strapped Loren, the neighborhood wimp, into the "electric chair," and put a small hubcap on his head to simulate the effect of electricity running head-to-toe through his body. So far, no harm. But, inexplicably, and with no warning, Steve took a hammer and began to nail the hubcap into Loren's head before we realized what was happening and stopped him. Loren ran home crying and bleeding. His mother showed up an hour later to curse us out and ask if we all were insane. Steve could be very funny at times, and he always treated me OK, but I realized he had dangerous tendencies and limited my activities with him. The last I heard he was in state prison.

Then there was Judy, the cutest girl in the neighborhood, experienced beyond her years, and with no parental supervision. Her dad, a professional wrestler, was rarely around and her mother was a professional drunk. Judy, who became my best friend in the neighborhood through my junior high school years, and my first sexual experience, was dating sailors when she was 16, taking heroin by 18 and turning tricks by 20. At one point, seeing the deep hole she was falling into, I wanted my parents to adopt her! My grandmother would tell me to stay away from Judy, warning me, "She's a bad girl," and I would respond, "But we can save her." The truth was no one could save her.

Judy and three older girls in my neighborhood, Linda, Carol and Barbara, did me one of the biggest favors ever—they taught me to dance. When I got to Sun Valley Jr. High School, there were Sports Nights every Friday night, which included games and dancing in the gym. The scene was typical: boys on one side, girls on the other, with an occasional couple of girls dancing together. One day, riding home on the bus, I mentioned that my parents had met on a dance floor, still danced at least once a week, and that I'd like to learn myself. No sooner had I said this, I was in Linda Wright's living room, with four girls teaching me the Lindy Hop and Jitterbug. Dancing became my meal-ticket, my way to get beyond shyness, meet girls and have fun. Wherever I went where music was playing and people were dancing, I could ask any girl to dance and, generally, impress her. Music transformed me, making me want to move, and dancing in sync with the music and a partner was exciting. Plus, I enjoyed the attention I got on the dance floor.

MY DAD HAD GROWN UP THE SON of a poor tailor, in a family of nine children. I grew up listening to stories of how grandpa Saperstein would rent a house or apartment without saying how many children he had, then move the family in during the middle of the night, only to be evicted when the landlord discovered how many kids grandpa and grandma Saperstein really had. The five Saperstein boys all had jobs by the time they were six. My dad got up at 4 a.m. with his older brother Rocky, took the street car out to the end of the line, bought a couple of large sacks of potatoes, and hawked them in the alleys to neighbors, pulling the potatoes in a wagon, before going to school. Being the handiest of the kids, my dad became the household carpenter, plumber, electrician, painter, roofer, and general fix-it person, while the other boys hustled their own jobs. The Saperstein boys became very entrepreneurial, the result of necessity, I suppose, and my dad's oldest brother, Abe, founded a barnstorming professional basketball team before he was twenty. That team became the Harlem Globetrotters, and Abe owned and managed them until his death in 1967.

By the late 1940s and 1950s, the Globetrotters were the world's best and most prosperous basketball team, and had four teams touring the world. They regularly came to Los Angeles in January, and I looked forward to that, as Abe would come over to the house for dinner with one of his basketball players or a beautiful actress, and I'd be hired as the Globetrotter "ball boy" for the Los Angeles games. My uncle Abe was a truly remarkable man. Three films have been made of his life. He was the first Caucasian inducted into the Negro Hall of Fame and he was inducted into the Basketball Hall of Fame in 1971. Hanging around the Globetrotters dispelled my illusions of becoming a professional basketball player. I remember going down to San Diego with my dad to help set up the basketball court and baskets on the infield of the San Diego Padres' baseball field. After we got the court and baskets set up, some of the Globetrotters showed up in the afternoon to see what the court looked like. Connie Hawkins, a 6' 9" forward with moves like Julius Erving, showed up in a three-piece suit and dress shoes, grabbed a basketball, and sank about ten 3-pointers in a row. I fancied myself a pretty good shooter, but I wasn't that good—plus, I wasn't 6' 9" and I didn't have any inside game. If a 6' 9" guy could shoot 3-pointers like that in a suit and dress shoes, no less, I figured I'd have to find some other line of work. Nevertheless, I've never given up my fantasies of being a basketball player.

Dad's childhood stories of his and his brothers' early entrepreneurial activities seemed to have an impact on me. By the time I was five, I was selling lemonade and Kool-Aid on hot summer days to passersby. Later, I sold Christmas cards, holiday decorations, and flags house-to-house from my red American Flyer wagon to neighbors, friends and relatives, and, during my first year in college, sold pots and pans, magazine subscriptions and encyclopedias. Once, at age eight, I filled up an ice chest with snow on a day trip to the mountains, brought it home and sold snowballs to the neighborhood kids. My neighbor, Eve Robertson, once said, "Whenever I see Guy coming down the street with his red wagon, I close the shades and turn out the lights!" Nevertheless, Eve couldn't escape me and she became my best customer. Perhaps as a result of these early entrepreneurial experiences, I never shied from the business aspects of running and financing a law practice.

I mowed lawns for my neighbors, washed and waxed their cars, and took care of their dogs when they went on vacation. My first experience feeding neighbor dogs, at age 6, almost was my last, however. My neighbors across the street, Eve and Bill Robertson, asked me to feed their two Labradors—King and Prince—during their vacation. Eve loaded me up with cans of their food—each dog ate two cans of dog food each day—and paper plates, and gave me instructions how to enter her side gate. The first day, I loaded two paper plates with two cans of dog food on each plate, quietly opened and closed the side gate, then started to walk along the side of their house, thinking I could set the food down in front of the doghouse. But, before I got more than five steps into the yard, King and Prince came bounding round the corner, barking loudly and running full-speed directly at me. I was frozen. Before I could re-act, King took a flying leap and knocked me to the ground. The dog food flew everywhere, and much of it landed on me, now laying prone in the dirt, with two huge labs eating dog food off my face, shirt and pants. Their meal finished, they walked calmly away, while I beat a fast retreat home, shaken by the experience, vowing to let the dogs starve for the rest of the week. By the next day, however, I knew I couldn't disappoint Eve by not feeding them, so I took the food over to the Robertson house, threw the food over the gate and called for the dogs, who devoured the food in a flash without trampling me. I took care of King and Prince for many years, and as I got older and larger, even ventured into the yard to feed them. King, Prince and I eventually became friends, but I never lost respect for their strength.

When I was in junior high school, I got a job delivering papers for the *Valley Times* on my bike. Thirty dollars a month, if everyone paid; if someone didn't pay, the cost of the papers I had delivered to them was taken out of my pay. When I turned fifteen, my neighbor, Bill Robertson, offered me a summer job working in the auto body shop he owned on Santa Monica Boulevard in downtown Hollywood; five days a week, plus a half-day on Saturday, for $50 a week. It sounded like a fortune to me, as I had been making $30 a month delivering papers. But I had to work my ass off for that $50. Every morning, I had to completely sweep out and clean up the large auto body shop and the adjacent gas service station, which Robertson also owned. Whenever someone pulled into the service station, I'd have to run from the body shop over to the service station and take care of the customer. The words "self service" hadn't been invented yet, so every customer got full service from me—I filled the gas tank, washed *all* the windows, checked the radiator, oil, and tire pressure (in all four tires) and added water, oil, and/or air, as needed, then asked, "Is there anything else I can do for you?" If anyone wanted an oil change or a lube job, I'd put the car up on the hydraulic hoist, raise the car, change the oil and lube the car. As soon as that was done, I was expected to get back to the body shop, clean any messes that had been created in my absence and assist in the hardest and most tedious auto body shop work— sanding and smoothing metal with a metal file and steel wool, rubbing out new paint with rubbing compound, then waxing the new paint. Mr. Robertson also expected me to find time to wash his new 1959 black Cadillac Eldorado convertible every day, plus wax his car every 2–3 weeks. So, I'd be washing a perfectly clean car every day, and waxing a car that didn't need waxing, every month. And his car had to be absolutely perfect when I finished. He would inspect it like a hawk, and if I left a single water spot on the car after I chamoised it dry, he'd call me over, point out the offending water spot, and inform me that he expected me to do a better job next time. Much of this work was done in 90 to 100 degree weather and I'd be soaked in sweat, but Mr. Robertson expected me to wear a clean Richfield Oil shirt at all times, so I'd often have to change clothes in the middle of the day to meet his cleanliness expectations. By the end of the summer I was asking myself, "Is this what real work is like? Am I going to have to work like this for the next fifty years?" Fortunately, that job turned out to be the most unpleasant job I ever had. Every job since that one has looked pretty good, in comparison.

After the summer was over and the job at Robertson's Auto Body ended, I got an after-school job working the sales counter and delivering liquor for Berg's Liquors. Berg's Liquors was run by two brothers, Bernie and Dave—each of whom supervised their own stores. Bernie was a warm, fuzzy, family-man type of guy, always interesting to talk to and interested in other people—just a great guy to work for. Dave, the older brother, was loud, flamboyant, obscene and funny; working for him gave me a chance to drive his bright red 1953 Cadillac convertible, a real pig to drive but a beautiful piece of metal. At Berg's Liquors, I worked the sales counter and made deliveries to the affluent neighborhoods in Studio City, Encino and Van Nuys. My job paid minimum wage, and tips were important. Most customers were regular tippers—a quarter, maybe 50 cents for a delivery—but I noticed the tipping practices of some of our movie and TV stars often depended on where I made deliveries to them; when I made private deliveries to their houses, I received no tips, but on those rare occasions when I made deliveries to them at their studios, with many people around, the same non-tippers would whip out a couple of bills, wave them around a little, and make sure everyone saw that I was getting a generous tip. I was happy to go along with the charade, but I'd think to myself, "What a phony." These also were the customers who ran tabs and often didn't pay. When reminded of tabs that often hadn't been paid for a year or more, they'd act offended that the subject even had been mentioned. Generally, Bernie and Dave would continue to carry them anyway.

The only downside to working at Berg's was occasionally having to work with Dave and Bernie's dad. The dad was retired, but worked the retail counter a few hours each week at Bernie's store. Dave refused to work with him because he was such a difficult person. I had a difficult time working with him, also. When I worked with Bernie or Dave, I waited on customers, made liquor and beverage recommendations to customers, and worked the cash register, in addition to making deliveries. But when Father Berg came around, he'd get mad at me if I waited on a customer, even if I knew the customer and he didn't, and even if the customer had approached me. He also would tell me to stay away from the cash register, as though he thought I would steal from it. And he'd tell me to clean up or reorganize the "bottle cage," where all beer and soda was stored outside, whether or not it needed cleaning or reorganization, or give me one menial task or another just to show me he was the boss, although I was then working twice as many hours per week as he was and knew the job duties better than he did. But I'd keep my mouth shut, do what he told me to do, and try to hide my resentment. Apparently I didn't hide it well enough, as, near the end of my second year and shortly before I was to graduate high school, Bernie approached me one night when his father was not around, and said, "Guy, you've been a good employee for me, and I've enjoyed having you work here. The problem is my dad; he complains about you all the time. I don't put much value in his complaints, but he's my dad and I can't fire him. You can continue working at Dave's store, but you can't work here any more." I told Bernie I understood his situation and why he was doing this, but inside I was devastated. I loved working with Bernie, loved the job and the customers, and thought it was unfair that I had to take the fall for the fact that Bernie's dad was a jerk and Bernie couldn't stand up to him. I was powerless to do anything about it, however Many years later, when I was representing workers who had been wrongfully terminated from employment, my own experience with job termination helped me understand the devastation my clients felt when they were fired from long-term jobs, often for insubstantial or political reasons.

In school, I was a lippy kid, constantly talking. My second-grade teacher, Mrs. Case, once broke a wooden yardstick over my head in class. I protested, "Why did you do that? Other kids are talking too!" "I know," she said, "but your voice carries!" Later, she was the first to tell me, "You should be a lawyer"—something I later heard from many of my teachers.

I was constantly getting into trouble in school and being sent to the principal's office. It seemed like whenever that happened, when I came home my mother would say, "The little birdy told me you were not a good boy in school today." I don't know if she was getting calls from the school, or was intuiting my problems from guilty expressions on my face, but, at the time, I believed in that "little birdy." I often sat in class looking out the window wondering which of the birds sitting on the nearby trees and utility lines was reporting to my mom. My mom had my number.

I had other problems in school, as well. As my fifth grade teacher, Mrs. Dawson, put it to my mother, "Guy is a classic under-achiever." Year after year, my mother was summoned to school to hear my teachers contrast my high IQ and aptitude test scores with low classroom performance. Mostly, they complained about my talking and the class disruptions I caused. Many seemed to have a love/hate relationship with me. They saw my potential, but I was the kid who could aggravate them a lot. Looking back, I don't think I was trying to be mean or disruptive; I was just bored stiff in school. Nevertheless, despite conflicts with teachers, I seemed to be a popular kid at least in elementary and junior high school, regularly being elected class president and captain of the baseball, basketball and football teams.

In the third grade, I had my first girlfriend, Georgia Riggins, the cutest brunette in my third-grade class, who later became a country western singer. In the fourth grade, I fell in love for the first time. The object of my affection was Anne Pinkerton, a classically beautiful blond and indisputably the cutest and nicest girl at Oxnard Elementary School. I became so smitten that I gave her my most prized possession—my complete collection of marbles. It was a great sacrifice for me, but, hey, the greater the sacrifice, the greater the expression of love. I doubt the marbles meant much to her or that she even understood the depth of my sacrifice—but she kept them. Unfortunately, Anne was a year older than me, which is a big difference at that age. In the middle of fourth grade, the school skipped me ahead to the fifth grade, which put me in Anne's class for half a year, but when she went on to junior high school, while I remained at Oxnard Elementary for another half year, the relationship lost all momentum. By the time I hit junior high school, she was well established there, continually surrounded by boys, and I was too shy to approach her. In the ninth grade, however, I did make one final, pathetic, attempt to capture her emotions. The setting was the annual baseball game between the A9 team (my class) and the B9 team (Anne's class). I was selected as pitcher for the A9 team. The whole school was in attendance watching the game, but I saw only one person in the crowd—Anne Pinkerton. In my mind, every strike I threw and each hit I got was dedicated to Anne, and all were evidence why she should rush onto the field and embrace me as her hero. My team lost, but I had a great game, pitching a complete game, getting three hits, and being voted the "Most Valuable Player in the Sun Valley Junior High School A9 v. B9 Baseball Game." But Anne didn't rush onto the field to embrace me or to even acknowledge my success; in fact, she left the game before it even was over. One more juvenile male fantasy into the trash can.

Sun Valley Junior High School was a new, but tough school, populated mostly by Latinos from the East Valley; its most famous alumni were Richie Valens and his girlfriend "Donna." In my first semester, there was a gang fight in a nearby park with knives and homemade "zip" guns. Of course, today these kids could buy Uzi's from mail-order gun dealers. In any case, the use of knives and guns made me reevaluate my own behavior. I had gotten into a lot of fights in elementary school, and, in the first week of junior high, even "chose-off" Freddy Piro, the toughest kid in the 7th grade, when he butted into the cafeteria line in front of me. I told him to get out of line, and he said, "I'll meet you after school behind the metal shop." I responded, "Why wait until after school? Let's go out to the bungalows and have it out right now." As we took the long walk to the bungalows, my best friend, Dieter Scholz, told me "You're going to get killed." I thanked him for his vote of confidence, then took the first swing at Freddy when we squared off. We fought for a while with no one getting hurt before a teacher broke it up and took us both to detention. Freddy and I became friends, and I had no conflicts with him for the rest of my three years at Sun Valley.

More instructive to me was a joust with a Latino kid from wood shop. He was a nasty, unlikable kid who was constantly picking fights with everyone, and when he picked a fight with me, I wasn't worried—I'd kick his ass. But when I naively showed up alone behind the metal shop after school, he was there with ten of his friends, who immediately surrounded the two of us in a circle. I swung the first punch and hit him square on the jaw, knocking him to the ground, but he came up waving a switchblade knife—the kind with a four-inch blade that looked about four feet long to me at the time—and started swinging it at me. My life raced before my eyes as I envisioned the knife slicing my chest, but before I got tagged, the metal shop teacher came out and everyone scattered. I contemplated how stupid I had been, getting into a fight and risking real harm from a kid I didn't even know and who was irrelevant to me. It was at that moment I decided I didn't need to fight every jerk at the school and that I could preserve myself better by learning how to talk my way *out* of fights, rather than into them. It was a good lesson and I've never regretted attending a tough school.

Learning how to steer clear of fights did not mean I became an angel, however. I still managed to get into trouble on a regular basis. I was First Trombone in the school orchestra, which put me in constant conflict with the orchestra conductor—a little fascist martinet named Victor DeVeritch. He kept moving me back to Second or Third Trombone position for talking too much and not following directions, only to have to move me back to First Trombone on Fridays, when challenge auditions were permitted. He called my mother in to tell her what an awful son she was raising; my mother was very offended.

My locker was in the hallway not far from DeVeritch's classroom. I had gone down to Tijuana with some older neighborhood kids and brought back a collection of firecrackers, some of which I kept in my school locker. Once, after an acrimonious exchange with DeVeritch earlier in the day, I took a cherry bomb out of my locker, lit it, opened the door to DeVeritch's classroom, threw it in, and casually walked away. By the time it exploded and DeVeritch came running into the hallway yelling and screaming, I was gone.

I thought I had scammed him good, but late that afternoon, I saw three Latino kids I knew from woodshop with their parents in Mr. Cosgrove's office, the Boy's Vice Principal. I waited around and asked them what had happened and was told, "We're getting suspended for tossing a firecracker into a classroom." I asked, "Which classroom?" "DeVeritch's," they told me.

They were innocent, of course, but they also were kids who got into a lot of trouble at school. They were being busted on general principles and because some firecrackers had been found in their locker. If they took the rap it would be no big deal, because they would never finish school anyway. Each of them already had spent time in Juvenile Hall for offenses much worse than tossing firecrackers.

I walked down the hall, telling myself the smart play was to let them take the rap. But I couldn't do it. I walked back to Cosgrove's office, knocked on the door and went in. "I'm the guy who did it. I tossed the cherry bomb into DeVeritch's classroom. Those three guys you suspended had nothing to do with it," I told Cosgrove. So my mother got called in and I got suspended. But I had done the right thing and my conscience was clear.

I got mostly A's and B's in junior high school, but continued to get U's ("uncooperative") in work habits and cooperation. I also was active in the wider universe of the school. I took drama class and starred as the male lead in two plays produced for the student body, teachers and parents, was sports editor of the school paper, captain of the basketball and baseball teams I played on, and was selected MVP of the 9th grade baseball and basketball games. I was regularly selected in pick-up basketball games ahead of Gail Goodrich, who later became an All-American at UCLA and All-Pro with the Los Angeles Lakers.

By the 9th grade I began a slide, and continued downhill for five years. A lot of the trouble was caused by my relationship with my father, and other authority figures. My dad is a good man, and was very loving with my mother. But he never really wanted to be a father. He agreed to have children because of my mother's insistence. And his approach to childrearing was typical of many men of his generation: "My way or the highway." Frequently, he repeated, "You'll do it my way, with no questions. When you're my age, you'll understand why." That approach was never going to work with a kid like me; I didn't want to wait until I was 45 to understand why, I wanted to know now. So I constantly asked "Why?" If my dad told me I had to do something by a specific date or in a certain way, I wanted a reasonable explanation—or at least some explanation. But he perceived my requests for explanations as challenges to his authority, and handled them with raised voice, threats and banishment to the bathroom, where I would stay for hours before being allowed out—until I kicked in the door at age 16. My dad was not physically abusive, but my life felt like a prison—with my father as warden.

My dad also expected me to be the best at whatever I was doing. I was a decent athlete, but one day, in a Little League baseball game with the score tied in the last inning, I was playing second base when a pop-up was hit down the first-base line. Running with my back to the plate, I tried to catch the ball over my head. It was a tough play, the kind even major league players miss, and I didn't make it. The ball hit my glove, bounced out, and we lost the game. To my dad, my failure was disgrace. He didn't say a word to me on the long drive home, and didn't talk to me for days.

Boy Scouts was even worse. For six years, my dad was Cub Scout and then Boy Scout Leader of the pack and troop I belonged to. I was a decent scout, becoming a Life Scout with 17 merit badges and getting elected Patrol Leader and Senior Patrol Leader, the highest position in the Troop. But I wasn't a perfect scout, and whenever I was too rambunctious, or made a mistake, my dad would hold me up as an example to the whole troop, calling me "the goof off." It became a self-fulfilling prophecy. As I became increasingly alienated from my dad and his misuse of authority, I began to "goof off" more and more, eventually becoming Patrol Leader of the "maverick" patrol, full of every malcontent and "goof off" in the troop, my patrol reveling in opposition to the parental leadership.

I wouldn't want to leave the impression, however, that my experience in the Scouts was all bad. Far from it. Boy Scout Troop 3 was my ticket out of the city, my opportunity to see more than my immediate neighborhood. My family did not take vacations, at least not ones with Tina and me; my dad was too busy working extra jobs to make ends meet. Troop 3 had a tradition of going camping at least once each month of the year, with a one or two-week trip in the summer. So, once a month, we'd find weekend campsites in areas within a one or two-hour drive from North Hollywood: the San Gabriel and San Bernardino mountains, the deserts out toward Palm Springs, as well as campsites along the ocean. In the summer, we'd go to Yosemite National Park, where we'd establish a camp in Yosemite Valley, then hike and backpack into the Yosemite backcountry. Some of the hikes were brutally hard for 10–13 year-olds carrying full packs, particularly the hikes out of Yosemite Valley to the high country, which all involved elevation climbs of 3,000–5,000 feet.

These were the days that predated modern, lightweight, backpacking equipment. Instead of the 3-pound down sleeping bag I now carry, which keeps me warm in temperatures down to 0 degrees, in Scouts I carried a large kapok sleeping bag that weighed 11 pounds in which I froze whenever temperatures dropped into the 30's. Instead of the 43-pound tent with superlight stakes and poles I now carry, in Scouts we had heavy canvas tents coated with some kind of green gunk that was supposed to be waterproof, but never was, with heavy wood stakes and poles, which weighed over ten pounds and didn't even have a floor! When it rained, we'd have to dig a trench around the perimeter of the tent to divert any water puddles from entering the tent and avoid touching the walls of the tent, because wherever the tent walls were touched, the tent would begin to leak and our kapok sleeping bags would start soaking up water. Many cold, sleepless nights were spent in these heavy, ineffective tents and sleeping bags.

The food we used to take added to our burdens. Instead of modern, lightweight, dehydrated food that backcountry hikers now carry, in the Scouts we generally carried heavy canned goods: Dinty Moore Beef Stew, Hormel's Beef Enchiladas, S&W's Canned Beans, Dole's Pineapple Chunks (in heavy syrup, of course). All our weight then was put into the crappiest pack ever invented—the infamous Boy Scout Yucca Pack. It was nothing but a glorified book bag—a big canvas sack with no waist belt to transfer weight to the hips, and canvas webbed shoulder straps about 1½-inch thick, which dug into our shoulder blades under the weight of the heavy packs, and which cost all of $5 to buy. Our packs must have weighed 40–50 pounds when full, and carried by 10–13 year-olds who often weighed less than 100 pounds. I remember one hike, a hike from the Valley floor to the top of Glacier Point—11 miles and 5,000-foot elevation gain—where some of the younger Scouts were crying in pain lugging their overweight equipment. Nevertheless, when we arrived at our destinations, the burdens of the trail were soon forgotten, and everyone got into the rhythm of climbing rocks, swimming in streams or lakes, cooking for ourselves, sitting around the campfire and telling stories late into the night, followed by laying in our sleeping bags, gazing at the millions of stars in the Milky Way visible in the brilliantly clear skies, pondering what the aliens who must live on some of those stars looked like and whether we'd ever meet them. Those trips, and experiences, were so memorable, I've been able to return many years later to the Yosemite backcountry, and not only find specific sites we camped at, but remember particular features of the campsites exactly as they still exist. I often can't remember where I put my pen or what I did an hour ago, but I remember some of the experiences I had in the Yosemite backcountry forty years ago as though they happened yesterday.

Our group became so well-bonded that when we turned 14,

we all continued with Explorers, the scouting experience for kids too old for Boy Scouts, and took a one-month driving trip to Alaska via the Al-Can Highway, which then was unpaved for 2,000 miles. We arrived in Big Delta Junction, Alaska, on July 7, 1958, the day Alaska became the 49th State. It was quite a day to arrive, as throughout Alaska there were celebrations that lasted for days. In Big Delta (population less than 100), a bonfire fifty feet high was built, followed by a barbeque with bear meat, moose meat, elk meat, and venison. It was a nice break from the noodle casseroles we had been eating.

Even after the Scout experience ended, I continued to hike and backpack with friends I had met in Scouts, and continue to this day to backpack in the Sierras. In fact, if someone ever told me I had a week to live and could take just one trip, I'd want to throw on my backpack and hike in the Sierras. The current homophobia of the Boy Scouts of America sometimes makes me embarrassed to say I was a Boy Scout, but the richness and indelibility of the experiences I had in nature with the Scouts makes me thankful my dad steered me into scouting.

Looking back on the totality of my relationship with my dad, I realize I learned many important lessons from him, despite the conflicts. I learned to work hard. My dad is the hardest working person I've ever known. He would work a full-time job during the week setting up displays in liquor stores or decorating windows in department stores, then take on carpentry projects at night and on weekends, fix everything in our house, do fix-it projects for relatives and friends, and still find time to run a boy scout troop with fifty kids.

I learned from my dad not to complain about bad breaks. My dad is very smart; in the U. S. Army his IQ was tested at 160. Even today, at age 89, he can remember a thousand jokes, and sit and tell one after another for hours, never repeating the same joke. Yet, as a result of his parents' poverty and his need to work to help support his family, plus the intervention of World War II, he never attended college or received any formal training. He is very inventive, and should have been an engineer, inventor or scientist, but, without formal education, he spent a lifetime in low-paying, mundane jobs. But rather than becoming bitter at his lack of opportunities, he made the best of his situation, worked hard, and didn't complain. "Work hard and you'll be rewarded, everyone has their setbacks in life, just deal with them," was his attitude. It was a great attitude, and years later, when I was working on legal cases and things went bad, people around me bemoaned the situation, became immobilized by bad luck, complained about a wrong decision or a stupid judge, and I'd say, "OK, things didn't turn out the way we wanted, but that's in the past. The question for us is what do we do now. Every setback is an opportunity—an opportunity to sink deeper into the hole, or an opportunity to figure out what went wrong and develop a different strategy for the future." Indeed, setbacks made problems more challenging to analyze and more exhilarating to overcome. My "don't feel sorry for yourself, make the best of the situation" attitude came from my dad.

I learned from my dad that life did not owe me anything. Life may be rough, but it is ultimately fair, according to my dad. You don't get something for nothing. Work hard and you'll be rewarded. I also learned to do the best I could. My dad would say, "Terry [my family called me by my middle name], I don't care if you become a shoe repairman. Just be the best shoe repairman you possibly can be."

Finally, my dad taught me to take responsibility for myself— no one owed me anything and there was no one but myself to blame for my own failures. Work diligently, ride the bumps, and things will work out fine. As I look back on my life, I can see this perspective gave me a great sense of independence and freedom from the fear of failure. It helped me accept more risk in my life choices than most people seem willing to tolerate.

DESPITE THE LONG-TERM LESSONS I was learning, my rebellion against my dad's overuse of authority became more acute. I ended up being threatened with non-graduation from junior high school; I was thrown out of the school orchestra, dismissed from the high school tennis, basketball and baseball teams, and threatened with non-graduation from high school for incurring more than 150 demerits—120 more than necessary to disqualify a student from graduation. This nearly prevented me from attending college, as well.

In the 9th grade, we all took the "Iowa Tests," a comprehensive "aptitude" test, and I scored in the 99th percentile in all categories. As a result, throughout high school, I was placed in advanced classes—a small group of about twenty students who were assigned to the best teachers, had more challenging and interesting assignments, and were rewarded with an additional grade point for each course. Most of the other students in the advanced classes were highly motivated by the classes. But I vowed never to take a book home during high school—a vow I nearly kept—and distinguished myself each day by taking the last seat in each class, often three or four rows behind the rest of the class. From that distant perch, I'd try to sleep, read a magazine or just watch the clock tick forward each 60-second cycle. I learned how to doze off with my eyes open, an ability that still comes in handy on occasion! The teachers learned to ignore me, except for Mr. Francis, my math teacher, who invited me to join his weekly adult poker game. Much of the time, I didn't go to class at all, preferring to join the day-time poker game off-campus at Harold Schlesinger's house, or going surfing in the '57 Ford I had bought with money I earned working at Robertson's Auto Body Shop and Berg's Liquors, or dancing at the local juke-joint across the street from school. My school counselor, Mr. Francis, who knew I was smart, at least in math, and knew I generally was following an unproductive path, ignored my misbehavior, did nothing to encourage me to pursue a college-oriented track, and, instead, seemed satisfied to play poker with me. Two years after I left North Hollywood High School, he killed himself in the school auto shop by closing all the doors and windows and running his car engine. He had more on his mind than my college education.

The stabilizing influence during this dark period of my adolescence was my mother. No matter how alienated I might be feeling about dad, school, boy scouts, or the world, she let me know she always understood me and was on my side. She never preached to me or told me what to do, she just listened to what I had to say and shared her thoughts and insights. I talked to her about nearly everything that was going on in my life until she died in 1996, at age 83. I talked to her about conflicts I had with teachers, problems with my dad, sexual experiences with women, career choices, political issues—everything. She usually waited for me to bring up issues for discussion before offering her opinions, but was not reluctant to become proactive when she thought I needed advice and the time was right. In my early 20s I fell in love with a beautiful actress and dancer. It was a passionate and exciting relationship, but difficult and tumultuous. Kim wanted to party and have fun, which I liked, but she wanted to do it every night, and that clashed with my efforts to finish my undergraduate work, and my plans to go to law school. My dad referred to Kim derisively as, "the showgirl," but after Kim stayed with me at my parents' house for a week, my mother sat me down on our back door step and said, "I know Kim wants to marry you and you know I love her. She has a great heart and is very sweet. But marrying her would be very impractical. Marriage is a partnership, and it requires a lot of work from both partners. Kim is not ready to share that responsibility." Many people had given me advice about this relationship, but it was my mother's advice that meant the most to me.

My mother was always busy helping someone—a neighbor, a relative, a bum who showed up at the front door looking for some food or yardwork, a member of her church, a homeless drug addict at the beach, a black girl who couldn't read, a Hispanic boy who was doing poorly in school. She did a lot of good deeds but always would be the last person to tell you about them—you almost had to catch her in the act. She didn't draw attention to herself or expect credit for doing what, in her opinion, simply was what one person should do to help another. The day after the Watts Riots killed forty-four people and burned down much of South Central Los Angles—at a time when most of the San Fernando Valley was worried that black militants would burn down their neighborhoods next—my mother drove to Watts, found a community center and asked, "Is there anything I can do?" She tutored kids for two years there every day for 4–6 hours, driving the 45 minutes each way by herself, never mentioning this to anyone except my dad and me. Later, after she and dad moved to Oxnard, she joined a long-haired hippy minister working with homeless kids and drug addicts who congregated on the beach, and then tutored minority children in the Oxnard schools for nearly twenty years. For her many community activities on behalf of people who were struggling to get their lives in order, as well as for founding Oxnard Beautiful, she was voted Oxnard "Woman of the Year." When she died, the Oxnard School District planted a grove of trees in her name, marked by a bronze plaque acknowledging her contributions, and the Mayor and City Council dedicated a bench and plaque to her on the Oxnard beach at her favorite spot. Without ever preaching or telling me what my responsibilities should be, she quietly provided the guidance and example I desperately needed.

My other stabilizing influence was the minister of the church I attended for fifteen years, the non-denominational Little Brown Church. Although my dad is Jewish, he never attended services, nor observed Jewish holidays, and deferred to my mother's Catholicism. Thus, I was baptized a Catholic and attended Catholic Mass in the spectacular St. Charles Church in Toluca Lake until I was five years old. The services were conducted in Latin and thus were completely incomprehensible to me. One day, my neighborhood friend, Jim Hopperstad, invited me to his Sunday School at the non-denominational Little Brown Church, and I began going there. Soon, my mother joined me, and, taken by the powerful sermons of the minister, John Wells, she abandoned Catholicism, attended Wells' sermons and taught Sunday School there for twenty-five years. I continued to attend the Little Brown Church regularly until I went away to college, but returned for services on my visits home, and, as I became an opponent of the Vietnam War, began to hand out antiwar literature after services.

John Wells was a truly remarkable man. His progressive politics and support of the Wobblies got him fired from three ministerial positions in the Midwest. He came to California with his wife, Donna, built a successful construction company, then hand-built "The Little Brown Church" in Studio City, a small, wood-frame building with pine interiors. Over the years, his powerful sermons led to many offers of large churches in the San Fernando Valley, as well as rebuilding his church on a grander scale. But Reverend Wells believed Christianity meant service to others, not large buildings; he never took a dime in salary from the church, and the money his church brought in went to service and missionary work. To Reverend Wells, and my Bible readings, Jesus Christ was an outsider, a revolutionary, an underdog who stood up for small, powerless, people against entrenched power—the man who washed the feet of his disciples and kicked the money lenders out of the temple. It was the same vision of Christianity that my mother's life presented—there were no small people, everyone deserved to be treated with respect, love, justice.

I REACHED MY SENIOR YEAR at North Hollywood High School with no plan about what to do next, only a vague notion about going to college. I took the SAT, scored in the 99th percentile, and suddenly doors opened. After years as a lousy student, all at once, I could get into nearly any college or university I might want to attend. I thought at the time how unfair it was that a good score on a three-hour aptitude test was more important to colleges than three years of hard study and good grades. I still think it's unfair.

Three of my high school friends and I drove up to the San Francisco Bay Area on Big Game Weekend to view the University of California and Stanford University. We arrived at the Psi Upsilon fraternity in Berkeley on a Friday afternoon, just in time for the Friday afternoon beer bust—full of drunken fraternity brothers and lots of good-looking sorority girls. This was followed by a large party, with dancing, more beer and more girls, followed by a gin fizz breakfast early Saturday morning, followed by the Cal–Stanford football game with more booze in orange juice cups, followed by a big dance party Saturday night. Cal appeared to be a non-stop party.

We woke up the next afternoon and drove to Stanford to spend Sunday night in the dorms with a friend. Badly hung over, the four of us moped around the Stanford campus. Where were the parties? Of course, it was Sunday night and everyone was studying! We drove back to North Hollywood the next day, and all agreed that Stanford was a really boring place. All four of us enrolled at Cal.

I graduated high school mid-term in January, 1961. As no one bothered to tell me my test scores made me eligible for various scholarships, I had to work throughout college. Since I would not start Cal until September, I took a job as a trainee-clerk in the Commercial Division of the Los Angeles Department of Water and Power. My responsibility was to manually record service change orders in my file of approximately 80,000 utility users. It was the most tedious job I've ever had—kind of like Stanford on a Sunday night. The only good part of the job was playing third base for the Commercial Division baseball team and walking around downtown Los Angeles at my extended lunch breaks. One day, standing on a corner three blocks away from our building, a loud, brash young black man told everyone who walked by that he was "The Greatest" and that he was going to knock out the local boxing favorite, Alejandro Lavorante, who then was the No. 2 ranked heavyweight boxer in the United States. That brash young man was Cassius Clay, now Muhammad Ali, and he did knock out Lavorante in exactly the round he predicted. I shook his hand, became a lifelong Clay/Ali fan, and still consider him to be the greatest, and most important, sports figure of my generation due to his achievements in boxing, his humor, brashness and charisma, and, most significantly, his political integrity and outspokenness.

After two weeks at the Los Angeles Department of Water & Power, I could do my job in half a day, so I'd sneak off to the mail room to take a nap among the mail sacks, or circulate throughout the Commercial Division, meeting the attractive young female employees. My boss, Mr. Niedermeyer, kept catching me and threatening me with termination. I would respond, "Mr. Niedermeyer, there are fourteen clerks in my department all doing substantially less work than me. Why am I the one being watched and disciplined?" Niedermeyer responded, "I know you complete your assignments on time and do good work. But, I don't care if you're working or not, I want you to *look* like you're working. So, when you're done with your files, sit at your desk, hold some file cards in your hand and *look* like you're working in case my boss walks through here!" He didn't care about performance, only appearance. Somehow, I managed to stay awake for eight months and saved almost enough money to get me through my first year of college.

2

Berkeley in the Sixties

"Any life, no matter how long and complex it may be,
is made up of a single moment—the moment in which
a man finds out, once and for all, who he is."
— Jorge Luis Borges

I DROVE UP TO BERKELEY the first week of September, 1961, with my friend, Dieter Scholz. After dropping him off at the Psi Upsilon fraternity, I drove back across campus to move into Room 314 of Griffiths Hall. Griffiths Hall was part of a new complex of four eight-story dorm towers—two filled with women, two with men—built around the cafeteria and recreation center and just two blocks from campus.

College life was liberating—probably too liberating for me. No parents, no curfew, no one telling me what to do, attractive coeds everywhere, and a group of guys on my floor who liked to party every night. This left little time for classes or studying. One of the guys on my floor, Geoff Rothman, had a large reel-to-reel tape recorder and an extensive collection of tapes full of rock-and-roll music, which he would set up in the recreation hall each night for dancing. I spent most of my weekday evenings dancing or watching TV in the hall. On the weekends, three of us, Geoff, Rich and I, would hit the dorm dances or travel to the local dance halls to pickup college or high school girls. We all were good dancers and frequently monopolized the dance contests—Rich winning the twist, Geoff the limbo, and me the jitterbug contests. During the day, I played basketball at Harmon Gym, practiced diving at the Harmon pool, then napped alongside the pool before my afternoon job as a referee and umpire at intramural sports events. My schedule left little time for classes.

I enrolled at Cal as an engineering major—my dream was to build bridges or become a patent attorney—but that didn't last long. The 8 a.m. start time for my chemistry class didn't mesh with my social life and the three-hour engineering labs in the afternoon conflicted with my work schedule. And I was having trouble with calculus, which I didn't expect. Math had been my strong subject—I had received straight A's in math throughout elementary, junior high and high school, and a perfect score on the math section of the SAT—but calculus was a mystery to me. Late in the first semester, about two weeks before final exams, my calculus TA (teaching assistant) took me aside and said, "Mr. Saperstein, you are failing calculus. At this point, you should just take your F and concentrate on your other courses." I did exactly the opposite—I neglected my other courses, bought a couple of primers on calculus, and studied calculus non-stop for two weeks. To my surprise, and to my TA's astonishment, I got an A on the calculus final and an A- in the course. Unfortunately, I got D's in everything else and was put on academic probation.

By my second semester, I abandoned engineering and switched to a political science major, which gave me greater flexibility in the variety of classes I could take, as well as the schedule of those classes. Nevertheless, my social life continued to be a priority over classes and I became Social Chairman of the dorms, ending my second semester on academic probation. I also fell in love with a beautiful coed and fabulous dance partner—I even bought her a diamond engagement ring—before breaking off the engagement right before the summer break. My friend Rich and I had made ourselves *personae non gratae* at Griffiths Hall by sailing trash can lids off the 8th floor balcony, rolling a bowling ball down the hall through the housemother's door, and projecting an X-rated movie on the side of the girl's dorm, so before I returned to Los Angeles for the summer, I signed up for fraternity rush in the fall.

I went back to work at the Los Angeles Department of Water & Power for the summer, but was placed in a different section of the Commercial Division, working the swing shift, 4 to 11:30 p.m. This section was populated mostly by blacks, who soon began to haze me with racial commentary. Never one to be silent, I took the hazing as a challenge and responded to each of their comments with comments of my own. They would tell me to "watch your back, the brothers are going to get you." I'd respond, "I've already given the Klan your home addresses." The intensity of the hazing increased when I started dating a very sexy black cheerleader who worked at the Department.

Midway through the summer, Lee, Maceo and Alvin began talking nearby about "MJQ" and "Night in Tunisia." I listened for a while, then interrupted and asked, "Who is MJQ?" They were astounded. "You don't know MJQ? You've never heard MJQ's version of 'Night in Tunisia'?" This was culture shock; this was two different worlds intersecting. After making fun of "the poor white boy" who didn't know MJQ, they took pity on me and explained that "MJQ" was short for the "Modern Jazz Quartet," and "Night in Tunisia" was a great jazz standard composed by Dizzy Gillespie. When they realized I wasn't even familiar with "jazz," they knew how culturally impoverished my life had been. This seemed to be the pivotal event that started to break down the barriers between us, for they immediately invited me to visit a jazz club with them after work.

We got off work around midnight, and drove to the "It Club" to see a jazz group from Texas called "The Jazz Crusaders." The "It Club" was a very dark, funky, smoke-filled club in South Central Los Angeles. I was the only white there and it wasn't long before someone challenged my right to be there. Before I could even respond, Lee Wax stepped in, and asserting his 6' 3", 220-pound stature, assured my challenger that, "He is with us. Leave him alone." Later, Maceo, who had been a U. S. Marine, showed me a few tricks about how to handle bigger, tougher guys.

The Jazz Crusaders took the stage and opened with "Young

Rabbits," a fast-moving, pulsating number with a great trombone solo. It was stunning. I never had heard this kind of music. The next day, I bought the Jazz Crusaders' first album and returned to work that afternoon asking questions about which other jazz groups I should look for, which albums I should buy, and so forth. Inspired by my enthusiasm, Lee, Maceo and Alvin proceeded to give me a short course in jazz history over the next several weeks and took me out after work to see other jazz groups playing in town. They even took me to an after-hours (2–6 a.m.) club, where I first heard Miles Davis. A whole new world of music that I never knew existed had been opened for me and I became, and remain, a dedicated jazz fan.

I learned about more than just music from my black friends at the Los Angeles Department of Water & Power. They gave me my first lessons about how racism operates. The blacks were running the department, but the young supervisor, Mr. Bloom, was white. Mr. Bloom was a nice guy, and he treated me well, but whenever anyone had a question about how to do something, they went to Alvin, not Mr. Bloom, because Alvin knew all aspects of the job and Mr. Bloom didn't. I looked around the Department of Water & Power and saw the same situation elsewhere. Blacks were hired in subordinate positions, but none as supervisors or managers—no matter how competent or experienced they were. I respected Alvin as a fine man and a supremely competent employee and I asked him one day, "How does it make you feel to know you are a much better employee than Mr. Bloom—indeed, we all rely on you for information and advice about how to do our jobs—but he is the supervisor and you're just a senior clerk?" Alvin looked at me and with an expression I can still see today, smiled his big tooth-filled smile and said, "That's just the way it is." I didn't know—but Alvin knew—that the Los Angeles Department of Water & Power was one of the few employers at the time in Los Angeles that would even hire blacks for white-collar work. He was not going to rock that boat! It would take a new generation of black employees and a civil rights attorney named Tom Hunt twenty years later to bust up employment discrimination at the Los Angeles Department of Water & Power, and other Los Angeles city departments, but the changes would come too late to help Alvin.

I learned a lot from the blacks I worked with at the Los Angeles Department of Water & Power. Blacks know not what America claims to be, but what America really is. Even though I grew up working-class poor, I never grew up thinking my life had boundaries; I always felt I could go as far as my talent took me. The blacks I worked with in Los Angeles grew up with boundaries all around them. They attended the worst schools, lived in the most dangerous neighborhoods, had the worst health care, received the least support for going to college, and were barred from employment in most white-collar corporate jobs and many government agencies— their reward for being captured and brought to America involuntarily, then having 200+ years of wages stolen from them by slavery.

I returned to Cal in September and entered fraternity rush. I received bids from Jewish fraternities, but elected to join a non-Jewish house. Only later did I learn I was the first Jew and that offering me a bid had been controversial among the active members. I liked the guys, they had good intramural sports teams and a good house GPA. Maybe the habits that led to their good GPA would rub off on me. Also, the house was next door to the Sigma Alpha Mu ("Sammie") house, where my best friend, Geoff, had pledged; the Sammies were known for great parties, plus they had a basketball court in their backyard where a nerdy little guy named Michael Milken hung out.

I had a great pledge class of fourteen guys, and I immediately fell into the active social life at of the fraternity; by the second semester, I was Social Chairman. Nevertheless, my grades improved moderately, probably as the result of mandatory study hours for pledges and the good study habits of my roommate, Tom, a near straight-A political science major.

I continued to work during the school year, but switched jobs from refereeing intramural sports to working after school twenty hours a week and Saturday as a recreation director for the Oakland Recreation Department. I returned to the Los Angeles Department of Water & Power for the summer, again working the swing shift. I had sold my '57 Ford and was riding a hot Ducati 250 Scrambler, a fast dirt bike which I raced occasionally in motocross events and hill climbs. There was no dress code on the swing shift and my regular outfit of jeans, boots and a t-shirt, coupled with the loud, fast motorcycle, earned me the nickname "Dean" from Lee Wax— his reference to James Dean.

I entered my junior year at Cal with a 1.8 GPA. Cal probably should have flunked me out, but once again the expectations created by my high test scores—in this case, the SAT—saved me. But I was in trouble academically. I wanted to attend a first-rate law school, and I knew not many top law schools were admitting students with 1.8 GPA's. I would have to get more serious with the books.

I signed up for 18 units, including a class in California constitutional history given by Professor Jacobus tenBroek, a difficult taskmaster and notoriously hard grader. TenBroek was blinded at age 7 by an arrow shot into his eye, and he asked students in his classes to sit in the same seats each class so he would know where everyone was and be able to call out their names when he wanted to call on them to speak or answer a question. He was a lawyer, had been a law professor at Harvard and Berkeley, and taught his classes using the Socratic method. Rather than lecturing or supplying answers to the students, he elicited answers from the students with focused questions. He was tall, perhaps 6' 3", with ramrod-straight posture and a steel-trap mind. He was rumored to have obtained the highest grades ever given a law student at Boalt, the University of California Berkeley law school, and he demanded prepared and thoughtful participation by the students in his classes, most of whom held him in awe and aspired to attend law school. He was also the first recipient of the student-initiated "Best Professor" award given at Cal, despite the fact that he rarely handed out A's.

For the first time in my life, I was engaged in class. The reading assignments were difficult and sometimes voluminous, but I read everything carefully so I would be able to participate in class discussion. By the third class, tenBroek had memorized where each of his students was sitting and could turn toward each student before calling on him or her. Sometimes, when I hadn't spoken for a while, he would turn to me in the middle of a class discussion and say, "Saperstein, what is your opinion about this?" remembering that a couple of classes earlier I had expressed an alternative point-of-view on the topic. He kept the discussion going so quickly, I forgot he was blind. I not only participated actively in class, I frequently went to his office hours to talk to him about reading materials that had stimulated me. He was one of my few professors who ever made himself available to students—most relied on their readers or TA's to deal with students—and he never failed to help me understand the subject better. One book, Alexander Meiklejohn's *Free Speech and Its Relation to Self-Government*, was particularly thought-provoking, and, after we talked about it in class and at his office hour, tenBroek said, "Why don't you give Alexander a call and take a walk with him. He lives by me in the Berkeley Hills and walks every morning. That is a great way to talk to him." Professor tenBroek gave me Alexander Meiklejohn's home telephone number and I called and made an appointment to meet him at his house. Meiklejohn had been President of Amherst, and in his 70s had become a constitutional scholar. He now was 93, yet able to walk up and down the hilly Berkeley streets as fast as me, while carrying on a conversation. His mind was quick and alert and I struggled to keep up with him—both in mind and body! He was kind enough to take several long walks to discuss his theories, which, in my opinion, remain the most profound and useful interpretation of the real purposes of the First Amendment.

During the semester, we had to write a half dozen papers about the various reading assignments, and, as the course final, tenBroek asked us to write a paper, of any length, explaining why the particular reading assignments had been chosen for the course—that is, to explain the thread of connections and interwoven ideas and concepts in the diverse reading assignments. At first, I thought it was a wide-open and easy topic, but as I reflected more, I realized it was a very focused and rigorous topic, as it required that we understand the very essence of the course. As I sat down to contemplate an essay, I didn't even know how to organize the material because the reading assignments had been so diverse and the lessons learned from each often seemed unrelated to other readings. I made a couple of false starts, then, late one night, studying by myself in the fraternity attic, everything seemed to come together in my mind and I wrote non-stop until dawn. The course reading assignments seemed seamless and clear as I made connections from one to another. TenBroek was asking us to understand the very essence of what constitutes a court, as distinguished from other types of decision-making bodies, many of which have many of the characteristics and attributes of courts. I felt a great sense of understanding and accomplishment—probably the first time I'd ever felt good about a learning experience. I typed up the paper and turned it in, along with a self-addressed postcard, the traditional way of receiving early notice of grades.

Three weeks later, I received my postcard in the mail: It read, "Grade on Final Paper A ; Grade in Course: A ." I was stunned. I hadn't received anything higher than a B- on any of my shorter papers. Later, I learned I had received the only A in the class of 93 students. I called tenBroek's secretary and scheduled an appointment. When I showed up, I told him I had been very surprised to receive an A on the paper and the course. TenBroek looked at me with a big smile and said, "Saperstein, you have a first-class mind. That is one of the best papers that ever has been written for me. I'd like to keep it." All my life I'd been told I had great potential, but I never had entirely believed it. Now, I knew it was possible for me to be a good student. My GPA for my last two years at Cal was a much-improved 3.6.

I CONTINUED TO WORK WEEKDAY AFTERNOONS and Saturdays as a recreation director for the Oakland Recreation Department. My first year had been spent at Broadway Terrace Elementary School, a white, upper-middle-class school in Oakland near Piedmont. I enjoyed it, but playground activity was slow; most of the kids had other activities planned for them and didn't hang out at the playground, as I had done as a kid. For my second year, I was assigned to Washington Elementary School, an inner-city school in a tough part of West Oakland. All the kids were black. Years later, I was told by the Recreation Department that I had been an "experiment," as the first white director to be assigned to a black school in West Oakland. Whether an "experiment" or not, I loved it. Instead of seeing 5–10 kids a day, as had been the case at Broadway Terrace, I had 200 kids a day on the Washington School playground. These kids had nowhere else to go and they devoured every activity I planned for them. These kids were so responsive; when I listened to them and showed them respect, it seemed like they were willing to do anything I asked.

I had basketball, baseball and football teams playing intramurally in a little league I set up, as well as competing in the Oakland City Leagues. I had track meets, I had a Tiny Tots program on Saturday, and I even had an adult softball game weekdays after work in the spring. And I had loads of talent on my sports teams. That year, I won the City basketball and football after-school league championships, even after benching my star quarterback on the eve of the championship football game for fighting with another kid. I had so much fun with these kids, I'd take them to ball games on Sunday, my only day off. When the Harlem Globetrotters came to town, I called my uncle Abe and said I'd like to have a few tickets for the Globetrotters game. He asked, "How many?" I said, "Fifty." Abe laughed, and said, "Sure." The only problem was, I only could round up three cars for the game, so we piled forty-seven kids, plus three adults, into three cars. I had nineteen 4th to 6th graders and two adults packed into my four-door 1951 Buick Roadmaster—one of the biggest cars ever made. When we drove by cops directing traffic near the stadium, with kids hanging out of the windows, I was certain I'd be stopped, but the cops just waved at us. When I got to the game, Uncle Abe not only had given us very good seats, he invited all the kids into the dressing room at half-time to meet the players and get programs and autographs. In later years, Uncle Abe loved telling the story how his nephew had asked for a "few" tickets and showed up with forty-seven kids.

I was having a great time on the playground working with the kids, as well as playing basketball or baseball every day. I also began learning about life in the inner city. The Oakland Police Department was a notoriously racist, violent police department and operated like an invading army—ever-present, asserting their authority, not just to control misbehavior but more often to let everyone know they were in charge, whacking people on the back or head with their batons if they received back-talk. Visiting some of my kids' houses, I saw what poverty looked like—small, run-down wood buildings with many people living in them—and many of the adults unemployed. I saw kids get sick, but not receive medical treatment. In talking to the fine principal at Washington School, Mr. Jefferson, I learned that many of these kids arrived at school unfed and without adequate sleep and were not physically ready to learn. The deck really was stacked against them. This was very disturbing to me, but, having grown up in a nonpolitical household, I didn't have any political perspective on the situation and couldn't fully interpret what I was seeing.

While I was gaining new and different insights into life in the inner cities of America, the Free Speech Movement erupted on campus. Cal students who had spent the previous summer working with civil rights groups in the South returned to campus in the fall, set up tables in Sproul Plaza—the main gathering place on the University of California campus—and began handing out literature and soliciting funds to support civil rights activities in the South. Prodded by complaints from local right-wing politicians and U.C. Regents, the Cal Chancellor ordered the tables to disband and the solicitation to stop. When the students refused, the tables were confiscated and the students cited for breaking campus rules. Speeches and demonstrations in Sproul Plaza began and continued for almost two months on a near-daily basis.

As the momentum of the demonstrations built, I began to spend more time in Sproul Plaza, listening to speeches, reading literature, talking to demonstrators, and trying to understand the issues. The First Amendment right for students to set up tables, hand out political literature, solicit contributions, and speak about civil rights issues seemed apparent—if students couldn't do that on campus, what was left of the First Amendment for them? How could the University be blind enough to not understand that students had a constitutional right to exercise these freedoms at appropriate times and places on campus? Indeed, exercising constitutional freedoms, and participating in important social issues seemed to me to be desirable not only on a social, but also on an educational level. The students made one compelling argument after another, and the University administration responded with stonewalling and gibberish. It was at this point that Mario Savio gave his famous Sproul Plaza speech.

It was at noon in Sproul Plaza on a brisk and sunny fall day. Savio stood on Sproul steps before a microphone wearing a brown corduroy coat, with his thin, uncombed hair blowing with the wind. Addressing 5,000 students gathered in front of him, he explained clearly the history of the events that had caused the confrontation with the University, the efforts to resolve the crisis with the University, and the University's intransigence in negotiations. He described how the University was run, what economic interests it served and drew connections to how political power in America was organized and how it operated, concluding with the words, "When the operation of the machine becomes so odious, you have to put your body in the gears and stop it."

The night of Savio's speech, I woke up and was so disturbed about what was happening, and what Savio had said, I had to talk to someone. The only person I could think of was my Sociology TA, Gerald Marx, so I called him and I woke him up at 3 a.m. After I explained what was bothering me, Mr. Marx asked, "Do you think this could wait until the morning? I could meet you for breakfast." I met him for breakfast at 8 a.m. on the terrace overlooking Sproul

Plaza, and for over two hours he listened to me and patiently helped me understand the connections the demonstrators were trying to make between organizing civil rights activities on campus, and social causes off–campus, and how important the table/leafletting activities on campus were to supporting civil rights struggles in the South. Now the issues were even more real and concrete, not just constitutional abstractions, for me. All of a sudden, what the students were demonstrating about was beginning to remind me about the living conditions and police behavior I was seeing daily in West Oakland.

A few days later, over 800 students occupied the University administration building and refused to leave, while thousands more conducted a supportive vigil outside in Sproul Plaza. After returning to campus from work that night, I joined the vigil. A few hours later, I saw two of my fraternity brothers circulating in the crowd, with cans marked "FSM Donations." Thinking they actually were supporting the demonstrators, I went up to them and asked why. "No, we're not supporting them. This is just an RF [short for "Rat Fuck"]. We're keeping the money," they told me, laughing. Eight-hundred students were risking expulsion and jail to protect First Amendment rights for university students and support the civil rights movement, and my fraternity brothers thought it all was a joke.

The next night at dinner, I sat nervously at the table, eating little, knowing I had to say something to my fraternity brothers sitting at the large U-shaped table. As dessert was about to be served, I rose to speak. I recounted the events of the past night, explaining how two of our brothers, as well as members of other fraternities, were mocking the Free Speech Movement, and, worse, ripping off their collections—which they certainly could have used for bail, as 800+ of them had been dragged out of Sproul Plaza and arrested. I explained, "These students, indeed, all of us, have a constitutional right to express political and social opinions and distributing literature on campus and collecting funds is part of that constitutional right. Whether you agree or not with the causes they are advocating, you must respect their integrity and courage and their right to exercise First Amendment freedoms. Collecting money under false pretenses is worse than just failing to support the First Amendment right to organize and express opinions—ripping them off is dishonest and cynical. Many of those students are still in jail and that money might have helped bail some of them out." The room, which had been very noisy, now was completely silent. Then, someone said, "Why do you have the big beak, Guy—it was a good RF," as laughter went around the room. Of the forty-five brothers sitting at dinner, no one spoke in support of me. Dessert was served; noise and talking resumed. I sat there looking around the room and realized this was the beginning of the end of my relationship with the fraternity. I was Rush Chairman, which normally is the last stepping-stone to becoming President, and I had had a lot of fun living there, but that night with my brothers, I realized I didn't really know these guys or understand their callousness and insensitivity. I moved out the next semester and never returned, except once two years later to be the "Grand Inquisitor" during the initiation of pledges.

I spent another summer working full-time as a recreation director and was reassigned to the combined Havenscourt Junior High School and Lockwood Elementary School playground, located at 67th and East 14th Avenue in East Oakland—probably the most crime-ridden and impoverished neighborhood in Oakland. The playground was very large, with two grass baseball diamonds, several asphalt baseball diamonds, a junior-high-school gym, outdoor basketball courts, and several recreation buildings for indoor activities. I was made head director, with six recreation directors under my supervision.

I had one of the best summers of my life there. I set up intramural baseball and basketball leagues, held a boxing tournament in the gym, organized a two-day track meet, started a nightly baseball game for adults returning from work, provided arts and crafts for young kids, a tiny-tots program for the small kids, and teen dances in the gym on Friday night. I regularly reported 400–500

kids on the playground and rarely did I go home at 8 p.m., the end
of my eight-hour day. I'd do the Tiny Tots program in the morning,
play basketball and baseball with the kids during the day, then join
the parents in the evening for the adult baseball game.

On Friday nights, I'd drive back to Berkeley on my motorcycle,
pick up my girlfriend, then open up Havenscourt gym at 9 p.m. for
2–3 hours of rocking to the beat of Motown—Marvin Gaye, The
Temptations, Aretha Franklin, Frankie Lymon, Sam Cooke, Brook
Benton, The Four Tops, Mary Wells, Sam & Dave. The kids called
me "Mr. Guy" and invariably put on Mary Wells' song, "My Guy,"
expecting me to get out on the floor with my lady to show what I
could do. If I made a good move, they greeted it with whoops and
hollers. The kids would form two lines for couples to peel off and
stroll down in-between, showing their moves. I would tell the kids,
"I can do anything you can do, so show me your moves!" There
was no choice but to learn all the dances—the Jerk, the Chicken,
the Pony, the Fish. Recently, my wife and I attended a benefit for
the San Francisco Symphony where Martha Reeves and the
Vandellas performed. Midway through her performance, she called
out, "Is there anyone who is going to get up on the stage and dance
with me?" My wife and I jumped on stage and ran through all the
'60s black dance steps with Reeves. I couldn't have done it without
those nights in the Havenscourt gym!

I had my own style of disciplining the kids. When fights broke
out on the playground, I'd take the combatants over to the gym,
put 16-ounce boxing gloves on them, and let them flail at each other
for a few rounds. The gloves were so large and padded, doing damage to someone was nearly impossible, and the kids would get so
tired swinging the heavy gloves, they'd back off in exhaustion, forgetting the underlying grievances.

The kids constantly asked to ride my motorcycle. After a month
of their pestering me, one morning I said OK and told one of the
toughest 9th graders to hop on the back. With 100 kids watching on
the street in front of the school, I popped the clutch and stood the
bike up on the back wheel and did a "wheelie" down the street for

about 100 yards. Then I turned my bike around and did it again. I pulled up to the gang of kids watching, who were all open-mouthed. I looked at my passenger and he was about as white as I was. That was the last time that summer anyone asked for a ride on my motorcycle!

The major problem I had at Havenscourt playground was with the Oakland Police. I wanted to establish good relations with them, so whenever I saw police officers in the neighborhood, I let them know I always had a pot of coffee in the recreation office and they were welcome to stop by. I thought if they got to know the kids—and the kids knew them—some of the mutual animosity might abate. And officers did stop by, but they would drive their cars on the playground to my office. I'd explain to them that I didn't let any of the kids ride bicycles on the playground, as that often led to accidents and injuries, that I walked my motorcycle to my office, and that they were setting a bad example, and making my job harder, by driving their cars on the playground. The officers generally gave me an ambiguous grunt, then drove on the playground the next time. Worse, some of them began to drive their cars throughout the playground, looking and acting like an imperialist army. Occasionally, a kid would yell something at the cops, which prompted the cops to jump out of their car and throw the kid against the car, handcuff him, and take him to juvenile hall. I began to object about this, explaining that I had the playground completely under control, I wasn't having problems, but that they were *creating* problems. I got nowhere talking to them and I realized that these guys had absolutely no interest in breaking down barriers between them and the community—as they might have done if they had gotten out of their cars, taken off their helmets, and walked around acting like human beings. Their behavior was calculated, instead, to intimidate the kids. After several confrontations with them about their provocative behavior, I told them I didn't want any Oakland police officers on my playground unless I had a situation I couldn't handle—in which case I'd call them from the telephone in my office.

The police stayed away for several weeks, then began driving on the playground again. The next day I went to the Oakland Police Department headquarters at 7th and Washington, and asked to speak with the officer in charge of the Patrol Division. I was directed upstairs, then was left to wait in the hallway for half an hour before being brought into a very small, windowless office to meet a sergeant. After introducing myself as a UC Berkeley student working as a recreation director at Havenscourt, I explained what had been happening on the playground. I told him that I had tried my best to be friendly and cooperative with the patrol officers, but that they were intentionally provoking confrontations with my kids and causing problems for me, in the short run, and for the community, in the long run. The officer listened with sullen politeness, but gave me no assurances that anything would change. I next went to Mrs. Pitts, the black woman who ran the Oakland Recreation Department, and explained the same thing. She understood what I was talking about, and seemed sympathic, but told me she wasn't sure she could do anything about the police.

A week later, Mrs. Pitts came out to Havenscourt on a Saturday. I was running a track meet for 200 kids. She watched for a while and I explained all the events. I was proud to have organized such a complicated event, and even prouder to have my boss standing there watching it with me—and watching it work so well. "This is fabulous, and you are doing a fabulous job out here," Mrs. Pitts told me after the meet was over, "but I came out today to tell you that I have to transfer you to Marshall Elementary School, starting Monday." "This is because of the cops, isn't it?" I asked. "I can't talk about it anymore, but I can tell you that you are doing an excellent job and this has nothing to do with your performance as a recreation director," she told me. I was stunned by the turn of events and felt totally powerless. I also was disappointed in Mrs. Pitts and really pissed off about losing my job at Havenscourt; I expected her to back me up and make an issue out of the police misbehavior. In retrospect, I understand my expectations were naive. Oakland was run by a Republican mayor and City Council, and Mrs. Pitts knew that in any confrontation between the Recreation and

Police departments, the police would prevail. She liked me, but she wasn't ready to lose her job supporting a part-time recreation director.

The following Monday, I reported to Marshall, a small elementary school in the Oakland Hills. The place was deserted. I spent the week playing chess with the few kids who stopped by, and quit my job the following week. Working at Washington Elementary School and Havenscourt Junior High had been the best jobs I'd ever had, but I knew the Recreation Department never would put me back at a school where I might have more confrontations with the cops; I would remain exiled in small schools in the middle-class, white neighborhoods in the Oakland hills, which I wasn't willing to do. It was very sad to be separated from my job and the kids at Havenscourt/Lockwood and to know there was nothing I could do about it. But I had learned a lot about the police and power in Oakland. I also began to see that becoming a lawyer was a way to overcome my sense of powerlessness, and, perhaps, someday represent the powerless people that society pushes around.

POLITICS NEVER HAD BEEN AN IMPORTANT PART of my upbringing. My parents subscribed to the *Valley Times*, which I read to keep up with sports and current events. But rarely did my family discuss political or social issues at home. My Dad even voted Republican. I must have followed his lead, as I recall in 1960 arguing with my boss at Berg's Liquors that Richard Nixon was "more qualified" to become President than Jack Kennedy, due to Nixon's longer tenure in Congress and experience as Vice President.

But now political events and my own experiences were clashing with the political complacency I had grown up with. The Watts Riots had forced me to read and think about the root causes of poverty, and my experiences with the Oakland Police Department confirmed the complaints about police abuses and demands for "civilian review boards" that were coming out of black neighborhoods throughout the nation. The Free Speech Movement had raised profound questions in my mind about who was running the

University of California, in whose interests it was being run, and the limits of basic freedoms that the University had tried to impose on students. In a larger context, the movement brought home the connection of free speech on campus and the civil rights movement. Watching the civil rights marches and demonstrations, and police hosings and beatings of demonstrators on TV, raised even more basic questions about America's commitment to the equal protection of the laws. And the developing conflict in Vietnam—which I might be called upon to fight—forced me to study the causes and purposes of America's involvement. Madame Ngu's visit to the Berkeley campus, her speech at Harmon Gym, and the attempts by the Vietnam Day Committee to stop troop trains as they rolled through Berkeley, heightened the immediacy of Vietnam. My perception of the world was changing. And so was I.

By 1965, my senior year, the war in Vietnam was beginning to escalate. Using an incident in the Gulf of Tonkin that history shows may never have occurred, President Lyndon Johnson called on Congress to pass the "Gulf of Tonkin" resolution authorizing the commitment of more U. S. combat troops in Vietnam. The military draft was reinstituted. I was 21 and knew I could be drafted as soon as my II-S (Student) deferment expired, so I began reading about Vietnam and attending demonstrations and teach-ins about the war. Senator Wayne Morse, one of only two U. S. Senators to vote against the Gulf of Tonkin resolution, spoke at Berkeley and provided a compelling indictment of our country's involvement. Robert Scheer, then editor of *Ramparts* magazine and one of the most articulate opponents of the war, wrote an eighty-page pamphlet explaining the origins of the conflict between North and South Vietnam, how the country had been partitioned by the French, how France had fought the nationalists led by Ho Chi Minh, and how the French were defeated at Dien Bien Phu. The terms of the Geneva Accords called for a two-year period of continued partitioning of Vietnam, then unification and elections—which everyone understood would be won by Ho Chi Minh. Indeed, President Eisenhower later wrote in his memoirs that if free elections had been held, Ho Chi Minh would have received 80% of the vote and the U.S.-supported Ngo Dinh Diem, who earlier had been part of the French colonial government, less than 20%. Unwilling to concede an election to Ho, the U.S. poured over $2 billion in aid to South Vietnam, providing 50–75% of the South Vietnam government budget, in an effort to prop up and popularize Diem and support Diem's frustration of a unification election. By 1959 it had become apparent that Diem, supported by the Americans, would not permit elections, and the Viet Cong insurgency emerged. By 1966, young American men were being asked to risk their lives to engage in a civil war—and to support the unpopular side in that war.

In an effort to learn more about Vietnam, I read every government pronouncement about the war, and attended speeches on campus by supporters of the war, including the Secretary of Defense, Robert McNamara. These people based their support for the war on the need to prevent the "domino effect," whereby China, which allegedly was using Vietnam as its proxy, would sweep throughout the Far East, turning every country into communist gulags, if they were not stopped in Vietnam. I thought the government's argument was preposterous. Vietnam had been fighting for independence for 1,000 years and historically had been an enemy of China. Ho Chi Minh was a Vietnamese nationalist who had studied in America and modeled the Vietnamese constitution on the American constitution. Ho Chi Minh was every bit as much the father of his country as George Washington had been ours, and he had no interest in fighting America for the purpose of expanding China's influence, let alone letting China take over his country. Indeed, America had taken over France's imperialist role in Vietnam, making sure we retained access to exploit Vietnam's natural resources and the ability to sell goods there. I began to think those reasons were insufficient to support our bombardment of Vietnam, which was causing hundreds of thousands of deaths and costing tens of billions of dollars of America's resources that should be going to the rebuilding of America's cities, the education of its youth, and healthcare. I also began to think that America's purposes were insufficient to justify the injuries and deaths of the young men who were being sent there to fight a war they neither understood nor supported.

In anticipation of going to law school, I took the Law School Admission Test in late 1965, hoping to score well enough to overcome my poor freshman and sophomore year grades and get into a first-class law school. I talked to one of Professor tenBroek's teaching assistants who had scored well on the LSAT and had gotten admitted to Harvard Law School, and he told me there was no way to prepare for the test, "Just get a good night's sleep and do the best you can." I remember asking him what he had scored and he said, "96 percentile." I thought to myself how fantastic it would be to get such a high score.

I took the test and waited for the results. Two months later, I received my computer-generated notice from the Scholastic Aptitude Testing Service. I opened the envelope slowly, knowing that the test score would determine whether, and where, I could go to law school. I looked at the score: I had scored in the 99.6th percentile. The next day, I filled out my law school application and took it, along with my LSAT score, to the admissions office at Boalt Hall School of Law on the University of California campus. The admission officer looked at the application, my recommendation from Professor tenBroek, and my LSAT score and said, "You're in."

I didn't want to leave Berkeley and was almost certain I wanted to attend Boalt, but decided to apply to some of the major eastern law schools thinking I that might want to live in the East for a while and that perhaps a degree from Harvard or Columbia might be more impressive on a resume. I applied to and was admitted to Harvard, Columbia and the University of Pennsylvania law schools. I visited the schools, sat in on some classes, but the students were too well dressed and the discussions were overly stiff, formal and competitive—very much like the portrayal of law schools in the movie *Paper Chase*, with John Houseman starring as the pedantic and authoritarian law professor. I chose to stay in Berkeley and go to Boalt Hall.

I graduated from U.C. Berkeley with a degree in political science mid-term in January 1966. Since law school would not begin until September, I applied to graduate school in English at San Francisco State University. I had taken only one English course at Cal, but I had enjoyed it immensely. My reading of good literature was not extensive, so I thought a semester of English courses would be a lot of fun and that I might improve my writing abilities in the process. I enrolled in three literature courses and two writing courses. I received A's on my first writing assignment in each of my writing courses and immediately decided I wasn't going to learn anything in those classes, so I stopped going, didn't bother to withdraw, and received F's. The two American lit courses were good and my one and only Shakespeare course was fantastic. Everyone in the class was a drama major working in a Shakespeare production which the professor, Mrs. Hiken, was directing. The students were all future actors. I soon began dating one of the actresses and the group accepted me as one of their own, inviting me to their parties and acting gigs.

My semester in the English Department was just pure fun, but the other students took the readings very seriously—dissecting the language as closely as any lawyer reads a contract. And, like lawyers who often are quite ingenious in fashioning arcane interpretations of statutes, cases and documents, while managing to miss the broader purposes of public policies, the English students often formulated tight interpretations of the use of language, while entirely missing the authors' intentions and the broader importance of the literature. Majoring in English would be good preparation for law school, but for the wrong reason!

When not in class, I worked as a reader and TA in an undergraduate constitutional history course at Cal. The course was considered a "mickey," as the professor was known for handing out a lot of high grades, especially to the football players and sorority girls who flocked to the course. I derived perverse pleasure in requiring that all course assignments, particularly the term papers, be completed before any credits for the course were received, and I gave out fair grades to everyone—not falsely inflated grades to the athletes. Their appeals to the professor were unavailing, as he was too lazy to read their papers.

My most serious activity during my seven months between graduation and law school was my political work against the war and my class at the Free University studying Marxism and American power structure under the tutelage of David Horowitz. Horowitz then was an avowed radical socialist and one of the leading scholars of power relationships in America, and he also wrote for *Ramparts*, then the leading left-wing popular magazine. He has since become a right-wing idealogue. His course was not-for-credit, it was education for the sake of education. I read every assignment, including the classic Marxist texts, the American socialist economists Paul Baran and Paul Sweezy, as well as *Monthly Review* and writers on American power structure such as C. Wright Mills, Carey McWilliams, and G. William Domhoff. Encouraged by Horowitz, I even obtained lengthy government reports from the Securities and Exchange Commission, Federal Trade Commission, and various U. S. Senate committees that revealed—although that was not their intention—much of the interconnections among wealthy families, strategic banks, corporations and foreign policy. I was beginning to understand "who rules America," and the dominant role of money in American politics. The stimulation of the course readings was enhanced by the students who frequented Horowitz's small classes, including Mario Savio, Mark Rudd and Tom Hayden. Savio then was working at Cody's Books on Telegraph Avenue, trying like me to understand the deeper relationships that led to the domination of power by wealthy elites. I stopped by frequently to talk to Savio about the readings, and he invariably had the most profound insights, and, never satisfied with pat answers, asked the most difficult questions. Savio was one of the most intelligent, thoughtful, fair-minded, and honest persons I've ever met, and the way he critically analyzed ideas, and refused always to accept easy answers regardless of whether offered by the Left, Right or Center, had a great impact on me. He encouraged me to analyze ideas from the Left just as critically as ideas from liberals, moderates or conservatives.

While I was developing a deeper political consciousness, through reading and discussion, the reality of the war in Vietnam pressed upon me. In the spring of 1966, an editor at *Ramparts*, Robert Scheer, announced he would run for Congress on an antiwar platform against a Democrat incumbent, Jeffery Cohelan, who was liberal on social issues, but supported the War. Scheer had been to Vietnam several times and was a brilliant critic of U.S. involvement there; as the campaign progressed, he became a knowledgeable critic of Congressman Cohelan's performance on many issues affecting his district. And, despite his New York intellectual background, and his full beard, he related very well with many types of people—I watched him at many house parties and rallies, as well as just talking to people one-on-one, and realized he was never patronizing or condescending with people. He didn't schmooze or glad-hand people, but he could communicate complex ideas with great clarity. But Scheer never had run for any political office, was unknown outside of left-wing circles in Berkeley, and was given no chance to beat an incumbent, especially one who regularly won with 70+% of the vote.

I had been critical of the antiwar movement at Berkeley. It had tried to stop troop trains, held demonstrations on campus, and marched through the streets of Oakland, but it wasn't talking to people. I attended a few meetings of the Vietnam Day Committee, and, each time, proposed that, instead of just marching through neighborhoods, we go *into* neighborhoods and talk to people one-on-one. I wanted the antiwar movement to be understood by people like my parents—good people, not necessarily political, but open-minded enough to listen to the reasons behind the protests. I said it wasn't enough to get attention by being controversial or outrageous, we had to talk to and persuade people. That was the only way to stop the war. But no one seemed interested in my prosaic notions of political change.

The Bob Scheer for Congress campaign provided an opportu-

nity to talk to ordinary people about the war. I signed up as a precinct worker going door-to-door in North Oakland. Our campaign
in North Oakland got off to a rocky start when we staged a Bob
Scheer rally in Bushrod Park, featuring the Country Joe and the
Fish band. Country Joe and the Fish were a long-hair hippie band
playing acid-rock and antiwar tunes and the black audience quietly watched, not quite knowing what to make of them. But Scheer,
demonstrating his ability to connect with all types of audiences,
gave a good speech about the war and racial injustice in Oakland
and the day was saved. Soon I was canvassing three precincts by
myself, and by the day of the election, I had gone to each address at
least three times to talk about issues. My precincts were working-
class, mostly black, and most of the people I spoke with did not
know much about the war, but were disturbed about what they did
know and they didn't understand the government's reasons any
better than I did. The more I talked to people face-to-face about
the war and Scheer, the more I began to think we had a real chance
to knock off Cohelan. Cohelan must have been getting worried too,
because during the last week of the campaign, he began to deliver
leaflets house-to-house, picturing him and Martin Luther King together, with the claim that Reverend Martin Luther King had en-
dorsed him. The claim was a complete lie, so the next morning, I
got up about 5 a.m. and began driving around the district locating
Cohelan's leafletters. He had no committed precinct workers, and,
instead, had hired day workers off the streets to deliver his literature. It was easy to offer each of these guys $20–$30 to give me all
their leaflets, which they did, and I collected about 30,000 of them.
I thought this was fair, since Cohelan was trying to steal the election with a false claim (King later repudiated Cohelan's endorsement claim in a letter to the Scheer campaign), but when our campaign manager found out about my maneuvers, he directed that
the literature be given back to Cohelan.

Aided by the return and distribution of the false King endorsement literature, Cohelan won 55–45%; my three precincts voted
between 57% and 61% in favor of Scheer. Even though 45% was a

loss, along with similar results in about a half dozen Democratic primaries around the country, a strong message was sent—Democratic candidates supporting the Vietnam war did so at their peril. Two years later, Hubert Humphrey lost the Presidential election to Nixon largely on this issue.

While I was involved with the war on a political level, I also had to deal with it personally. Some fraternity brothers of mine had enrolled in an Air Force Reserve program, the 349th Air Wing, at nearby Hamilton Air Force Base. As reserves, they committed themselves to a period of training, then monthly meetings and two weeks of summer camp. The program guaranteed that the participants never would be drafted into the Army and sent to a foxhole in Vietnam, and it paid each reserve $600–$800 a month. This seemed like the most benign way to satisfy my military obligation and avoid landing in a muddy foxhole in Vietnam, where I might get my balls shot off.

I drove out to Hamilton AFB, spoke to a recruiter, who assured me that the 349th Air Wing that I would be applying for never had been activated for military service. Monthly meetings and summer camp sounded a lot better than taking the chance of fighting in a war I didn't believe in, so I took the pilot aptitude test, scored in the 99th percentile, and was invited back for a medical exam, which I passed. Shortly after this, I received a postcard notifying me that I had been accepted into the pilot training program of the reserves. I put the card on the shelf above my desk, and looked at it several times each day, weighing my personal salvation against my political convictions. I didn't want to support the military, even the Air Force Reserves, but ducking the draft or becoming a war resister could lead to jail and the forfeiture of my dream of becoming a lawyer.

When I started law school in September, my military decision still was unresolved. During the first week of law school, a draft card turn-in was organized by the National Lawyers Guild, and a press conference against the war was held in a classroom at Boalt Hall. I listened to speeches given by a number of law students who had decided to turn their draft cards in explain their reasons, and watched as nearly 100 students turned in their draft cards in opposition to the war. I decided I couldn't sit on the fence any longer. I walked home, took the Air Force Reserve pilot acceptance card off the shelf and threw it into the wastebasket, stuffed an envelope addressed to my draft board with some antiwar literature, my draft card, and a note, stating, "I will no longer carry a draft card or cooperate with the draft in any way." I walked to a mailbox a block away and dropped my letter in with a sinking feeling that soon I would be classified I-A, drafted, and prosecuted criminally when I refused to report for the draft.

I heard nothing for several months, then I received a reclassification as I-Y—temporary disability. I had no idea why I had been reclassified I-Y, how long it would last, or whether I would be prosecuted as a draft resister. Years later, when I was defending draft resisters in federal court, I learned that the government had made a political decision not to prosecute draft resisters at that time, and, instead, to deny that draft resistance was having any effect. Only later, in 1967, when draft resistance became so widespread that the government could not ignore it, did prosecution of resisters begin. I had no way of knowing it at the time, but I had turned in my draft card at a very propitious moment. And my I-Y reclassification notice was the last time I ever heard from the Selective Service System.

In 1968, a U. S. Navy ship, the USS Pueblo, ventured too close to North Korea and was captured by North Korea. It was an international incident and one reserve unit was mobilized in response—the 349th Air Wing of the Air Force Reserve. Those guys spent four years on active duty in South Korea and Vietnam. Had I been one of them, as I came close to being, I have no doubt I would have acted out against the war in some way and been court-martialed, resulting in perhaps years in military jail, a dishonorable discharge, and possible disqualification from admission to the Bar. So the smart play—the Air Force Reserve option—had not turned out to be so smart after all. This was a pivotal moment for me: I decided that since it was impossible to accurately predict the future, I might as well do the right thing, follow my convictions, and live with the consequences, whatever they might be. This experience enhanced my tolerance for risk and helped me follow my intuition and sense of fairness without being overburdened with thoughts about what could go wrong.

3

My Law School Years

"Life can only be understood backwards, but it must be lived forwards."
—Søren Kierkegaard

ROM DAY ONE, law school was a disappointment to me. The curriculum was oriented toward developing lawyers who would serve property interests and large corporations. Classes were taught by pedants who reveled in their own brilliance and enjoyed demonstrating how ill-prepared and sloppy the thought processes of their students were. I recently attended my 30th law school reunion and one of my classmates, Eric Seitz, who I sat next to in my first-year classes, recalled how I sat in class, high in the back rows, muttering, "This is bullshit. I'm never going to last through three years of this crap. I can't stand this." I became openly contemptuous of the instruction, often walking into class late and leaving early. In the third week of class in my first year, I walked in late to my Real Property class, and was immediately called on by Professor Stefan Riesenfeld—a brilliant man, but someone more interested in teaching arcane property concepts from 15th-century England than preparing attorneys for property transactions in the 20th century. Professor Riesenfeld asked me to state the facts of a case assignment and explain the holding. I told Riesenfeld, "You better call on someone else. I haven't read the assignment. Besides, I don't even believe in your real property system!" The class exploded in laughter. Thereafter, whenever I showed up in property class, Riesenfeld turned to me and asked, "Mr. Saperstein, what is the Socialist point of view on this issue?" This gave me license to say anything I wanted, whether or not I had read the class assignment—which, most often, I had not. My third year, I barely attended classes, spending seven months on a strike in support of the proposed Third World College and engaging in extracurricular political activities. I learned the course materials on my own.

During my first year at Boalt, I helped establish Oakland Draft Help and raised money, mostly from Quaker organizations, to set up a draft counseling office across the street from the Oakland Induction Center in downtown Oakland. The induction calls were at 6 a.m. each weekday morning, so the draft center would open before that to provide last-minute advice to young men who had been drafted and ordered to appear for induction into the Army. We provided straight advice to individuals about deferment options, medical disabilities, conscientious objector status, draft resistance, including jail, as well as the possible consequences, and military alternatives to the draft. Occasionally, inductees showed up with their own draft deferment innovations. One young man brought a sheet of aluminum foil, shredded some of it just before 6 a.m., swallowed it, then left for the Induction Center, returning to our office late in the day to announce he had been disqualified for medical reasons. We asked what he had done with the aluminum foil, and he said, "I told them I had ulcers, and aluminum foil shows up on an X-ray looking like ulcers." Another young man showed up with a dozen raw eggs, ate a few of them before going into the Center, returned a few hours later to throw down a few more, then returned at lunch to swallow the remaining eggs. Apparently, after each ingestion of raw eggs, he had returned to the Induction Center and barfed his guts out. He, too, got a medical deferment. We never counseled this kind of strategy, but we got a big laugh out of such ingenuity.

In addition to last-minute, desperation draft counseling, I developed a program to explain alternatives to the draft and military to high school students. High schools regularly allowed the military services to explain their programs to students. I met with high school principals and explained that I was a law student at Boalt, that this program was run by law students, but that not all speakers would be lawyers or law students. I explained that not all of their students were looking for careers in the military and that those kids needed to know what the alternatives to the draft or voluntary military service were. Most principals let us speak, generally to auditorium-size student audiences, and often also to individual classes.

My program consisted of me or another law student explaining the qualifications for different types of military deferments, a conscientious objector discussing the qualifications and requirements for CO status, and an 18-year-old high school student from Berkeley, Jeff Mertens, who had become a war resister, explaining the basis for his decision not to cooperate with the draft. Later, we added some military veterans of the Vietnam War to talk about their experiences in Vietnam, including Donald Duncan, the famous Green Beret who had publicly quit the Army in disillusionment with the war. The students would listen politely to me as I laid out the legal deferments rap, but they were more interested in Jeff, who was so close in age to them and whose personal statement of courage was so powerful, and in the military speakers, who effectively explained the reality—and took the glory out—of the war. We generally got a great response from the students, and many accepted our offer of free draft counseling; some teachers even invited us to their classrooms to spend more time on the subject in a smaller classroom environment. Most of the high school principals thought our presentation was fair and a good balance to the military recruiters they allowed to solicit in their schools, but some thought we were too political or antiwar, and those principals didn't invite us back.

Many years later, when I was defending draft cases in federal court, I got some insight into how effective the anti-war movement had been: fewer than 50% of the inductees drafted for the Oakland Induction Center had appeared and stepped forward; on many days, only 10–20% of those called appeared, were qualified, and were inducted. Relatively few ever were found and prosecuted.

In early 1967, a coalition of antiwar groups in Berkeley organized a march and demonstration at the Oakland Induction Center. The police intervened, tear-gassed the crowd, and many people were arrested and/or bopped on the head by police batons. Our office across the street from the Induction Center became a refuge for demonstrators seeking to avoid the cops, although not a refuge against the tear-gas canisters the Oakland cops were shooting up and down the street. Following the "Oakland draft riots," the Alameda County District Attorney filed criminal conspiracy charges against seven of the organizers of the march and the "Oakland 7" trial ensued. Representing the prosecution was D. Lowell Jensen, a very fine veteran prosecutor who later became a federal judge; representing defendants was Charles Garry, perhaps the finest leftist attorney in the country. Garry was reputed to have defended more than seventy-five first-degree murder cases without a single first-degree murder conviction. Previously, he had successfully defended Huey P. Newton, Chairman of the Oakland-based Black Panther Party, from first-degree murder charges for killing an Oakland cop in a case also prosecuted by Jensen. I couldn't miss the opportunity to watch one of the great criminal trial attorneys, and I cut a lot of law classes to attend the trial.

The prosecution's star witness was a young man who had infiltrated the leadership of the antiwar coalition, even becoming a member of the steering committee. He had eaten meals with them, stayed at their houses, smoked pot with them, partied with them. They thought he was a friend, not a spy for the Oakland Police Department.

Every seat in the courtroom was filled when prosecutor Jensen called him to the stand as the first prosecution witness. He laid out in detail the internal discussions and planning that had led to the Oakland Induction Center march and protest, in an attempt to tie together seemingly innocent events, such as buying cardboard for signs, printing notices of the event, speaking at the demonstration, etc., with the unplanned disruption and violence—largely induced by provocative police misbehavior—that occurred at the demonstration. Such is the nature of conspiracy charges—the ability to tie together innocent "overt acts" to subsequent disruption to prove a plan to cause illegal behavior. He testified for most of two days, and then it was time for Charlie Garry to cross-examine.

The judge intoned, "Your witness, Mr. Garry." The courtroom was packed, with all eyes on Garry. Garry was a balding man of medium build in his early 60s with a serious demeanor, wearing a slightly baggy, dark suit. He sat at counsel's desk looking down, not moving. A minute passed in silence. Then he slowly rose. With an expression of pain and disgust on his face, he sauntered over to the witness box, and slowly removed his glasses. Leaning forward and looking at the witness directly in the eyes, he asked, "Do you know what the term 'rat fink' means?" "Objection," said Jensen; "Sustained," said the judge.

"Do you consider yourself a rat fink?" asked Garry, each time emphasizing the word "rat fink."

"Objection!" cried Jensen.

"Sustained," replied the judge.

"Have you ever worked as a rat fink before?" continued Garry, ignoring Jensen and the judge.

"Objection!"

"Sustained."

"Don't you think someone who befriends another, even going to his parents' house for family dinners, then uses that intimacy to gather information and testify against him is the very definition of a rat fink?"

"Objection!"

"Sustained."

I don't think Charlie Garry got a single one of the "rat fink" series of questions answered by the rat fink, but the point was made and it was indelible. The jury did not forget. After a long trial, the defendants were acquitted on all charges. Garry's performance left a lasting impression on me also, and I dreamed of such trial moments myself—with me controlling the courtroom and destroying witnesses as effectively as Charlie Garry. Later I would discover that such trial theatrics were not as easy to pull off as Charlie Garry made them seem. Nevertheless, it was dramatic moments like this, and the opportunity and ability to represent the causes I believed in, that reminded me why I wanted to be a lawyer, and kept me enrolled in law school.

The other thing that kept me motivated in school was my occasional attendance at conferences put on by groups such as the California Trial Lawyers Association, the American Trial Lawyers Association, California Continuing Education of the Bar, and the Practicing Law Institute. Unlike law school, which mainly was taught by cerebral pedants who never had seen the inside of a courtroom, these legal conferences were run by practicing attorneys, mostly trial attorneys, talking about practical trial issues, such as jury selection, opening statements, putting on direct evidence, cross-examining witnesses, dealing with expert witnesses, and final argument. The attorneys used real cases they were working on as examples to illustrate points, and the educational experience they created was animated and exciting.

For the summer of 1967, I had job offers to work in a poverty law program in Appalachia, and a Law Students Civil Rights Research Program project in Los Angeles with welfare recipients. I had just broken up with a long-term girlfriend and didn't relish the thought of being stuck alone in a small town in Appalachia, where I thought all the single women might be missing their front teeth, so I chose the Los Angeles job. As training, I was sent to New Haven, Connecticut to be educated by poverty lawyers and community activists. The training generally was good, but the sessions with some of the black community activists were overdone and counterproductive. At one day-long session, black activists berated the twenty law students for being white, stupid, ignorant of problems of poverty, and morally deficient. This went on for most of one day, and in the afternoon, a "black power" community activist launched into a vitriolic attack on a white law student from Yale

Law School who had dared to ask a naive question, visiting upon him all the sins of slavery and hundreds of years of oppression of black people, and even condemning him as "morally depraved." The student was in tears, while the other law students cowered, afraid to say anything for fear they would be subjected to the same blistering attack. A little voice in the back of my head told me to shut up, but I was incensed that this law student could be bullied like this and that our supervisors condoned it. At this point, I spoke up:

"This student may be a little naive about the problems of poverty, but he is not evil and it is unfair and irresponsible for you to treat him as though he were a white slaver. He could be working this summer in a high-paying law office in New York City; instead, he is here in the ghetto trying to learn how lawyers can help solve some of the legal problems of the poor. Instead of being thanked for his time and social concern, he is being treated as morally depraved white trash. Before you cast such harsh judgments on him, I want you to ask yourself, if you were a person of privilege and had the option of working downtown in a high-paying job, would you be here, working and living in the ghetto for low pay, as he is? You should be helping him, and the rest of us, to understand the legal problems of the poor so we can do a better job. If you don't want our help, you should just say so. I'm sure all of us could find work elsewhere."

That evening, my supervisor came to the housing project where I was staying, and asked me, "Do you think you are fit to work in this program?" I asked her, "What makes you think I'm not?" "The way you talked back to the black community activist today made you sound like a racist," she said. I said, "In other words, you think that we have no right to talk back to a black activist, even if he is unfairly abusing us? If that's your position, you're the racist, not me, because I'm willing to tell someone he's talking nonsense even if he's black, while you think that being black gives him a special racial exemption to talk nonsense and be abusive." She said she would think about it. Apparently, she did, as I remained in the program.

I arrived in Los Angeles the third week of June with my friend and fellow Boalt law student, Les Harrison, and immediately was assigned to work with the Welfare Rights Organization, an organization of welfare mothers led by Johnnie Tillman. The organization was planning a march from downtown Los Angeles to the federal building, where a picket line would be set up and speeches made. I worked all week going house to house in South Central Los Angeles, telling people about the march, as well as explaining the legal rights of welfare recipients to the people who had questions.

When Friday morning arrived, several thousand people assembled in a park downtown, then spread out for the march to the federal building. Arriving at the federal building, I noticed Les in the picket line ahead of me talking to a very attractive young woman. As I got closer, I thought to myself, "This is a very foxy welfare mother." I walked alongside Les for awhile as he talked to her and realized she wasn't a welfare mother at all, but a social worker who was on the march to support the political demands of the welfare recipients. And, she was a graduate of UC Berkeley! At this point, I decided I needed to know her a lot more than Les needed to know her, as Les had a long-term girlfriend, Polly, living in Los Angeles (they later married), and I was womanless. As Jeanine likes to tell the story, "I was talking to Les, a very attractive, interesting fellow, and, all of a sudden, Guy steps right in between me and Les, and begins talking so fast Les couldn't say anything. It didn't take me long to figure out that Guy and I had a lot in common and decide I wanted to know him better."

Jeanine not only had graduated from Berkeley the same year I had, she also had attended North Hollywood High School, living in a Studio City neighborhood where I had worked delivering groceries and liquor. We did not meet in high school, as North Hollywood High had over 3,000 students and she was a year and a half behind me, but our paths must have crossed many times.

I would have asked Jeanine out that night, but I had scheduled a weekend at Lake Arrowhead with an old girlfriend. The weekend proved to be a total fiasco. In the years since I last had seen her, my former girlfriend had turned into a Jesus freak, preaching her salvation and her version of the gospel in every sentence like some steroid-fortified athlete who, when asked how he won the game says, "I owe it all to God"—as though God actually gave a shit about who won. After two days of listening to talk of her enlightenment, I cut the trip short early Sunday, dropped her off, drove home, called Jeanine and asked her out that night. We went to dinner and a movie and ended the evening by my loudly reading Allen Ginsberg poems to her under the streetlight in front of her apartment in central Los Angeles.

Jeanine and I went out thirty nights in a row, and then I decided her job and mine were interfering with our romance and asked her to quit her job and drive to Expo '67 in Montreal with me. We'd take a month driving up through Oregon and Washington to British Columbia, then drive the 3,000 mile Trans-Canadian highway to Montreal, visit the world exposition, then return through the United States, camping out along the way. Jeanine thought it was a great idea—as she had decided to quit and move to Berkeley in the fall before she met me—and gave notice at the Welfare Department. Three weeks later, driving along the Trans-Canadian highway at high speed, I looked at her and said, "I think I'm falling in love with you." Later, she told me this really scared her!

Jeanine moved back with me to Berkeley and stayed with me and my roommate, Rich, and his girlfriend, Marsha, in our two-bedroom flat on Woolsey Street, while she and Marsha looked for an apartment together. A couple of weeks of apartment hunting went by, when Jeanine and Marsha returned and announced they had found an apartment and would be moving out after Jeanine went down to Los Angeles over the weekend to see her parents and pick up some of her stuff. As I left her at the airport, I said, "I have something I want to talk about when you get back." When she returned, I told her, "I'm in love with you. I don't want you to move out. I want to marry you." I had known Jeanine for less than ninety days, but there was no doubt in my mind. There was a lot of doubt in her mind, but, fortunately, she kept her doubts to herself and said, "I want to marry you, too." With the help of Jeanine's mother arranging everything, we got married a mere 2½ months later at a wedding with 250 people for dinner and dancing.

Jeanine and I spent the following summer traveling in Europe blowing the whole $1,500 we had received as wedding gifts. Half of that went to airfare and the remainder sustained two people in Europe for 2½ months. Arthur Frommer's book, *Europe on $5 A Day*, became our bible, and we actually averaged $5 a day for all expenses, including travel in Europe, meals, lodging and souvenirs! We avoided youth hostels, which generally separated men and women, and searched out small, cheap pensions that Frommer's book recommended. We walked for hours, checking out cheap recommended restaurants, and frequently hitchhiked to save money. With Jeanine's good legs and miniskirts, we rarely had trouble getting rides, but some of the drivers we encountered were really dangerous. As a class, the Italians were the fastest drivers and biggest risk-takers, especially with a pretty woman in the car they wanted to impress. But the most dangerous ride we got was from a German who picked us up at a castle about 150 kilometers from Munich, and drove the curvy four-lane highway at 180–220 km/hr while simultaneously fondling his girlfriend in the front seat and turning around to carry on a conversation with us in the back. I'm a very fast driver myself—I have collected many speeding tickets throughout the West despite my radar/laser detector, have raced sports cars (I now drive a Ferrari), and I've even driven Formula 1 race cars in France—but I thought the ride with this German would be my last. Nevertheless, he got us to Munich alive and happy to be able to step on firm ground. For the next few weeks, we took trains.

We were planning to stay in Munich for 3–4 days, but ended up spending part of eight days in the Deutsches Museum, a fantastic German industrial museum with working models of chemical plants and automobile plants, various German inventions, musical instrument collections, etc. We became so entranced with the ingenuity of the exhibits, we even attended museum lectures in German, although neither of us speaks any German. While in Munich, we ran into one of my classmates, Henry Holmes, who had a car and was leaving the next morning for Prague. He invited us, and we were tempted, but the next morning we told him we wanted to go back to the Deutsches Museum for another day and would join him in Prague in a few days. Henry left for Prague without us, and the day he arrived, the Russians invaded Czechoslovakia. Henry wrote first-hand accounts of the invasion which were published in the *San Francisco Chronicle*. We felt we should have been in Prague with Henry watching history being made.

In Paris, we ran into another Boalt classmate of mine, and childhood friend of Jeanine's, Jeff Brand, and his wife Sue, who also were in Europe travelling on their honeymoon. They had rented a two-cylinder Citroen, the kind with the top made of canvas that could be rolled down, and we traveled with them for a month through France, Switzerland and Italy. Many years later, Jeff joined my law firm and we successfully prosecuted a four-month trial.

DURING MY THIRD YEAR AT LAW SCHOOL, minority students at the University of California called for the establishment of a Third World College to promote the study of different ethnic cultures. When the University resisted, the students organized public demonstrations in support of a Third World College, and when the University continued to reject their demands, the students called for a boycott of classes. After the boycott had lasted several months, and several hundred students had been arrested on picket lines and in public demonstrations, a number of law students organized a visit to Sacramento to meet Governor Ronald Reagan to explain the demands of the minority students and possibly mediate the dispute. I thought it was a good public relations ploy to have law students—supposedly more conservative than the minority students—supporting the Third World College demands, and hoped the Governor would listen and try to understand the reasons in favor of increasing ethnic studies. We alerted the media and scheduled a press conference to follow our meeting with him.

About thirty of us chartered a bus and drove to Sacramento, about eighty miles away. On the way, I was asked to make the main presentation to Reagan. We arrived at the statehouse and were ushered into a large meeting room, with chairs arranged in a wide circle. Reagan entered with several staff members, one of whom I recognized as Alex Sheriffs, Reagan's education advisor and a former assistant dean at UC Berkeley. Reagan went around the room shaking hands.

On meeting him for the first time, my impression was that he looked much older in person than he did on TV. On TV, he was tall, erect, dark and handsome, with chiseled features—the look of a leader. In person, his face was deeply lined and his neck was flabby and wrinkled—a chicken neck. He looked like an old man. In my mind, I immediately contrasted him with the former Governor, Edmund "Pat" Brown, who I had met several times and watched on TV many times. In person, Pat Brown's face was clear and smooth, his eyes twinkled brightly, and he quickly revealed charm and intelligence—but on TV, he appeared fat, short, slow-moving and older than his age.

After courtesies and introductions, I began to explain that the history of America's ethnic populations had been largely ignored by the University and that students had been taught history from the perspective of white European immigrants. I said that this not only denied the ethnic populations their heritage, it provided white students like me only a partial understanding of history, and the history of important components of America's population, such as Native Americans, African-Americans, Latinos and Asians, was underrepresented. It was only natural that these populations would, at some point, demand to be included and demand to be part of the process of evaluating and teaching their own history. This should be applauded and accepted as expanding the mission of the University, not stonewalled and impeded. Other law students volunteered similar comments.

After listening to us for thirty minutes or so, I could see that Reagan was becoming very agitated. He fidgeted in his chair, grinding his teeth and shaking his head. Abruptly, he dragged his chair across the room and planted it six to eight feet in front of mine. With a face contorted in anger, he looked me directly in the eye and in a loud and passionate voice, declared:

"Don't you understand that these are just Communists and that's the way they act? They have fooled and manipulated you and gotten you to come here to do their bidding! I know how they operate better than you because I watched them for years infiltrate the Screen Actors Guild and watched them manipulate well-meaning and innocent people to take positions that were straight out of the Communist program. Maybe you are naive enough to be fooled by these people, but I'm not!"

Reagan was more than angry. He was almost frothing at the mouth in his disdain for "the Communists," as well as our naivete and stupidity. As our meeting began to spin totally out of control, and before Reagan could make more embarrassing, and misdirected comments, his aides grabbed him from both sides and led him out of the room. Reagan exited, looking like a prizefighter whose handlers were taking him out of the ring involuntarily while he still had a lot more fight left in him. We were stunned. We had tried to be informative and nonconfrontational, but Reagan had treated us as dupes of the Communist Party and had failed to respond to a single substantive point we made.

We left his office and went directly to the press room where I made a statement and television, radio and newspapers journalists followed up with questions. I told the media that Governor Reagan did not understand the underlying purposes of the proposed Third World College and appeared not to want to understand those purposes, the minority students, or even us. He was locked in the same rigid stance as the University, except he was even more pugnacious, appearing to savor his conflicts with intellectuals and students, rather than trying to understand and mediate them. We gave him a pretty negative portrayal in the media that day, but I knew his rigidity and hostility would not be good for the Third World College, the minority students, or even the University. I left Sacramento with a new sense of astonishment that someone as narrow-minded and irrational as Ronald Reagan had become governor of California. Little did I imagine at the time that the same superficial qualities that took him to the California statehouse would propel him into the White House.

During my third year at Boalt, most of my time was spent administering the Boalt Hall Community Assistance Project (BHCAP) to which I had been elected President, and continuing my anti-draft work in high schools and at Oakland Draft Help. BHCAP was a student-run project that put law students into the community doing clinical legal work. Since the law school had no clinical program, and many of the students were just as bored as I was with the classroom curriculum, BHCAP had 150 law students actively involved.

While BHCAP was an implicit criticism of the sterility and corporate orientation of the law-school curriculum, many students, including me, made our criticisms explicit in the *Boalt Hall Writ*, the law student newspaper. Each month, the *Writ* was full of critiques of the orientation of the law school toward servicing the needs of corporate America and the teaching techniques themselves. The law school was put so much on the defensive that, late in my third year, it closed down for a three-day colloquium on the subject of legal education, and I was asked to debate the Dean-elect, Professor Sanford Kadish. Kadish, a very smart man and a more interesting teacher than most who taught criminal law, despite never having practiced criminal law. He had made a career for himself writing law review articles on due process, but couldn't answer practical questions. Calling him "The Due-Process Theologian," I explained how I had gone to him many times seeking advice about how to handle practical criminal law issues that had arisen in BHCAP work, draft cases, and some of the legal defense committees organized to defend student and antiwar demonstrators, but that he never could provide useful information. Among other things, I said, "It's fine to write law review articles about due process, but many of the students in your courses actually want to practice criminal law and you are not competent to teach those students." The comment kind of summed up my attitude toward Boalt.

DURING MY THIRD YEAR OF LAW SCHOOL, a vacant lot a block away from my flat was developed by neighbors into vegetable and flower gardens, a children's play area, complete with swings and a climbing structure, and a grass play area for adults. The neighborhood had no parks, and a vacant lot overrun with weeds and trash had been transformed into a neighborhood amenity—"People's Park." The lot was owned by the University of California, but the University's plans to build an intramural soccer field on the lot had not been funded and was years away. Nevertheless, the University continued to assert ownership and contended that neighborhood use was unauthorized and illegal.

On May 8, 1969, U.C. Chancellor Roger Heyns, Sim Van der Ryn (Chair of the Chancellor's Committee on Housing and the Environment), a student government representative, and Wendy Schlessinger of the People's Park Committee met to discuss ways to produce a park plan under Van der Ryn's direction. Heyns proposed a three-week period for the development of a park plan. Despite this three-week planning agreement, five days later, Heyns issued a statement that the University was going to put up a fence around the park and proceed with its own plan for site development. The next day, the University posted "No Trespassing" signs throughout the Park, and early the next day, 250 Berkeley Police and California Highway Patrol officers, dressed in bulletproof flak jackets and armed with rifles and tear gas, entered the Park, cordoned off an eight-block area around the Park, and constructed an 8-foot chain-link fence around it.

At noon, a rally was held on Sproul Hall steps, and my friend, Student Body President-elect Dan Siegel, gave a speech which discussed alternative actions. The crowd began chanting, "We want the Park," and Dan said that the people, without committing crimes or causing injuries, should "take the Park." The crowd of 6,000 began to walk toward the Park, three blocks away, but were stopped by police barricades a block away. As the crowd and police stood at an impasse, someone opened a fire hydrant and the police moved into the crowd to shut it off. Some rocks were thrown and the police retaliated by firing tear gas into the crowd. The situation quickly deteriorated and became a roving street battle, with demonstrators throwing objects at the police and the police saturating the area with tear gas. At this point, a large contingent of Alameda County Sheriff's Deputies arrived, armed with shotguns, and began firing live ammunition into crowds and at individuals. Many people were seriously wounded, including Allan Blanchard, who was permanently blinded, and James Rector, a rooftop observer, who was fatally shot. At least 128 people were treated at hospitals, including three journalists, mostly for gunshot wounds.

The area around the Park and south campus became a war zone—the air a fog of tear gas, cars overturned, debris on the streets and sidewalks, with bands of demonstrators—including me—running from street to street yelling and throwing rocks at the police, and the police shooting back with tear gas and shotguns. It looked like Budapest, Prague, Beirut. Someone said to hold a wet handkerchief over nose and eyes to deflect the effects of the tear gas; not having a handkerchief on me, I wetted my shirt and put it over my face as I ran through the tear gas. By 5:30 p.m., the confrontations and violence ended and a dull silence came over the city. Jeanine came home from work and was upset that she had missed the whole thing.

That evening, Governor Ronald Reagan activated the National Guard and three battalions of the 40th Infantry Brigade arrived to support the 800 Sheriff's Deputies and police officers. The National Guard laid large rolls of barbed wire around a perimeter two blocks from the Park. Our flat at 2323 Bowditch, just a block from People's Park, was within the barbed wire and we had to provide identification with our address to be permitted to go to and from our house.

My friend and classmate at Boalt, Dan Siegel, who had given

the "Take the Park" speech that day and who lived upstairs with his wife Beth in our three-flat house, came downstairs and said he'd like to speak with me privately in the backyard. Out in the yard, he said quietly, "A number of people want to burn down the Chancellor's house tonight. What do you think?" I was a little taken aback. This was a serious idea. I thought about it for a few moments, then told Dan, "We're all really angry about what happened, but burning down the Chancellor's house would only play into the hands of Reagan and the right-wingers who really want to clamp down on Berkeley students. Besides, the Chancellor's house will probably be heavily guarded and it's made of stone and concrete, so it would be hard to burn down, in any case." That seemed to make sense to Dan, and I didn't hear any more talk of burning down buildings. I was grateful because I didn't want to go to jail or lose my chance of becoming a lawyer in a vainglorious attempt to burn down a building. Instead, Jeanine and I walked down to Telegraph Avenue, a block away, to argue with the police and Sheriff's deputies now occupying the city. After confrontations with several of them, and warnings that we were violating the curfew, we returned to our house inside the barbed-wire barricades.

Five days later, a vigil in memory of James Rector was held by the Berkeley faculty on Sproul Hall steps. When the 4,000 people attending the vigil attempted to leave, we were blocked by National Guardsmen. The crowd moved north toward the Chancellor's house where police began to disperse the crowd with batons and tear gas. I walked back toward the main campus plaza, where a University-wide referendum on the Park was being voted upon, then continued to lower Sproul Plaza, where I heard the sound of a helicopter. I looked back and saw a large Army Sikorsky-type helicopter about 200 feet above the ground, flying near the Campanile in my direction, dispersing gas. I ran south and escaped the gas, but many were not so lucky. The Army was using CS tear gas, a type banned for wartime use by the Geneva Convention, and the people it hit suffered vomiting, nausea and severe eye pain. Tear gas fumes spread to patients at the campus hospital, students in nearby elementary and secondary schools, and a childrens' recreation area near campus.

A few days later, the results of the University referendum were announced: By a vote of 12,710 to 2,250, UC students favored keeping People's Park; by 642–95, the UC faculty supported the Park. A week later, 30,000 people peacefully demonstrated support for People's Park by marching through Berkeley and around the Park. Nevertheless, the UC Regents voted to turn the Park into a parking lot and soccer field.

While the People's Park demonstrations were going on, some law students proposed that final exams at the law school be cancelled or rescheduled. Indeed, during much of the two-week period prior to exams, tear gas had wafted into the law school library, making study impossible. In a school-wide meeting, Law School Dean Edward Halbach said exams would not be cancelled or postponed and that it was our job as students "to disregard the events on campus, concentrate on your studies, and take the exams." When I heard his pronouncement, I thought to myself, "What else should I expect from a guy who's spent his life writing estate plans for rich people!"

In the end, individual professors were allowed to give exams as scheduled or permit students to take them at a later date. I chose to take mine on the scheduled dates, despite the campus turmoil, in order to get them over with and end the law school experience. I received the best grades of my three years.

I had not attended my junior high school, high school, and undergraduate college graduations, so I decided to attend my law school graduation and invited my parents. On graduation day, about 25 of the graduating law students, including myself, showed up dressed in suits and ties, but without black robes and mortarboards. Instead of paying $30 each to rent graduation attire, we had donated that money to support the students' protest in favor of the establishment of the Third World College. As we waited at the side of the law school for the graduation ceremonies to begin and for the graduates to make their entrance, Walter Ingalls, the third-year class president, and someone I considered to be a real toady for the law school administration, came back to where I was standing and announced, "Dean Halbach has decided that, since you are not wearing proper graduation attire, he will not read your names and you will not be permitted to go through graduation ceremonies." Paul Bardacke and I picked up Walter, turned him upside down, and stuffed him into a trash can, head-first. As Walter struggled to extricate himself from the trash can, I yelled at him, "Tell Dean Halbach that we don't care if he reads our names or not. If he doesn't want to read our names, we will seize the microphone and I will read off the names of the graduating protestors." Five minutes later, Walter returned to tell us that Dean Halbach would read our names, and we would be permitted to participate in the graduation ceremonies, after all—and my parents finally got to see me graduate.

Many years later, I became active in local politics in Berkeley, was appointed to the Berkeley Planning Commission, and participated in the development of a Traffic Management Plan to limit and control vehicular traffic in Berkeley. One of the traffic control devices used in the plan were traffic diverters—big round cement bollards that were placed in the middle of selected residential neighborhoods for the purpose of diverting traffic out of neighborhoods and onto arterial streets. The plan, once implemented, became very controversial—people love their cars and don't like their commute patterns disrupted—and two referenda were placed on election ballots seeking to abolish the traffic diverters. I became co-manager of both campaigns seeking to save the Traffic Management Plan, and the controversial traffic diverters. Both campaigns won by substantial majorities after heated campaigns, but that didn't stop the opponents of traffic diverters, who next filed a lawsuit challenging Berkeley's diverters as illegal traffic control devices under the California State Streets and Highways Code. The Berkeley City Attorney's office was obligated to defend the lawsuit, but in the expectation that their lawyers would be ineffectual, I organized a group of well-respected Berkeley attorneys to defend the diverters as *amici curiae*.

The case was tried in the Alameda County Superior Court, with me as lead trial attorney defending the diverters, but we encountered a judge, Robert Barber, who was unremittingly hostile to Berkeley's traffic diverters, and, after a weeklong trial, we lost. We obtained a stay of the order to remove the diverters and took an immediate appeal to the California Court of Appeals, where we reversed the trial court, as the Court of Appeals decided the diverters were legal "traffic control devices." The story did not end there, however, as the diverter opponents took an appeal to the California State Supreme Court, which subsequently reversed the Court of Appeals by a 4–3 vote. The deciding vote was rendered by Justice Frank Newman, former Dean of Boalt School of Law, who wrote the majority opinion holding Berkeley's diverters to be traffic control devices unauthorized by the California Streets and Highways Code. Many people told me afterwards that Newman frequently had fulminated about how the diverters disrupted his commute from Orinda to the law school, where he often did research. If these reports were true, Newman should have disqualified himself from consideration of the case, but, as I was learning, not all judges with a bias or interest in one direction or another always did the forthright and honorable thing. In any case, I was too busy trying to protect the traffic diverters to think much about Justice Newman's ethics.

I called my local State Assemblyman, Tom Bates, and asked if it would be possible to get an emergency piece of legislation run through the California State Legislature and signed by the Governor before the devices were removed. Tom said he would pursue this, we drafted some corrective legislation, and a few days later Tom called back to tell me that the bill would go to the Assembly Transportation Committee and that I should talk to the Chairman of that committee as soon as possible. I asked, "Who's the Chairman?" "Walter Ingalls," replied Tom—the same guy I had stuffed into a trash can on graduation day! I called Walter's office to get an appointment, fully expecting him either to not talk to me and/or screw me and the traffic bill I so desperately wanted. But, to my surprise, Walter took my call. I said, "I'm sure you remember me. I'm the guy who stuffed you in a trash can!" Walter laughed loudly, and, when he had stopped laughing, said, "Oh, don't worry, I'll never forget you or the trash can incident." "Well, is it possible for us to get beyond the trash can and talk about a traffic bill?" I asked. "Guy, we are already beyond the trash can and I harbor no ill will whatsoever about it. You were always passionate about what you believed in and I guess I just got in the way of your passion that day. Tell me about the bill you want," said Walter. I explained the bill to him, and why I wanted his help, and he got it through the State Assembly in five days. The bill was signed by the Governor six days after I talked to Walter and eleven days after we submitted it. Berkeley's traffic diverters were added to the Streets and Highways Code as legal traffic control devices, where they continue to protect residential neighborhoods from heavy traffic, and I was left with new respect for the magnanimity and generosity of a law school classmate.

Still, I would not recommend stuffing classmates in garbage cans, particularly if you think there is any chance they might end up in your state legislature one day!

4

My Reggie Fellowship

"You were once wild here. Don't let them tame you."
—Isadora Duncan

I NEVER CONSIDERED working for a large law firm. In fact, I interviewed for only one job while at Boalt—a Reginald Heber Smith Community Law Fellowship, funded by the federal Legal Services Corporation. The "Reggie" Fellowships were designed for "impact" legal work in the fight on poverty; the "Reggies" were supposed to be the legal shock troops of the Office for Economic Opportunity attack on poverty. There were 250 Reggies selected in 1969 and they were sent to legal-services programs throughout the United States, not to work on daily service-type cases, but, instead, to bring the type of cases—generally class actions—that were designed to facilitate structural changes in the private and governmental institutions and programs that affected lives of low-income people.

In 1969, the Reggie Fellowship was quite popular and competitive. In fact, five of the top ten academic students in the 1969 Boalt Hall class became Reggies. On the strength of my leadership in the Boalt Hall Community Assistance Program (not my grades), I was selected and given the choice of participating in legal services programs in New York City, San Francisco or Colorado.

I was inclined to stay in the Bay Area and work for San Francisco Neighborhood Legal Assistance, a well-established and respected legal services program. Before committing to San Francisco, however, I phoned the Director of the Colorado rural program, Jonathan B. ("Skip") Chase to inquire about the legal issues he anticipated his program would be dealing with in its first few years and what role he foresaw for the two Reggies that he hoped to get. I spent two hours talking to Skip, and, after talking to Jeanine, we decided to go to Colorado. Skip was energetic, open, charismatic and persuasive in talking about his vision for Colorado Rural Legal Services (CRLS); his enthusiasm and passion for improving the lives of migrant farm workers was inspiring. The program was set to begin September 1, 1969, so I would be there at its inception, and presumably have an opportunity to influence its development. By virtue of having followed the efforts of Cesar Chavez and the United Farmworkers Organizing Committee to organize farm workers in California, I was somewhat familiar with the legal issues facing farm workers. I also knew something about the legal issues California Rural Legal Services had handled in support of farm workers. Skip impressed me as someone who understood the legal problems of farm workers and was willing to confront these problems by prosecuting class actions, not simply providing service to individuals affected by institutional problems. Also, both Jeanine and I had lived nearly all our lives in California and thought going to a different environment for a year or two would be exciting. I became so enthusiastic about Skip and Colorado Rural Legal Services, I didn't even investigate the New York City option, despite the fact that I had always wanted to live in New York, at least for a time.

The Reggie program began with a four-week training program at Haverford College, Pennsylvania. The training, which ran 8–10 hours per day, focused on the legal problems of the poor—with emphasis on impact litigation. Class action lawyers from all over the country lectured us on housing, employment, healthcare, farmlabor, and welfare issues. Unlike law school, which had emphasized a curriculum designed to maintain and service corporate interests, these lawyers were on the cutting edge of legal strategies challenging the status quo. I was excited in a way that never seemed possible in law school. This was an opportunity to represent the powerless people who got pushed around by society and had no way to protect their rights. This is why I had become a lawyer.

One of my Reggie classmates was a young lawyer from Philadelphia named Jerry Rivera—later to become the "Geraldo" Rivera of talk-show fame. Jerry was one of the most obnoxious characters any of us ever had met. One hot and sunny morning, a group of us were having breakfast on the porch of the dining hall, when Jerry approached, pointed to the women wearing blouses without bras, and began shouting, "Look everyone. These are feminists. You always can tell because they don't wear bras. Look at their nipples! Bra-less feminists, ha ha!" He jumped around as he yelled. Clearly, the sight of fully-clothed women without bras was too much sexual excitement for him to handle at that stage of his life.

A week later, when the black Reggies sought to take over the Reggie program in true '60's style, Jerry—middle-class to the core—instantantaneously metamorphosed into the Hispanic "Geraldo" in an effort to gain acceptance by the more radical black Reggies. His politics were undefined, but his racial posturing was obvious. Jerry/Geraldo practiced law as a Reggie for a year, before going into broadcasting, where he became famous for sensational and sleazy reporting. To his credit, in the mid-1990s, rejecting much of his own past low journalistic standards, he began to do honest legal reporting and commentary on his show "Geraldo." His show did the best commentary and discussion on the O.J. trials and Whitewater allegations and became one of the best talk shows on television emphasizing legal and political issues.

The Reggie training was followed immediately by the California Bar Examination. Despite little study, and a 38% pass rate on the August 1969 exam, I managed to pass. My friends, who had watched me go out many a night at the Reggie seminar instead of studying for the bar, were surprised. I was a little surprised myself.

For the trip to Colorado, Jeanine and I sold her flower-power 1962 Comet, bought a used 1965 Volvo 122S station wagon, filled it to the roof with our worldly possessions (with a place for Mighty Moth, our cat), and headed across the Sierras, camping along the way. Once in Boulder, we rented a small two-bedroom brick house on Arapahoe Avenue, with Boulder Creek in our backyard, and I began work at CRLS. Jeanine, having left social work, began her teaching career at Jarrow School, Boulder's Montessori preschool.

On my arrival, CRLS was nothing more than an empty suite of offices at an old Catholic school for girls, now owned by the University of Colorado, with a $450,000 grant to set up a rural legal services program to represent the rural poor of Colorado. Our first task was to set up four field offices, and, to that end, our director, Skip, and Bill Prakken, who had been a Reggie the year before, and I set out to scout the state. Before leaving, we were told by some Chicano members of our Board to, "Stay out of the cowboy bars, and the Chicano bars, too." We could understand why the cowboy bars might be dangerous for a bunch of lawyers who looked like hippies (Skip and I both had long hair and big beards), but we couldn't understand why we might be unwelcome in the Chicano bars. After all, we were there to save them, or at least the low-income Chicanos. Moreover, there was nothing much to do at night in the small rural towns we were visiting other than to visit the local bars.

Unfortunately, the advice we had been given was sound. Whenever we walked into a Chicano bar, someone would direct some swear words in Spanish at us, and Skip, who spoke fluent Spanish and who then was the reigning national AAU middleweight wrestling champion despite his 5' 6" height, would go directly to whoever uttered the slander and demand an apology. We then would be faced with the prospect of an argument or fight, as we tried to explain what good guys we really were, while we also tried to drag Skip away from his tormentors. As for the cowboys, we were rudely introduced to the state of their hostility in Monte Vista, a small town in southwest Colorado.

Monte Vista was the hometown of Lt. William Calley, the man who had led his troops to execute 600 Vietnamese—nearly all women, children and old men—at My Lai. He was a war criminal, but in Monte Vista he was a hero. A large banner hung across the main street saying, "Support Lt. Calley In His Time of Need," and every restaurant we went into had pro-Calley posters, with contribution cans for his criminal defense.

Fearing to spend time in the cowboy bars, and there being no Chicano bars in town, we decided, instead, to catch a movie at the local cinema. Showing was *Easy Rider*, which none of us had seen. The movie ends with a couple of rednecks in a pick-up truck murdering Peter Fonda and Dennis Hopper because they were hippies and Hopper had flipped off the rednecks. We were devastated by the violent end of the movie, but the cowboy audience liked it a lot; everyone else in the theater stood up and applauded as the hippies were murdered. When the movie ended, we sat quietly in our seats, trying to look as inconspicuous as possible. It was a long walk back to our hotel and I don't remember us going out the next night.

CRLS had originated from two influential law review articles Skip had written for the *University of Colorado Law Review* analyzing the legal problems, and possible theories of legal solutions, of migrant farm workers. The articles were noteworthy not only for the legal analyses, but also for Skip's intimate understanding of the living and working conditions the migrants suffered under—an understanding gained from the time he had spent in migrant labor camps and work fields while writing his law review articles.

Skip thought his lawyers should have some of those experiences, so I found myself spending four days working in the sugar beet fields of Southern Colorado, living in a migrant camp. The work was arduous. Digging for sugar beets was then done with a short-handled hoe, which meant bending over for ten hours a day or more, digging the subterranean beets. At the end of the day, I found it almost impossible to stand up and I felt like I was ready for a back implant. And my hands were red with blisters. Then it was back to the fields the next day for the same work and the same pain. The work was hard not only for inexperienced legal services attorneys; it was difficult also for the migrants. Indeed, I saw very few workers over 40 years old digging sugar beets, as their bodies gave out long before that. As a result of litigation later brought by CRLS and a parallel legal services program in California, California Rural Legal Assistance, as well as rule-making by various state legislatures and agriculture departments, use of the short hoe was banned in favor of the long hoe, which works nearly as well as the short-handled hoe and saves backs. Nevertheless, even today, as I drive the backroads of California, I continue to see the short hoe in use—its ban not enforced by government agencies.

The living conditions in the migrant camps were as bad as the working conditions. The sleeping accommodations were unheated, uninsulated barracks; no privacy, no hot water—and a wake-up alarm at 5:30 a.m., when it is quite cold in Colorado even in the summer, but especially in spring and fall. A few flush toilets were available in the camps, but the workfields had no toilet facilities, not even outhouses; the workers were left to urinate and defecate in the fields, a system that provided neither privacy for the workers, nor sanitation for consumers. This was nearly twenty years after Edward R. Murrow had exposed similar conditions in the Florida agriculture fields on national television in a famous CBS Reports documentary called *Fields of Shame*. Thirty years later, on a wall in my office, I still have a photograph of a farm worker bent over, working with a shorthanded hoe, to remind me of the working and living conditions of farm workers and the real value of labor.

Bad as the living conditions in the labor camps were, the living conditions of the migrants outside the labor camps were often worse. My leading plaintiff in many of my CRLS class actions, Lionel Sanchez, and his family of nine, lived in a public storage garage approximately 18 × 20'. No water, no heat, no toilet, and one light bulb overhead. Everyone in the family, including the young children, worked, but the work was seasonal and the wages low. Plus, the migrants normally were paid through farm labor contractors, who often extracted high fees from the migrant workers' wages for the "service" of providing the migrant labor to the farmer.

Shortly after I returned to Boulder, CRLS filed its first lawsuit—a class action against Great Western Sugar Company and other large landowners, attacking conditions at a farm labor camp in Fort Lupton, a small town north of Denver. This lawsuit was later settled, with Great Western agreeing to make substantial improvements in the labor camp. Unfortunately, as we were to find out, Great Western was one of the few employers willing to consider reasonable improvements to the working and living conditions of the migrants.

At about the same time we filed the Fort Lupton labor camp case, we filed an action in Greeley seeking to rescind the purchase of a car by a blind man. It was not a class action, but the facts were compelling. The car engine was running when our blind client and his sighted wife tested it, it was left running when they negotiated the purchase, and it continued to run while they drove it home. It never ran again. On inspection by a mechanic, it was found to have a dead battery, serious engine problems, and sawdust in the rear differential to muffle the sound of major damage. We thought it was an open-and-shut case for rescission of the contract, as none of the car's serious problems had been disclosed.

The judge presiding over the case was Jewish—the only Jewish judge I met in two years practicing law in Colorado. He immediately extended his friendship, inviting me to dinner and, taking notice of my Jewish last name, asking me to join his synagogue. Only later did I find out that at the same time he was showing friendship and religious bonding, he also was accepting bribes from the defendant used-car dealership!

Unaware of the back-room pay-off, we went to trial in Greeley, seeking rescission, an equitable remedy tried to the judge, not a jury. The evidence was overwhelming that the car was defective and the dealership had misrepresented the condition of the car, and our blind plaintiff was very sympathetic—but to our amazement, the judge ruled for the defendant. Three years later, after I had returned to California, someone sent me a newspaper article reporting that this judge had been thrown off the bench and dis-barred for taking bribes from the used-car dealership we had sued. In our case, he had sold out for a $300 Buick.

Another lawsuit we filed in Fall 1969 was a class action against thirty-five of the largest farms in Colorado, challenging their use of various pesticides. We claimed the pesticides were potentially carcinogenic to anyone who breathed and touched them, particu-larly farm workers who worked in the fields breathing and han-dling sprayed vegetables, occasionally even getting sprayed them-selves during aerial applications. The lawsuit was prepared mainly by fellow-Reggie, David Mastbaum, with me lending a hand, and David and I took the Complaint to the United States Courthouse in Denver to file it. As it was both a plaintiff and defendant class action, with thirty-five named defendants, we had 40+ copies of each document, so filing was complicated and voluminous. It took over an hour just to file it with the Clerk's Office and get all copies stamped, and, as we were leaving, the clerk we had been working with said, "Boys, next time you file something like this, you really should bring the attorneys with you." (I guess David and I, in our jeans, beards, long hair and boots, didn't fit the image of federal litigators in Colorado—or perhaps anywhere else.)

There were very few federal or state statutes that directly ben-efited farm workers, though there were a number of federal statues that provided protections for farm workers. These, however, did not expressly provide remedies for noncompliance that farm work-ers could enforce directly themselves. In most cases, enforcement was through the U. S. Department of Agriculture or the Immigra-tion and Naturalization Services. Unfortunately, both these agen-cies were completely unresponsive to the needs and complaints of farm workers, as we found out by filing administrative complaints with the agencies.

Farm workers were the intended beneficiaries of specific leg-islation, and Skip, on leave as a professor of Contracts at the Uni-versity of Colorado School of Law, thought we could directly en-force these statutory protections by suing on their behalf as third-party beneficiaries—a conventional contract theory, albeit a relatively novel theory of statutory enforcement. As a companion to this theory, we also argued that farm workers had a "private right of action" to enforce statutory provisions that clearly were designed for their benefit. To support the private right of action theory, we had a long line of securities cases, where individuals had been able to enforce securities statutes, despite the fact that no private enforcement mechanism was expressly provided by statute and despite the existence of the Securities and Exchange Commission, which had been provided express authority to enforce the securities law. We thought a legal theory that worked so well to protect investors was equally applicable to protect farm workers.

The 1948 Sugar Beet Act, for example, provided many protections for farm workers (assurances that they would be paid for their work, have adequate housing and sanitation facilities, etc.), but the mechanism of enforcement was through complaints to countywide Sugar Beet Committees, the members of which were farmers whose interests often were in direct conflict with the Sugar Beet Act protections for farm workers. There was a right to appeal adverse decisions of the local committees to the Department of Agriculture in Washington D.C., but the Washington D.C. hearing officers were southerners with roots in farming. They were unsympathetic to claims brought on behalf of farm workers; indeed, many were surprised that farm workers even thought they had rights under the Act. So the clear farm worker protections found in the Sugar Beet Act were unenforced and illusory. Our lawsuit to challenge this lack of enforcement through application of third-party beneficiary and private right of action theories was unsuccessful in the trial court and the Circuit Court of Appeal for the Tenth Circuit. Apparently, the courts found it odd that we would think the rights of low-paid farm workers to enforce statutory protections was comparable to the rights of investors.

Likewise, immigration statutes set up a wide variety of limitations on immigration and provide substantial funds for the INS to locate and return non-documented aliens, but we found hundreds of non-documented farm workers living in unsafe housing on farms and depressing wages for farm workers, or, in some cases, acting as strike-breakers, yet the INS did nothing when notified of farmers who were harboring them. This, too, we attacked with contract and private right-of-action theories and were equally unsuccessful in the trial and appellate courts.

One statute that we succeeded in enforcing with our novel theories was the Hill-Burton Act. The case arose out of grotesque, and tragic, facts. A farm worker, seriously injured by some farm machinery and, bleeding heavily, was taken to the hospital in Monte Vista, where he was refused admission. The next closest hospital was in Alamosa, thirty miles away. He bled to death before reaching Alamosa.

This obviously gave rise to a wrongful death action, which we were required to refer to the private bar, as the case was fee-generating. We were not satisfied with that remedy, however. We didn't think farm workers had to die or be seriously injured before they had a right to medical care, and we didn't think a wrongful death action would be an adequate remedy in any case, as the life of an Hispanic farm worker was not likely to be valued very highly by a Monte Vista jury. We researched the federal Hill-Burton Act, which had provided billions of dollars of funds for the construction of hospitals throughout the United States, such as the Monte Vista hospital, and we found that hospitals which accepted federal construction funds were required to allocate 10% of their services to low-income people, such as the dead farm worker. Despite this requirement, virtually no low-income persons without cash or medical insurance ever had been treated at the Monte Vista hospital. The hospital had been happy to take the federal money but had ignored requirements they didn't like, and no one had enforced those requirements. Our case, again brought on contract and private right-of-action theories, along with similar cases brought by rural legal services attorneys in Florida and California, was successful in directly enforcing the federal service requirements. As a consequence, practices changed at the Monte Vista hospital, and hospitals throughout the country that had accepted Hill-Burton funds.

MY FIRST TRIAL IN FEDERAL COURT and, indeed, the first-ever federal trial for CRLS, started just a few months after I began to practice law, and only days after receiving notice that I had passed the Colorado bar exam. The case involved Gregory and Randall Cranson. Gregory was Student Body President of La Junta High School and an A student; his twin brother, Randall, was captain of the La Junta High School wrestling team and also an A student. Nevertheless, on returning to La Junta High School in Fall 1969 with hair covering their ears, they were told by the school to cut their hair or find another school. Believing the right to style their hair as they chose was a form of expression protected by the First Amendment, and supported by their parents in this decision, they kept their long hair and got kicked out of their senior year at La Junta High School. Nearly every student in the senior class signed petitions supporting the Cranson boys, but that failed to persuade the La Junta School Board that they were worthy of an education.

The Cranson family found their way into our La Junta office, which referred the matter to me, the putative First Amendment and "student rights" expert. Within days, I filed a complaint in United States District Court, accompanied by a motion for a preliminary and permanent injunction enjoining the La Junta School Board from ejecting the Cranson boys from school. The case was assigned to United States District Judge William A. Doyle, a former District Attorney in Denver, and trial on the request for an injunction was scheduled two weeks later in Denver. Within days, I was getting calls from Judge Doyle reminding me he had ruled a year earlier against students in a similar case arising in Denver and imploring me to tell the kids to just "cut their hair." I have no doubt Judge Doyle was trying to be helpful. But I also suspect he was trying to save himself court time. My clients and I had no interest in avoiding a righteous fight with the school, so I gave Judge Doyle a firm "no."

Two weeks later, I was in trial before Judge Doyle, presenting evidence and contending that long hair was a form of expression protected by the First Amendment. Relying on a recent United States Supreme Court decision, *Tinker v. Des Moines School Board*, which had held that an American Flag patch sewed on a jacket was a form of protest and expression protected by the First Amendment, I contended that long hair was a cultural statement and a protected form of political expression. To the credit of the La Junta High School, the whole senior class of approximately 100 students was bussed to Denver from La Junta—a distance of approximately 120 miles each way—to attend the trial, which lasted a week. Due to the large audience, the trial was moved into the ceremonial courtroom.

The school tried to justify its prohibition of long hair, and the expulsion of my clients, as necessary to prevent "disruption of the educational environment." Its main spokesman was the Boys' Vice-Principal, a large man with a pasty white face, clothes a size too big, and absolutely no sense of irony or humor. He testified that long hair could fall onto the desk of students sitting behind and "disrupt" that student's learning experience and that long hair, in general, would make it impossible to concentrate on learning.

On cross-examination, I had a field day. I pointed out to the Boys' Vice Principal that the Cranson boys' hair barely came over their ears and was at least ten inches too short to fall onto another students' desk. I asked him if he felt the same about girls' hair and asked him to explain why girls at La Junta High School could have hair of any length, while boys had to keep their hair cut above their ears. "Girls' hair can, in fact, fall into the desk of other students. Can you explain why that doesn't disrupt anyone? Why haven't the girls been expelled?" The VP's answers were rote: long hair on boys disrupts education; long hair on girls has no disruptive effect.

I established that he knew George Washington wore long hair and asked, "Do you mean to say that the father of our country would be expelled from La Junta High School?" Answer: "Yes." "Do you mean that Thomas Jefferson, the man responsible for drafting the

United States Constitution, could not get an education at La Junta High School because he wore long hair?" Answer: "Yes." "Do you mean that Benjamin Franklin's long hair would disrupt the education environment at La Junta High School?" Answer: "Yes." At this point, Judge Doyle interrupted, saying, "Mr. Saperstein, I think I get the point."

A few days later, it was time to make final arguments, so I summarized the testimony and the evidence, concluding with a flourish: "The Boys' Vice-Principal's testimony showed the absurdity of the school's position, as he testified that the father of our country, the author of our Constitution, and one of the most brilliant thinkers and inventors in our nation's history all would have been expelled by La Junta High School for their 'disruptive' long hair." This was too much for Judge Doyle, who interrupted me again and said, "Oh come on, Mr. Saperstein, if this had been you, wouldn't your parents just have told you to cut your hair and go back to school?"

Unbeknownst to Judge Doyle, my mother had flown in the night before from California to visit me over the weekend and was sitting in the last row of the audience. So I told Judge Doyle, "I don't know, but my mother is right here, let's find out." I turned around and my mother already was standing. One hundred pairs of eyes turned to her, and she said clearly, "I would have supported Guy, just like the Cranson parents are supporting their sons!" The whole courtroom erupted in applause. Judge Doyle slammed down his gavel and, exiting as quickly as he could, said, "The court will be in recess."

I had been a big hit with my mother, the audience of La Junta High School students, even reporters and the court personnel, but a week later Judge Doyle ruled against the Cranson boys, holding that long hair was not a form of expression protected by the First Amendment. We took an appeal to the Tenth Circuit Court of Appeals, but a year later, the United States Supreme Court, in a similar case, refused to extend the *Tinker* rationale to cover long hair. Judge Doyle accurately had forecast what the Supreme Court would do with this issue. I was disappointed, but not surprised. A couple of years later, the La Junta newspaper published an editorial which argued that the local school's long-hair ban had been stupid. The school board had spent $40,000 defending the no-long-hair rule and now, two years later, all the boys had long hair anyway. Long hair had lost the constitutional argument, but won the cultural war.

At the same time I was waging a battle for freedom of expression at La Junta High School, I was having similar problems of my own with my boss, Skip. Before becoming a hippie law professor, Skip had practiced law at Cravath & Swain, a large and stuffy New York City law firm. From that experience, he developed the belief that our written product should be just as error-free as the written product at Cravath, and that the CRLS attorneys should dress as impeccably in court as the Cravath attorneys in New York City. His first expectation led to many arguments with our staff of secretaries, who generally were highly educated spouses of University of Colorado teachers with little secretarial experience. His "dress-for-success" expectation ran into direct conflict with my wardrobe, which consisted of one suit (the suit my mother-in-law made me buy for my wedding) and an old pair of Redwing cowboy boots.

The cowboy boots offended Skip. They definitely were not pretty, but I tried to explain to Skip that I had very difficult feet to fit—size 11AA—and that the Redwing boots were the only "dress" shoes I had that fit. I also explained that regular dress shoes wouldn't work for me, anyway, as Jeanine and I (having moved from town to the nearby mountains) were living in a cabin up Coal Creek Canyon, 9,100 feet high, with about 200 feet of snow to walk through each morning just to get to my car parked on the road and that my feet would get wet if I wore regular dress shoes, which I didn't have anyway.

My explanations had no impact whatsoever on Skip, who told me each morning as we drove to the Cranson trial on the Boulder–Denver highway to "get some decent dress shoes." His threats escalated to the point that, by the end of the fourth day of trial, he told me, "If you wear those fucked-up boots tomorrow, I'm going to fire you." This threat, of course, made it an absolute certainty that I would wear my fucked-up Redwing boots to court the next day. After all, how could we, as lawyers, contend that schools could not regulate the hair length of their students, while compelling the same lawyers—on threat of termination—to wear "decent dress shoes?"

I drove down from my cabin early the next morning to pick up Skip at his house in Boulder. He took one look at my boots, told me this would be my last day at CRLS, then refused to talk to me as we drove to Denver for me to make my first-ever closing argument in a federal court trial. I could have used some help that morning discussing the argument; instead, I spent the 45-minute drive pondering what an asshole Skip was, and I'm sure Skip silently reciprocated. What an inauspicious first-ever federal trial experience for me and CRLS!

After closing arguments by both sides, Skip announced he was returning to the office, while I stayed to talk with reporters and the Cranson family. On returning to the office late in the afternoon, I was met by our office administrator, Linda Chavez, who announced, "I'm sorry about this, Guy, but you've been fired; Skip wants you to clear out your desk." I was outraged by what I considered Skip's flagrant hypocrisy, and proceeded to round up all the attorneys and staff for a meeting to discuss Skip's behavior and my termination. Skip, dressed in his usual office attire—jeans and bright blue and yellow wool Mexican poncho—joined the meeting to defend his decision. He said his decision to fire me was based on his expectation that CRLS would be just as high-quality a law firm as Cravath Swain, that our work product would be impeccable, and that we would dress like Cravath lawyers, at least when we went to court, ignoring the fact that his regular in-office lawyer outfit closely approximated the dress of a Mexican bandito.

Skip had no chance. He lost the clerical staff with his "impeccable work product" standard, and the lawyers were just too free-spirited, not to mention poorly dressed, to jump on board the "dress-for-success" model he advocated. After four hours of debate, which ran long past dinnertime, the vote was 13–2 in my favor. Skip was just enough of a democrat to accept the vote, and I stayed at CRLS, although Skip didn't speak to me for a month.

Despite this inauspicious beginning, Skip and I became good friends, and several years later, Jeanine and I returned to Boulder for a visit, and were invited to a wonderful dinner at Skip and Nancy's beautiful house. After dinner and a couple of joints, I said, "Skip, remember when you tried to fire me?" At that point, Nancy interrupted, saying very forcefully, "Guy, it would not be a good idea to talk about that. It's a real sore point with Skip." Refusing the warning, I explained as follows: "Skip, I realize now that you were absolutely right in insisting on a good dress code and trying to fire me, except you just hadn't figured out your best argument. Your best argument was that our client—poor people—would have preferred to have their lawyers look like lawyers, but they didn't have the choice. They had to take what they could get. By insisting on our own cultural diversity, and dressing poorly, we were just rubbing their noses in their own poverty. We were telling them, you've got to take us even if we look like hippies and even if we wear banged-up cowboy boots. You should have fired me and made the rest of the CRLS lawyers, including yourself, dress like real lawyers." Skip gave me a big hug and we had a good laugh at our mutual follies.

Later, I would feel much differently about dress at my own law firm. Although I learned to dress impeccably for court appearances, throughout the twenty-three years I ran my firm, I never insisted that anyone dress any particular way, and many of the lawyers, paralegals and staff frequently came to work dressed quite casually, including T-shirts. In fact, in the late 1980s, when once-a-month "dress-down" days were beginning to be popular in corporate law firms, I used to joke, "I just wish I could get my employees to dress *up* once a month!" I felt differently about my law firm because none of our clients were compelled—by poverty or otherwise—to be represented by lawyers who did not dress like corporate attorneys. If appearances were important, potential clients could find many law firms that would impress them with beautiful suits and expensive office space. If they wanted the best civil rights law firm, we were it. I think even Skip could have lived with that.

I GOT MY FIRST TASTE OF THE INTERMIX of politics and law in Colorado. On arriving in Boulder, I became involved with the local anti-war movement and almost immediately moved into a leadership position. This was no great achievement, as the anti-war movement was just being born at the University of Colorado and I had had four years involvement with anti-war groups in Berkeley, experiences which had educated me on the issues and taught me some organizational skills. Meeting primarily with a handful of student leaders, including the editor of the *Colorado Daily*, John Hillson, we quickly organized a rally in the downtown Boulder city park band shell, headlining the rally with a speech by Bob Scheer, then Editor of the radical *Ramparts* magazine and former peace candidate for Congress, followed the next day by educational teach-ins on Vietnam War issues.

The late November day was overcast and cold, but a good audience of about 300 people showed up at noon on a Friday. As MC of the event, I made the mistake of letting two leaders of student groups precede Scheer to the podium, and, rather than making short comments, the two rambled on for over an hour total, despite my handing them notes to "wind it up." Their speeches were passionate, sincere, and full of self-righteousness, but neither compelling nor interesting. I was afraid we would lose the audience before Scheer, whom I considered the most informed and articulate opponent of the Vietnam War, even had a chance to speak. But the audience sat through the cold weather and boring speeches, waiting patiently for Scheer.

Scheer took the mike at 1:15 p.m. and spoke until 2:30 p.m. The audience never moved. They were concentrating on what he had to say, and he had a lot of disturbing things to say about the war. They stayed en masse until 3:00 p.m.—three hours outside in the cold—asking serious questions. I think it was at that moment, as I sat on the podium watching the faces of these middle-Americans in what then was a Republican town, that I first began to believe the war could be stopped.

The teach-ins the next day at the University of Colorado confirmed that belief. In my group of perhaps thirty, there were mainly working people, middle-income people, little-league moms and dads, plus students. They were there on a Saturday morning listening to a long-hair radical lawyer from Berkeley trying to explain Vietnamese history, the colonial origins of the war, and our country's role in destroying the 1954 Geneva Accords between France and the Viet Minh that provided for free elections in North and South Vietnam, which everyone understood would have resulted in an overwhelming vote for Ho Chi Minh. These were not the ideologues I had known in Berkeley, willing to spend nearly all of their time fighting among themselves over ideological trivia rather than talk to the kind of people who sat in this room with me, the kind whose votes and protests could stop the war. These were not political activists; these were people with sons who were facing the draft and daughters worried about being widowed by war; these were the people reading about the mounting war casualties, watching body bags being unloaded from planes on TV, and asking, "Why are we expending our resources and our young men on a war whose purposes and objectives are murky and which our leaders can't or won't explain?" They were concerned, disturbed and serious. They wanted to learn more and they were going to talk to their neighbors and their friends; their doubts about the war were going to spread until both political parties would have to promise to "stop the war," which both Presidential candidates did in 1972. (The winner, Nixon, reneged on the deal, but that's a longer story.) Much as I had loved Berkeley, it was refreshing to be confronted with the real politics of change

My political involvement in Colorado extended to the National Lawyers Guild, a national organization of progressive lawyers which had distinguished itself in the defense of civil rights and civil liberties, most notably the defense of alleged Communists in the McCarthy era, civil rights activists in the South, and student and military protestors of the Vietnam War. I had been active in the Guild Chapter at Boalt Hall, so my involvement with the Guild in Colorado came naturally. To the mostly Denver-based Guild member-attorneys, I seemed to represent energy and enthusiasm, and I soon was elected President of the Colorado Chapter.

The main clients of the Guild attorneys at this time (1969–71) were conscientious objectors, draft resisters, soldiers who had turned against the war, and two radical organizations, the Black Panther Party and the hispanic Crusade for Justice. The Black Panther Party in Denver was small in members and weak in organizational and political ability. Nevertheless, like Black Panther Party chapters throughout the country, they were being hounded and harassed by the FBI and local police at every opportunity. The Crusade for Justice was a more formidable organization in Denver. Led by the charismatic Corky Gonzalez, and fortified by the fact that its members were indigenous to the Denver barrio, it was a more serious threat to the status quo than the Panthers. This threat ultimately led to a police attack on the Crusade's headquarters and a major gun battle between the police and the Crusade, with many resulting criminal prosecutions against Crusade members.

The intensity of these political battles, and the criminal prosecutions of Black Panthers and Crusade for Justice activities, led the Guild to challenge the selection system for grand juries and trial juries in Denver. I worked on the challenge to the grand jury selection system in the federal courts in Denver. At that time, the grand jury was selected by the Chief Judge of the United States District Court, the Honorable Alfred A. Arraj (known to us as "Triple A"), who mostly chose grand jury members from his friends and acquaintances. There was no malice or discrimination intended by Judge Arraj, but the grand juries that resulted in this system looked a lot like Triple A—white, male, older, upper-middle class. It wasn't exactly representative of Colorado, let alone a jury of peers for minority defendants.

Our legal challenge to the federal grand jury selection system was a slam-dunk, as prior United States Supreme Court decisions had made clear that selection systems resulting in the over-representation of whites and the under-representations of minorities denied criminal defendants due process of law. The lawsuit was such a slam-dunk, the local United States Attorney capitulated and agreed to reform the system, and adopt constitutionally appropriate selection procedures. This, however, didn't stop Triple A from taking our constitutionally valid challenge as a personal attack on his friends and his own fairness.

Soon thereafter, I found myself in trial before Judge Arraj, defending Michael Francis, a conscientious objector to the draft from Colorado Springs, on the criminal charge of refusing an order to report for military service. Judge Arraj made his displeasure with me evident by turning his back toward me whenever I spoke during the trial. He was most especially displeased with how long I was taking to present my defense. Triple A was known for once bragging to the *Denver Post* that he could try three draft cases in a morning; he couldn't understand why or how I wanted to take three days to present my defense to a charge that could result in five years in federal prison! I explained that the Colorado Springs draft board had made many procedural errors and had demonstrated bias towards, and ignorance of, the standards for conscientious objection status. In fact, in the 20+ years that the Colorado Springs draft board had operated, they *never* had approved a single application for conscientious-objector status. In some respects, this was not too surprising, as Colorado Springs was a heavily military town dominated by retired brass from nearby Fort Carson and Cheyenne Mountain, the national command headquarters of the Air Force Strategic Air Command. Surprising or not, however, the draft board had been biased, did not understand the correct standards, and had made serious errors, and it was my job to demonstrate these facts, even if Triple A couldn't play golf in the afternoon—or whatever he usually did after sending three kids to the slammer in the morning.

I and my co-counsel, John O. Kuenhold, then a fellow attorney at CRLS and now judge on the Colorado Court of Appeals, put on a pretty decent trial, given our relative inexperience, and at the conclusion of trial the Court permitted closing arguments. The United States Attorney prosecuting the case, Gordon Allott, Jr., son of then-United States Senator, Gordon Allott, and a living monument to the shortcomings of nepotism, then got up and, taking a full thirty seconds for his closing argument, said, "The Colorado Springs draft board are good people. They knew what they were doing." I responded with a one-and-a–half-hour discussion of the many legal errors the Colorado Springs Board had committed—all of my scholarly discussion, of course, bouncing off the back of Triple A. At the conclusion of my argument, Triple A turned around and intoned, "Let the record reflect that this Court has sat here patiently for one and a half hours as Mr. Saperstein lectured it on selective service law."

To no one's surprise, he found Michael Francis guilty, but sentenced him to only six months in jail, which was a surprise, as Judge Arraj's normal sentence in such cases then was five years of incarceration. He must have listened to something! Perhaps Mike's quiet, sincere explanation of why he sought CO status impressed him. In any case, Mike Francis served four months in a minimum-security federal prison, with conjugal visits with his wife, and was released early for good behavior.

Despite the light sentence, we took an appeal to the Circuit Court of Appeals for the Tenth Circuit, which then was the most reactionary of the federal circuits on selective service issues. Indeed, as the Tenth Circuit argument was about to begin, the appellate attorney the Department of Justice had flown out from Washington, D.C. for the argument said, "It's a shame you've got this case in the Tenth Circuit. You'd win it in any other Circuit!" He was right, and our next stop was the United States Supreme Court, where Justice William O. Douglas, one of my great legal heroes, wrote an opinion on behalf of three Justices arguing that the Supreme Court should grant the petition for *certiorari* and hear the appeal. Unfortunately, four votes are required, the petition was denied, and the Mike Francis case ended.

While John and I were trying the selective service case in front of Judge Arraj, a medical malpractice trial was taking place next door, with the plaintiff being represented by a prominent local Guild attorney, Walt Gerash, and Melvin Belli. During breaks in my trial,

I'd go next door to watch the malpractice trial and Walt would keep me apprised of developments in that case at lunch and after court. He told me to make sure not to miss closing arguments. My trial ended in time for me to watch the closing arguments, and I was not disappointed.

The plaintiff in the malpractice action was from California and originally had been a client of Belli, who referred the matter to Walt, perhaps the leading personal injury lawyer in Colorado at the time. The case was in federal court on diversity jurisdiction (i.e., the plaintiff and the defendant resided in different states). Walt did the trial, and Belli flew in from San Francisco only for the closing argument—a strange division of trial work that I've never seen repeated in any other case, before or since.

Walt, a short, balding man with a handlebar mustache, showed up in court at 8:45 a.m. dressed in a white linen double-breasted suit, red silk handkerchief, and a wide-brim white Panama hat adorned with a beautiful red feather. The outfit cried out for attention, but Belli topped him.

Belli did not appear until the judge and the jury had been seated and the case was called. At that point, Belli, a large erect man with silver-white flowing hair, walked through the swinging doors at the back of the courtroom wearing a dark electric-blue silk suit that absolutely shimmered in the lights, a bright red silk tie, with matching red silk handkerchief overflowing his suit jacket pocket, and a diamond ring that lit up like it was powered by a small generator. At his side was a totally spectacular platinum blond, no more than 22 years old, dressed immaculately in a tight-fitting blue suit that emphasized all her curves. Belli escorted her to a front row seat, doted on her for a few minutes, making sure she was comfortable, while every eye in the courtroom, including the judge and jury's, watched his every movement. Then, he turned to face the court, saying, "Good morning, your Honor, and good morning, ladies and gentlemen of the jury."

I've never seen such a grandstanding entrance by an attorney in my life, but it didn't endear him to our little group of left-wing legal services attorneys there to watch. We hated him for his arrogance, his flashy display of wealth, and his use of the blond as a prop. But he certainly had our attention. Could this guy deliver the goods? Could his argument match his flashy entrance?

We listened as he began to explain the nature of the particular type of brain injury the plaintiff had suffered, what constituted appropriate medical treatment, and what the defendants, the operating doctor and the hospital, had done wrong. It was technical stuff which, despite the use of graphic illustrations, demanded thought and attention. Then, two attorneys made the defense side of closing arguments. Neither argument dented Belli. At the conclusion of the arguments, the court took a recess and we walked out into the hallway to discuss the case. We were amazed at our reactions; every one of us was completely persuaded by Belli. Despite his flamboyance and our biases, we had to admit Belli had a technical command of the subject matter that clearly surpassed that of his opposition, and he used that mastery effectively to persuade the jury that the defendants had not met the appropriate standard of care. Jury instructions were read to the jury after lunch and the jury began deliberations late in the afternoon. That evening, Walt called me at home to tell me the defendants had agreed to pay the then-largest medical malpractice settlement in Colorado history while the jury still was deliberating.

Belli had delivered the goods in a style that worked for him. It got him attention and provided entertainment for the jury, but the core of his presentation was his great mastery of the subject, which should have been no surprise, as he had authored a multi-volume text on medical malpractice cases. His style would not work for others, and, despite my efforts to convince Jeanine that my trial skills would be enhanced by having a young blond model accompany me at all times, I knew I would have to find a different style—my own.

The criminal and political cases I worked on with the Guild and with draft and military resisters were done in my spare time. Back at my real job at CRLS, I was still litigating class actions in federal court. Unfortunately, a disproportionately large number of CRLS federal cases were being assigned to United States District Judge Hatfield Chilson. Judge Arraj was a moderate, compared to Chilson. Chilson had been a farmer from northern Colorado, who still wore cowboy boots on the bench, and we seemed to have no chance with him. Every class action we filed that was assigned to him was dismissed, generally with little argument permitted at a short hearing. We were discouraged, not only because we were losing, but also because it seemed that Judge Chilson gave our claims and theories no thought or consideration.

I was told that Chilson still owned farm land in Colorado, so I suggested to a *Denver Post* labor reporter that he take a look at Judge Chilson's land holdings and see if he was a beneficiary of any of the farm subsidy programs we had been challenging in our lawsuits, which would be a disqualifying conflict-of-intent. On finding some evidence to support my suspicions, the *Denver Post* ran the story of Judge Chilson's conflicts of interest on the front page. Within days Judge Chilson had to recuse himself from our cases.

This was not the last I would hear of this matter, however. Within days I got a phone call from Chief Judge Arraj's secretary informing me that Chief Judge Arraj wanted to speak with me "this afternoon." I arrived at his office on the appointed hour and was shown into Judge Arraj's chamber, which, like most federal court chambers, was immense, with ceilings eighteen feet high. As I entered the office, I announced myself to Judge Arraj, who again had his back completely turned to me, as he hunched over the credenza behind his desk. He didn't offer me a chair, or say anything, so I just stood there quietly as the tension built, looking around the room, but staying alert for him to turn around. After what seemed like an eternity, but probably was four to five minutes, Judge Arraj turned in his swivel chair to face me, his flabby jowls wobbling as his feet moved. Looking at me directly without an ounce of friendliness in his eyes, he said coldly, "Mr. Saperstein, you really know how to stab a man in the back."

I felt no remorse.

I WAS ENJOYING MY CLASS ACTION practice at CRLS' headquarters in Boulder, but I wanted to see how law was practiced in our field offices, so I asked Skip if he would let me pinch-hit for some of our field staff attorneys when they took vacations. This led to several one- and two-week stints in our field offices in Grand Junction, Greeley, La Junta and Alamosa. The caseloads were typical legal services fare: landlord–tenant problems, harassment by creditors, and government benefit claims, such as welfare and social security disability benefits. Each lawyer had over 200 cases. I would get phone calls, "This is Sanchez." Of course, I had fourteen clients named Sanchez. Everyone worked hard and did their best, but it was all fingers-in-the-dike service work—important for the clients, but not the type of legal work that ever would lead to any structural change in the status and living conditions of poor people. Nevertheless, working on small cases was a necessary part of my development as a lawyer, and as I was later to learn even more powerfully, an important building block in my evolution as a successful class-action attorney, as they provided valuable legal training, as well as experience in dealing with a wide variety of people.

Working at CRLS also gave me the opportunity to get out of my office and meet our client community. Skip believed that the poor had to develop their own community organizations to create political pressure for change, not just expect lawyers to file silver-bullet class actions to change the conditions of poverty. To back up this belief, Skip hired a Chicano community organizer, Magdaleno ("Len") Avila, to inspire, encourage and assist the development of community organizations. Len and I got along well and I requested to accompany him on some of his travels to the rural areas of Colorado. Len and I developed a little road show. We would show the movie, "Salt of the Earth," a true story made into an inspiring film about a labor union strike in a silver mine in Silver City, New Mexico in the late 1940s, and about how the workers, mostly Mexican-Americans, and their wives and families, had to work together to maintain strength to sustain the strike. The film virtually defines the concepts of cooperation and solidarity, and it always inspired our audiences about the power of people working together for common goals.

We followed the showing of the film with Len giving his "Chicano Power Rap." Len was a big guy, over six feet, around 240 pounds, with a flowing black mustache and black hair—a former football player. He had a commanding presence, accentuated by a powerful voice and strong articulation. After Len fired the audience up, I would introduce CRLS and describe the kind of practices we thought were illegal and which we wanted to challenge. Later, I would be accused of "soliciting cases" this way by the Colorado Bar, to which I responded that it was my constitutional right to inform the people affected by these practices that they had a right to challenge them in court and that we were prepared to do it. Indeed, I considered it my obligation to provide this kind of information to the people adversely affected by illegal practices. I wouldn't be doing my job if I didn't actively provide such information, even if some members of the Bar wanted to deter us with spurious charges of "solicitation." I was warned to be "cautious" in continuing such practices—a warning I vowed to ignore. Thus began a pattern I would adhere to throughout my career as a class action attorney; I decided what kinds of abuses I wanted to attack and what kind of cases to bring, then I went out and found plaintiffs to file those cases.

By Spring of 1971, Jeanine and I had to face the issue of staying in Colorado or returning to California. She had a good job teaching at Jarrow Montessori School and I had several job offers from interesting private law firms in Boulder and Denver. We both loved Boulder and its proximity to the mountains. During the winter, we could put on cross-country skis at our 550-square-foot cabin above Coal Creek Canyon we shared with our two Siamese cats and climb Mt. Thorodin (10,500 feet), then ski home non-stop down a fire road. My next door neighbor owned 1,500 acres, and across the road was all National Forest land, so hiking opportunities were abundant all around us. Even better, we were just twenty minutes from fabulous hiking and cross-country skiing trails near the Continental Divide, and less than an hour from Rocky National Mountain Park, which almost became our backyard. Colorado had reinvigorated the love of the mountains I had developed backpacking in the Sierra as a Boy Scout, but which I mostly had forgotten during my college years. Plus, we had made some very good friends in Colorado.

But the pull of California was strong. Jeanine missed living near the ocean and was also very close to her large, extended California family. And she was getting tired of taking off and putting on forty pairs of mittens and snowsuits for her students each winter day. I would have been happy to stay in Colorado, at least for another two to three years, but I didn't put up much of a fight, as part of me wanted to see if I could succeed as a lawyer in a major-league venue like the San Francisco Bay Area. Denver in 1971 was still pretty much a cow town and I knew if I stayed, my law practice would consist primarily of individual personal injury and criminal defense cases. The Bay Area offered the greater possibility of being involved in larger political issues and legal cases. I wanted my legal career to have an impact on society and I also wanted to find out whether I had enough talent and ability to play a meaningful role in these bigger fights.

Jeanine's school year ended in June and I decided to quit my fellowship at the end of that month, first to help plan the national convention of the National Lawyers Guild, which was scheduled to take place at the University of Colorado campus in July, and then to "see the Rockies" before returning to California. Jeanine was pregnant with our first child, and knowing that children would fundamentally alter our lives, we knew this would be the last opportunity for a long time to get away for an extended trip, let alone a physically demanding adventure.

While I was attending the Guild Convention, noted criminal defense attorney and prison law activist Fay Stender asked me if I would be interested in working for the Prison Law Project in the Bay Area, which then was working with black prison law activists at San Quentin. Fay explained to me that these black prisoners were "the vanguard of the revolution" and the most important role models for black activists outside prison. While flattered by her interest in me, I told Fay I didn't buy the "vanguard of the revolution" theory. I had read enough history to know that, while many revolutionaries had spent time in prison, no revolution ever had been led by a prison-based movement. I also had worked with enough prisoners in Colorado to know that most prisoners were too disorganized even to take care of themselves, let alone lead a revolutionary movement; furthermore, some were pretty dangerous characters. But, mostly, I didn't want to fall into a niche law practice raising prison mistreatment issues. I wanted to see if I could learn to be a trial lawyer and I wanted to work on issues that affected large numbers of working people.

Later, I heard many stories of internecine warfare within the Black Panther Party and sectarian violence within and among militant black prison rights groups. Many people were killed in this self-destructive process, including Fay Stender, who was gunned down several years later in her living room in Berkeley by an assassin. Fay did not immediately die, but suffered irreparable spinal injuries, including paralysis, surviving in terrible pain for two years on heavy medication, and committing suicide to escape her pain and disillusionment. When she died, I thought back to Fay's offer to join her in the prison rights struggle, my disagreement with that political strategy, and my fortunate choice of a different career path. But I respected Fay's work and identified with her struggle and her tragedy.

Unburdened by these future tragedies, Jeanine and I planned to backpack through Wyoming, Colorado, New Mexico and Arizona for three months, generally in trips of 7–10 days, consisting of 60 to 80 miles of hiking. Many of our Guild friends from law school came out for the Boulder convention, and as soon as the convention ended, about ten of us backpacked into Rocky Mountain Park for a week filled with hiking, swimming in ice-cold alpine lakes, some mountain climbing, and a reasonable amount of weed, mescaline, and acid. One day, most of the group took acid and spent the day in a high-alpine meadow concentrating on the beauty of every type of vegetation, especially the wildflowers, and "skiing" down small hills of snow in our hiking boots. The next day, me and Steve Bingham, one of my law-school pals and a fellow Reggie, climbed Longs Peak (14,256 feet) on a cold, gray, but magnificent, day. Steve, a better climber than me, made sure to avoid the easier routes, and I found myself holding onto rocks with my boots and fingernails, looking down at more height exposure than I really wanted to deal with. But we made it to the top in good time and returned to camp well before dinner. I had known Steve for three years at Boalt, but never knew what a joyful and competent mountaineer he was until that day.

After a week in Rocky Mountain National Park, Jeanine and I bid our California friends goodbye and headed to the Wind River Range in Wyoming for ten days of backpacking. This turned out to be much more complicated and arduous than in Rocky Mountain National Park, due to the fact that the Wind River Range had not yet been mapped by the United States Geological Service, which forced us to travel with Forest Service maps that contained no elevation information. We also had heavy rain, which lasted for nearly eight days. We were forced to walk through many rain-swollen creeks, and our boots stayed wet for the whole trip, as we dragged ourselves back to trailhead walking on heavily blistered feet. The last day of the trip, when we had to hike twelve miles and climb over 3,000 feet, felt like the Bataan Death March to Jeanine and me, but once in our trusty Volvo 122S station wagon, our spirits rose and we headed for the nearest restaurant and motel for a newspaper, meal and hot shower. After an hour driving a dirt road, we emerged on a paved highway and the sight of a restaurant. As Jeanine went inside to grab a table, I spotted a newspaper rack and went over to buy one. Lifting the cover, I saw the heavy black print headline, "Fugitive Lawyer Sought," and a photo of Steve Bingham.

The news story indicated there had been a shoot-out at San Quentin Prison, and three persons had been killed, including the Black Panther Party leader, George Jackson. Steve was alleged to have met with Jackson shortly before the shootings and to have brought him a 9mm German lugar hidden in a tape recorder. I knew intuitively the charges were preposterous, as Steve was much too smart for a stunt like this, which surely would have led to Jackson's death. I immediately suspected the guards planted a gun in Jackson's cell as a pretext for murdering him, and now were trying to pin the rap on Steve.

Nevertheless, fearing that black militants might believe he brought the gun to Jackson, Steve fled the country, not to return for fifteen years. On his return, he was prosecuted for murder and acquitted after a long trial. The government's theory was implausible—the 9mm lugar found on Jackson would not fit inside Steve's tape recorder, nor on Jackson's head under a wig the prison official's claimed Jackson wore after leaving his meeting with Steve, and Steve was simply too credible for the jury to believe him guilty of such a foolhardy plot. It was a chilling reminder that political and legal struggles did not stop just because Jeanine and I decided to go back-packing.

We spent a couple of days in Jackson Hole restocking our supplies and equipment and making telephone calls back to California to try to obtain information about Steve, then did a 60-mile loop around the Grand Tetons with some friends from Texas. Emerging after eight days in idyllic conditions, with wildflowers in full bloom, I volunteered to hitchhike back to the car, which had been left at a different trailhead. The first car that approached me as I stood on the road with my thumb out was a black limousine with small American flags on the front fenders. The back window was open and inside were the architects of the continuing war on Vietnam: President Nixon and Secretary of State Henry Kissinger! Reality had struck again. As soon as I got a newspaper, I learned they were in Jackson Hole as guests of Nelson Rockefeller, who owned a big ranch nearby.

We continued to hike in the Rockies for another two months, and when snow began to fall, headed south for two weeks hiking the abandoned trails of the Grand Canyon, then a week in the Gila

Wilderness in southern New Mexico. Our travels over, and with Jeanine's pregnancy becoming a greater factor in our lives, we headed back to the Bay Area with no jobs, no prospects and no money—but with the feeling we were coming home.

5

Private Law Firm: The Early Years

*"We are all sculptors and partners, and our material
is our own flesh and blood."*
—Henry David Thoreau

JEANINE AND I rented a small house in a poor and mainly black
section of West Berkeley, near San Pablo Park. Jeanine went back
to work in the welfare department, despite being late in her pregnancy, and I began to practice law out of my house—when I was
not too busy playing basketball with the neighborhood teenagers.

My law school friend, Paul Harris, who had just finished
clerking for United States District Judge Alphonso Zirpoli, soon
got me on the federal public defender conflicts panel in San Francisco, due to my expertise in selective service law. This panel of
private attorneys had been established for the purpose of representing clients of the Federal Public Defender Office when special-
ized legal experience was required or when the Public Defender
had a conflict of interest, which frequently occurred when there
were multiple defendants in a case. Since the Bay Area was a hot-
bed of opposition to the continuing Vietnam War, many draft reg-
istrants were refusing induction into the armed services, and criminal prosecutions for draft refusal were at an all-time high. I immediately began to be appointed by federal judges as defense counsel
in draft refusal cases.

My first draft case was assigned to U. S. District Judge Robert Schnacke. Judge Schnacke already had distinguished himself as the most right-wing judge on the Northern District of California federal bench. His credits included sentencing C. Arnholdt Smith, a major contributor to Republican causes, to six months probation for defrauding the depositors at San Diego National Bank, which he owned, of millions of dollars; but Schnacke regularly sentenced draft resisters—many of whom resisted the Vietnam War as a moral imperative—to the maximum five years in prison. A few years later, Judge Schnacke made the front page of the local papers when he was arrested in a porno theater a few blocks away from the United States Courthouse—not a place federal judges normally frequent. A lot of us had a good laugh at that, although no one wanted to deny him his right to be aroused.

I received notice of my new case appointment on a Wednesday and appeared the following Monday for the arraignment. Judge Schnacke took the bench and his demeanor fit the political description I had been given. He was a large man and the elevation of his chair and bench above the courtroom floor enhanced his size. His head was large, bald, and unsmiling; his tone of voice deep and gruff. There were no pleasantries and he did not even acknowledge my "Good morning, your Honor." After I introduced myself and entered a plea of "not guilty" for my client, Judge Schnacke told his court deputy, "I want the first available trial date." The deputy answered, "I have Monday available." "OK, trial will begin on Monday," Judge Schnacke said. "What Monday?" I asked. "Next Monday!" Judge Schnacke snapped.

I thought seven days was pretty quick for an offense that carried up to a five-year prison term, but I knew the subject well and I wasn't exactly overwhelmed with cases, so I didn't object. I just explained to Judge Schnacke what information about the alleged offense I needed and he ordered the Assistant United States Attorney to "get that material for Mr. Saperstein today." I went down to the United States Attorney's Office on the 16th floor, reviewed the selective service file, copies of all documents were made for me, and

I went back home to begin writing a motion to dismiss the charges.

The criminal charges against my client were defective in several regards, most notably the "order of call." The defendant had been called for induction out of order, a clear-cut defense to his failure to step forward and be inducted. In a thirty-page memorandum of points and authorities supporting my motion to dismiss, I explained the defects and demanded that the criminal complaint be dismissed. I filed the memorandum on Wednesday, and by Friday the Assistant United States Attorney phoned to tell me that the Government would acquiesce in my motion and dismiss the case.

On the following Monday morning, the defendant, the Assistant United States Attorney and I appeared before Judge Schnacke and I explained that the prosecution was defective, the defect was not curable, and the complaint had to be dismissed. Judge Schnacke turned to the government attorney, who stated, "The Government concurs in what Mr. Saperstein has said and moves to dismiss the case." Judge Schnacke became quite upset at this turn of events; indeed, he seemed to be even more upset at the prosecutor than he was with me, although he clearly was not happy with me either. In a voice even more gruff and deep than usual, he demanded more explanation from the government attorney, and when further explanation didn't please him, refused to dismiss the case, ordering the United States Attorney's office to research the matter in greater depth to determine if there was any basis for continuing the prosecution. I was astounded. I had never seen—or even heard of—a judge refuse to acquiesce in a prosecution motion to dismiss a case.

A week later, we all returned to do the same dance before Judge Schnacke, and the prosecutor, this time supported by his own legal memorandum explaining the incurable defects in the government's case, was forced to take further abuse from the eminent judge. I felt sorry for the prosecutor, who was in a completely untenable situation, having a clearly defective prosecution case in front of a judge bent on convicting draft resisters. But the prosecutor persevered, and after grilling and insulting the prosecutor Schnacke had no choice but to dismiss the case. Nevertheless, despite the unassailable merit of my motion to dismiss the charges, which showed conclusively that the government had tried to induct my client illegally, Judge Schnacke scowled at me and told my client, "You're lucky your lawyer got you off on a technicality!" I thought to myself, "Gee, I thought the government's obligation to comply with the law was more than a 'technicality'." I also thought right-wing judges believed that rules—even technical rules—were supposed to be followed.

The federal court fee schedule set rates for appointed cases at $20/hour for out-of-court time and $30/hour in-court; I calculated my bill at $752, filled out the appropriate government form, and sent it to Judge Schnacke for approval. He sent it back a week later, cutting my fee to $300—less than $10/hour for keeping a young man out of prison for five years. I was nearly broke. I was happy to get the $300.

Over the next several years, I defended approximately forty selective service cases. In a majority of these cases, I was able to find technical defects in the induction process that led to dismissals; in the cases where I couldn't uncover any defects, I was lucky to face the more moderate federal judges, who generally sentenced the draft resisters to up to two years in prison and often placed defendants on probation for eighteen months of those two years, leaving only six months to be served, with time off for good behavior.

I represented one young man who refused to fit into this pattern, however. This defendant was a member of the Resistance, as I had been, and he refused to cooperate with the draft in any way. He was neatly, although informally, dressed, with sandy blond hair appropriately long for the period. He was a person of strong conscience, articulate political views, and came from a caring and close family. He had no defense to the charges, but he received a predictably favorable report from the probation officer assigned to his case and a recommendation of the two-year sentence, with six months to be served and eighteen months on probation, a standard condition of which required defendants not to engage in illegal activity while on probation.

His parents and I were quite happy with the probation recommendation and we appeared before United States District Judge Albert Wollenberg fully expecting the recommendation would become the order of the Court. And, indeed, Judge Wollenberg was prepared to follow the probation department recommendation. However, as the Judge was about to announce the sentence, the defendant politely interrupted and asked if he could say something to the Court before sentence was pronounced. Judge Wollenberg said, "Of course," and my client quietly, but forcefully, explained he would not be able to accept probation, as accepting probation would be a form of cooperation and accommodation with the draft and he conscientiously could not do that. All of us, including Judge Wollenberg, were stunned. Judge Wollenberg advised my client to speak with his parents and his attorney, while the Court took a recess. There was no one else in the courtroom, so while the Court was in recess, I talked with my client about his unexpected decision. I explained that non-cooperation with the draft could take many forms. In my case, it had consisted of mailing my draft certificate back to my draft board with a statement that I refused to carry the card and would refuse induction. In his case, he already had gone further than that, as he actually had refused induction. Moreover, he was not cooperating with the selective service system, or the military, in any way, as he had refused induction into the army, pled guilty to the crime of refusing induction, and now was about to be sentenced to six months in prison for that act of non-cooperation. "In no way," I argued, "are you cooperating with either the selective service system or the armed forces." His parents agreed, but said little, deferring to me to make the case for accepting probation. We spoke for nearly a half hour and then one of the judge's law clerks came out of chambers and asked me if we had made any progress. I said "no" and a few minutes later, the defendant, his parents, and I were invited into Judge Wollenberg's chambers. Judge Wollenberg asked him if he "really had to do this."

"Isn't there another way? Do you fully understand the consequences of what you are doing?" My client politely repeated his vow of non-cooperation with the draft and added that he intended to continue opposing the draft actively and that it was highly unlikely he would be able to honor the terms of his probation, if he were to accept probation, anyway. Judge Wollenberg normally had the face of a kind and benevolent favorite uncle, and the pain and concern on his face now was evident, but he said he would honor the intentions of the defendant.

We all went back into open court, and Judge Wollenberg pronounced sentence—two years in federal prison, no probation—adding, "I wish there was some other way, but this young man has thought about this very carefully, and, while I do not agree with the decision he is making here today, I respect and honor it." I was much closer in age to my client than was Judge Wollenberg, and I was thinking back to my own recent escape from the draft, but my feelings were the same as Judge Wollenberg's—I would not have chosen two years of prison to demonstrate my principles, particularly if I had been offered the option of probation. Yet I admired his courage and the primacy of his principles.

Not every opponent of the war was as honorable as that young man. In addition to my selective service cases, I began to represent resisters in the armed forces. My first case was a Navy pilot on leave while the aircraft carrier he was stationed on was undergoing minor repairs in the Bay Area. Knowing that his ship would be sailing for the South China Sea, and feeling that he would be flying over and bombing Vietnam villages, he had begun to explore his feelings about war and had decided he was a Conscientious Objector. Before approaching me, he had filed a formal request for CO status, which had been rejected summarily by the Navy.

His ship was scheduled to sail in three days, so I immediately filed a petition for writ of habeas corpus in federal court in San Francisco seeking to have his CO claim reviewed, and the case was assigned to "CBR," short for United States District Judge Charles B. Renfrew. I never had appeared before Judge Renfrew, one of the newer federal judges, but I had heard of his reputation for intelligent legal analysis and fabulous work habits. I was not disappointed.

My petition was filed midday, and by 4 p.m. that afternoon I received a call from Judge Renfrew's courtroom deputy, James Robinson, telling me, "Judge Renfrew has a jury trial going on this week, starting each morning at 9:30 a.m., so he can hear your case tomorrow at 7 a.m."! I never had met a judge willing to convene court that early, and I was not in the habit of working that early either. Nevertheless, when I appeared in court the next morning at 7 a.m. and was shepherded into Judge Renfrew's library by his secretary, Judge Renfrew and one of his law clerks already were pulling books off the shelves and reading military habeas corpus cases. Judge Renfrew was tall, blond, handsome, very fit, and appeared younger than his 40+ years. He was extremely articulate, very courteous, and set high standards for himself and the attorneys who appeared before him.

The issues I had raised in my petition were (1) Was the petitioner entitled to an administrative review of his application for conscientious objector status; (2) If so, what form of review was required; and, (3) Where and when should that review take place?

I began to discuss these issues, as did the attorney representing the Navy. Judge Renfrew listened, asked questions, then summoned his law clerk to pull cases for him, which he would read on the spot—shooting questions at us as they came to him. When 9:30 a.m. rolled around, the Judge excused himself, saying, "I have a jury to attend to." The Navy attorney and I waited in the library, and at 10:45 a.m., while the jury took its morning break, Judge Renfrew returned, then returned again at the lunch break, to discuss further the difficult issues presented by the *habeas corpus* petition, to read more cases and to ask more questions. The jury went home at 4 p.m., and we all worked until 7 p.m., when Judge Renfrew ruled that (1) The petitioner had raised a legitimate claim for conscientious objector status and was entitled to an administrative review; (2) He was entitled to a hearing, not simply a paper review of his claim; and (3) The hearing would take place on the aircraft carrier in three days, with the Navy ordered to fly me to and from the aircraft carrier as it steamed toward the Far East.

I was elated. While I didn't get all that I had asked for, as I had requested that a hearing be convened at Treasure Island, a Navy base in the middle of the San Francisco Bay, I certainly got a fair ruling and all the remedy that reasonably could have been expected. I was also excited about the prospect of landing on, and taking off from, an aircraft carrier.

My client, dressed in casual civilian clothes, was waiting for me at my office when I returned around 8 p.m. He was not as happy as I was, as he plainly did not want to get back on the boat, scheduled to sail the next morning. I explained that the Navy rarely had federal judges intervene in this way, and that whatever they did would be subject to review by Judge Renfrew. "Knowing that the Navy will grant you due process and a fair hearing, and that a very diligent federal judge will be watching what the Navy does, I feel confident we will win your claim." I further explained to him that if he went AWOL (absent without leave) the next morning, we would lose everything we had won today, he would never get a chance to establish his CO status, and he could face criminal prosecution and/or dishonorable discharge when he was caught.

Nevertheless, he went AWOL the next morning and I never heard from him again. Sadly, I had to phone Judge Renfrew and inform him that his painstaking and timely work (and mine) had been wasted. I could sense surprise and disappointment in Judge Renfrew's voice when I gave him this news. My reaction was much stronger. I was pissed off that I had been dragged into this fight and then had been abandoned; moreover, I hadn't even charged a fee. I also was afraid I might have used up some goodwill with a prominent federal judge who might not be so responsive next time I came seeking an emergency order.

I had been naive about this client and had not done a good job of explaining what realistically could be accomplished with a *habeas corpus* petition. I had assumed he was committed to the legal process he had initiated and that he would understand that obtaining a review of his CO claim—supervised by a federal judge—was a major win. I assumed he understood that we could not expect to obtain 100% of what we sought and that he could not assume that any rehearing ordered by the judge would be away from his ship. And I assumed that he trusted me, valued my advice, and would comply with a reasonable court order. I failed to understand how afraid he was about getting back on his ship and how suspicious he was about further legal proceedings.

I realized that, in the future, I needed to have a full discussion with my clients about the objectives of any legal action and get a commitment from them to realistic objectives. If they were not going to be realistic at the beginning of our relationship, it was unlikely they would be realistic at the end. And I realized I should have gotten this Navy pilot more involved in his own case by bringing him to the *habeas corpus* hearing. If he had seen how hard Judge Renfrew and I had worked on his behalf, and how reasoned and responsible Judge Renfew had been in rendering his decision, I think he would have shared my confidence in Judge Renfrew and realized that if he didn't get a fair hearing from the Navy, he had recourse to a powerful and fair federal judge. Instead, by not discussing objectives, not charging him a fee, and not involving him in the federal court hearing, I made sure the Navy pilot had little commitment to the case, or to me, and he just walked out when he didn't get 100% of what he wanted.

A COUPLE OF MONTHS INTO MY HOME LAW PRACTICE, I was solicited by two groups of young lawyers who were considering establishing law firms. I spent a month developing plans to begin a law firm with the first group, which included a friend of mine from law school, but our plans exploded when the my friend's marriage broke apart for reasons unrelated to the incipient law firm. The other group was being organized by Barry Willdorf and Charles Farnsworth. I had worked with Barry on a military case in San Francisco, but had never met Farnsworth. What Barry told me about Chuck sounded great: a graduate of Stanford Law School, he had worked for California Rural Legal Assistance, doing legal work on behalf of farm workers that was similar to what I had been doing in Colorado. After leaving CRLA, Chuck had gone to work for the United Farmworkers Union as legal counsel and had been on the front lines of their legal battles, which then involved an historic attempt to organize farm workers, a group of workers who had never previously been organized, led, of course, by the legendary Cesar Chavez. Chuck was a member of the National Lawyers Guild, had defended military cases, and also had some experience in personal injury and worker's compensation law, which I lacked. There were lots of parallels and similarities in our legal experiences and political views, and I even had a connection with his wife, Elizabeth, now an anchor for *The News Hour* with Jim Lehrer. Elizabeth had been working with the North American Congress on Latin American (NACLA). NACLA published a small, dense, informative newsletter on political and social issues in Latin America, which I subscribed to from Colorado. Apparently, they had wondered about the subscriber from Colorado, as I was the only NACLA Newsletter subscriber in Colorado. Elizabeth, an expert in Latin America, was surprised to learn that that subscriber was the same person her husband was now contemplating establishing a law firm with.

Barry, Chuck and I met, liked one another, found we had much in common and similar goals, and we soon began looking for cheap office space in the Fruitvale section of East Oakland. We selected this area because it was multiracial, working class, and the population of lawyers was low. Plus, rents were cheap. Around the same time, an attorney position became available at San Francisco Neighborhood Legal Assistance Foundation. I applied and was invited to interview for it. The first question I was asked was, "What knowledge and experience would you bring to this program?" I answered, "Well, I think I know more about the 1948 Sugar Beet Act than anyone you'll interview, and if you have a lot of sugar beet cases, I'm your guy." Despite my smart-ass answer, I was offered the job. I was fortunate to get the offer, as attorney positions in good legal services programs like SFNLAF rarely became available, but I already had spent two years working in a legal services program and I wanted to broaden my legal experiences. I asked for a week to consider the offer, then another week, then a third week, as I got to know Chuck and Barry better and as we moved closer to starting a firm. I discussed with Jeanine the risks of starting my own firm versus taking a secure job with a regular salary. She did not hesitate to encourage me to take a risk for something I believed in. She always was willing to help support me and support my career choices.

After weeks of looking at different office possibilities with Barry and Chuck—mostly storefronts—we found a little building with a reception area and three offices, formerly a doctor's office, but unoccupied for years. It wasn't even on the rental market, but we tracked down the owner through county property records, contacted him, and determined that he was willing to rent it for $200 per month, with a two-year lease. The catch was he would make no repairs, do no maintenance and pay no utilities. If we wanted the space, we could have it "as is." We asked for a few days to make a decision.

The next day, late on the afternoon of March 2, 1972, I got a phone call at home from Barry. He announced he was withdrawing from the law firm he had proposed and organized. I was stunned, as Barry had said nothing in the past month and a half to indicate any doubts or reservations about our plans for the new law firm. I asked him why he had made this decision. Barry explained that he wanted to focus on military law exclusively and that Chuck and I were interested in a broader scope of cases. He said he understood that Chuck and I were willing to do military cases as part of a law practice, but he wanted a practice that focussed exclusively on military law. I told Barry I was a little ticked off that he had not revealed these feelings to Chuck or me earlier. More important, I tried to explain that a law firm that did nothing but military law simply was not economically viable, as we all had learned in our own military cases that few military clients could pay anything more than a nominal fee, and many could not afford to pay any fee. Barry admitted that might well be true, but he and his wife, who had agreed to work with him, were committed to this course. While I admired the underlying basis for Barry's decision—opposition to the Vietnam War—the differences in philosophy between Barry and me were irreconcilable and I had no choice but to accept his decision. (Fifteen years later, Barry and his law partner hired me to represent their firm in a very important sex discrimination and attorneys' fees appeal that was before the United States Circuit Court of Appeals for the Ninth Circuit. During the course of my representation of Barry's firm, Barry told me, "Remember when I decided to withdraw from the firm with you and Chuck? Well, you were absolutely right, it was not possible to maintain a firm on military cases alone.")

As soon as I got off the phone with Barry, I told Jeanine what had happened. I told her the law firm now was in doubt, as Barry had been the catalyst organizer and I knew Chuck much less well than I knew Barry. As soon as I finished my explanation, Jeanine went into labor. We drove to Alta Bates Hospital as quickly as we could, and after checking in, went into our Lamaze procedures. Unfortunately, as the baby had decided to arrive six weeks early, we only had completed half the Lamaze class, but we did our best. I tried to do my part as the Lamaze coach, timing the contractions, helping Jeanine to breathe properly, putting cool washcloths on her forehead—while taking photographs. I hope I did a better job of coaching than I did as a photographer. I was so nervous that I didn't get the film on the spool properly and snapped a roll of film without the film ever advancing. We have no pictures, but I can still remember looking with wonder at the doctor handing me my first son with the umbilical cord still attached just seconds after he had been born. We named him, "Leon Douglas" after Leon Trotsky and William O'Douglas.

After leaving the delivery room while Jeanine rested, I went to a pay phone to call Chuck to ask what he wanted to do now that Barry was going his own way. Chuck's reaction was firm: "Let's go ahead." I agreed. That made two births in one day: my first son and a law firm.

A few days later, Chuck and I signed the lease for our little Art Deco office at 2201 Fruitvale Avenue, in Oakland, and immediately began resurrecting it. Chuck and I cleaned and painted the building inside and out, I refinished three old desks, purchased used for about $35–$75 each, my dad drove up from Los Angeles and fixed the plumbing and the roof, Jeanine made curtains for the windows, and we paid an out-of-work architect $50 to paint in large letters on the outside of the building, "Farnsworth & Saperstein, Attorneys at Law." It took a month to transform the ghost building into law quarters for our fledging firm. When we finished the last scraping of paint off the outside window trim and Chuck and I stood back on the sidewalk to admire our handiwork, a large, white Cadillac pulled up to the curb and a matronly, well-dressed lady leaned out the window and summoned us. "I've been watching you boys paint this building for the past two weeks and I've been impressed with your work," she told us. "I have a large house in Piedmont and I'd like to hire you to paint it." I laughed as I explained we were the lawyers, not painters, and we declined the job. This might have been a mistake, because we would have made a lot more money painting houses than we did practicing law the first few years.

Our doors opened the first week in April, 1972. There were no fanfares, dancing ladies, or lights projecting into the sky, just a few people from the neighborhood who occasionally stuck their heads in the front door and asked who we were and what we were doing, plus a local wino who frequently lounged on our front steps in the afternoon when the sun was in just the right position to warm him. He would barely move as Chuck and I stepped over him to get into the office.

WE HAD A RECEPTION AREA AND RECEPTIONIST DESK, but no receptionist or secretary to greet clients, answer the phones, or type letters and briefs. Chuck and I did our own typing on our manual typewriters, I on the Smith-Corona portable my mother had given me when

I graduated high school. Fortunately, I am a good typist and Chuck was even better, so this was less of a burden on us than it might have been on others. Nevertheless, we were both very happy six months later when we were able to hire a young Hispanic woman from the neighborhood, Gloria Zamora. Gloria, then a sophomore at Cal, worked fifteen hours a week for us. Gloria was absolutely perfect for our job: she was smart, efficient, attractive, pleasant with clients, indigenous to the community—and inexpensive. We splurged and bought her a reconditioned IBM Model C electric typewriter for $300—a major step forward in the firm's technological capability, but a significant expense at the time, as Chuck and I each were making only about $300 a month.

Work came in slowly and we had much time to tune in on the Watergate hearings, then running every day on TV, enjoy long lunch conversations, and occasionally watch a prominent lawyer try a case in court. I also had time to leave work and go home to help Jeanine with Leon whenever she called. After six months, Chuck's good friend, Frank Denison, joined the firm as the third partner. Frank was a terrific conversationalist, and, because he was more politically conservative than Chuck and I, our lunch breaks became even longer as we discussed and debated such light topics as the continuing Vietnam War, the allocation of public money to military and social welfare purposes, the maldistribution of wealth in America, the role of wealth in politics and the media, class in America, etc.

Chuck knew Frank from the United Farmworkers Union, where Frank had worked directly for Cesar, doing the business and organizational legal work for the Union as well as setting up and overseeing the Union's health and welfare and pension plans. Adding Frank to the firm brought in the Farmworkers Union as our first institutional client. Frank did the business work for the Union, as well as the health/welfare and pension plans, Chuck began doing a lot of federal class action litigation for the Union, directed against enemies of the Union and targets of the Union's nationwide grape boycott, and I occasionally was called upon to represent Union members and supporters arrested in political demonstrations. The health/welfare and pension plan work paid a low, but decent, hourly rate, although I doubt that Frank—a 99.9% perfectionist—ever charged the plans for more than half his time; the class action work, which at one point had Chuck working 60–70 hour weeks, paid almost nothing; and, my criminal representation work did, in fact, pay nothing. But we never felt exploited. How could we? The Union then paid its employees, including Cesar, $5 a week, plus room and board. We all felt honored to be able to help "La Causa," which then was the most important labor organizing effort in America.

Our work for the Union enabled me to meet Cesar twice, once at our office, and once at the Farmworkers Union convention. I was impressed by his humility, interest in others, sense of grace, and serene demeanor, regardless of stress or overwork. He had one of the most peaceful, pleasant expressions I've ever seen on a man and it reminded me of John Coltrane, another hero of mine. I had had the good fortune of seeing Coltrane perform twenty to thirty times in the early 1960s at the Jazz Workshop, on Broadway in San Francisco, and I remember watching his face as he and his great quartet played powerful avant-garde music. The music would drive and pulsate as Coltrane played the most exhilarating solos in jazz saxophone history. His face would sweat profusely, yet there was a peacefulness and serenity in his face that was mesmerizing—the closest I've ever seen to complete joy, compassion and love expressed in a person's face. Cesar's face expressed the same kind of serenity and compassion.

I continued to take criminal defense cases from the federal public defender conflicts panel, litigate military habeas corpus cases, as well as court-martial defense cases before military tribunals, and I accepted court appointments for appeals of criminal convictions. I also began doing cases that came to us from the neighborhood. I represented the local drug dealer, the local drunks, the neighborhood hookers; I represented clients in bankruptcies, divorces, child custody trials, personal injury cases, and got on the Alameda County Public Defender conflicts panel, which provided a wide range of criminal defense work. None of these cases paid much, and some paid nothing, but they provided training and trial experience that would give me skills and confidence that would be very important later when bigger cases became available to me.

Being appointed to the Alameda County Public Defender conflicts panel resulted in my representation of a lot of prostitutes. The Oakland Police Department then was conducting a crusade against prostitution, spurred on by local merchants and neighbors along the most popular streets for the hookers to congregate—MacArthur Boulevard, San Pablo Avenue, and East 14th Street. The police were rounding prostitutes up *en masse*, often by entrapping them with undercover "johns," frequently by observing a pick-up, then arresting the woman as the "solicitor"—"solicitation" of an act of prostitution being a crime—despite the fact that the woman normally did little more than dress alluringly and appear available, while the john initiated the contact and asked for a "date." It was a one-sided and sexually discriminatory enforcement of the anti-solicitation statute, and the Alameda County Public Defender's Office, along with a group of private attorneys, including me, brought a constitutional challenge to the police department's disparate treatment of men and women. The case, ironically, was called *Hartway v. Superior Court*, named after the lead plaintiff, Cynthia Hartway. The case provided me an opportunity to watch more experienced criminal defense attorneys cross-examine police officers, contest prosecution claims, and build an evidentiary record.

The attorney who most impressed me was Mike Ballachey, then a criminal defense attorney and now a respected judge of the Alameda County Superior Court. Mike knew how to confront hostile witnesses firmly, in this case police officers, while using humor and a street-savvy style to put witnesses at ease and, to some extent, disarm them. It was an entertaining, effective method, one that showed respect for the witness, while attacking what the witness had done on a particular occasion. Mike, with a lot of experience cross-examining cops, knew how to walk the edge between respect and attack, and was a good example for a young attorney to emulate—particularly someone like myself, with my anti-cop bias. I knew I was driven by a strong anti-establishment perspective, but I also knew I would have to learn to control that perspective, or at least make it less obvious, if I was going to be effective in court. The *Hartway* challenge, unfortunately, went all the way to the California Supreme Court, which decided against the women's claims.

My criminal law practice taught me who controlled the courtroom. It wasn't the judges. It was the deputy district attorneys. They decided how to charge the case, what kind of plea bargain to offer, and the judges, particularly in high-volume, inner-city municipal courts like Oakland, followed their recommendations. Rarely did the judges deviate from the disposition sought by the prosecutors and more rarely still did they grant defense motions. I thought this all would change when liberal Democrat Jerry Brown became Governor of California in 1974 and began appointing Democrats to the bench, but I was disappointed. The new judges Brown appointed gave defense attorneys like me more sympathetic hearings, then followed the DA's recommendations, just like the Republican judges. The results were the same, but the new Democratic judges wanted us to feel better about it.

One exception to this dismal tendency was Marilyn Hall Patel, a newly appointed municipal court judge who had practiced trade and patent law in San Francisco before her appointment. I first appeared before Judge Patel a few months after her appointment on a motion to dismiss the criminal complaint against a group of women accused of soliciting acts of prostitution. I put a couple of the women on the stand to testify about the circumstances of their arrest and a pretty clear story emerged about the dissimilar treatment of the women, now charged with crimes, and the johns, now home with casual warnings from the cops. One of the arresting officers testified for the prosecution, but was not particularly effective in undermining the women's story of discrimination as well as physical mistreatment by the police.

As soon as the prosecution and I had finished our brief arguments about the constitutionality of the police conduct, Judge Patel said loud and clear, "This Court will not tolerate this kind of police behavior. The motion is granted and all cases are dismissed," then slammed down her gavel. I was astounded, but the deputy DA was so shocked he could speak only in gurgles. He finally pulled himself together and demanded that the hearing "be put on the record." No court reporter had recorded the hearings, and this was a demand that a reporter be brought in to record the proceedings in this case, including the evidentiary hearing, and was an open challenge to Judge Patel. The underlying message was: "You better not do this, because if you do, we'll take an appeal. How dare you dismiss cases like this? Who do you think runs this court?" Judge Patel dutifully said a court reporter would be brought in and a rehearing would commence at 1:30 p.m.

We all returned at 1:30 p.m., and with a court reporter present, the morning's events were repeated: the women testified, the arresting officer testified, and I and the deputy DA provided legal arguments, only this time the DA's argument and demeanor were full of arrogance, bluster, vitriol and challenge. It was as though the deputy DA was saying, "We've got to clear the streets of prostitutes. How dare you challenge police conduct or the authority of the District Attorney's Office?" I sat listening, thinking to myself, "The judge doesn't know me, doesn't owe me anything, and doesn't want to be labeled 'anti-police' and blackballed by the DA's office—which could be the kiss of death to any ambitions for future judicial appointments to higher courts. She'll cave." But, as soon as the DA concluded his remarks and smugly sat down, Judge Patel stated loud and clear, "This Court will not tolerate this kind of police behavior. The motion is granted and all cases are dismissed. If you want to take an appeal, you now have a record." Before letting my excitement overtake me, I thought to myself, "This woman is a real judge!" It was truly inspirational. Constitutional rights counted. There were limits to what the police could do, even against weak and unpopular people. One judge was willing to tell the police department and the District Attorney what some of those limits were and enforce them. One strong lawyer—in this case a judge—made the difference.

Judge Patel went on to earn approval ratings of nearly 95% in the annual Alameda County Bar evaluation poll, one of the highest ratings ever, and later was appointed to the United States District Court by President Carter. She continues as one of the smartest, toughest, and most respected federal judges in California.

I OFTEN HAVE CHARACTERIZED PRACTICING LAW as a "whole life" experience, meaning that knowledge and experiences obtained outside law school and outside the law practice often can be more important in winning cases than so-called "legal knowledge." A criminal trial I did in Solano County early in my private law career illustrates that point.

Dennis Crowder, a young black airman stationed at Hamilton Air Force Base, was accused of attempted murder and assault with a deadly weapon arising out of a busted drug deal. Crowder claimed the victim had been acting strangely and had threatened to attack him with a knife before Crowder shot him twice in the chest in self-defense. Crowder claimed there were witnesses to the victim's pre-shooting behavior, but in four months of investigating the case, Crowder never produced any of these witnesses, nor even showed up in my office for an appointment to discuss the case. This aggravated me, since this was going to be my first serious felony trial in state court and I had the time and willingness to pursue all investigative possibilities.

The preliminary hearing was held in municipal court, and on the basis of the victim's testimony and the identification of a gun found in Crowder's possession the day after the shooting, Crowder was bound over for arraignment and trial in superior court. Shortly after the arraignment and "not guilty" plea, Crowder got cold feet and called me to tell me to "make a deal" with the DA. Because two shots had been fired and the victim nearly had died, as well as the indication that the dispute had arisen over the sale of hard drugs, the deputy district attorney insisted on state prison time, but indicated his willingness to follow the probation report recommendation. This was acceptable to Crowder, but when we appeared before Judge Thomas Healey to enter a plea, Crowder had second thoughts and refused to acknowledge on the record that he was waiving specific constitutional rights in order to change his plea. The judge had no choice but to set a trial date, which arrived two months later without Crowder having located any of the witnesses he claimed could support his story and without Crowder even returning my phone calls. My investigator, Don Hamitt, and I searched for the witnesses based on the names Crowder had provided at our first meeting, along with the "vicinity," but no address. I talked to many people, but was not successful in locating any witnesses. Trial began with no corroboration of Crowder's version of events.

I was nervous the morning of the first day of trial. As the deputy DA and I went into the chambers of Judge Raymond Sherwin to discuss pretrial motions and jury instructions, the deputy DA, Jon Unterman, added to my nervousness by pointedly mentioning a couple of times that he had "thirteen straight trial convictions and this was going to be number fourteen, the easiest one of all." The judge was friendly to Unterman and indicated to me that Unterman was a tough, but fair, prosecutor. I accepted that as true, even though Unterman clearly was preying on my inexperience and trying to intimidate me.

I told Judge Sherwin this was going to be my first felony jury trial in California. I hoped this might buy me a little compassion. As we sat discussing motions and instructions, I noticed several photographs on the wall behind the judge's desk. I recognized one of them as Columbine Lake, a very inaccessible lake in the High Sierras that I had hiked to the summer before with my friend Bill deCarion. Columbine Lake is reached by hiking a cross-country route up and over a 12,000-foot pass, so few backpackers ever see it, despite its extraordinary beauty. After about an hour of wrangling over legal issues, the prosecutor said he had to make a phone call, and as he was making his call from the judge's conference table, I asked Judge Sherwin, "Is that Columbine Lake in that photo?" He said, "Why yes, but how did you know? Nobody ever has recognized that lake before." This gave me an opportunity to tell him I had hiked there and to talk about some of my backpacking trips in the Sierras and Rockies, and for the Judge and I to share some of our experiences. The DA sat quietly for twenty minutes as the Judge and I told stories about hiking and backpacking. I walked out of chambers feeling much more comfortable, and Judge Sherwin treated me extremely well throughout the six-day trial, never embarrassing me when I made inappropriate evidentiary objections or overstepped the limits of proper arguments.

The jury panel was all-white, and I had a black defendant, so I talked to the jurors during jury selection about their attitudes and experiences with black people, borrowing heavily from the questions Charles Garry had developed in trying to expose and sensitize jurors about racism, including their own. I asked questions such as: "If you were walking on a city street late at night and saw a black man walking toward you, would you feel some fear or want to walk to the other side of the street?" Such juror questioning was discretionary with the judge, and many judges would not allow it. Judge Sherwin let me ask the questions I wanted to ask. Despite the whiteness of the jury panel, I thought they might be OK, except for juror number 12, a male farmer who obviously had racist attitudes. I spent a lot of time with him and I thought by exposing some of his anti-black attitudes and getting his explicit promise to put those feelings aside and treat Mr. Crowder the same way he would treat a white man—plus the fact that the other jurors had observed him expose some of his biases and would monitor him, and that the alleged crime was a black-on-black dispute, would be enough to keep him in line, so when the DA said he would accept the jury panel, after briefly consulting with Crowder we agreed to take the panel. I later would learn that not using a preemptory challenge on this juror had been a mistake, but fortunately not a fatal mistake.

After opening statements, the prosecution presented its case, relying most heavily on forensic evidence tying the gun found in my client's car to the bullets taken out of the victim's chest, and the testimony of the victim. The victim offered the story that he had loaned money to the defendant, who subsequently refused to repay the money, there had been an argument, Crowder said he was going to kill him and pulled out a gun and shot him twice. On cross-examination, I was able to plant some doubt about the "loan," as the victim didn't seem to know Crowder well enough to be loaning money to him, and to establish that he did have a knife in his possession, although he claimed that he had not taken it out of his pocket (it was in his pocket when the police got to him). Probably the only thing that really helped the self-defense theory was that the alleged victim was about 6 feet 3 inches tall, over 200 pounds, and very muscular, while Crowder was shorter, quite thin and not muscular at all. The prosecution closed its case on Friday afternoon, which gave me one last chance to locate witnesses over the weekend.

After trial on Friday, Crowder provided me with a better description and a new address of the woman he claimed had been threatened by the victim shortly before the shooting, but, characteristically, failed to appear at my office Saturday morning for our planned trip to East Oakland to locate her. I went by myself to the housing project where the woman supposedly lived, but couldn't find her. I knocked on doors for several hours, but no one would help me. In that all-black neighborhood, I looked like a cop. In frustration, I walked over to a neighborhood playground office and asked to use the phone to call Crowder again and try to get him out there. As I was making my call, someone yelled, "Guy!" I turned around and it was Joyce, who had been my assistant playground director at Washington Elementary School. She had been a thin, very quiet and deferential young woman when I had worked with her eight years earlier, but now she was an articulate, confident and well-dressed professional. She explained to me she had obtained her bachelor and masters degrees in public administration and now was working full time as a manager in the Oakland Recreation Department. She then proceeded to introduce me to the recreation directors at the playground, telling each of them that I was "the best recreation director the Oakland Recreation Department ever has had"—one of the most cherished compliments I've ever received. Joyce also told me I could have a job as a recreation director any time I wanted. I told her I would take it when I learned how to live on $3.15 an hour. What I didn't tell her was that I was making *less* than $3.15 an hour on the Crowder case!

After reminiscing about our days at Washington High, I explained my dilemma to Joyce, who grabbed me by the arm and walked with me back to the housing project, where she began inquiring about the woman I was seeking. The fact that Joyce was black and known in the community seemed to stimulate cooperation, and within an hour of knocking on doors we located the home of the elusive witness. She was not home, so I left a long note about my interest in helping Dennis Crowder and asked her to call me at home. Later that evening, she called and we arranged a meeting in my office the next morning.

Sunday morning, sitting across from me, the woman explained her fears about testifying against the victim, as well as her interest in helping Dennis. I did the best I could to allay her fears and she began telling me the story of what she saw the afternoon of the shooting. She told me she had known both the victim and my client for some time and had been a close friend of the victim until he scared her away with his violent and abusive behavior. About two hours before the shooting, he had broken into her home, ranted and raved about "taking care" of Dennis Crowder, and had struck her in the face with his fist several times, leaving major black-and-blue marks. He also had threatened to kill her with a knife he waved around. She said he appeared to be high on drugs, was angry and uncontrollable, and she had feared for her life. She also said his grievance with Dennis had to do with a drug deal, but I was somewhat less interested in this than the victim's threats and violent behavior. She was an attractive, well-spoken woman, about 5' 5" and 120 pounds, almost appearing to be a college student, and I thought she would be a very credible witness. After again explaining the importance of her testimony, I asked her to appear in court in Fairfield the next morning, fifty miles away. Hoping to stay in her good graces, I did not serve a supoena on her, but immediately had a supoena served on the victim.

Monday morning, I called the victim as my first witness, surprising both the judge and the prosecutor, who promptly objected on the ground that I had cross-examined the victim on Friday and there was no purpose in reopening cross-examination. I explained to the judge that new evidence had become available to me and my examination would go beyond my prior cross-examination. It was not hard for Judge Sherwin to order the victim to retake the stand, and, as he was being resworn as a witness, my new witness walked into the quiet courtroom and took a seat in the front row. Her entrance was noted by everyone—most importantly, by the victim and me. The simple act of her walking into the courtroom simultaneously provided me the greatest source of relief, as I was not 100% certain she would appear, while causing the victim to show surprise and fear in his eyes and face. He was a big, tough guy, probably a real bully, and I hadn't been able to dent him much on cross-examination. Now I felt exhilarated at the prospect of seriously damaging his prior testimony.

While he was still unnerved by the presence of the new witness, I quickly moved to the heart of my questioning about his violent behavior shortly before the shooting, his abuse of the woman, his threats to kill her, his knife, and his threats to "take care" of Crowder. As to each question, he answered, "I refuse to answer on the ground that my answer will incriminate me." Once I realized he was going to rely on the Fifth Amendment privilege against self-incrimination and wasn't going to answer any of my questions, I just kept asking more questions about his violent, threatening behavior that day, including threats made directly to Crowder immediately before the shooting. All questions were answered in the same way: "I refuse to answer on the ground that my answer will incriminate me." I hoped the jury would interpret this as, "the truth will incriminate me," or, at the very least, raise doubts about the candor and veracity of his prior testimony. At the conclusion of my examination, the victim clenched his teeth and glowered threateningly at me as he walked across the courtroom. I hoped some of the jurors had seen this.

I next called the woman, who proceeded to tell her story exactly as she had explained it to me in my office. Her testimony was as credible and effective as I had hoped it would be. The DA did little to damage her testimony, other than make the obvious point that she had not witnessed the shooting itself, nor what, if anything, might have provoked it. I followed with Crowder, dressed in his blue Air Force uniform, testifying about himself and his Air Force career and the circumstances of the shooting, which he testified was provoked by the victim making threats and then coming toward him with a knife. I then followed Crowder with two character witnesses, who reinforced the idea that Crowder was a good airman with a reputation for truthfulness.

On rebuttal the next day, the prosecution recalled the victim, who now testified that he never had made any threats to Crowder or the woman. I don't think anyone believed him, but my first question was, "Why did you tell us yesterday that answering these questions and telling the truth would incriminate you?" The prosecutor's objection was sustained, but the point was made. We did closing arguments that afternoon, the prosecution going first and last. Whereas my opening statement had been stiff and heavily dependent on my notes, my closing argument was animated, passionate, and made directly to the jury without reliance on any notes. I felt like I was talking to each of them. The prosecutor made his rebuttal and the court read instructions to the jury before dismissing them for deliberations. At that point, Mr. Unterman walked over to the defense table, extended a hand to me and said, "That was a very good argument." Suddenly, I realized I might win the case.

The jury deliberated for about three hours, and returned with a verdict of "Not Guilty" on all counts. Crowder embraced me, congratulated me on my work, and promised to be in my office the next day to pay my bill. Afterward, I spoke with several jurors, who explained that the first vote was 10–2 for acquittal, that it quickly went to 11–1, but the hold-out juror was the racist farmer I thought

I had turned around in *voir dire*. Although he eventually capitulated to the majority, I learned an important lesson—*voir dire*, even extensive *voir dire* on attitudes and experiences about blacks, was unlikely to compensate for a lifetime of racist attitudes.

The next day Dennis showed up at my office, dressed in casual civilian clothes, thanked me again, told me I was "like a brother" to him, and promised to pay me the $350 he still owed me (he had paid $400 of my $750 total fee) by signing over the pink slip to his new Pontiac Bonneville—a much better car than I owned—which was parked in front of my office. I took a look at the car and was moved by the offer, but I told Dennis, 'I don't want to take your car. I trust you to pay me." My trust was misplaced; it was the last time I ever saw or heard from Dennis Crowder.

The Crowder case reinforced a lesson I was to learn many times over the course of my legal career: often the result is determined by life experiences, not what was learned in law school. In this case, it was my love of hiking and my familiarity with an obscure mountain lake that had enabled me to make a good connection with the trial judge and which led to his kind and fair treatment of me, even when I made the mistakes of an inexperienced trial attorney. More significantly, it was my work in the Oakland community that gave me a chance to make a strong connection with a respected black woman who found the witness who turned the case. I also realized that the kind of irresponsible behavior Crowder had demonstrated—failing to help me find witnesses even though it was his liberty that was at stake—eventually would drive me away from criminal law.

A few weeks after the Crowder trial, I calculated what I had made on the case. Deducting only direct costs for transportation to and from Fairfield, typing of legal briefs and jury instructions, and a small bill from an investigator, I had made less than 50 cents an hour; even if Dennis had paid my bill in full, I would have made less than a $1 an hour. I had gotten some good trial experience, but I was going to have to learn to be a better businessman.

My next trial, however, was even more of an economic folly for me—but it remains one of my all-time favorites. My client was Clint Wilson, a political friend of mine, who had tried to make some money for his political work by running the "Berkeley Erotic Film Festival" in the Berkeley Community Theater. This "Festival" consisted of two showings of thirteen erotic films. After the conclusion of the second show, two plainclothes Berkeley vice officers who had sat through both shows—fourteen hours of film—busted Clint and his projectionist for exhibiting "obscene" films. Three minors, aged 11, 15, and 16, were found inside the theater, so a charge of exhibiting obscene materials to minors was added.

I had studied obscenity cases in my constitutional law class enough to know that the courts have had great difficulty defining what is obscene. United States Supreme Court Justice Potter Stewart once wrote, "I don't know how to define it, but I know it when I see it." Such subjective judgment, of course, provided almost no guideline to filmmakers, theatre operators, and the public about what was, or was not, obscene. Another United States Supreme Court Justice, Hugo Black, a recognized authority on the First Amendment, refused to "see it" at all because it was his opinion that the First Amendment protected all speech, even allegedly obscene forms of expression.

I also had learned from personal observation how transient the definitions of obscenity were and how quickly community standards can change. I watched Lenny Bruce on the stage of Basin Street West in San Francisco two nights before he killed himself with an overdose of drugs. He devoted his entire performance to reading transcripts from his many obscenity trials, commenting throughout about the hypocrisy of obscenity law enforcement. It was tragic to watch how this funny and insightful man had been driven to the edge of madness by criminal persecution for using words on stage that every boy I knew had been using privately since junior high school. Bruce had been thrown into bankruptcy by the cost of defending obscenity prosecutions, and by being made virtually unemployable because of the threat of obscenity prosecutions against comedy clubs where he had worked. In his last year of

life, only a few clubs in America would book him. His alleged offense, his "obscenity," was using four-letter words in his monologues
in a way that people commonly speak and to emphasize certain
points. His real offense was being ten years ahead of his time, because within ten years the same four-letter words were being used
by comedians in clubs throughout America, and in many commercial films. Today, we don't even consider this an issue—certainly
not a criminal issue.

By the time my case arose, the United States Supreme Court
had evolved a three-part test for "obscenity." It must be determined
that (1) the average person, applying contemporary community
standards, would find that the work, taken as a whole, appeals to
the prurient interests; (2) the work depicts or describes sexual conduct in a patently offensive way; and (3) the work, taken as a whole,
lacks serious literary, artistic, political, or scientific value. Both pruriency and patent offensiveness are defined by contemporary community standards, thus raising factual questions for the jury regarding whether the depiction of sexual conduct in the film "goes
substantially beyond customary limits of candor and affronts contemporary community standards of decency." The jury would also
be asked to decide whether the films had any serious literary, artistic, political, or scientific value. (This legal definition of "obscenity," of course, never has included the thousands of murders,
maimings, and acts of physical abuse available throughout the day
to children and adults on television.)

While I knew the relevant legal standards, I did not know how
to conduct an obscenity trial. I asked some criminal defense attorneys I knew to identify attorneys who had handled obscenity cases
and learned that there was a very small group of "First Amendment" lawyers in the Bay Area who had had experience defending
books or films. I called them all and two of them agreed to meet
with me. The most helpful was Joe Rhine, of Kennedy & Rhine,
who, curiously, was the older brother of the woman who had been
ranked number one in my law school class, Barbara Rhine. Joe
agreed to meet with me for lunch, and ended up giving me three

hours of his valuable time. Joe walked me through all phases of such a case, and, most importantly, identified the expert witnesses available for testimony in obscenity cases, along with providing me with insights regarding jury selection in sex cases.

Joe also suggested that I file a "motion to declare films non-obscene as a matter of law," which had been done successfully once before in an obscenity case prosecuted in Fresno. The idea behind the motion was to show to the court, in a separate pretrial hearing, films that had been found non-obscene by California juries, then show the thirteen films I had to defend, and argue that my films were not more offensive than the films that had been acquitted, thus did not violate contemporary community standards of pruriency. Joe introduced me to one of his clients, Jim Mitchell, who operated the Mitchell Brothers Theater in San Francisco, and Jim provided me with copies of eight hardcore films that had been found non-obscene by California juries. I subsequently reviewed these films with my trial experts, and we found the acquitted films to be neither more nor less offensive than the thirteen films I was defending, so I decided to file the pretrial motion Joe Rhine had suggested.

The day arrived for the hearing on my motion to declare my films "Non-Obscene As a Matter of Law" and when I arrived at the courtroom with the films and my projectionist, the doors were locked to the public. Through the window I could see the courtroom was nearly full with police officers, probation officers, bailiffs, sheriffs deputies, court clerks, public defenders, deputy district attorneys, defense attorneys, and the judge from the adjacent courtroom—all waiting for the show to begin! Walking around the hallway to the judge's chamber door, I was let in and soon the courtroom was dark and Clint was operating the projector. Judge George Bruun was on the bench, as we all began watching the first of twenty-one films.

I decided to show the eight "acquitted" films first in order to establish the standard of what juries accepted as falling within community norms and also to desensitize Judge Bruun to the offensiveness of the films I was defending. The hearing got off to a rollicking good start. The "acquitted" films included just about everything one could expect in hard-core films—oral copulation and intercourse filmed from all possible angles, group sex, heterosexual sex, homosexual sex, even sex with animals. By the time we got to the film portraying sex with animals, Karl Payne, the deputy DA prosecuting the case, was taking a razzing from nearly everyone in the courtroom, most urging him to dismiss my case on the ground that juries seemed willing to accept nearly anything as not patently offensive. Karl, who had just finished prosecuting a string of first degree murder cases and who did not appear to think prosecution of this case was especially important to the well-being of the citizens of the Berkeley–Albany Municipal Court district, took the razzing in good humor but did not have authority from his boss to dismiss the case. Clearly, he was hoping, and perhaps expecting, Judge Bruun to dismiss it.

The films were shown continuously for nearly ten hours. The whole time the courtroom remained nearly full with court personnel, lawyers and law enforcement officers, plus Judge Holmstrom from the court next door, who bounced in throughout the day so frequently I have no idea how, or whether, he got any work done in his courtroom that day. The thirteen films I was defending, like the eight acquitted films, included a near-full range of sex acts. I wanted to end the show with the most benign of the films, and chose an art film that had won several film festival awards, and which had no sex acts in it. The film was beautifully photographed in the outdoors and consisted mainly of naked people running through forests, filmed from long range, accompanied by music and poetic narration. The only close-up shot in the film was a short sequence of naked young children in a room, some of whom had their hands on their genitals. The film was so inoffensive, or so I thought, that it almost could have been made by National Geographic.

As soon as the last film was over and the lights went on, I made my constitutional argument that the films I was defending could not violate contemporary community standards of decency, as they were no more graphic in their depiction of sex acts than the films that had been acquitted in California communities that were far more conservative than liberal Berkeley. Furthermore, how could anyone contend these films violated community norms when the whole courtroom had been filled with court and law enforcement personnel—none of whom had any reason to be there other than their interest in these films? Indeed, the court audience seemed to enjoy the films and nearly everyone, including Judge Bruun, had made jokes about the films, with the deputy DA—who was completely undeserving of criticism—taking the brunt of most of the jokes. The charges had to be dismissed. Karl Payne responded with perfunctory comments, concluding that he did not have authority to dismiss the charges, and that if they were to be dismissed, the court would have to do it. His comments almost were an invitation to Judge Bruun to dismiss the case and save him the burden of having to prosecute the charges to a jury.

Fully expecting Judge Bruun, a well-respected judge whose reputation was that of an ACLU liberal, to dismiss the charges as violations of First Amendment protections, I was astonished to hear him go off in a wholly unexpected direction. He began, "In my opinion, the people who should be prosecuted for these crimes are the parents of the children in that last film, who permitted these children to masturbate and be filmed masturbating!" He then proceeded to expound on the evils of masturbation and how those children's lives would be damaged by having participated in the film. At the conclusion of his tirade, he denied the motion, leaving it to a jury to address the relevant factual and constitutional issues. We all had learned much about Judge Bruun's disapproval of masturbation and nothing about his thoughts on the constitutional issues presented by the films I had shown and the motions I had made.

I think the prosecutor was just as stunned at Judge Bruun's reaction as I was. In any case, he again told me he could not dismiss the case, but now offered to let each defendant off with a $100 fine and six months probation. It was about the lightest sentence he possibly could offer and I firmly rejected it. I was pissed off about what Judge Bruun had done and I was ready to defend the First Amendment in trial. Clint, Neil, and I gathered up the projector and films and left the courthouse. Outside, Clint, a big strong guy, yet at the same time a sweet, gentle person, said quietly to me, "Don't you think we should take that offer?" In my hyperventilated state of mind, I explained that we had a responsibility to defend the Constitution. That seemed enough for Clint and Neil, who never again raised the issue of a plea bargain.

A few weeks before the scheduled trial date, I thought it would be a good idea to try to talk to the children who were found in the theater at the time of the arrests. I did not look forward to this, as I expected that the parents might not be very happy that my clients showed these films and their boys saw them, but I knew I must make the attempt to speak with them before trial. Two of them, the 11 and 15-year-olds, were brothers and lived on McKinley Street in Berkeley, a block from the Berkeley Community Theater and just two blocks from the Berkeley Police Department. I stopped by their house on my way home from work, knocked on the front door, and introduced myself to the woman who opened it as the attorney representing the two men arrested for showing the allegedly obscene movies at the Berkeley Community Theater. I asked if the boys were available and if I could talk with them. The woman, who was a bit surprised at my visit, introduced herself as Mary Lou Goertzen, the boys' mother. She said they were just finishing dinner but that I could wait for them in the living room.

While I waited, I explored the bookshelves and noticed a significant number of books about pacifism and a number of pamphlets published by the Central Committee for Conscientious Objectors (CCCO), a Quaker-funded organization I had worked with in my years of draft counselling at Oakland Draft Help. When Mrs. Goertzen came into the living room, I told her that I was familiar with CCCO, as I had been a draft counsellor for several years and CCCO published the best materials on conscientious objectors and other alternatives to military service. She told me her family were

Quakers, her church had helped fund CCCO, and she was beginning to explore conscientious-objector status for her boys. I told her I would be happy to recommend several draft counsellors to her, but for CO status the counsellors at CCCO were the best. It certainly was a nice way to start what I anticipated would be an awkward conversation.

The boys had not yet come into the room, so I asked Mrs. Goertzen, "How do you feel about what happened?" She said it had been a shock to her and her husband to be called at 2 a.m. by the Berkeley Police and to be told that her boys had been found inside a theater watching pornographic films and were now at the police station waiting to be picked up. When they got the boys home, they decided to speak with them about the experience. They spoke as a family for several hours, and Mrs. Goertzen said it was a very healthy discussion. "For a while, we had been intending to have a long discussion with the boys about sex and sexuality, but, like many parents, we had not gotten around to it. This experience forced us to talk about these topics and the boys learned a lot by the whole experience, including the films." I asked her how she felt about boys aged 11 and 15 seeing such explicit materials, and she told me the older boy handled it well, but that the films were a little overwhelming for the 11-year-old. "I would not have chosen to have the 11-year-old see such films. Nevertheless, it forced us to talk about sexuality as a family and much was learned by both boys." I asked her if she would consider testifying at the trial and telling this story, just as she had told it to me. She was very surprised at my request, but promised to think about it.

The boys and the father came into the room and I asked the parents if it would be all right for me to ask the boys a few questions. They said it would be fine, and I asked them to tell me the circumstances of how they got into the theater. I was most relieved to have them tell me exactly what my clients had told me. The boys had not paid to get in; they had sneaked in when the ticket-taker was not looking.

I left the Goertzen home that night with a wonderful feeling.

Not only did I get confirmation of my clients' version of what happened, I had also met a wonderful Quaker family.

JOE RHINE HAD TOLD ME IT WAS IMPORTANT in an obscenity trial to *voir dire* the jury extensively about their attitudes about sexual behavior, both to determine which jurors had libertarian attitudes about consensual sexual behavior even when it went beyond their own experiences, and to desensitize the jury to the films they were about to see. He also told me that Asians generally had more mature and tolerant attitudes about sex than other nationalities and that they had been good defense jurors in obscenity cases. I never really had thought about this, but Joe's comments reminded me that a lot of very fine Asian art I had seen, even ancient art, was quite erotic in its depiction of sex. Taking his comments on faith, I accepted every Asian who was impaneled in the jury box, even an Asian Republican Catholic housewife with four kids from Albany, a local pocket of conservatism. I figured, even if Joe's Asian stereotype didn't fit this woman, she wouldn't be a "control" juror. She would be a follower, not a leader.

One juror I felt very confident about was a tough, 40-ish merchant marine, who never had been married and who had traveled the world as a merchant marine for over twenty years. I figured he had seen a lot of erotic films and hit every whorehouse from here to Hong Kong. Indeed, in *voir dire*, he admitted having seen many erotic films. He later was to provide another jury surprise for me.

Sitting in the last row of the courtroom quietly knitting among the prospective jurors was someone I recognized—Mary Lou Goertzen. I approached her at the lunch break and asked her if she had considered my request. She said she had and that she was willing to testify.

Joe had told me that the low point in any obscenity prosecution is the showing of the films. No matter how well you have tried to desensitize the sex acts in *voir dire* and the opening statement, the films would still be shocking to jurors who had never seen such films. Joe was right. Seven of the films were shown to the jury the morning of the second day of trial. The lights went on and I looked at the jury. Their eyes were blank, their faces expressionless. Deer looking into headlights. The jurors slowly began to file out of the jury box, except one woman, the Asian Catholic housewife from Albany. She sat stiffly, staring straight ahead, her eyes unblinking; it was not clear whether she still was breathing. I kept glancing at her as I reviewed documents in preparation for the cross-examination of the arresting vice officers, which would follow the completion of the showing of the films. Still she didn't move, blink, change her glazed expression or demonstrate any visible signs of life. After ten minutes, another juror came back, gently held her by the arm and shoulder, and led her out of the courtroom. This had to be the low point; it couldn't get worse!

But it didn't get better. The next day, after all the films had been shown and the vice officers had testified under the direction of Deputy District Attorney Henry Johnson, it was my turn to cross-examine them. As I stepped forward to begin my questioning, I had nothing but contempt for these hypocritical creeps. By the time they testified at trial, they had seen all thirteen films at least *nine* times: they watched the complete show at the Berkeley Community Theater *twice* before arresting my clients and seizing the films, watched all thirteen films when they were shown to me at the police station, watched all of them when shown to the prosecuting attorney, watched them all again once when they were shown to the prosecution psychiatrist, twice again when the films were shown to my expert witnesses, once again at the pretrial hearing (where they got the bonus of seeing the eight acquitted films), and then again at trial. I have no idea how many more times they might have watched the films on their own. They had spent fifty hours of their time repeatedly watching the same "patently offensive" films unnecessarily. They really had to love this stuff, because the films, in my opinion, were pretty boring.

I began my cross-examination of the first vice officer by establishing that both vice officers had seen the films at least nine times each, then established that they had no reason to sit through eight of the nine showings. He admitted that an arrest was appropriate after one complete showing, perhaps even after one film had been shown, and could not explain why they sat through two identical shows—fourteen hours of film—before making the arrests; nor could he explain why they sat through the two showings to the attorneys, the three showings to the expert witnesses, or the pre-trial hearing, where the vice officers played no role whatsoever. I then asked with the greatest amount of sarcasm I could inject into my voice, "Don't you think the reason you watched each of these films eight times unnecessarily is because you *enjoyed* watching these films? And since you obviously enjoyed watching these films so much, why did you think they were 'patently offensive,' as defined by the statute you arrested them under? Do you think they are patently offensive, and, if so, why did you watch them so many times? You are a member of this community and you obviously enjoyed them, so how can you claim the content of the films goes beyond community norms?" And so forth... Some of the questions were objected to by the DA; some were answered—poorly—by the hypocrites masquerading as defenders of public morality. I thought my point was being made with my brilliantly contemptuous cross-examination. The fact these guys had repeatedly gone out of their way to watch these films proved that the films did not violate accepted community norms and/or contained serious material worth their valuable time. But the jury didn't think I was so brilliant. Speaking with them after the trial, they wanted to know, "Why were you so angry at the vice officers? What were you trying to do?"

My cross-examination had been a big zero—or worse—with the jury. I had failed to build my cross-examination slowly enough so the jury could better see why the cops' behavior contradicted the basis of the criminal charges and why I might be angry, or at least contemptuous, of their testimony. I had let my anger about the hypocrisy of their behavior, and the whole prosecution of these charges, inflame my anti-police biases and impair the distance and objectivity I needed to be effective. It's not pleasant to be told you have been ineffective or stupid, but I appreciated the candid criticism I received from this jury after the trial. Like most good criticism, it helped me to understand better how my behavior was being perceived and how I might handle the situation more effectively next time.

I also learned that what might work for one attorney wouldn't necessarily work for me. Charles Garry, with the confidence, skills and reputation gathered from eighty first-degree murder cases, might be able to cut an undercover cop off at the knees with his demonstration of contempt, as he did so effectively to the "rat fink" undercover cop in the Oakland Seven trial, but that didn't mean I could pull it off—at least not yet.

The prosecution followed with the testimony of a psychiatrist from a state hospital, who provided his opinion of "prurient interest" and why these films had no redeeming social value whatsoever, and closed their case by calling to the stand the 11-year-old boy to establish that he and his brothers had watched the films. The state hospital shrink was the kind of guy who believed watching erotic films caused warts and hair to grow on young men's hands and he did me no damage, but the 11-year-old boy carried a strong emotional charge. Every juror would be thinking of their own kids and how they wouldn't want them to be watching these films. While the boy clearly established his presence in the theater, on my cross-examination he admitted he and his friends had sneaked into a side door of the theater when Clint's back was turned and they had ducked down in their seats each time Clint or Neil came into the theater. Clint may have been negligent in not staffing his film show adequately, but I thought the boy's testimony put my clients' criminal culpability seriously in doubt, at least on the minors' charge. And, I had a surprise waiting for the DA on this issue!

I began the defense case with someone I considered to be star-quality—John Wasserman, chief film and music critic for the *San Francisco Chronicle*. John agreed to testify for free because he believed so strongly that the First Amendment protected all forms of artistic expression, even very bad films and films depicting sex. I was thrilled to have John as a witness, as I read his music and film reviews nearly every day and considered him to be one of the funniest and most entertaining writers the *Chronicle* has ever had. I thought his testimony was fabulous. He placed the type of films I was defending into historic context, explaining how candid depictions of sex in art, books, and film often had been castigated and oppressed but had gained acceptance over time. "Artists push the barriers of what is acceptable and we need that." And he explained how large the audience was for such films, both in theaters and in home video, which then was beginning to grow quickly. With such a large audience, how could such films be said to lack any artistic merit, or violate community norms? John was funny, entertaining and quick with opinions. As I was to learn later, however, the jury perceived him as arrogant, didn't like the fact his definition of artistic merit seemed to have no limits, and didn't like the fact he had testified at so many prior obscenity trials—always for the defense. He appeared to be too partisan on this topic.

I followed John with two psychiatrists, one to testify about "prurient interest," the other to describe how he used such films in marital counseling. The first psychiatrist had testified for the defense in many obscenity cases; he was so polished and experienced he almost needed no questions from me. His most useful observation was that there had been many studies of the effect of sexually explicit films on behavior, but none ever had found that explicit films led to violence against women, or violence in general. The second witness was a young psychiatrist in a local family counseling practice whom I had heard was using sexually explicit films in couples' therapy. He never had testified in a criminal trial and was nervous. When I reassured him that I just wanted him to explain how he used such films in his work, he calmed down and agreed to testify. His nervousness showed as he was sworn in as a witness and began to answer my preliminary questions, but as soon as we reached the topic of how he began to use sexually explicit films in therapy, and the positive results he had witnessed from the use of such films, he relaxed and became quite animated. He explained how he had used the films with couples experiencing sexual problems, among other things, to educate them about different sexual possibilities and positions, to encourage couples to act out harmless sexual fantasies, or sometimes to get couples interested in sex again. He explained he was using such films with normal working-class and middle-class couples, many of whom never had seen such films before, and that he thought his use of such films had been very effective with many couples. He provided the basis for me to argue that the films had a serious purpose and scientific value.

I then called Mrs. Goertzen, who explained how her boys seeing the films had led to an important and healthy family discussion about sex. She didn't promote the viewing of such films—particularly for her 11-year-old—but she allayed any fears the jury may have had in this case that the minor boys had been harmed by the experience. I concluded by calling Clint to the stand, who testified with his inherent sincerity about how bad he felt about the minors getting into the theater. His contrition was genuine. I felt that any anger that might have remained on the jury after Mrs. Goertzen's testimony now was gone.

After a half day of deliberations, the jury returned not guilty verdicts on all counts. Clint thanked each juror, energetically telling them he'd never show sex films again. I spoke with as many jurors as I could to find out what did, and did not, influence their decision. It was clear the jury threw out all the testimony of the "professional" witnesses who had testified in many previous obscenity trials as mere "hired guns," promoting their own political or social agendas. The testimony of Mrs. Goertzen and Clint was very important, but the witness who influenced the jury most profoundly was the young psychiatrist whose testimony, they felt, was derived from his own empirical observations, not any ideology about the value of such films or any preconceived version of the First Amendment. I was impressed by the commonsense and pragmatism of the jury—qualities I later would observe in many juries.

For years after this trial, whenever I ran into Karl Payne or

Harry Johnson, the two Deputy District Attorneys who had prosecuted the case, we'd laugh at the memory of it. I'd see Harry coming down the hall 100 feet away, and as soon as he spotted me, he'd be laughing. Nobody even needed to say anything. It was that kind of case.

I had charged a total fee in this case of $100 and invested 400+ hours in it—25¢ an hour—but I had learned a lot. My willingness to talk to a parent about what this experience meant to the family—not just the legal point about how the boys got into the theater—led to surprising and important testimony. And practical testimony from an inexperienced expert witness proved far more persuasive than the witnesses, on both sides, who were so clearly identified by their prior testimony with either the prosecution or defense theory of obscenity. From this point forward, I rarely feared using inexperienced expert witnesses, and often looked for new witnesses on well-traveled topics.

I also gained a greater understanding that what might be entertaining to me—such as Wasserman's testimony—might be far less entertaining or persuasive to jurors who did not share his opinions or enjoy his arrogance. I had to learn to look at issues from the perspective of the people I was likely to have on the jury. Later, as I began to litigate and settle major employment discrimination cases against large companies, I had to learn to look at those cases from the perspective of the company/defendants, not just the plaintiffs' perspective. This sounds simple, but most lawyers, like most people, are not very good at understanding an opponent's perspective, let alone distinguishing the legitimate from illegitimate interests and concerns of people with radically different points of view.

This trial also confirmed the value of seeking help when you need it. I never could have handled a trial as complex as an obscenity trial without the advice I received from Joe Rhine. Throughout my career, if someone knew more about a topic that affected a case of mine, I wanted to talk to that person. I found that attorneys, even busy trial attorneys, were willing to share advice generously, so long as I asked pertinent questions and didn't waste their time.

ONE MORNING, IN THE MIDST OF WORKING on some of my small cases, I got a call from Moses Durst, president of the Moonie Church in America. Mr. Durst said that I had been highly recommended to him by Richard Burda, then the General Counsel to Synanon, a drug treatment organization, and he wanted to speak with me as soon as possible about a major case. That afternoon, he and his associates were in my office describing how "deprogrammers," paid by parents, were kidnapping young adult followers of the Moonie religion, incarcerating them for weeks, and using psychological "deprogramming" and "brainwashing" techniques to convince them to leave the Moonie religion. Mr. Durst, on behalf of the Church, wanted me to file a lawsuit against the deprogrammer organizations to stop these practices. He knew the case would be a major undertaking, involving thousands of hours of legal work, but he assured me I was the attorney they wanted and they were prepared to pay top-level fees. I told him I wanted to think about his proposal overnight and would call him the next day.

At dinner that night, I described this proposed case to Jeanine, explaining that whatever one thought of the Moonies, the people being kidnapped were adults with a constitutional right to associate with any church or religion they wanted to join, that while the parents had a right to persuade their children to leave the Moonie church, they had no right to have them kidnapped, held incommunicado, subjected to sleep-deprivation and brainwashed into leaving the church. I added, "Even if you think joining the Moonie church is a mistake, people have a right to make their own mistakes without being kidnapped and brainwashed." I also mentioned that it was my first opportunity to be paid a real fee for a case. I thought this was relevant, as I was making about $400 a month at that point. None of my arguments had any impact on Jeanine. She responded, "The Moonie church is a right-wing cult, it uses brainwashing techniques of its own, and if my kids got sucked into such an organization, I'd hire a deprogrammer, too, just like those parents. I would be appalled if you took this case, regardless of how much money they are willing to pay."

Deciding that continued poverty with domestic tranquility was preferable to affluence and domestic strife, the next morning, I called Mr. Durst and declined the case. The Moonies subsequently hired two prominent San Francisco attorneys, who filed, tried and won the case against the deprogrammers. Their legal bill exceeded $1 million. It was the only time in my legal career Jeanine objected to my taking a case.

Chuck and I continued to take as many personal injury cases as we could get, hoping that one substantial case could put the firm on a tenable financial basis. But we seemed to attract small cases— slip and falls, fender-benders, etc. I recall one case where Chuck represented a 70-year-old drunk driver who had driven his car into a ditch left open by the local utility and suffered minor injuries. Chuck settled the case on the day of trial for $3,500, even waiving his attorney fee to facilitate settlement. The settlement judge, Lew Lercara, took Chuck into chambers and said, "You're a fine attorney. I have some good advice for you. Don't take dogshit cases." "Judge, all our cases are dogshit cases," Chuck responded.

That was pretty close to the truth. I remember speaking with one prospective client who explained to me that he wanted to sue the Soviet KGB because they were transmitting coded messages through the fillings in his teeth. I told him "You don't have a legal problem, you have a dental problem." Another complained that ten years earlier on a commercial airplane he had bumped his head on the overhead cabinet; he sustained no injuries, but ten years later expected a lawyer to redress his grievance. Our "case flow" was weak, to say the least. Indeed, the quality of our cases, combined with our dismal billing practices, and a lot of free work for the Farmworker's Union, led to our small incomes—$3,300 the first year, $6,000 the second, $9,000 the third. I was getting some good legal experience, but making very little money.

In the long run, the experiences were more important than the money; but in the short run, Jeanine and I had to live very cheaply. We had bought a four-bedroom house in South Berkeley across the street from the Smokehouse, a local burger pit on Telegraph

Avenue, with money for the down payment borrowed from our parents. Jeanine developed a downstairs room into a half-day Montesorri preschool for eight children and we rented out one bedroom to a Hispanic graduate student. Jose was a terrific housemate, but he fell in love with a friend of ours and moved in with her after one semester, to be replaced by a young couple. John played drums in a local band and he generously shared his drums with Leon, then aged two, who actually learned to play quite deftly, his artistic talents showing early. We were disappointed to see John and his wife leave after a year. Our next roommates, Roz and Fred, a husband–wife psychiatrist–psychologist team, were part of the "Radical Psychiatry" Movement, and I immediately became their involuntary patient. This led to some sharp dialogue about our respective values, roles, politics, relationships, and the like, but when they accused me of "dominant male-chauvinist behavior" because I played basketball each Saturday morning at a nearby playground, I realized they were full of shit, stopped taking them seriously, and just tried to enjoy the verbal combat. It wasn't the most pleasant arrangement, but we needed the rent.

To their credit, Roz and Fred had an interesting group of friends, and, after a year, Fred and Roz moved out and two of their friends, Fred and Linda, moved in. Fred was a brilliant mathematician, then working on his Ph.D. at UC Berkeley, and I stayed up late many a night talking with him for hours about a wide range of topics. Fred and Linda lived with us for a year and then got married in our backyard. The wedding was great, but we made the mistake of letting their relatives move in with us for the week before the wedding. This had the unintended, but probably inevitable, effect of putting Jeanine and me in the middle of the tensions and conflicts between their two families. As much as I liked Fred, our house was a lot more quiet and peaceful when Fred and Linda— and their families—moved out after the wedding and we no longer had to share our house with another family.

One advantage of having housemates was that the cooking, housework and yard work was shared. With the housemates gone,

Jeanine and I found ourselves spending many of our evenings cooking and cleaning house and me doing the yard work and house repair and maintenance on the weekends. This became increasingly burdensome as my law practice grew and my 40-hour weeks turned into 50 and 60-hour weeks. Nevertheless, we always tried to leave time for fun. Saturday nights were sacrosanct; no matter how busy we might be, we went out every Saturday night dancing, to parties, to see movies, or to have dinner with friends. I played basketball Saturday mornings at St. Augustine School, the local playground, and Sunday at Live Oak Park, then the toughest inner-city game in Berkeley. Later, Chuck—an excellent athlete who had played varsity baseball at the University of Kansas—and I organized a team of lawyers and we competed for many years in the Oakland adult basketball leagues. Basketball always has been a tonic for me, particularly during periods of hard work and stress, and there were many times Jeanine kicked me out of the house to go play basketball, knowing I'd return relaxed and happy.

We had no extra money for vacations, so we went backpacking or car-camping. Neither cost anything, other than gas, and Leon and Jacobus Muir, who happily arrived in 1975, loved both. Jeanine and I both were fit and we took Leon on his first backpacking trip when he was one month old, a 70-mile backpacking trip in the Sierras with Leon on our backs—including a climb to the top of Mt. Whitney (14,495') when he was five months old, hiked to the bottom of the Grand Canyon for a week when he was one year old, and took many other hiking and cross-country trips with him until Jacobus was born. At that point, we found it too difficult to carry two children, plus equipment, so we began to pack our gear, and kids, into our well-dented twenty-year-old seventeen-foot aluminum Grumman canoe (purchased used), and take one to two-week canoe trips along the rivers and lakes of Western United States, as well as continue car camping.

Our friends were taking trips to Europe, living in bigger houses in better neighborhoods, hiring housecleaners, gardeners and nannies, and buying new cars, but we never felt deprived, jealous or inferior. Jeanine and I each believed in what we were doing and enjoyed our jobs. We were healthy, we had two terrific kids, and we had fun together. Two careers of self-employment, while raising a family, was hard work, but we never expected it not to be.

6

Development of My Employment Law Practice

"It is not how busy you are—but why you are busy.
The bee is praised. The mosquito is swatted."

—Marie O'Conner

SOON AFTER OPENING OUR OFFICE on Fruitvale Avenue, I received a call from Russ Galloway and Steve Ronfeldt, two attorneys at the Legal Aid Society of Alameda County. Russ and Steve were litigating a number of Title VII employment discrimination class actions ("Title VII" refers to Title VII of the 1964 Civil Rights Act), and had additional cases to file. They asked me if I would be interested in working on one with them. I said I never had done a Title VII case and really didn't know much about Title VII caselaw. Their response was that I knew a lot about class actions and federal civil procedure and that they would be available whenever I had questions. Furthermore, they would assign three "experienced Title VII lawyers" to work with me on any case I chose, as well as front the litigation costs of the case—which was important to me, as my low-overhead law practice could not afford to fund a case of this magnitude. I met with them at their office, selected a possible case against Trans International Airlines (TIA), then the world's largest charter airline, and met my co-counsel, Margy Gelb, Janice Cooper and Les Hausrath—all young attorneys like myself.

We reviewed TIA's workforce statistics and it was obvious TIA was deficient in its employment of blacks in all job categories—clerks, mechanics, flight attendants and flight crew. At that point, we did not know what their applicant flow of blacks had been, but being headquartered at the Oakland International Airport, just a stone's throw from heavily black East Oakland, we knew blacks would be readily available for work in most job categories at TIA, with the possible exception of pilots. We decided to file a Title VII class action complaint against TIA, the Federal Aviation Administration (FAA), and the Port of Oakland.

We had a conventional cause of action under Title VII and Section 1981 (the 1866 Civil Rights Act) for the underhiring of blacks by TIA, but we added innovative theories against the FAA and the Port of Oakland. Since 1948, Executive Order 11246 had required all companies doing business with the federal government to provide equal employment opportunities to racial minorities; compliance was measured by affirmative action plans each contractor was required to develop. On paper, these affirmative action plans generally were fine, but the problem was that they were not enforced by the appropriate federal agency, which, in the case of an airline was the FAA. Relying on legal theories I had pursued at CRLS, we contended that the intended beneficiaries of the Executive Order, in this case blacks, had a private right of action to enforce compliance with the Executive Order and the airline's affirmative action plan. The remedy we sought against the FAA was an order mandating the FAA to enforce compliance with the requirements of the Executive Order by initiating the process to withdraw all federal contracts with TIA. Since most of TIA's business consisted of work for the federal government, we knew this hammer, or even the real threat of using it, would be sufficiently powerful to induce compliance with the Executive Order.

Against the Port, relying on the authority of *Burton v. Wilmington Parking Authority*, we contended that the Port, as TIA's landlord, was jointly liable for overt racially discriminatory employment practices of its tenant, TIA. In *Burton*, a restaurant located in a publicly owned and operated parking structure refused service to a black customer, and the United States Supreme Court held that the state, as the restaurant's landlord, was a "joint participant" in the restaurant's racial discrimination:

> By its inaction, the [parking] Authority, and through it the State, has not only made itself a party to the refusal of service, but has elected to place its power, property and prestige behind the admitted discrimination.

We thought the principles set forth by the Supreme Court in *Burton* applied equally well to our case: The State, acting through the Port of Oakland Authority as landlord to the airline, had placed its "power, property and prestige behind the...discrimination" and had become a party to the discrimination by the tenant airline. As such, the Port's inaction in the face of the airline's racial discrimination violated the Equal Protection clause of the Fourteenth Amendment to the United States Constitution. The *Burton* case never had been applied in an employment discrimination case in this way, but we saw no conceptual reason why the landlord–tenant relationship in our case created any less obligation than the obligation enforced in *Burton*, and that forcing publicly funded airports to monitor discriminatory conduct by its tenant airlines would have an impact on employment discrimination that would extend far beyond our case. We thought the principles set forth by the United States Supreme Court in *Burton* applied equally well to our case.

In the federal court system, new cases are assigned randomly to District Court judges upon the filing of the complaint. The court clerk for the Civil Division (i.e., noncriminal) would accept the complaint and filing fee, stamp all documents as filed, stamp a case number on the documents, then reach into a box containing small pieces of folded paper with the initials of a judge inside each folded piece of paper, open it to reveal the initials of the assigned judge, and then complete the filing process by stamping the judge's initials on the front page of the documents (called "pleadings"). In most cases, the judge assigned to the case when the complaint is filed remains the judge throughout the case. The main exceptions to this rule occur when a judge dies, retires or is promoted to an appellate court, or when a decision by the District Court judge is appealed to one of the twelve United States Circuit Courts of Appeals.

Federal judges exercise a significant amount of discretion on most issues presented to them, and thus wield a tremendous amount of power in the cases assigned to them. This was even more true in Title VII cases, as Congress did not provide a right to a jury trial in Title VII cases until 1991. Prior to 1991, all Title VII cases were heard, and decided, by the federal judge assigned to the case. While most federal judges are hard-working and competent, there have always been significant variations in ability and political/legal perspectives among them. Thus, the judge assignment is one of the most important—some would argue *the* most important—factor in any federal case.

Knowing how important the judge assignment would be to the result of a case, in my early years of practice I approached the filing of a case with great anxiety, watching the clerk's hand reach into the box and open the paper. Sometimes I would delay filing a case for a few days, waiting for a day that felt good to me. Frequently I'd get to the clerk's office and watch a few filings and judge assignments in other cases, just to get a feel for how the assignments were running. Sometimes a string of unfavorable judge assignments in other cases made me feel like the next one would be good, and I'd step forward. Sometimes, it would be just the opposite: a few assignments of "good" judges would make me feel confident the tide that day was running in my direction. Maybe none of this can be explained rationally, but in over twenty-five years of filing federal cases in California, I was satisfied with the judge assigned to my cases about 90% of the time.

There was another civil rights attorney I knew who seemed to do even better than me in judge assignments. Oliver Jones, a black attorney practicing in Richmond (near Oakland), was filing major civil rights cases and getting good results, mostly actions against police departments for mistreatment of black people, and consistently drawing the best federal judges available. I watched this for many years, and one day Oliver came to my office to discuss one of his cases, and I asked him, "Oliver, I've been watching you for a long time, and you get the best judge assignments I've ever seen. How do you do it?" Oliver said, "Guy, no one ever has asked me that and I'm going to tell you something I've never told anyone. I hope you won't laugh. Before filing any case, I consult with Madam Fatima, a palm reader and fortune teller. It costs me $1,000 and for that she will pick a good day for the filing, then go with me to the clerk's office, where we will sit, sometimes for hours, until she tells me, 'Now is the time.' Then I file it." I didn't laugh one bit. Whatever Oliver and Madame Fatima were doing, it was working very well!

In the TIA case, when the clerk unfolded the little piece of paper, the initials "CBR"—short for United States District Judge Charles B. Renfrew—were revealed. I was quite satisfied with that, as my experience with Judge Renfrew in my military case had confirmed his reputation as a smart, fair, thoughtful, and hardworking judge. If I lost a case before a judge like that, it would either be my own fault or just the lack of facts to support my clients' claims.

In responding to our complaint, the defendants—TIA, the Port and the FAA—requested several extensions of time, then filed a motion to dismiss all allegations, supported by a 100-page memorandum of law. We responded with our own lengthy legal memorandum in opposition to the defense motion, the defendants filed a lengthy reply memorandum—as the moving party is permitted to do—and the matter went to a hearing before Judge Renfrew. My co-counsel asked me to argue most of it. Defendants were represented at the hearing by James Madison, a Senior Partner at Orrick, Herrington & Sutcliffe—a major corporate law firm headquartered in San Francisco.

Judge Renfrew called our case last on the morning calendar—usually an indication the judge intends to give the case more time for oral argument than the preceding cases. I've always preferred being called last, thinking that more time would provide a greater opportunity for me to clear up any questions or uncertainties the court might have about the issues. I also hoped I would be more flexible and persuasive in argument than my opponent and the longer the argument, the more of an advantage I would have. The oral argument began with Judge Renfrew and Mr. Madison expressing pleasantries toward each other that indicated close friendship and mutual respect. This type of familiarity between judge and opposing counsel used to bother me in small town courts in rural Colorado, where friendships count for much and outsiders are at a major disadvantage, but as the hearing went forward, and the legal issues were debated, whatever friendship relationship Judge Renfrew had with Madison seemed to play no part in the Judge's consideration of the issues.

Madison's legal memorandum had been comprehensive and well argued and his oral presentation achieved the same high standard. The only chinks in his argument were the result of what I call "Senior Partneritus." This is a condition caused by having younger law associates and partners do most of the legal writing, then having the lead partner orally argue it. Because the lead partner did not write much, if any, of the legal memoranda, often he had not read all the cases cited in the parties' written memoranda and had not made the editorial decisions that always are made in writing a complex argument, such as the decision to spin an argument in a specific direction to avoid latent problems, or to not over-argue the meaning of a particular case precedent because in other parts of that same precedent are rulings or statements (called *dicta*) that are not helpful, or even adverse. Thus, as a young attorney arguing cases against more experienced lawyers and law firms with hundreds of lawyers and unlimited resources, I often felt that I was the one who had the advantage. I did not have the luxury of farming out research and writing to an associate, so I was the one who had to research, think and write the arguments from the ground up. I was the one who had to read every case and think through every possible argument long before appearing in court for oral argument. Thus, the great resources of large corporate defendants and the large law firms they hire—and the hierarchical structure of assignments—often operates against them, in my opinion, when faced with a quick, mobile and prepared opponent. The fact that losing a class action at that stage of my career would have bankrupted me also added a level of motivation that most corporate defense counsel didn't have. It was the difference between General Westmoreland and the ponderous, conscripted United States Seventh Army and the Viet Cong fighting for their homeland.

When it was my turn to step up to the podium, Judge Renfrew was most interested in my novel theories—the private right of action under Executive Order 11246, third-party beneficiaries, and the *Burton v. Wilmington Parking Authority* landlord–tenant-based theories. He was particularly intrigued with the argument that the Executive Order was a law enforceable by private parties, despite the fact that Executive Orders are issued by the President without the normal congressional process or legislation, and the fact that no private enforcement remedy was explicitly provided in the Order—despite the fact that minorities affected by racially discriminatory employment practices, such as our plaintiffs, clearly were the intended beneficiaries of the Order. In fact, he was so interested in those theories, it seemed he had read most, if not all, of the cited cases himself—an extraordinary amount of preparation for a busy federal judge. Renfrew was questioning me not only about the holdings of specific cases, but also about the detailed facts in those cases. He was so well prepared, and his questions so detailed, as well as comprehensive, that the hearing lasted three hours—well into the lunch hour. It was like being in law school, with Judge Renfrew as Dean. I loved it, because my work and preparation were being rewarded by the intensity of the examination, but it was a tough examination.

At the conclusion of the long hearing, Judge Renfrew ruled from the bench. He held that the defendants' motion to dismiss would be denied as to the plaintiffs' Title VII and Section 1981 claims. Regarding the Executive Order, private-right-of-action, third-party beneficiary and landlord–tenant theories, he said, "The Court will take those under advisement," meaning he was not ready to rule on our innovative theories. The order permitted the case to proceed to trial, and, by not dismissing the innovative theories, discovery on those issues was allowed to proceed.

Shortly after Judge Renfrew denied defendants' motion to dismiss the case, TIA fired Orrick, Herrington & Sutcliffe and hired Hal Perry, a black sole-practitioner practicing in Oakland, as their defense counsel. This was unfair to Orrick Herrington, which had done a good job, but I was told TIA thought it would be smart to be represented by a black attorney in a case where the main issue was racial discrimination.

Hal immediately called and invited me over to his nearby office, also in East Oakland, to talk about the case. When I arrived, he couldn't possibly have been nicer. Hal had been an All-American basketball player on the great University of San Francisco teams with Bill Russell and K. C. Jones that had won two NCAA basketball championships, and he told me that my uncle, Abe, founder and owner of the Harlem Globetrotters, had been one of the greatest men he ever had known. According to Hal, it was my uncle who had encouraged him to go to law school and had given him money to leave basketball and enter law school. Hal and I talked basketball for over an hour and he invited me to play in a game he had going at the Oakland Athletic Club, which I later did. As for the TIA case, Hal assured me, "We'll work that out, don't worry."

Despite the bonhomie, I commenced formal discovery against TIA by serving a Request for Documents and First Set of Interrogatories, neither of which TIA responded to. After sending several letters to Hal demanding answers to my discovery requests—none of which were answered—I had no choice but to file a Motion to Compel Discovery. The motion was granted and TIA ordered to produce the requested documents within fifteen days. Nevertheless, no documents were forthcoming. After sending a letter to Hal indicating I would seek sanctions from the Court, and again receiving no response, I filed another Motion to Compel Discovery, this time seeking discovery sanctions against TIA and Hal Perry.

The motion came on for hearing at 9 a.m., as scheduled, but Hal was not in court when the case was called. I explained to Judge Renfrew that his discovery order had not been complied with and he promptly reordered production of the documents and assessed $1,500 in sanctions against the absent Mr. Perry.

My co-counsel and I appeared in Hal's office the next afternoon, but neither Hal nor the documents were there. His secretary assured us Hal had the documents and would be there momentarily. We waited for two hours, then left. That evening, I attended the annual Founder's Day Banquet put on by my college fraternity—the only time I've ever attended this event. Sitting across the table from me was someone I did not know, but whose name, "Merritt Smalley," I recognized as a named defendant in the TIA case! Introducing myself, I asked him if he was the same Merritt Smalley who was the Senior Vice-President of TIA, and he told me he was. I then told him I was one of the plaintiffs' attorneys in the race discrimination class action against TIA. Brother Merritt asked me, "How are you getting along with Hal?"

I told him I had to be careful in answering that question, as an attorney representing one party normally is not permitted to speak with an opposing party who is represented by his own counsel without that counsel being present. Merritt waived off my cautiousness, saying, "Don't worry about that, I'm an attorney myself and I'm not about to give away any TIA secrets." Being only too happy to answer his question about Hal Perry, I then explained that Hal, although a very likeable man and a terrific basketball player, had been totally unresponsive to our discovery requests, and just the day before had been sanctioned $1,500 by the Court, only to follow that up by stiffing us that afternoon at his office. Merritt was incredulous, assuring me that he had no idea Perry was not producing discovery, and assuring me the documents would be produced the next day. Good to his word, a set of the requested documents arrived at my office the next day, along with a check for $1,500, signed by Brother Merritt, along with his personal letter of apology. Hal Perry was fired a few days later, replaced by Oakland's largest defense firm, Crosby, Heafey, Roach & May. The lead attorney was my former law school trial practice instructor, Ed Heafey, Jr.— the best teacher I had in law school, and reputed to be one of the best trial attorneys in California. Crosby Heafey would be a formidable opponent, but there would be no more abuses of the discovery process. I felt bad for Hal, who had blown a great billing opportunity for himself, but I was happy now to begin moving the case forward without unnecessary discovery delays.

Seeking to establish that the Executive Order was not being enforced—and, thus, that private enforcement was necessary—I noticed the deposition of the Chief Compliance Officer of the FAA, Jose Alvarez. He appeared in my office, as scheduled, and I began to question him about his responsibilities. He testified that his major job responsibility was conducting "compliance reviews" of the employment practices of airlines and that this required nearly 100% of his time. I asked him how he conducted compliance reviews, and he explained that he would visit the corporate headquarters of an airline, review their EEO-1 Reports (a summary of workforce demographics that all federal contractors are required to submit to the federal government), review documents and reports regarding hiring, promotion, job assignment and termination of workers, and talk with company officials about any problems or deficiencies he uncovered. I asked him how long a typical compliance review took from start to finish, and he testified, "One and a half days." I asked him how many compliance reviews he had conducted the past year, and he answered, "Ten." "How many the year before that?" "Eight." "And this responsibility is nearly 100% of your job?" "Yes," he said. "Mr. Alvarez, you have accounted for only fifteen days of work in 1973 and twelve days in 1972. Is that correct?" "Yes." "Can you explain what you did the other 250 work days of the year?" Answer, "No."

I also asked him if the FAA ever had rescinded a contract with an airline, despite the broad-based underemployment of racial minorities in the airline industry, and he answered, "No." Indeed, at this time (1973) no contract ever had been rescinded by any agency of the federal government for noncompliance with Executive Order 11246. By his own admission, it was clear very little effort was being taken by the FAA to enforce compliance with Executive Order 11246 and that none of the efforts ever had led to meaningful enforcement. Thus, the airline industry was ignoring the Order with impunity, and the rights of minority job applicants, like my clients, were worth less than the paper Executive Order 11246 was written on—unless, of course, they were permitted to enforce the Order themselves.

With Crosby Heafey representing TIA, appropriate discovery was produced promptly, time-consuming but frivolous motions were not filed, and the case proceeded quickly to a scheduled trial date. Taking a hard and realistic look at their patterns of employment, which demonstrated under-hiring of blacks in all entry-level jobs, the under-promotion of women in white-collar positions, and even the failure to hire or promote available blacks into the flight crew, TIA agreed—one week before trial—to a comprehensive settlement of claims. All named plaintiffs received cash awards and jobs, and TIA agreed to a court-enforced order requiring the increase of women and blacks in all jobs for which under-representation existed. Plaintiffs' attorneys would receive $30,000 for attorney's fees and costs, of which my co-counsel agreed I would get $22,000. This order, which was complied with by TIA, resulted in several hundred jobs for blacks and women over the course of the following five years.

The settlement of any federal class action requires notice to the class, an opportunity for class members to object to the proposed settlement at a Fairness Hearing and court approval of the settlement terms, including attorneys' fees. No objections were filed, Judge Renfrew found the Consent Decree to be "fair, adequate and reasonable," and adopted it as the order of the Court. Following the Fairness Hearing, Judge Renfrew's clerk announced that Judge Renfrew would like all counsel to meet him in his chambers.

We all went into chambers and I took a seat. Judge Renfrew was sitting at his desk, his black robe off, with a cigar in hand. He was effusive in his praise of the attorneys for bringing this complex case to a reasonable and fair resolution without the acrimony that trials encourage. Judge Renfrew said something that had an immediate and lasting effect on my legal career—particularly on how I perceived my responsibilities in communicating with judges. "I may appear formidable sitting up there on the bench. I try to prepare for each issue as well as I can so I can ask probing and relevant questions and reach the correct decision; sometimes I may even appear to be all-knowing. But the truth is, I never can know and understand your case as well as you do because I have 350 cases to handle. That is why I must rely on the work of good, well-prepared lawyers like yourselves to bring to my attention the relevant facts and most pertinent cases and arguments."

This was a supremely important lesson for me. Judge Renfrew had a formidable reputation among attorneys for his often commanding control of legal arguments and he certainly could appear to be "all-knowing," particularly to a young lawyer. But, he was telling us how much he relied on good lawyering; he was demystifying his own appearance of omnipotence and asking for good preparation and sound arguments from us. This gave me—still a relatively inexperienced attorney—a real sense of empowerment and responsibility. I felt more powerful because a judge I respected was telling me I always would know my case better than the judge, and I felt more responsibility because I saw more clearly that it was my job to communicate effectively with the judge. As time went on, this lesson became even more obvious and important to me—particularly, in talking with other lawyers about cases and mentoring younger lawyers in my own firm. Complaining about judges is an inveterate vice of lawyers. Often I would hear a sad story from a lawyer about how he or she got screwed by a judge, usually punctuated by statements such as, "Judge So and So is a stupid SOB," or "Judge So and So is biased, prejudiced, etc." These statements often were cop-outs for not taking the responsibility for figuring out what went wrong or how the lawyer could have influenced a different result. I'd tell my lawyers, "You're right, Judge So and So may be dumb and lazy, and maybe he's not very interested in this kind of case. That all may be true. But *your* job is to figure out how to communicate effectively with him—even if he is a dumb SOB."

I never enjoyed losing legal arguments, but when I did—and it happens to everyone—I always asked myself, "What could I have done better? What should I have done differently? How could I have communicated with that judge more effectively? More clearly? What could I have done that would have changed the result?" It was my responsibility to figure out the answers, not just blame the judge.

Judge Renfrew also had some particularly complimentary things to say to us: "Most attorneys would be satisfied with the standard approaches to an employment case and rely only on Title VII and Section 1981. But you were not satisfied with the conventional; you brought new and innovative theories of civil rights enforcement. This is in the greatest tradition of the common law. This is how the law grows and evolves." As we all sat there in the glow of his generous remarks, a little voice in the back of my head told me to "shut up and accept the compliment." But overriding the little voice, I asked Judge Renfrew, "If you liked our innovative theories so much, why weren't we winning them?" The glow in the room disappeared and in the hallway afterwards, my co-counsel wanted to kill me for my bad manners. I thought it was a fair question, but I already knew the answer: Judge Renfrew knew our case was well-grounded in Title VII and Section 1981 and he didn't need, and wasn't ready, to become the first United States District Judge in the country to establish a private right-of-action under the Executive Order or establish other new theories of civil rights enforcement.

A year later, I was back in front of Judge Renfrew defending a group of doctors in a Medicare fraud criminal prosecution. The indictment was extremely broad and vague, so I filed a Motion for Bill of Particulars, which, if granted, would have forced the United States Attorney to specify the criminal charges in greater detail. Once the charges were clearly set out, I felt confident I would be able to defense the case, as the Medicare regulations on which the criminal charges were based, were unconstitutionally vague. I had

had a good relationship with Judge Renfrew in the TIA case, so when I appeared for the hearing on the Motion for Bill of Particulars, I expected my arguments to be fully heard and considered by the Judge. But Judge Renfrew was in no mood to hear the specifics of my motion, and denied it summarily. Six months later, on the Friday before trial was scheduled to begin the following Monday, I was back in front of Judge Renfew with a Motion to Dismiss, based on the unconstitutional vagueness of the Medicare regulations. Since trial was imminent, Judge Renfrew this time listened carefully to my arguments, and, at the conclusion of the hearing, told John Lockie, the Assistant United States Attorney, "You had better be able to answer Mr. Saperstein's arguments by Monday morning, otherwise the case will be dismissed." (All criminal charges were, in fact, dismissed the following Monday.) Judge Rendrew then turned to me with an apology: "Mr. Saperstein, I recall you bringing a Motion for Bill of Particulars many months ago, which, if granted, would have revealed the constitutional defects of the government's indictment. I'm sorry that I didn't give your motion more serious consideration at that time." Here was perhaps the most hardworking and learned judge I've ever appeared in front of apologizing to me and warning the government that he was about to dismiss all charges against my clients. What more could I ask for? The responsible reaction would have been to thank the Judge for his apology and for recognizing the defects in the government's case—indeed, many, if not most, federal judges would have missed the technical defects in the charges—but that was not my reaction. I said, "Thank you, Your Honor, but you would have saved me a lot of time and work if you had done this six months ago." Judge Renfrew, unfettered by my bad manners, apologized a second time.

This is one time my outspokenness probably went over the line into impudence—especially in light of Judge Renfrew's graciousness. But that was just me being me. I said what I thought, and, although my outspokenness got me in trouble on many occasions, it also gained me a reputation as being honest and straightforward. My word was good, it could be counted on, I didn't make representations that later would be shown to be less than fully truthful. I found that as my career evolved, lawyers and judges didn't necessarily like me, but they respected me, and in law, respect is the coin of the realm.

After the TIA hearing I walked to the parking lot with Tim Murphy, the youngest of the three Crosby Heafey lawyers who had worked on the case. I had gotten to know Tim during the case, liked him, and felt I had permission to ask a question that was important to me. "Tim, would you mind telling me what the attorneys' fees for the defense were?" Tim replied, "Guy, you don't want to know." "I guess the answer is going to hurt, but I still want to know," I replied. Tim said, "More than $300,000. The defense fees just for the motion to dismiss were $30,000." "Thanks, Tim, I'll never make that mistake again," I said.

I had litigated the case for 2½ years, and had obtained wall-to-wall relief for my clients, but the fee we recovered for ourselves was less than 10% of the fee charged by the defense attorneys. Nevertheless, it didn't bother me. I was happy with my $30 an hour, I had learned a lot about employment discrimination cases, and I had learned not to undersell myself the next time. Those were valuable lessons, even though the last one had come at a high price.

I had loved working on the TIA case. Unlike most of my cases, where the stakes were too small to expend a lot of time and do top-quality work, in the TIA case the stakes were large enough, and the legal and factual questions complicated enough, to justify spending as much time as necessary to do first-rate legal work. Plus, I preferred the generally higher level of preparation required of everyone in federal court: defense counsel wrote better briefs, I was required to write better briefs, generally more time for oral argument was available, the judge had two very smart law clerks to prepare bench memoranda analyzing the issues, and the judge had more time to digest and consider the issues than do the often-overworked and understaffed state court judges. Most significantly, the end result was important: hundreds of minorities and women would get jobs that had historically been closed off to them.

I WANTED TO DO MORE EMPLOYMENT discrimination cases, and I soon received a phone call from Kathleen Connelly, Executive Director of a small organization called "Women Organized for Employment" (WOE). Kathleen had heard that I was willing to prosecute employment class actions and had done a good job in the TIA case, and she asked if I would be interested in meeting her at her office and talking about what WOE was doing. Within a day or two, I was at her small office in the downtown financial district of San Francisco meeting with Kathleen and her staff. Kathleen explained that WOE was a relatively new organization, with only a small membership of women working mostly in white-collar occupations, but that the issue they were addressing—the underutilization of women in large companies—was systemic in nature and affected large numbers of women. I needed no convincing of this, as I had seen much of what she was talking about and had arrived at the same conclusions. What most impressed me about the organization was Kathleen. She was a very astute political organizer who understood the issues well, wanted to address them with well-placed direct action and litigation, who had the charisma and personal confidence to inspire the women around her to stop sitting around and complaining to one another and, instead, to begin taking effective steps to stop the employment practices they bemoaned.

During our meeting, Kathleen told me about the company that was WOE's main target, Fireman's Fund Insurance Company. Fireman's Fund was one of the nation's largest casualty insurance companies and was headquartered in San Francisco, so a nationwide class action properly could be venued in the United States District Court in San Francisco. She wanted me to file a sex discrimination class action against Fireman's Fund, but first I would have to meet, and gain the confidence of, the woman employees of Fireman's Fund who had complained to WOE about the lack of promotion opportunities for women at Fireman's Fund. These women had been meeting regularly after work to discuss their employment problems and Kathleen suggested I join one of their regular meetings.

I met this group of eight to ten women at a small apartment in the Richmond District of San Francisco on a weekday evening after work. The women were all dressed in their insurance company attire and I tried to look like a successful trial lawyer, although my wardrobe had not quite gotten there yet. Kathleen graciously introduced me to the women as a successful employment discrimination lawyer, and the women to me as current employees of Fireman's Fund who had been directly impacted by Fireman's Fund discriminatory employment practices.

I asked each of the women to describe their complaints to me, and each provided familiar stories of how they had worked for years at various jobs with Fireman's Fund, only to find men—generally younger, less experienced men—hired or promoted ahead of them. In many cases, inexperienced men had been brought into departments for on-the-job training by the women, only to be made the supervisor of the women as soon as he was "trained." All the women agreed that one of them, Susan Westerlund, had been the person most unfairly treated.

Susan appeared somewhat embarrassed at being identified as "the most discriminated against," but managed quietly to recount her history of mistreatment at Fireman's Fund. And it was compelling. Susan had been an exemplary employee, the recipient of consistently "outstanding" performance appraisals, and the employee the other workers in her claims department job regularly sought for help. Her male supervisor, by contrast, did not understand his own job, and generally was ignored by staff; indeed, he often depended on Susan to complete his assignments. Everyone, including Susan, assumed Susan would become the department supervisor when her boss retired, but, to everyone's amazement, a young manager who had a job history of poor performance appraisals and failure in two other supervisory jobs at Fireman's Fund was moved laterally into the supervisor position above Susan. He was a poor personnel manager, as well as unknowledgeable about the department's duties, and became almost completely dependent on Susan to get his job done. Susan became increasingly distraught about his mismanagement of the department, as well as the unfairness of not having been seriously considered for the job she was so obviously qualified for. Indeed, discovery later would show that he had been dumped in this department because no one else wanted him and because he would have a strong, knowledgeable employee—Susan—to be trained by and to rely on!

The meeting was full of pathos and compelling examples of blatantly unequal treatment, but I could sense that the women were using these meetings as an encounter group—telling their stories, baring their souls, and receiving sympathy and understanding from one another—but no one was prepared to take the next step and do something about their complaints. After several hours of listening to their complaints, and, hopefully, gaining their confidence, I began forcing the issue: "Your stories are compelling, I believe them, plus I know women at Fireman's Fund, like women in nearly all insurance companies, are underhired, underpromoted and underpaid. But what are you going to do about it? Sitting in this room and complaining to one another may make you feel better for a short while, but soon you'll get fed up with this kind of treatment at Fireman's Fund, you'll quit and go to work for another bank or insurance company where you'll probably encounter the same kind of underemployment and mistreatment. Are you going to spend a lifetime complaining or are you going to do something to change the way large employers, like Fireman's Fund, treat women?" I explained that a Title VII class action provided the chance to completely change the employment practices of Fireman's Fund, to make sure women got hired and promoted fairly and to obtain back pay for their own experiences of being underhired, underpromoted, and underpaid. I also explained that the law prohibited retaliation for filing an employment discrimination lawsuit, that I would confront any attempts at retaliation aggressively, that I would advance all costs of litigation and be paid attorneys' fees only if I won the case (by court order assessing fees and costs against Fireman's Fund). I realized this was a risky strategy, as I had just met these women and all of a sudden I was telling them to stop being doormats and to take legal action. I waited for their responses.

No one disagreed with what I said, but no one stepped forward either. Instead, they continued to restate their complaints and promote Susan as the No. 1 victim—as though no one needed to do anything unless Susan did something. I decided Susan would have to be the leader.

Susan was an unlikely leader, however. Clerical in appearance, overweight, already experiencing stress-related stomach disorders at a young age, soft-spoken and timid in meetings, she met no one's image of a feminist pioneer. And yet, I knew that it was women like Susan that companies like Fireman's Fund depended on, even as they exploited them. I saw in Susan the same thing I had seen in Alvin, Maceo and Lee, my black friends at the Los Angeles Department of Water & Power—the people who got the work out while the fat, white supervisor was schmoozing with the pretty female clerks. These guys were lifers, largely because there were few other places they could go; they knew their jobs cold and they did them, day in and day out, while less experienced whites passed them by on the way up the promotion ladder.

Susan was petrified at being thrust into the position of leadership, and her discomfort only increased as the meeting wore on, as the other women continued to tell and retell the many incidents of mistreatment she had been subjected to and I emphasized both her social responsibility to take action and her own personal desperation: "You are not far from an emotional breakdown over the mistreatment you are receiving at Fireman's Fund, you have little or no hope of being properly rewarded for your hard work and commitment to your job, you won't last long at Fireman's Fund, in any case, so what do you have to lose?" I said. "I want you to be the first-named, lead plaintiff, and if you do this, everyone will join you," I said, not knowing if anyone would join her. Susan turned to the other women and asked, "Is that right?" and each one slowly agreed with my statement. With that, Susan agreed to sue Fireman's Fund—indeed, to become the lead plaintiff in a nationwide class action, *Westerlund v. Fireman's Fund Insurance Company.*

I don't know for sure if it was the lateness of the hour, the constant emphasis by the other women of how badly she had been beat up by Fireman's Fund, or my badgering to get up off the floor and do something that caused Susan to take the crucial first step toward litigation, but I like to think she had had enough, wasn't going to take it anymore, and just decided she wasn't going to live her life afraid. I know one thing—after Susan took that step, she never looked back, never complained, never showed fear, and slowly became a different person as the case progressed.

MANY YEARS AFTER THE FIREMAN'S FUND case was concluded, Susan visited me. She looked younger, thinner, more fit and better dressed. She was married and living in a middle-income white suburb near Peoria, Illinois. A black professional family had moved into her neighborhood and immediately had been subjected to threats and then a fire-bombing of their house. Susan became the leader of an ad-hoc community group dedicated to protecting the civil rights of this family, as well as raising broad issues of racism in the community. She told the story with the confidence of someone who had become comfortable with the role of leader and seemed unfazed even by the physical threat the people who fire-bombed the black family's house might pose to her. It was an amazing transformation from the Susan Westerlund I had met in 1975. I thought to myself, "Maybe I should run an ad: 'Make money, increase your self-esteem, lose weight and become more powerful. File a sex-discrimination class action against your employer!'"

With Susan as the lead plaintiff, and six other employees and WOE as co-plaintiffs, I filed a natonwide class action against Fireman's Fund. Rather than hiring a process server to serve the complaint on the company, WOE organized a press conference in front of the Fireman's Fund Insurance Co. national headquarters on California Street in San Francisco. We drew all the local television stations, and Kathleen and I each made statements to the press about Fireman's Fund's brand of gender-based employment discrimination. Then Kathleen and about fifteen members of WOE pushed their way past a couple of overweight, befuddled security guards through the front door and into the lobby, then took elevators upstairs to the office of the CEO, Myron DuBain, where they demanded to see Mr. DuBain and serve the class action complaint on him. It was great theater: much pushing and jostling between the women and security guards—with TV cameras being knocked at odd angles, attempts by secretaries to keep the group from WOE out of the CEO's office, women sitting on the floor of the CEO's anteroom demanding to see Mr. DuBain and restating complaints, and a Fireman's Fund spokesman providing feeble responses to the women's demands. The little demonstration ran as the lead story on the 6 p.m. news for all four local TV networks, and the next day my and WOE's phones were lit up with women employees of Fireman's Fund anxious to explain how Fireman's Fund had discriminated against them, also. I was off and running with my first nationwide class action.

Defining the plaintiff class as nationwide in scope offered the advantage of aggregating pattern evidence and potentially obtaining company-wide remedies, but it presented problems for me. The geographical scope of the case would be spread out over hundreds of offices of various sizes, employing in total 15,000 people in over 1,500 different job titles. The task of showing that the practices of discrimination my seven plaintiffs had suffered were typical of the discrimination suffered by thousands of female Fireman's Fund employees throughout the country would be difficult, to say the least. Fireman's Fund would try to dice up the class, dividing it up by geographic location, job positions, job descriptions, job qualifications and employment patterns in an effort to show that the complaints of the seven plaintiffs were aberrational—not representative of the way women employees had been treated throughout the country and, thus, not appropriate for treatment as a class action. If successful, my case would be reduced to seven individual complaints, be worth relatively little, and lead to no meaningful company-wide change.

Fireman's Fund hired a large San Francisco firm, Bronson,

Bronson & McKinnon, to defend the case and soon I was facing off with their top employment attorneys, Edwin L. ("Larry") Currey and Gilmore ("Gil") F. Diekmann. Each had had more experience in Title VII cases than I had, and would prove to be formidable, as well as honorable, opponents. Larry had been a labor lawyer long before Title VII was enacted; he had a droll sense of humor and confidence bred by long experience in labor trench warfare. Gil was my age, but whereas I had graduated from Berkeley—a bastion of liberalism—Gil was a University of Chicago Law School graduate, a member of their law review, and a reflection of that school's then very conservative political orientation. He was tough, smart, no-nonsense. Fortunately, he dealt with the law and facts of the case and did not let his political perspective intrude on his legal judgments. Both Larry and Gil had lived through the civil rights movement of the 1960s, understood why Title VII had been enacted, and respected the law and the purposes underlying it. That didn't stop them from defending their client, but it led to an adversarial relationship that was based on the actual conflicts between the plaintiffs and defendants, not the type of personal allegations of bad faith that I later saw become so common in litigation in the mid-1980s and 1990s.

On behalf of Fireman's Fund, Diekmann and Currey promptly filed a motion to dismiss the entire case brought under Title VII on the ground it was filed prematurely, and the representative claims brought under the Equal Pay Act on the ground that the Act required the filing of written consents by each putative class member. Fireman's Fund asserted that Title VII prohibited the filing of a lawsuit until 180 days after the date charges were filed with the Equal Employment Opportunity Commission (EEOC), noting I clearly had bypassed this deferral period and had obtained a Right to Sue letter from the EEOC without waiting 180 days. In anticipation that Fireman's Fund would file such a motion, I had obtained an affidavit from Sherry Gendelman, Regional Director of the EEOC, stating that the EEOC was so backlogged with charges it would be unable to investigate or conciliate the Westerlund charges for 18–

24 months. Faced with that reality, United States District Judge Oliver J. Carter held that requiring plaintiffs to wait 180 days would be a futile act, as the EEOC would do nothing during that period, and that any interest Fireman's Fund had in informal settlement would not be prejudiced by the premature filing of the action, as Fireman's Fund was free at any time to engage in settlement discussions with plaintiffs, citing Judge Renfrew's decision on the same issue in my prior case, *Murray v. Trans International Airline*, as authority. On the Equal Pay Act issue, Judge Carter held for Fireman's Fund, ruling that written consents from individual class members would be required.

As I was preparing to undertake discovery, Diekmann and Currey went to trial in an employment discrimination class action prosecuted by a friend of mine, Bill Carder. Bill, formerly an attorney with the National Labor Relations Board and the United Farmworkers Union, was a smart, experienced, hardworking attorney, but he had relied on the manual inspection of personnel files to create his database of hire, assignment, transfer, and promotion decisions. At trial, this manual compilation of data proved to be disastrous, as the people doing the work—law students and clerks—had miscoded information, made inconsistent and often inexplicable subjective decisions about categorizing data, and generally created a database that was not reliable. I watched Bill's investigators get methodically carved up by Diekmann. It was not a pretty sight, and I felt terrible for Bill, as I knew that a successful job of impeaching the accuracy and credibility of the database on cross-examination would lead to the Court's conclusion that plaintiffs' crucial statistical proofs—which all were based on the questionable database—could not be relied on and the class action verdict would be for the defense. It was no surprise, therefore, when Judge Orrick issued a defense verdict after a long trial. With it went Bill's large investment in time and expenses preparing the case—a total loss. It was the last Title VII class action Bill ever did, as he subsequently moved into a traditional labor law practice where the cases—and risks—were much smaller. I admired Currey and

Diekmann's skill, but I really felt Bill's loss. A very fine plaintiff attorney would never again be available for an employment discrimination class action. Rationally, intellectually, I knew this could happen to me, too. But I never thought or worried about that possibility. I never thought I would lose a case.

I commenced discovery in the Fireman's Fund case by serving the defendant with a set of "computer interrogatories" and requests for production of the company's computerized personnel database. The interrogatories sought an explanation of what type of personnel data was maintained in computer-readable form, along with many technical questions regarding how to read the computer tapes once we got them. This type of discovery was essential if I was to have a chance litigating the case on a company-wide basis.

The development of computers, and the extensive use of computers by American business, has, of course, been one of the most important developments in the last thirty years. Computers permit businesses to keep track of inventory, analyze systems of production, and keep track and retrieve large amounts of information efficiently. One of the first widespread uses of computers in large companies was the development of personnel databases. Databases were used to print checks, keep track of payroll, and maintain detailed information about work histories, salaries and benefits of the tens of thousands of workers employed by large companies. They were not intended to be used by Title VII plaintiff lawyers, but without this type of computerized database I doubt I could have prosecuted a case like *Westerlund v. Fireman's Fund*, or any of the large employment discrimination cases my firm later would prosecute. Nor could I have had a serious impact on employment discrimination against women, minorities or older workers that was systemic in so many companies during the '70s, '80s and '90s. Computers made it possible to process large amounts of employee data in a relatively cheap and accurate way and permitted this data to be evaluated and shaped into powerful evidence of employment discrimination. If this information had not been available in computer-readable form, I would not have had the human resources to manually collect and tabulate this amount of information, and, even if I had had the human and financial resources for manual search and tabulation, I would have encountered the type of accuracy problems that sank my friend Bill Carder.

Fireman's Fund resisted production of computer-based discovery, but after I obtained a court order compelling this discovery, Fireman's Fund produced its personnel database on four very large spools of computer tape, along with answers to my interrogatories which permitted my statisticians to read and understand the format of the data. Understanding a company's data format never is perfect, so, with the cooperation of defense counsel, I arranged to have my statisticians, Richard Drogin and Richard Kakigi speak directly to Fireman's Fund computer experts.

In the 1970s, computers that could process the personnel tape of a large company like Fireman's Fund were neither cheap nor widely available. In fact, the only computer near my office and available to me on a rental basis that had enough memory to handle such a large personnel database was owned by the University of California at Berkeley. Drogin and Kakigi would load the tape on the University's computers, then wait until 3 or 5 a.m. for the computer to run programs for my cases. I would get the reports I requested within a few days, would review them, and often modify my analyses to look at employment patterns in a different way, then have new reports produced. The level of analysis could be very sophisticated, the analyses could be modified in almost an infinite variety of ways, and the data reprocessed—and new reports produced—quickly. I never could hope to have the litigation resources of a large company like Fireman's Fund, but computerized analyses of personnel data tapes provided me an accurate picture of how men and women, minorities and whites, were treated differently, and even, in some cases, to put a monetary valuation on the effects of discriminatory employment patterns. Through my Title VII career, I attempted, with the constant prodding of my office administrator, Helen Thompson, to stay on the cutting edge of the development of office computer technology—even when I had to borrow money, or mortgage our house, to do it. Computers were expensive for me, but they were the great equalizer; they made prosecution of my class actions against large companies possible.

Once the Fireman's Fund tapes were fully operational and we could run reports, certain patterns of unequal employment treatment of women appeared in the data. Even controlling for age, education and experience in our regression analyses, women were assigned to lower-paid positions than men, and, after initial assignment, progressed up the employment ladder slower than men. Comparing women and men by level of education, revealed huge salary disparities at every level. In fact, female employees with graduate degrees were earning, on average, less than men with high school degrees. Although the men, on average, had longer work histories and more experience at Fireman's Fund, these differences were insufficient to account for the salary disparities. Certain discrete patterns of disparate treatment of men and women also were shown by the data. For example, the company had many categories of claims adjusters, and in each category, there were "inside" adjusters and "outside" adjusters; usually, both inside and outside adjuster positions had identical job descriptions and requirements. The inside adjusters stayed in offices; the outside adjusters worked both inside and outside Fireman's Fund offices (which all seemed to agree made the outside adjuster work more interesting), had company cars and car allowances, and higher salaries. We also observed in the data that only outside adjusters were promoted to management positions in the claims department. We could not miss an obvious fact: nearly all the outside adjusters were men, while the inside adjusters were predominantly women.

In all, we developed approximately twenty statistical analyses demonstrating patterns of gender discrimination, including a very complex wage-regression analysis, which factored in all objective components of the background and experience of Fireman's Fund employees, including formal education, insurance training, prior work history, job positions at Fireman's Fund, and performance appraisals, and which placed a monetary value on the effect of gender on wage and job opportunities at Fireman's. I was convinced we had a strong case, but I was mindful of the inherent problems in trying to certify such a large and diverse class of women covering over 1,000 job categories. Currey and Diekmann, while aware of the problems I would have in certifying the class, also had been conducting their own statistical analyses with SRI International, a statistical and econometric consulting firm at Stanford; I had no doubt their analysis was showing some of the same patterns we had observed, although their statistical experts undoubtedly would be prepared to provide alternative interpretations of the data. Currey and Diekmann also knew that if I was successful in certifying a nationwide class, their client's liability for class damages would increase greatly. Thus, with both sides facing uncertainty, and with substantial risks on both sides, we agreed to meet and discuss the evidence before a motion for class certification was filed.

Sensing the seriousness of their interest in possible settlement of the case, but also knowing they were capable of doing any of the analyses I had done themselves, I took the calculated risk of showing them our statistical analyses. My purpose was straightforward; if I could convince them that we had sound analyses demonstrating discriminatory patterns of employment, their client would be more likely to settle the case. Meeting them with my statistical expert, Richard Drogin, we walked through each of the analyses, with me providing interpretations and conclusions. Currey and Diekmann were just as sophisticated in their understanding of such statistical evidence, if not more so, and they didn't waste time trying to argue that the analyses were meaningless, choosing instead to point out where the Court might not choose to derive the same conclusions as Richard and I. Nevertheless, after our first discussion of evidence, we never returned to the topic, and instead spent our time discussing the settlement of issues and the remedy for the underemployment of women.

Their price for a settlement that included goals and timetables requiring the hiring and promotion of women on a companywide basis was no recovery of class damages—a common trade-off in

Title VII settlements at that time. Recognizing this as the norm but also mindful that an injunctive remedy that included goals and timetables would dramatically increase the employment opportunities and upward mobility of women at Fireman's Fund now, not many years later, I was willing to make that trade. Only later, when faced with unreasonable opposition by another large insurance company, did I begin fundamentally to alter my view of trading class damages for injunctive relief. In any case, after months of debate about what each named plaintiff was entitled to in settlement, what the "availability" of women was for each category of jobs, and what goals for increased hiring and promotion needed to be established to provide fair, equal and compensatory employment opportunities for women, a lengthy consent decree was agreed to and presented to the Court for approval. Individual notices of the proposed decree were mailed to the thousands of identifiable class members, and notices were published in national publications explaining the terms of the decree and inviting comments and/or objections to be filed. No substantive objections were filed, and the decree was approved. It would result in thousands of jobs and promotions for women at Fireman's Fund.

The Fireman's Fund case was not over for me, however. One issue had not been negotiated or settled—my attorney's fee. Title VII provides that the "prevailing party" is entitled to an award of reasonable attorney's fees and costs, and there was no dispute I was entitled to fees and costs as the "prevailing party," but the issue of "how much" remained for United States District Judge William A. Ingram to decide, as Judge Carter had died during the pendency of the case. I considered Judge Ingram to be a very fair man, but while in private practice he had defended insurance companies. Plus, he had been appointed to the federal bench by President Nixon—no friend of civil rights attorneys. Judge Ingram was a new federal judge, with no track record awarding fees in public interest cases, so it was anybody's guess what he would do with my application for fees.

Remembering my experience in the TIA case, where I had

greatly undervalued my services, I decided to consult other civil rights attorneys about their experiences in fees litigation and review fees applications they had written. They were quite willing to help, but after talking to them and reviewing their fees applications, I realized the civil rights bar didn't understand money and the role it played in large-scale litigation any more than I had in my TIA case. Many civil rights attorneys suffered from what I call the "legal aid mentality"—the belief that legal services should be provided for free or near-free, that it was impure to seek high rates, and/or that any attorney obtaining high fees must be sacrificing relief for his or her clients for fees. I, too, had suffered from this malady; in my early years of private practice, I found it difficult to set and collect a fair fee from my working-class clients. But collecting a fair fee from a major insurance company after creating thousands of promotion opportunities for women—opportunities that were worth hundreds of millions of dollars—was something I had no reservations about. Moreover, I had learned how much time and expenses had to be advanced to prosecute employment class actions. I wanted to continue doing them, not abandon class actions, as nearly all of the civil rights attorneys I had talked to had done because they no longer were willing to advance expenses and live with anxiety for years before a case was conducted, only to be paid an inadequate fee after all.

I decided the civil rights bar would be no help, and went looking instead for class action attorneys who had been successful in obtaining reasonable fees—securities and antitrust attorneys. San Francisco had a strong securities and antitrust plaintiffs bar, so I called several prominent securities and antitrust attorneys, talked to them and obtained copies of their fees applications. These were the guys who understood prevailing hourly rates, the risks of contingent-fee litigation, the burden of advancing hundreds of thousands of dollars in expenses, the cost of delay in getting paid, the value of obtaining relief for thousands of people in a class action, and the need to award plaintiff attorneys "multipliers" or "enhancements" of their hourly rates to reflect such factors as risk of loss, delay in receipt of payment, and results achieved for large numbers of people. If I wanted to make a career out of doing civil rights class actions, I would have to learn how to obtain reasonable attorney's fees from attorneys like them, not the civil rights bar.

One thing several of the securities attorneys had told me was to consider hiring another attorney to represent me on my fees application, as it sometimes is easier for another attorney to brag about your results than it is to do it yourself. With that in mind, I hired another law firm, Altschuler & Berzon, to help prepare the fees petition and collect declarations from attorneys attesting to the hourly rate I was seeking, the quality of the settlement I had obtained, and the appropriateness of awarding multipliers of hourly rates to reflect the risk of loss, delay in receipt of payment and the exceptional results. I supported this with an eighty-five–page written declaration of my own, detailing the history of the litigation and explaining the value of the results achieved. I believe it was the first time that a civil rights attorney in Northern California had sought a big firm hourly rate (which then was $125 an hour for a large corporate firm attorney of my age and experience), enhanced by a multiplier of two.

Larry Currey and Gil Diekmann must have been quite surprised to receive this fee application, and its request for a high rate—doubled—because the opposition brief they filed was filed with claims of "outrageous" and "unreasonable," followed by a proposal that I be paid a low hourly rate, that half my hours not be paid at all as "non-productive," and no multiplier awarded ("an unprecedented request," they claimed). This was supported by a declaration from Gil that was as long and detailed as my lengthy declaration, except in Gil's version of the history of the case, my work had been simple and straightforward, with few risks and little delay. Further, I had been snookered in the settlement, obtaining only weak and ineffective relief for the class of women I represented. Some of this was defense attorney boilerplate, but I think part of it was based on Gil's honest feeling that if I claimed I had done a good job of lawyering and obtained good relief, it meant he had done a bad job and had been beaten at the settlement table. Despite the fact that the Consent Decree declared my clients "the prevailing parties," thus entitling us to an award of fees and costs, the two competing versions of history took on the look of "Who Won the Fireman's Fund Case?" The truth was, we both had done a good job lawyering the case and both had protected the interests of our clients in the settlement, which, of course, required substantial compromises on both sides.

In that posture, I appeared in Judge Ingram's courtroom in San Jose to sit and listen to my attorney brag about my work. However, as soon as the hearing began, Judge Ingram turned to me, sitting at the counsel table, and said, "I know you hired an attorney to represent you because you probably thought it unseemly to brag about your own achievements, but I read your long declaration and you do quite a grand job of tooting your own horn!" I would have been upset at the comment, except Judge Ingram was smiling when he said it so I thought maybe I'd be all right. He then began to question me about "This multiplier, what is that?" I made several attempts to explain the concept, each time drawing blank expressions from Judge Ingram's face. Then, with my last explanation, a light bulb went off in his head, his face brightened, and he said, "Oh, you mean you want a bonus so you can create a litigation fund to sue more insurance companies?" My motives thus exposed, I wanly replied, "Yes." With that the hearing ended and I was left to wonder whether I'd be able to pay for the larger house Jeanine and I had just bid on at an estate auction.

JEANINE AND I HAD DECIDED we needed a larger house to accommodate her Montessori preschool, which she wanted to expand to eighteen students. The house we found in North Berkeley had a large basement and garage on the lower floor, which we could convert for the school, and a large, beautiful yard for the kids to use. It was perfect for our family, now consisting of our two sons, and our niece, Unmi—who Jeanine's brother and sister-in-law had adopted in

Korea, but who now lived with us part-time—and for Jeanine's school, but the price was a stretch for us. The asking price had been $195,000, but bids by nine bidders had driven the price to $265,000 and at least $40,000 was required for immediate repairs. Excited by the possibilities of this house, and with a loan from my law partner, Frank Denison, I won the Probate Court bidding auction by bidding 35% over the listing price. But now I had a big dilemma— I had to get a bank loan within thirty days, or lose the 10% cash deposit I had paid to the Probate Court.

I submitted loan applications to every bank and savings and loan in sight, and was rejected by all of them. The problem was our income. Our highest joint income had been $26,000 a year and the mortgage, utility and insurance payments on the new loan alone would be more than that! My best hope had been my bank, Bank of America, but when they turned me down, I was really up against the wall. I asked the loan officer to speak with the bank manager, and after being told by the bank manager that my income didn't qualify me for the loan, I asked, "Who really makes these decisions?" I was told they were made in a regional office out on Hegenberger Road, near the Oakland Airport. I took my loan file, drove out to Hegenberger Road, and asked to speak to the man in charge of residential loans. They were not used to consumers dropping in like this, but they took me to the man they told me made these decisions. I handed him my loan file, and he asked, "What can I do for you?"

I said, "I know my earnings history doesn't qualify me for this loan by conventional lending standards. In fact, by conventional standards, I'm not even close to qualifying. But the mortgage I'm applying for will be paid with future income, not past income, so the Bank should assess my future prospects, not just past income. While my past income has been low, that has largely been the result of my long-term investment in large class actions, which are expensive to prosecute and require many years to complete. But I have been investing in these cases now for eight years and several are about to be completed, including my employment discrimination case against Fireman's Fund Insurance Company, in which I am seeking over $300,000 in fees. I wouldn't be seeking, nor would I obligate myself, to such a large mortgage unless I was confident my income would increase and I could pay it. I'm coming to the Bank of America with this unusual request because of the Bank's heritage. This Bank was founded by A. P. Giannini as the first retail bank in California, with small branch officers located throughout California with the mission of servicing the needs of small people. Giannini had the reputation of lending to many small businesses that wouldn't qualify for loans under conventional bank lending standards. By being unconventional himself, and investing in small people, he built a major bank. Investing in me really is no different than what the Bank has been doing for years, indeed, it is no different than the very mission and purpose of the Bank of America."

The loan manager leaned back in his chair and, reviewing my file, said, "You are quite right to say you do not qualify for the loan you are seeking. Nevertheless, I am impressed by your confidence. About once a year I do something like this—I'm going to play a hunch and make this loan. Anyone with as much confidence in himself as you have deserves a chance." He authorized approval of the loan and told me to take it back to the branch officer. I thanked him. I wish I could remember his name so I could find him and thank him again, because we lived in that house for sixteen years and it was the perfect house for our family and Jeanine's school.

A month after the Fireman's Fund fee hearing—an unusually short period to wait for such an order—I received Judge Ingram's decision in the mail: I was awarded $125/hour for my time, no deductions of my time, not even 1/10th of an hour, and a 50% bonus (1.5 multiplier). It was the highest hourly rate and multiplier ever awarded a public interest lawyer up to that time in the Northern District of California. The decision included one typo, and the next day I got a call from Judge Ingram explaining and apologizing for the typo ("Gee, Judge, no apology is necessary!" I thought). More important than the apology, and even the fee award, Judge Ingram told me, "The legal papers you filed in this case were a model of how a Title VII class action should be prosecuted and I have told my clerks to keep copies in my chambers as a reference for future Title VII cases that come before me."

The total award was $282,500, enough to pay law firm debts, but as I was basking in the glory of the fee award and Judge Ingram's gracious comments, I got a call from Gil Diekmann which sent a chill up my spine. "Fireman's Fund is considering an appeal of the fee award, but I thought you and I should talk about it first," he said. "OK, what's on your mind?" I replied. "Well, I am willing to recommend that the company accept the award if you are willing to concede a few issues that add up to around 5% of the award." We talked those issues through, I compromised on a number of them, and we settled the fee for $270,000, to be paid within fifteen days.

Before the fifteen days ran, Gil invited me to lunch at an exclusive men's club—the type that normally excludes people like me and my clients. After an enjoyable lunch and chat, Gil invited me back to his office. Once there, he handed me my check and made a little speech about the work I had done in the Fireman's Fund case, which included telling me that "you prepared this case better than I've ever seen a Title VII case prepared." It was a very classy and touching thing for him to do and his comments meant a lot to me; I had developed great respect for his intelligence and the quality of his work during the four years spent litigating the case—respect that transcended our political disagreements and the representation of conflicting interests. The lunch and comment were an example of the type of collegiality and respect that could develop between competing litigators twenty-five years ago that seems to have become rare these days.

Collegiality and money aside, the Fireman's Fund case was my most important achievement to date, as it opened up employment opportunities to thousands of women throughout the country. The result was satisfying in every respect—thousands of job opportunities were created for women in the insurance industry and I received a fair fee—but my experience with employment discrimination in the insurance industry was just beginning.

WHILE I WAS DEVELOPING MY CLASS ACTION CASES, I began to do individual race, sex, age and disability discrimination cases. I also began to take wrongful termination cases and participated in the development of wrongful termination law in California.

My first individual employment discrimination case was a race case on behalf of Skip Rosales, a tough, young Hispanic steamfitter, against his employer, Contra Costa County. Skip had been fired allegedly for screwing up a job, but my investigation of his claims revealed a vicious pattern of race discrimination directed toward him by his boss and supported by white co-workers. Some of the hostility toward Skip was engendered by the fact that he was shop steward for the steamfitter's union, some because of his "take-no-shit" attitude, and most because he was a minority who demanded to be treated fairly. I spoke with other minority co-workers, and even some of the white co-workers, and they confirmed that the mistakes he allegedly made that led to his firing were not mistakes at all. Quite to the contrary: he was fired for refusing to install a heavy air-conditioning unit by drilling holes in a large "glu-lam" (laminated wood) beam. He was correct, and his boss was wrong: drilling holes in the laminated beam would have weakened the beam, which was supporting the roof. Furthermore, even more serious mistakes by white workers had not led to their terminations; Skip was being singled out and his alleged "mistake" was a pretext for racial discrimination.

The case was assigned to United States District Judge Stanley A. Weigel. Weigel had been a cracker-jack antitrust lawyer before he became a federal judge and his reputation as a judge was as a harsh, brilliant, demanding, even tyrannical, jurist who had no hesitation telling lawyers how to practice law or publicly correcting their errors. Several lawyers told me he was the last judge they would want to appear in front of.

Nothing serious was offered in settlement of the case, so Skip and I and his family appeared in court ready to begin trial. The case had been pled as both a Title VII and Section 1981 case. Section 1981 is derived from the Civil Rights Act of 1866 and provides a right to a trial by jury, but as jurors were filing into the jury box, I dismissed the Section 1981 cause-of-action. Judge Weigel immediately commented, "I've never seen anyone do that!" I had grown to like and respect Skip very much as someone who had spent his life fighting racism in the trenches, but he was a tough, angry guy and I was afraid some jurors might view him an angry man with a big chip on his shoulder just looking for trouble. Since jury verdicts in federal court must be unanimous, and jury *voir dire* is very limited, the chance of pulling one or two unsympathetic jurors was too great, in my opinion. In consultation with Skip, we agreed to take our chances with Judge Weigel on the Title VII claim.

This was my first federal discrimination trial and the facts were a bit complicated, so I had prepared a complete opening statement. Typed, it ran forty pages. I stepped to the lectern, introduced myself and my client, and began to deliver my opening statement. I had spoken for about ten minutes, when Judge Weigel interrupted me, saying, "Counsel, if you are reading your opening statement, I'd prefer that you just hand it up to me. I can read faster than you can talk." My client and his family were in the courtroom, as were some of the trial witnesses, not to mention the defense attorneys, and I felt embarrassed—my inexperience had been exposed for everyone to see!

I turned my opening statement upside down, and responded to Judge Weigel, "I'm not reading my opening statement," then gave the rest of my opening statement—which lasted thirty to forty minutes—without looking down at my notes. Judge Weigel interrupted me several times, but each time to ask a probing, intelligent question about the case. I sat down, a bit shaken, but confident I had explained my theory of the case.

The defense attorney stood up, moved to the lectern, and began to explain why plaintiff should not prevail. He was a very experienced trial attorney, a name partner in a 100-attorney law firm, impeccably dressed in a dark blue suit, a distinguished looking man in his early 60s, very articulate and appearing very confident. I respected—even feared—his trial experience and his smoothness in court, but he lacked two qualities I brought to the case: experience in discrimination law, and detailed knowledge of the facts of the case.

He began his opening statement with a gracious introduction of himself and his client to the Court, then launched into a series of broad generalizations about discrimination law and the facts of the case. Judge Weigel listened impatiently for five minutes, then interrupted, saying, "Counsel, I listened to Mr. Saperstein carefully for more than a half hour. He presented a coherent explanation of the facts of this case and how, if those facts are proved, Mr. Rosales would be entitled to a verdict in his favor. I understand his case. You now must answer Mr. Saperstein and explain why his case is factually or legally flawed and why your client is entitled to a verdict."

Defense counsel restarted his argument, but the quality of the presentation did not improve. It continued to be full of generalizations and sparse on the facts of this case. Three minutes of argument passed, when Judge Weigel interrupted him again, saying, "Counsel, you are not answering Mr. Saperstein. I want you to address his argument directly and explain why he is wrong. If you can't do that, I want you to sit down!" His voice was louder, more agitated. I could see his patience was very limited.

Defense counsel started a third time, but now, clearly disturbed by the Judge's strident demands, he became even more general in his presentation, relying on defense attorney boilerplate—"the burden is on plaintiff to prove all elements of his case;" "the plaintiff must prove it was more likely than not that his termination was caused by race discrimination, rather than his poor job performance," etc. It was the kind of general boilerplate lawyers must explain to jurors unknowledgeable about burdens of proof, but the argument was just repeating things the Court knew well and was avoiding the subject the Court needed to hear—the facts of the defense side of this case. Judge Weigel listened for a minute, then slammed his gavel on his desk, and bellowed, "Counsel, I've heard enough. Sit down!" I was stunned. I realized defense counsel was not providing a very informed or useful opening statement, but I had never seen a judge refuse to let an attorney complete an opening statement. I had some mixed feelings about this: on the one hand, I realized I had gained an advantage in the opening statements, but I also felt a little compassion for the harsh treatment the defense attorney had received. The incident also increased my apprehension about Judge Weigel: Would I be treated the same way if I fell short of his expectations?

Judge Weigel turned to me and said, "Call your first witness." I called Skip Rosales, who stepped forward, was sworn, and sat down in the witness chair. I began to question him, first introducing him as a person by having him explain his background, his work history, his skills, the kind of work he did, and his union activities. I then began to question him about his employment with Contra Costa County and the specific facts of the case. But I couldn't get more than one or two questions out of my mouth without defense counsel standing up and objecting to my questions: "Objection, Your Honor, the question calls for hearsay;" "Objection, Your Honor, the question is vague and ambiguous;" "Objection, Your Honor, the question calls for conjecture;" "Objection, Your Honor, the question assumes facts not in evidence." To each objection, Judge Weigel responded, "Denied." Over the course of the first two hours of Skip's testimony, defense counsel made approximately fifty objections, and each one was denied. Shortly before the lunch break, I asked another question, and defense counsel rose to make another objection. As he rose from his seat, Judge Weigel and I turned to look at him. Quietly, he said, "Would it serve any useful purpose for me to make any more objections?" Judge Weigel replied firmly, "Absolutely not!"

We took a break for lunch, then resumed with Skip's testimony for the rest of the afternoon. Skip was a tough, combative person who I had been afraid might alienate some jurors, but I thought there was a chance his personal qualities, and the strength of his testimony, would impress Judge Weigel—a tough, combative guy himself. I could see Weigel was interested in Skip's story. If I passed through important parts of his testimony too quickly, the Judge would interrupt and ask a few questions of his own. His questions were relevant and probing—I could see why he had had a strong reputation as a trial lawyer—and I could see there was respect developing between Skip and the Judge. Skip was courteous, but not deferential to the Judge. He was blue-collar, whereas the Judge came from a white-collar elite profession, but Skip carried himself with respect and dignity. Through his testimony, it became clear Skip was a person who wasn't going to be pushed around as a union shop steward or intimidated by racism; he would stand up and speak out for fairness, which is what got him fired. As I elicited Skip's story and watched Judge Weigel, I thought to myself, "I bet Judge Weigel is thinking, 'If the circumstances of my life had found me as a Hispanic steamfitter working in a racist environment, I probably would have challenged my boss, too, and gotten fired just like Rosales.' " At least, that was what I was hoping Judge Weigel was thinking! In any case, Skip's testimony stated his case well, the Judge was listening carefully all day, and I had no doubt Skip had made a big impression on him. We had had a great day by the time Judge Weigel stopped trial for the day at 5 p.m.

I guess the defense interpreted the day the same as I did, because as soon as Judge Weigel adjourned trial, the defense attorney approached me and asked, "What will it take to settle this case?" I replied, "100% of Skip's back pay losses, 100% of my attorney's fees and costs, reinstatement of Skip to his job, with full seniority credit, and removal of his boss." He asked, "Are you willing to speak with a settlement judge about this?" I said yes, so long as the settlement judge was United State District Judge Alphonso Zirpoli. Judge Zirpoli, who was known as a totally brilliant and courageous liberal judge, had represented unions before becoming a federal judge, and I knew he would understand Skip's case. The defense attorney agreed, and we walked directly to Judge Zirpoli's chambers.

Judge Zirpoli was just finishing a long day of his own, but he agreed to talk with the attorneys. We went into his chambers, while Skip and his family, and representatives from Contra Costa County, waited in the reception room. Once in chambers, defense counsel explained that we were in trial before Judge Weigel, but defendant wanted to explore settlement now. Judge Zirpoli said, "Fine," then turned to us and asked, "What do you want, counsel?" I repeated my demand: 100% of back pay, 100% of fees and costs, reinstatement with full seniority, and removal of the head of the steamfitters department. The Judge responded, "That's a pretty tough demand. Do you really expect the County to reinstate Mr. Rosales AND get rid of his boss?" "That's up to them," I said, "but if they want to settle the case, that's what they have to do."

The defense attorney excused himself and went outside to talk to his client, returning thirty minutes later to say, "We agree to all of Mr. Saperstein's demands." I was blown away! I never believed for a minute that they ever would agree to reinstate Skip and remove the head of the department. I went out into the hall to tell the great news to Skip, but Skip greeted the news impassively, and told me to refuse the deal! I demanded to know why. "I've been waiting 2½ years for this day and we're kicking their teeth out. I want to keep kicking them until the Judge rules that they committed discrimination," he told me. "But the County is offering you more than 100%, because even if Judge Weigel rules in your favor, the most he could do is award you reinstatement, plus 100% of back pay and attorney's fees and costs. He would have no authority to remove your boss," I counseled. "I don't care. They humiliated me and I intend to humiliate them!" Skip replied.

I realized that I was making no progress standing in the hallway, so I told Skip I wanted to meet with him in my office at 8 p.m. that night, and I wanted him to bring his wife and his brother, who also worked in the steamfitter shop at Contra Costa County. I then went back into chambers to tell Judge Zirpoli and defense counsel that my client had rejected the offer. Both were dumbfounded by this unlikely development, but Judge Zirpoli said, "Speak with your client tonight, then I want all of you here tomorrow at 9 a.m."

Promptly at 8 p.m., Skip, looking glum and stubborn, appeared at my office with his wife and brother. I could see from the expressions on all their faces that they had been talking about the County's offer and that Skip hadn't moved an inch. We began the discussion with me telling Skip how well he had done as a witness and how impressed I thought Judge Weigel had been with his story. "You said earlier that we were kicking their teeth out, and I think that is an accurate assessment," I told him. "But there also comes a time when a settlement makes sense. While the trial is going very well, and I am confident we will win, there are no guarantees in this business. We haven't heard them present their defense and there's always the possibility of some surprises. In this case, the defendant is offering you *more* than you could obtain from a trial verdict. That is extraordinary. I've never seen that happen before and you can be proud that it is because the County recognizes you have a strong case and probably also that they have a real problem with your boss and are willing to take this opportunity to move him elsewhere. The County's offer is phenomenal and is a total victory, plus." Skip was unmoved by my eloquence.

Skip's brother added, "The minute you walk back into the shop, everyone will know you kicked their ass, and getting rid of the supervisor is just unbelievable." Then Skip's wife spoke. She had attended many office meetings and court hearings, but had remained largely silent. "Skip, this has been a very hard 2½ years for you, first getting fired and having to hear about your boss and some of your co-workers make derogatory comments about you, and then living through this lawsuit. But this lawsuit also has been very hard on me and our children. You are a good father, but there have been many times that you were angry and distant from me and the kids. For our sake, as well as yours, you need to end this." I was near tears listening to her, and I could see Skip was deeply moved by her, but he stood fast. "This is something I just have to do and I apologize for all the pain I've caused you and the kids," he said. There was nothing more I could say or do, but to prepare for the next day of trial.

The next morning, before showing up in Judge Zirpoli's office at 9 a.m., I stopped by Judge Weigel's office to tell him that we had met with Judge Zirpoli last night and were meeting with him again this morning, but I'd be ready to recommence trial at 10 a.m., as scheduled. He said, "Take whatever time you need with Judge Zirpoli, so long as you're making progress. Let me know at noon where you stand."

We announced ourselves to Judge Zirpoli's secretary at 9 a.m. and he came out of his office wearing no judicial robe, shook hands, then invited everyone, including Skip, his wife and brother, and his kids, and defense counsel and his client, into chambers. I explained that I had met last night with Skip, his wife and brother, but that I could make no progress; Skip was determined to go back to trial. Judge Zirpoli pondered that for awhile, then said, "Would anyone mind if I talked to Skip alone?" No one objected, and we all left.

A half hour passed, then another half hour, then another. Then the door opened, and out walked Judge Zirpoli with his arm around Skip's shoulders, a big smile on his face, and a smile on Skip's face. Judge Zirpoli announced, "Skip will accept the County's offer." Skip looked at the Judge, shook his hand warmly, turned to me and said, "Judge Zirpoli really understands the working man!" Then he embraced his wife and brother.

Later, I tried to get Skip to tell me everything that had happened in Judge Zirpoli's chambers, but Skip kept telling me what a fine man Judge Zirpoli was and how he really understood working people. I thought to myself, "I hope someday I can communicate with people as well as Judge Zirpoli obviously communicated with Skip."

SEYMOUR FRIEDMAN HAD BEEN WORKING for eighteen years as a clothing salesman for Sewell Manufacturing Co., when he was suddenly fired at age 69. Sewell Manufacturing Co. was located in Georgia, outside Atlanta, and was owned and run by W. C. Sewell. Mr. Sewell personally had fired Seymour by sending him a letter claiming that Seymour's sales were slightly down and that, besides, he was of the age when he should be retired and "should be spending more time with your lovely wife. You'll be much happier this way." The letter, signed by Mr. Sewell, stated, "I pray for you everyday and May God Bless You." Of course, Mr. Sewell didn't ask Seymour if he would be "much happier" getting fired, nor did he account for the fact that Seymour was still working at age 69 because he didn't have enough money to retire.

Seymour presented himself to me as a lively, charming, very dapper gentlemen who looked much younger than his age. I liked him immediately and never stopped enjoying his visits to my office. I asked him if Sewell's claim that his sales performance was down was accurate, and Seymour said it wasn't. Subsequent discovery would prove that his sales performance was not down and was comparable with other Sewell salesmen.

I filed the case in federal court in San Francisco under the federal Age Discrimination in Employment Act, and the companion state statute, and drew United States District Judge Eugene F. Lynch as the judge. I didn't know Lynch, but he was a Republican, appointed by Ronald Reagan both as a state court judge and also to the federal bench. That didn't comfort me, but I surveyed some other attorneys and was told that he wasn't the most intellectual of judges, but he didn't carry any political agenda or bias against civil rights litigants. He sounded fair enough for me. As time went on, he was to become one of my all-time favorite judges.

I knew I would need to go to Georgia to take Mr. Sewell's deposition, as he had been the one who fired Seymour, so I phoned some labor attorneys in Atlanta to see what they knew about Sewell. They told me that Mr. Sewell, then 85 himself, was almost legendary as an autocratic, anti-labor, racist owner of Sewell Manufacturing Co., a company that manufactured men's suits and employed approximately 3,500 people. They all told me deposing him would be quite a challenge. The description of Sewell was so colorful and his termination letter to Seymour had been so full of Christian righteousness, I decided to take a video deposition of him. A videotape deposition would be much more expensive for me, but I knew I might not be able to compel his attendance at trial in San Francisco, so a video deposition would be the best way to let a San Francisco jury see what this guy was really like. I called defense counsel—a fine trial attorney named Bill Bush—and he had no objection to the video deposition. In fact, he suggested it be taken at King & Spaulding, the mega-law firm that represented Sewell Manufacturing Co. in Georgia. Normally, I would want to take such a deposition in a plaintiff attorney's office so that the witness might feel less comfortable than being in his own lawyer's office, but I had heard a lot about King & Spaulding and thought it might be interesting to hang out there for a few days while I deposed Mr. Sewell. I scheduled Mr. Sewell for three days of deposition, hoping to finish in two days, and flew to Atlanta with my video technician.

I woke up early in Atlanta and decided to walk the six blocks to the King & Spaulding offices. I wasn't ready for Atlanta weather in August. Although it was 8:30 a.m., my six-block walk left me drenched in sweat. Nevertheless, the King & Spaulding lawyers, who would be defending the deposition, greeted me warmly, even inviting me into a senior partner's office to sit and talk and get to know one another. I was impressed by their cordiality and graciousness, but it didn't last long. Once inside the deposition room, and the witness was sworn, collegiality disappeared and the lawyers began a familiar line of objections to my questions.

The witness, Mr. Sewell, was a tall erect man, despite his 85 years, wearing an ill-fitting black suit, even in the hot weather. I could see he was used to being in charge, as he seemed distracted by his lawyers' objections and interventions, preferring to focus on me and answer my questions directly. I'm sure he thought that, once I heard his side of the story, I'd understand what a fine Christian man he was and abandon this silly lawsuit. Witnesses with this level of arrogance are just nourishment for good attorneys. I was anxious to get on with the questioning, but knew I had to control my impatience, not look overeager and be gracious at all times, not only to maximize the amount of information I would get from him, but also to appear courteous to the jury that one day would watch the videotape. I wanted to carve him up like a turkey, but not appear to embarrass him. Let his testimony embarrass him.

I began with questions about his background, focusing on how he started the company and how he ran it. I gently asked what unions represented workers at his company, and Mr. Sewell sat erect and proudly stated, "Mr. Saperstein, in my thirty-five years of running Sewell Manufacturing Co., I have never allowed a union in my company!" I knew San Francisco jurors would love that!

We took a lunch break, and after lunch, Mr. Sewell returned with coffee and food stains all over his tie and white shirt. I began questioning him about Seymour Friedman and one of the first things he said was that Seymour was "slovenly." I asked what he meant by that, and he testified, "Seymour was just not careful about his appearance. His clothes didn't fit right and I'd often see him with coffee or food stains on his shirts." As I continued to question Mr. Sewell about Seymour's ill-fitting clothes and food and coffee stains, I passed a note to my video technician: "Take close-ups of the food and coffee stains on his tie and shirt and the suit jacket collar that doesn't fit his neck." Never once in his half-hour discourse on Seymour's cleanliness habits did he mention, or apologize for his filthy shirt and tie, and not once did I point out the condition of his own clothes. I knew the video images would be worth ten thousand words!

After exhausting the issues of dress and cleanliness, I moved on to the bases for Seymour's termination and Mr. Sewell's unctuous termination letter. Presenting him with sales records that showed Seymour's sales performance to be comparable to the sales of younger Sewell salesmen, he was unable to explain why Seymour's performance was inferior to younger salesmen who were not fired. When pushed, he fell into ageist explanations, suggesting that, at 69, it was getting harder for Seymour to travel and make sales calls. I asked him whether, at 85, it was becoming more difficult for him to travel or run his company, and he said, "Not at all." I asked him about the 30-year-old who replaced Seymour, and Mr. Sewell was forced to admit he had lost accounts and sales from Seymour's territory had fallen.

I asked Mr. Sewell why he had written in his termination letter that Seymour "should be spending more time with your lovely wife," and Mr. Sewell told me that "at his age, he should slow down and be with family." I asked him if he had ever asked Seymour or his wife if they felt that way, and he admitted he had not. I asked Mr. Sewell what he meant when he wrote that Seymour would be "much happier this way," and he testified, "Well, you know, he could be gardening, or playing golf, or visiting with his grandchildren." I asked him if he had any idea if Seymour gardened, golfed or had grandchildren, and he said, "I don't know." I asked him, "So how did you know if he would be 'much happier' being fired?" Sewell answered, "I guess I didn't know." I asked him if he would have been "much happier" being involuntarily retired at age 69, and he said, "No." I asked him if it was true that he had prayed for Seymour "every day," and he said, "I don't remember." I asked him why he wrote "May God Bless You" in the same letter in which he fired Seymour, and Mr. Sewell answered, "I just wanted to make the old rascal feel good." "In other words, you wanted to make him feel good about getting fired?" I asked. "Yes," he answered. "Does it bother you that Mr. Friedman doesn't feel good about getting fired?" I asked. "Not particularly," Mr. Sewell replied.

I thought the picture of Mr. Sewell as a Christian hypocrite had been painted, and we adjourned the deposition for the day. As soon as the deposition stopped, the defense attorney invited me into his office for a chat. Once in his large and comfortable office, the hostility he had demonstrated toward me during the deposition disappeared, and he walked to his liquor cabinet and offered me a drink. We sat talking for an hour and a half, with him giving me advice about restaurants, sights to see, and even offering to drive me around sightseeing. It was an odd juxtaposition—professionally hostile in deposition, then gracious and friendly as soon as we weren't working. A litigator's version of southern hospitality, I guess.

Six months later, I was in Judge Lynch's courtroom ready to start trial. I faced a number of hurdles: the defendant had filed eighteen motions *in limine* to limit the introduction of much of plaintiff's evidence and Seymour was in a hospital in Southern

California seriously ill with phlebitis. The motion *in limine*, if granted, would have gutted the best evidence I had from the case. As Bill Bush and I argued the merits of each motion, I could see Judge Lynch was going to let me get to the jury with enough evidence to make a good case. In the end, I won fourteen of the eighteen contested motions; I was in good shape for the jury trial. The defense apparently thought I was in better than good shape, as they immediately increased the settlement offer, from $40,000 to $400,000, which Judge Lunch correctly said was a lot of money for the case, as I would have the difficult job of convincing a jury that Seymour wanted to work to age 80 in order to build up his wage loss claims. Nevertheless, I told defense counsel and Judge Lynch I wanted to reject it, but would phone my client. I made sure not to mention that Seymour was in a hospital! I went out to a phone in the hallway, called Seymour and told him that Sewell had offered $400,000 to settle the claims. Seymour was quite surprised and asked for my opinion. I recommended against taking the offer: I said I thought Sewell had no credible explanation for firing him, that it clearly was based on Seymour's age. More significantly, in my opinion, was Mr. Sewell himself; his video deposition revealed him as a nasty, arbitrary, anti-labor, Christian hypocrite, with no credible explanation for firing Seymour, and expressing false concerns for Seymour's welfare. I knew San Francisco jurors would hate him and a large punitive damage award, in addition to back pay and emotional distress damages, was possible. Seymour listened to what I had to say, then asked me to call back in twenty minutes.

Twenty minutes later, I called back and Seymour's doctor and wife got on the phone. The doctor told me that the stress of a trial could kill Seymour, and strongly advised against a trial; Seymour's wife got on the line and tearfully said, "You have to settle the case, Guy." Then Seymour said, with disappointment and apology in his voice, "I hate to disappoint you, Guy, but I think I need to do what my doctor says." Of course, the reality was that Seymour never had made more than $25,000 a year and the settlement would be far more than that and would allow him to retire. I went back into court, told Bill Bush and Judge Lynch that my client would take the offer, then groused that I would have killed Sewell in trial. Of course, taking the offer was the right decision for Seymour (who went on to have a nice retirement and—in fact—play a lot of golf).

THROUGHOUT MY LEGAL CAREER, I represented plaintiffs in employment cases. However, on one occasion, I represented the defendant in an employment case. The circumstances that caused me to do so were unusual.

Mother Jones magazine had fired their Editor in Chief, Michael Moore, and then sought me out for legal representation. *Mother Jones*, a left-wing magazine headquartered in San Francisco that I read and supported, was being savaged by a few left-wing journalists for the termination of Moore. I was approached by Adam Hochschild, a co-founder of the magazine, and Don Hazen, its publisher, who explained to me that hiring Moore had been a terrible mistake and the magazine had had no choice but to fire him. I told Don and Adam, "You currently are being represented by Pillsbury, Madison & Sutro, who will do a good job, why do you need me?" Their answer was: "Pillsbury is a good firm, but it is a corporate defense firm. We would be criticized among some liberals and progressives if we used a large corporate defense firm to represent us. You have the reputation as a strong attorney, but also as a plaintiff's attorney with very progressive politics. Your reputation is more consistent with *Mother Jones*' politics." As I was to learn, criticism of *Mother Jones*' firing of Moore by some left-wing critics, particularly Alexander Cockburn, had exasperated those at the magazine and raised the stakes in the case. It was important for *Mother Jones* not only to avoid getting tagged with a big jury verdict or settlement, but also to demonstrate to their readers and the public that the firing of Moore was justified.

I pondered their request, then said, "I would be willing to represent *Mother Jones* on one condition." "What is that condition?"

asked Adam. "If I investigated the case and determined that the termination of Moore was wrong or unfair, I would have to have the authority to settle the case, even if you disagreed with my assessment. Can you accept that condition?" I asked. "Absolutely. If we've done something wrong, we will admit it." I agreed to represent *Mother Jones* magazine and began my investigation.

I told Don and Adam I first wanted to speak privately with Deirdre English, the editor Michael Moore had replaced, and the *Mother Jones* department heads who Moore had directly worked with. Deirdre was the first person I spoke with.

Deirdre, an attractive, very articulate woman in her early 40s, had been the *Mother Jones* Editor in Chief for nearly six years. She explained that she had worked very hard at *Mother Jones* and needed a break from the pressure of putting out a monthly magazine. She had immensely enjoyed her tenure as Editor, thought her staff was hard working, supportive and competent, and was sad to leave. She had participated in the selection process that settled on Moore and had voted in favor of hiring him, but she had some reservations about his appointment. On the plus side, she said that Moore had founded and published a gritty underground newspaper in Flint, Michigan that emphasized working-class issues. She and others liked his politics and the liveliness of the Flint paper. Moore's perspective fit nicely with the magazine's desire to reflect the interests and concerns of working-class people, and Adam, in particular, liked Moore's political perspective, and pushed for his hire.

Deirdre's doubts about Moore concerned his ability to handle interpersonal relations. She said he had been very clumsy and antagonistic dealing with her and other *Mother Jones'* staffers. She had wanted to help and support Michael in making the transition, but Michael resented her help and resented also the affection and loyalty the staff showed her. Instead of interpreting staff affection for her as a natural and admirable response to someone they had worked with for some years, Moore acted like it was a threat to him. Moore was moving from a small, local paper, with only a few part-time staffers, to a national magazine with nearly one hundred employees. He had much to learn in making the transition, yet he cut himself off from Deirdre, the person who could most assist him in learning the responsibilities of his new job. Moore also came to *Mother Jones* with the attitude that he was the savior of a floundering magazine, that his vision and perspective represented a fundamental departure from what the magazine had been doing, and that everyone had to learn to do things "the way we did it in Flint."

Other *Mother Jones'* staffers painted the same picture: Moore was egotistical, insecure, suspicious of anyone who had been close to Deirdre, non-collaborative, and unwilling or incapable of listening to or accepting advice from others. He was in over his head running a national magazine, yet he became increasingly isolated from the people who wanted to help him. Everyone admired and supported his working-class politics, but all agreed the magazine had no choice but to replace him. With that as background, I noticed Michael's deposition.

Michael appeared in my office with his attorney, Dan Siegel. I knew Dan extremely well. Dan and I had gone to law school together, had both been active in the National Lawyer's Guild chapter in law school, and we had shared a house near campus during my third year of law school, with Dan and his wife living in the upstairs flat, and Jeanine and me in the ground-floor flat. Dan also had been Student Body President at the University of California during the People's Park protests. Dan was a friend and I had a lot of respect for him.

Michael showed up dressed in baggy jeans, worn tennis shoes, a shirt hanging out of his jeans, and a baseball cap cocked at an angle on his head. I think this probably was his "working-class hero" outfit, but he certainly didn't look like an editor of a national magazine. Michael sat down, turned sideways, crossed his legs, and gave the appearance of complete indifference. I began to ask questions and I could see he was trying hard to impress me with his wit and charm. He often was funny, and he had a bit of roguish Irish charm, but he was doing a terrible job of making a case for himself and his tenure as Editor at *Mother Jones*. When he couldn't be comedic with

top: Guy (right) with father, sister, and mother, 1961
bottom: as legal services attorney in Colorado, 1969

top: with partner Charles Farnsworth in front of law office in East Oakland, 1972; bottom: with Farnsworth and Jeff Brand (center), and staff, 1975

Insurer Will Pay Tens of Millions In Sex Bias Suit

Women and State Farm Settle a Complaint

By KATHERINE BISHOP
Special to The New York Times

SAN FRANCISCO, Jan. 19 — In a multimillion dollar settlement, the State Farm Insurance Company has agreed to pay damages and back pay to women who were refused jobs as insurance sales agents in California over a 13-year period.

Wilda Tipton, left, and Muriel E. Kraszewski, with their lawyer, Guy T. Saperstein, at a news conference yesterday. The women will receive the maximum award from State Farm Insurance to settle their suit.

Associated Press

top: front-page article in *The New York Times* announcing the State Farm settlement, January 20, 1988; bottom: interior photo with plaintiffs Wilda Tipton and Muriel Kraszewski.

top: with wife Jeanine, Hillary Clinton, and Senator Barbara Boxer, 1998; bottom: with family Jacobus, Jeanine, and Leon.

an answer, he gave his responses little thought or attention. He was full of bluster, but very short on information or explanations defending his work performance and his relations with staff at the magazine. I deposed him for three days, and while he was one of the most entertaining witnesses I had ever deposed, he also was one of the worst. I viewed him as a person some jurors might like, whose arrogance would repel others—and determined that virtually none would accept his thinly-explained version of events when his testimony was arrayed against the testimony of many conscientious co-workers who liked Michael but found him hopelessly ill-suited to running an organization. The very qualities that Michael liked so much about himself—his iconoclastic rebelliousness, his obvious disdain for the opinions of others, his quick wit at the expense of thoughtful explanations—would sink him in front of a jury. I viewed him as kind of a big, overgrown kid—smart and articulate, but insecure and emotionally immature. I even felt some sympathy for him being thrown into a job he clearly was not ready to handle. But, of course, he had sought the job and talked his way into it. I told Don and Adam, "Don't offer anything. I'll defense this case. You will get the vindication you seek from your left-wing critics."

Michael's deposition was not complete and he had to return a couple of months later for a fourth and fifth day of questioning. As he sat down to be re-sworn as a witness, he didn't look good. I began asking questions about his allegations of emotional distress. He previously had testified that his termination had caused him emotional distress, which, if proven, might entitle him to recover damages. So I asked him if he was feeling OK. He answered, "No." I asked him if he was still suffering symptoms of emotional distress, and he said, "Yes." I asked him when he most recently had experienced symptoms of distress, and he said, "Early this morning." "Would you please explain what happened?" I asked. "I wasn't able to sleep last night. I woke up many times and I woke up at 3 a.m. nauseous and with a bad case of the runs," he testified. "Is this condition related to your termination at *Mother Jones*," I asked. "Yes," he answered. "How is your nausea and diarrhea related to your lawsuit?" I asked. "My nausea and diarrhea were caused by the prospect of coming here and facing you for a fourth day," offered Moore. "Thank you, Michael," I said, "you're the first witness this year who has admitted I made him shit in his pants!"

The case was called to trial in San Francisco Superior Court a year later. Before sending us out to a trial department, the Master Calendar judge sent us to Judge Stuart Pollak for settlement negotiations. Before any discussions could begin, I announced to Judge Pollak, "My client will not offer a cent. This is not negotiable, so there's no purpose to be served by me being here. I'm leaving so I can work on my opening statement. If you can get some money out of the insurance company, that's OK, but my client won't pay anything." I got up to leave, and Judge Pollak said, "I've never seen this happen before. I've never seen anyone walk out like this!" I said, "I'm sorry. I'm not trying to be rude, but I'm leaving," and I left. An hour later, Judge Pollak came out of chambers, walked over to me and said, "I've got some money from the insurance company. I think I can settle this case if *Mother Jones* will kick in $10,000." I replied, "No." "$5,000?" asked the judge. "No," I replied again.

In the end, the magazine's insurance company came up with $58,000, and the case settled without *Mother Jones* contributing a cent. Michael used his share of this amount as seed money for his film, *Roger and Me*, concerning his futile efforts to talk to the CEO of General Motors about the effect GM layoffs were having on Michael's hometown of Flint. It was a terrific little film, which Michael reputedly sold for $3 million, and he has gone on to have an important career as a muckraking producer of iconoclastic television shows and the great film documentary *Bowling for Columbine*. I'm glad he found a way to use his talents so productively.

I CONTINUED TO REPRESENT INDIVIDUALS IN WRONGFUL termination and discrimination cases for many years. By the mid-1980s, I had become the Co-editor of, and written three chapters in, the leading book on wrongful termination cases in California, *Wrongful Employment Termination Practice*, published by California Continuing Education of the Bar, and regularly was representing high-level corporate executives, including corporate CEO's and General Counsel, as well as individuals complaining of race, sex and age discrimination in employment and a lot of sexual harassment cases. Many of my best cases were referred to me by judges and employment defense attorneys, which I interpreted as professional compliments. I received a number of complaints from one of my female law associates about representing white male executives in wrongful termination and age discrimination cases. She said, "I came to work here because I wanted to represent women and lesbians in civil rights cases, and I find myself spending some of my time doing work for white males." "That's the difference between you and me," I told her, "You want to represent certain categories of people. I'm willing to represent anyone who gets pushed around unfairly."

By the mid-1980s, I was receiving over 100 new case referrals every month and these individual cases had become the most lucrative part of my law practice. But as much as I enjoyed them, and despite the amount of money I was making doing them, I decided to stop accepting them. A strong plaintiff employment bar was emerging in California, as many attorneys were attracted to the large settlement and verdicts that were being obtained in such cases. These attorneys, many from the personal injury bar, were willing to front the costs and take the risks of litigating individual cases, but they were not doing class actions. They didn't know how to litigate class actions and they didn't want to front costs which often were in the millions, accept delays that often ran many years, or risk tens of thousands of hours of work on one class action case. These lawyers were doing a good job prosecuting individual cases, so I was no longer needed. I felt that the large class actions that others avoided were what my firm should be doing. Those were the cases where I could have the most impact and those were cases that might not be prosecuted if I didn't take them.

People used to ask me, "What type of law practice do you have?" I would respond, "I do the cases that no one else wants." It sounded glib and facetious, but it was the truth.

7

Taking on Two Insurance Giants

"Work like you don't need the money.
Love like you've never been hurt.
Dance like nobody's watching."

—Satchel Paige

WHILE THE FIREMAN'S FUND CASE was still in progress, I was presented with sex discrimination allegations against the largest life insurance company in the world (Prudential Insurance Company of America) and the largest casualty insurance company in the world (State Farm Insurance Companies). One would be resolved eleven months after the complaint was filed; the other would become the most heavily fought employment discrimination case ever, would last sixteen years (twenty-three years, including monitoring of an affirmative action order), and result in the then-largest monetary recovery in a civil rights case in American history.

Murray v. Prudential Insurance Company

The case against Prudential began when I received a phone call from Madelyn Murray. Ms. Murray, a black woman, had applied to become a Prudential sales agent, but had been rejected. I immediately flew Ms. Murray up to my office in Oakland to discuss her complaints against Prudential. Before Ms. Murray's appointment, I went to the telephone company's main office in Oakland and reviewed the yellow pages listing of Prudential sales agents in the most populated cities in California and found very few female names.

I was very impressed with Ms. Murray personally and by her story. She was well educated, extremely attractive in appearance, professional in demeanor, and very well dressed. She spoke clearly and articulately, and appeared to me to be someone who would represent any company well. I couldn't imagine why Prudential would not hire her. Knowing that I would want to file an across-the-board case against Prudential alleging race and sex discrimination both in sales and operations jobs, I asked Ms. Murray if she knew of other women or blacks who may have suffered employment discrimination by Prudential. She said she did and a few days later she phoned to identify others and describe their complaints. I asked her to find out when it would be convenient for all of them to meet with me and told her I would fly to Los Angeles to speak with them.

Feeling confident I was going to pursue this case, and knowing I would need local counsel in Los Angeles, I collected the names of attorneys in Southern California reputed to do Title VII cases, made appointments with them, and flew to Los Angeles for two days of interviewing attorneys. My search for local counsel was pretty dispiriting; most of the employment attorneys I spoke with knew nothing about employment class actions and one used class action allegations merely as a bargaining chip to try to leverage damages for his individual clients. I was disgusted by this tactic, as it fundamentally violated the tenets of a class action brought pursuant to Rule 23 of the Federal Rules of Civil Procedure. One of the essential requirements of Rule 23 was that the plaintiff be an "adequate representative" of the class. Among other things, this requires the class representative/plaintiff to prosecute the interests of the class as vigorously and honestly as she/he prosecutes his/her individual interests. What this attorney told me was that he regularly would make sham class allegations solely for the purpose of raising the potential stakes for the defendant company, then agree to dismiss the class allegations with no relief for the class in trade for money for his individual client. I told this attorney, who described this *modus operandi* with great pride, that he was a disgrace to the class action bar and that tactics like his would give all serious class actions, and class action attorneys, a bad name. He showed no remorse, commenting weakly, "I guess I won't be working on the Prudential case with you."

The last attorney I was scheduled to speak to in Los Angeles was A. Thomas Hunt. Meeting Tom was a joy and a revelation. Tom had been litigating Title VII cases since his graduation in 1965 from Harvard Law School, first with the Civil Rights division of the United States Department of Justice, and then with the Center for Law in the Public Interest (CLIPI), which, coincedentally, had been founded by three law school classmates of mine, John Phillips, Brent Rushforth, and Stuart Tobisman. Tom had been litigating major Title VII cases all his career; while at CLIPI Tom almost single-handedly had brought racial integration to the Los Angeles Police Department, Fire Department, and Department of Water & Power with his class action Title VII lawsuits. These were tough cases, and I knew I was talking to a veteran of Title VII battles and a very shrewd lawyer. His list of accomplishments was long, perhaps as long and important as any Title VII attorney in the country. He knew the federal judges in the Central District of California, as well as the employment attorneys in the major Los Angeles law firms. Talking with Tom about the Prudential case, and other cases each of us had litigated, was fun and illuminating. I became a regular guest at Tom's house on my many trips to Los Angeles and we would talk late into the night about our cases.. Tom, who had adopted two children, including an African-American boy, lived and breathed discrimination cases; prosecuting them was his life passion and purpose.

Despite Tom's greater experience, I insisted that I be lead counsel in the case against Prudential, which would give me ultimate authority over litigation and settlement strategy. I took this position because the clients were mine and because I anticipated a disagreement might arise between Tom and me regarding the settlement of the case. Tom believed that the purpose of Title VII was to integrate the workforce, and regularly would waive damages in favor of strong hiring and promotion orders. While I agreed that the predominant purpose of Title VII was to get jobs for women and minorities, I was beginning to rethink damage waivers. Tom, who never before had accepted second-chair status in a Title VII class action, reluctantly agreed to my terms, perhaps because of the friendship we were developing or perhaps in the belief that ultimately I would agree with him on all important questions of strategy and settlement.

From information contained in Madelyn Murray's EEOC investigation file, I determined that Steve Tallent and Jack Halgren, both from the mega-firm Gibson, Dunn & Crutcher, would be representing Prudential. As a courtesy, I called Steve to introduce myself and to tell him of my intention to file a Title VII class action against Prudential encompassing its eleven-state Western Region. Steve tried to talk me out of filing any lawsuit until we had explored settlement possibilities. I told Steve I wanted to have a lawsuit on file so that Prudential would know that I was serious about this case and so that I could pursue formal discovery, if necessary. I also told Steve I considered my case to be extraordinarily strong, as the EEOC investigation files, and my own investigation, had revealed a substantial underrepresentation of blacks and women in nearly all job categories. Nevertheless, I agreed to meet with Steve before filing the case.

I met with Steve twice before the lawsuit was filed. The first meeting was in his corner-suite office, high above Century City. I never had met Steve before, and he didn't fit the usual description of a corporate defense attorney. He had a full beard, wore professorial reading glasses, wore a cardigan sweater with no tie, and was puffing contentedly on a pipe. He looked more like a university professor than trial attorney, and I thought I might be in Berkeley, not on the 35th floor of a steel and glass Century City office tower.

Steve was cordial, relaxed, erudite, and a bit full of himself. He began explaining his background in employment cases, which was extensive, and proceeded to explain what a liberal he was. "I will not accept a case without authority to settle it, if I think a violation of the law has occurred. I will not defend a company that has discriminated and I have held to this position even when it meant losing a client. We don't like to lose clients, but Gibson Dunn is so big, and our services are in such demand, we can afford to stand on our principles and lose clients, if necessary," he said. I listened to him tout his principles, and the risks he had taken in adhering to them, for nearly two hours, then he finally paused to let the full gravity of his refined intelligence and liberalism weigh upon me. Instead, I pondered the strength of my case against Prudential and Steve's obvious interest in avoiding litigation. The room was silent for a moment before I said, "Well, Steve, if you want to be a liberal, I guess this is the right case for you to be a liberal." I think this was too much impertinence for Steve, who probably viewed me as more of a student or disciple of his than a worthy adversary, and the meeting ended abruptly.

Our next meeting began at 9 a.m. the day I had told Steve the case would be filed. The express purpose of this meeting was to discuss informal discovery; Steve's purpose, however, was to dissuade me from filing the complaint. Prior to this meeting, I had sent Steve copies of my interrogatories and requests for documents which identified the type of computer-readable personnel information I needed to evaluate—and, ultimately, to prove—the case. Taking my discovery requests as the first agenda item, Steve and Jack launched into a very long and complicated explanation of Prudential's data-retrieval capabilities. The thesis of this argument essentially was, (1) Prudential had the most sophisticated and complicated computer equipment known to mankind; (2) Prudential maintained more information in its computerized database than any company in the world; and (3) the equipment was so complicated and the database so huge, Prudential would not be able to retrieve the personnel data that I was seeking. I sat there wondering what farm they thought I just finished pitching hay and shoveling cowshit at. At the end of this absurd presentation, I said, "I don't care how simple or complicated your data retrieval system is. The purpose of having such a system was to permit the retrieval of information. I have little doubt Prudential's computer people know how to do it and that my computer people will figure out a way to do it also. In the meantime, I'm off to file my lawsuit." At that, Tom and I left their office, drove to the Clerk's Office, filed our lawsuit against Prudential, alleging a pattern and practice of race and sex discrimination, and issued a press release to the media.

Despite the initial obfuscations and self-congratulations by the Gibson Dunn lawyers, and my impertinent responses, Tallent and Halgren turned out to be two of the smartest, most honest, and most creative lawyers I've ever had on the other side of a case. In the end, they helped achieve an honorable settlement and performed great service for their client.

Shortly after the complaint was filed, I formally served Prudential with a set of computer interrogatories and requests for documents explaining the personnel database and how to retrieve information. Tallent answered the formal discovery requests, but instead of providing me with copies of Prudential's personnel data tapes, he proposed that we commence a process to settle the case in which we would request, and Prudential would provide, all information reasonably necessary for Tom and me to evaluate the liability issues and propose specific remedies for discriminatory employment patterns. If we weren't satisfied with the computer reports Prudential would give us in response to our questions, we would retain the right to seek production of Prudential's data tapes through formal discovery. Tom and I found this proposal acceptable, as it would avoid the delay caused by technical problems in trying to read and understand someone else's data system, and it would save us the cost of having our computer experts run a huge amount of data—a cost I estimated would be at least $100,000 just for preliminary evaluation. The system proposed by Tallent proved to be workable; Prudential promptly produced computer reports in response to our questions over the course of several months and the data we were being provided revealed an extensive pattern of hiring and promoting women and minorities at rates that were significantly below the availability of women and minorities for specific jobs and career paths.

While not conceding liability, Tallent and Halgren approached the data, and the conclusions Tom and I were making, realistically, and soon the discussion turned to appropriate remedies. Tom and I proposed goals and timetables for increased hiring and promotion of women and minorities, for a period of five years, along with specific damages for the named plaintiffs and a modest damage fund for identifiable victims of discrimination. Tallent and Halgren were surprised at the damage fund demand, as it had been Tom's practice to waive class damages when adequate injunctive (i.e., remedial) relief was obtained. I explained that this demand was coming from me, that Tom did not agree with me, but, as lead counsel, it was my call and my demand and the case would not settle without it.

Tallent and Halgren accepted the concept of classwide goals and timetables, but there was much disagreement about what the appropriate goals should be—as there is in every negotiation of a Title VII consent decree. Frequently in a hiring discrimination case, the flow of applications by women and minorities to the defendant company will be depressed by the knowledge by women and minorities that the company rarely, or sometimes never, hires anyone other than white males for entry-level jobs—particularly sales and entry-level management positions. In such cases, the company argues that women and minorities are "not interested and available" for these jobs—as evidenced by their low applicant flow! The Title VII plaintiff attorney then must show that women and minorities were interested and available and would have applied had they not been deterred by the company's reputation and/or active discrimination. Proof of "availability" often comes from civilian labor force data found in the ten-year census, and updated census surveys.

For some of the entry-level jobs of Prudential, an unusual "availability" issue was presented. For several years, Prudential's job recruitment efforts had included the use of mobile personnel offices which had been located in South Central Los Angeles—an area of high black population. This commendable recruitment effort—indeed, a recruitment effort that was unique in the Los Angeles region—had resulted in an "applicant flow" of blacks that was, in some respects, higher than true availability, in that many blacks without relevant qualifications had applied for jobs. In setting goals, exclusive reliance on the percentage of black applications, without regard for at least the minimum qualifications of the job applied for, would not accurately measure "qualified availability" and would, in effect, penalize Prudential for recruitment efforts that were extraordinary. Setting goals thus required review of many actual job applications, as well as reliance on civilian labor force data.

The largest single category of entry-level jobs at Prudential, other than clerical, was the sales agent position. Prudential neither hired nor retained many women or minority sales agents—as then was common in the insurance industry—and I felt confident that it could be proven that women and minorities were interested in sales jobs. But Prudential's personnel data history revealed a serious problem in the sales job—to wit, extremely high turnover. In order to keep one new sales agent on the job for two years, *six* agents had to be hired! I knew I was in a position to force Prudential to hire women agents, but I didn't want just to place them in this fast-moving revolving door, only to be thrown out on the sidewalk before they could establish themselves as successful agents. I worried further that the already high turnover rate for male agents would be even higher for women due to the fact that new agents were trained by male agency managers in an apprenticeship environment. These male agency managers, feeling that women or minorities who couldn't sell insurance were being forced on him by an unwanted court order, would passively resist the order, or worse, decide that their own incomes, which derived in part from the sales of the agents under his supervision, would decrease as the direct result of hiring unqualified women and minorities. We had to figure out a way to overcome the expected resistance by Prudential agency managers to a hiring order. Hiring women and minority agents, just to watch them rapidly leave, would do neither Prudential nor the class of women and minorities I represented any good.

Steve Tallent saw the same problem, but he bettered me by coming up with the solution: provide cash incentives for the agency managers to *retain* newly hired, successful female and minority agents. Understanding that agency managers largely were driven by financial considerations, Steve proposed that financial incentives be created at levels sufficient to encourage agency managers to do the right thing—hire, train and retain successful female and minority agents.

Steve recognized that neither Prudential nor I had any interest in hiring and retaining unsuccessful agents, nor did we want to encourage agency managers to do so. So the economic incentives we designed kicked in when a woman or minority agent sold insurance at 100% of the average sales of new agents and increased proportionately with increased sales performance. Thus, if an agency manager hired and trained a woman or minority agent, and after one year that agent was selling at 100% of the average of new agents, the agency manager received a $2,000 bonus. If the female or minority agent were selling at 120% of the average, the agency manager's bonus would be $2,400; if sales were 200% of the average, the bonus would rise to $4,000 per year. The bonus system would stay in place for the full two-year training program, thus offering agency managers the potential of making $4–8,000 in bonuses for hiring and retaining each successful female and minority agent. Since agency managers typically trained 2–4 new agents every two years, the total bonus available to each agency manager could be as high as $16,000 per year, or $32,000 over two years.

If the system worked, everyone would benefit. My clients would get hired, properly trained, and would become successful agents. Agency managers would be rewarded for their good training and encouragement, and Prudential would cut down the high turnover rate of agents—which would save money on recruitment and training—and obtain more successful insurance agents. It was a win-

win-win solution.

The plan was radical for an affirmative action decree in that it provided financial incentives to the men who had created the problem in the first place to change their behavior. Neither Steve nor I ever had seen such incentives used in a Title VII consent decree— and it required some selling to Prudential. Steve went back to Prudential's headquarters in Newark, New Jersey, and spent two weeks talking to everyone with authority to approve our proposal. In the end, he obtained approval and one of the most innovative hiring decrees I've ever seen was submitted to, and approved by, the Court.

In addition to establishing hiring and promotion goals in most job positions in Prudential's western region, two new recruitment programs were established and $400,000 was set aside for distribution to class members for past discrimination. A formula-based distribution system was established, to be administered by a young attorney in Tom's office on behalf of plaintiffs and by Jack Halgren on behalf of Prudential. The money was distributed promptly and with little conflict. In my opinion, Steve Tallent and Jack Halgren, by realistically assessing the problems Prudential would have in litigation, and being willing to negotiate a prompt and reasonable solution to the problem of the underhiring of women and minorities, did an absolutely fabulous job of representing Prudential's interests and avoiding what was a potentially much costlier legal problem.

Just how good a job Tallent and Halgren did representing Prudential can be fully appreciated when contrasted with a similar case I had against State Farm Insurance Companies.

Thus begins my twenty-year saga with State Farm.

Kraszewski v. State Farm Insurance Companies

As a result of my highly-publicized litigation with Fireman's Fund Insurance Company and Prudential Insurance Company, I was beginning to develop a reputation as a civil rights lawyer willing to take on large companies. In a feature article about insurance and employment discrimination, the *San Francisco Examiner* described me as "the Ralph Nader of the insurance industry." That characterization was more generous than accurate, but it certainly did not hurt my flow of business. I began to see a steady stream of new clients with complaints about employment discrimination. It would have been easy just to select my cases from the clients who came to me, but I chose a different path.

If the cases I chose to litigate were determined by the complaints I listened to in my office from potential clients, I might have prosecuted a number of cases against the large General Motors assembly plant located in nearby Fremont, as I received a steady flow of black GM workers with race discrimination complaints. I knew that one of the reasons I was seeing so many complaints from black workers at GM was that, unlike many other employers, GM had hired a lot of black workers. Further, these workers were backed up by a strong union, the United Auto Workers, and were less afraid and more willing to prosecute complaints against their employer than workers in many other companies. I'm certain that many of the individual complaints by the GM workers of on-the-job discrimination were valid, but I was more interested in suing companies that excluded women and minorities altogether. Those were the kind of cases that would be most provable and where I could have the greatest impact in promoting equal employment opportunities.

During the prosecution of my case against Fireman's Fund, I learned much about the insurance industry. Among other things, I learned who the largest companies were, which companies paid the most, and which companies had reputations for not hiring women and minorities. Among those companies, State Farm was by far the biggest, it paid the most, and it had one of the worst reputations for hiring women and minorities. I put State Farm at the top of my list of companies to target for a Title VII class action.

I asked the plaintiffs in my Fireman's Fund and Prudential cases if they ever had had problems with State Farm, and one of my Prudential plaintiffs, Inga Lisa McDaniel, told me about her unsuccessful efforts to get hired as a State Farm agent many years earlier. Her claims extended beyond the statute of limitations, and were not actionable, but I asked her if anyone else she knew had had similar employment problems with State Farm. Inga told me that someone she knew, Daisy O. Jackson, had been trying for years to become a State Farm agent without success. I asked Inga to talk to Daisy and tell her of my interest in State Farm.

Within days, Daisy was in my office telling me the first specific story of discrimination by State Farm I ever heard, and, in many respects, the most amazing story of discrimination at State Farm I ever was to hear, about how she had been doing 100% of the work of a State Farm agent, yet couldn't get hired as an agent by them. Daisy was a woman close to 60 years old, originally from Oklahoma, plainly dressed, wearing no make-up, with a powerful story to tell. In fact, it was so powerful, I wasn't sure I should believe all of it. But, as later events would prove, every single thing she told me was true.

Daisy told me she had worked for 2½ years as a "solicitor" in a State Farm agency in Palo Alto. Daisy said she had done all the insurance selling at the agency, since the sales agent, Ed Borgia, was never around. Ed, she said, "would come into the office once a month for two to three hours on a Sunday to look over the books and write checks. That's the only time we ever saw him." I asked her why Ed didn't come into the office, and Daisy told me, "He's also a lawyer and has a law practice in San Jose." I asked her if Ed's State Farm agency had been successful and she said, "Yes, it's one of the most successful agencies in the Peninsula. The agency even won State Farm awards for high sales—based entirely on *my* sales." I asked her what Ed had paid her and Lorraine, the office manager, and what Ed made from the agency last year. Daisy told me she and Lorraine each had been paid about $15,000, while Ed had made over $60,000 a year, for his two- to three-hours-a-month commitment.

Daisy said she had tried repeatedly to become a State Farm agent. She had talked to State Farm Agency Manager Don Wilson about the possibility of becoming a State Farm agent. He told her she was better off remaining a secretary in Borgia's office, that he didn't want to take a good secretary away from an agent, and that "State Farm is not hiring women agents." Later that year, George Seifert, an agent in Don Wilson's district, died, creating a vacant agency position nearby. Agency Manager Wilson never told Daisy that he intended to fill this vacancy with a new agent ("trainee agent"), and, instead, offered the job to his son, Roger, who was then living out of state, had no community contacts in the area, and had to be persuaded to return to California.

In 1975, Daisy learned that State Farm was considering promoting agent Borgia to a position as Agency Manager—despite the fact that he had not run his agency, or sold insurance, for over two years. Daisy asked Borgia if she would be able to take over the agency, as most of the agency's clients has been dealing with her for over two years and thought she was the agent anyway, but Borgia told her that would not be possible because she needed a college degree, State Farm frowned upon making secretaries agents, and that it was against State Farm's policy to hire women agents because women could not do the job—despite the obvious fact that Daisy had been doing the agent job, successfully, for over two years. Borgia told her that "insurance is like law and medicine, no one wants to talk to a woman," ignoring the obvious fact that clients had been talking to her about insurance for years.

Despite this discouragement, Daisy persisted in her attempts to become a State Farm agent, and finally was permitted to take the Aptitude Index Battery ("AIB") of tests, which was one of the first steps in the application process for trainee agents. She scored well on the tests, and, to Ed Borgia's credit, she received a rare recommendation from him:

> "Daisy has a unique gift for selling and gaining the confidence of people. Her ability to work is awesome… I believe Daisy has the potential of becoming the greatest female agent in the Company and one of the best agents in any category."
> (Ed Borgia letter to State Farm, dated 1/5/76).

In Spring 1976, three years after she first sought a State Farm agent position, Daisy Jackson was appointed a trainee agent. However, even at that point she was subjected to egregious discrimination. It was State Farm's normal practice to start their trainee agents with a "book" of existing insurance accounts—normally 300 to 700 policies, and sometimes as many as 2,000 existing insurance policies—so that trainee agents did not start "cold," and, instead, could use the existing accounts as a base in building their new agencies. Doing this with Daisy made even more sense than usual, as she had been selling to, and servicing, all of Ed Borgia's accounts for over two years. Since Borgia was leaving his agency to become a State Farm Agency Manager, what could be more obvious than to give Daisy all or part of his accounts, as well as his agency office so that the clients would be able to continue dealing with the same person they had been dealing with for the past 2½ years?

While the logic and fairness of this should have been obvious to anyone, even State Farm, that is not how State Farm decided to treat Daisy. Instead of giving her all, or at least part, of the policies Daisy had worked on for 2½ years at the Borgia agency, State Farm divided the Borgia agency accounts among three male trainee agents, and gave Daisy precisely nothing. Instead of permitting her to continue to work in the Borgia agency office (which Borgia had vacated), where State Farm clients knew to find Daisy, they put two male trainee agents in that office and assigned Daisy to the worst section of Palo Alto to begin her agency from scratch with no accounts. Nevertheless, despite the gross unfairness of State Farm's treatment of her, Daisy didn't complain. She told me, "Even starting an agency from scratch in a bad neighborhood didn't discourage me because I knew I could sell insurance, and, while it might take longer, my agency would be successful."

One thing Daisy had not factored into this equation was illness. Six weeks after being appointed a trainee agent, on the way home from an agent training class, she suffered a pulmonary embolism (blood clot) in her lung. The embolism destroyed one half of a lung, left her in a coma for a week, and nearly killed her. She remained in the hospital for two weeks, when, against doctor's orders, she returned to work. She "feared that not returning to work would jeopardize my position as a trainee agent." She worked for two weeks, then suffered another pulmonary embolism, causing another one week hospital stay. Once again, against her doctor's orders, she returned to work, fearing that more time off the job would give State Farm an excuse to fire her.

Her fears were well founded. As soon as Daisy returned from her second hospitalization, she was told by Agency Manager Borgia that she would be terminated in ninety days unless her sales production increased, despite her weakened condition. State Farm, however, didn't give Daisy ninety days; she was terminated only thirty days after the ninety-day probation period began. Daisy had been ill or in he hospital for 4½ months of her 6 months as a trainee agent. Later, in formal discovery, both Agency Manager Borgia and Agency Director Butler testified that they did not take her illness into account in evaluating her sales performance and terminating her. Her 2½ years of exemplary sales performance at the Borgia agency, and even Borgia's rave review ("Daisy has a unique gift for selling… [She] has the potential for becoming the greatest female agent in the Company and one of the best agents in any category") were apparently forgotten.

This did not mean, however, that Borgia and Butler were simply harsh and unsympathetic men. Indeed, they had a softer side—but this soft side evidently was reserved for men. As the case progressed, I was to learn in discovery that at the same time Daisy was being terminated, one of the male trainee agents in the Palo Alto area who had received several hundred of Ed Borgia's active policies was also falling short of sales expectations due to illness.

Michael Bonasera's sales performance before he became ill was 30 to 62% below the "minimum expected" level for a State Farm trainee agent four of his first five months and his life insurance sales was "one of the lowest we've experienced for a new trainee," according to his agency manager. He was off work for four months due to illness, then returned for two months, during which his sales were off 18–35%. Even at this point—with seven months of grossly unsatisfactory sales—his agency manager still did not consider terminating him. "I wanted to be absolutely sure before terminating him," his manager testified. Only after another month of sales that was 39% short of minimum was Bonasera put on ninety-day probation. Bonasera, however, was given nine *months* of probation before his continuing low sales caused State Farm to give up on him. Bonasera had been given a healthy fifteen months to prove his sales abilities (nineteen total months); Daisy had had six healthy weeks to sell before her hospitalization and illness streak, and her 2½ years successfully selling State Farm insurance were ignored. After her termination by State Farm, Daisy was hired as a sales agent by Farmers Insurance and was highly successful.

After listening to Daisy's experiences with State Farm, I decided to do some research. I went to the telephone company's main office in Oakland, and asked to see copies of the Yellow Pages for every city and county in California. They politely directed me to a room, where a clerk delivered approximately one hundred phone books. With each, I turned to the "Insurance" section, and looked for the names of agents listed under "State Farm Insurance." Of the approximately 1,500 State Farm agents, only five or six had names that appeared to be female. State Farm's sales force was more than 99% male. That wasn't an accident and Daisy Jackson's encounter with State Farm's gender discrimination was not an aberration. Sex discrimination in sales jobs was State Farm's normal mode of operation.

I needed no more convincing that this was a case I wanted to act on, but I also knew I wanted to have a plaintiff for each of State Farm's three California regions. I filed individual and classwide charges of sex discrimination on behalf of Daisy with the U. S. Equal Employment Opportunity Commission (EEOC) and immediately called the Regional Director of their San Francisco office, Sherry Gendleman. I told Sherry I had filed classwide allegations of sex discrimination in sales jobs by State Farm, that I intended to file a Title VII class action lawsuit, and that I wanted to know if the EEOC had any other similar charges of sex discrimination against State Farm in California. Sherry said she would find out.

A few days later, I received a phone call from a woman who identified herself as "Muriel Kraszewski." Muriel said she had received a call from someone at the EEOC, who told her about the charges I had filed against State Farm and my intention of filing a Title VII lawsuit. She told me she had worked for many years in State Farm offices in Southern California, and had tried repeatedly to become a State Farm agent, but each time was discouraged or rebuffed. In frustration, she had left State Farm and became a Farmers Insurance agent. I asked her how she was doing. "I'm second in sales in my district, out of thirty-five agents," she said. I told her that her experience with State Farm was remarkably similar to Daisy Jackson's and that I would like to meet her as soon as possible. Two days later, Muriel and her husband, Bob, flew to Oakland and were in my office telling me what had happened to her at State Farm.

Muriel, a cheerful, 30-ish woman, had worked in several State Farm agency offices as a secretary, solicitor, and office manager for twelve years. Her job duties had included quoting prices on policies, explaining insurance averages to potential customers, writing insurance policies, soliciting new sales, and selling all lines of State Farm insurance. For three years, 1971–74, Muriel had worked for an agent whose horse-ranch home was more than a two-hour drive away. Muriel said he was in the office infrequently, preferring to stay at his horse ranch rather than sell insurance.

Realizing that she could sell State Farm insurance as well or better than any of the agents she worked for, Muriel made numerous attempts to apply to become a State Farm Trainee Agent. She told State Farm Agency Director Eugene Miller of her interest in becoming a sales agent. Miller told her that state Farm did not hire women agents. She approached State Farm Agency Manager Robert Carver at a training session for State Farm agency employees and expressed her interest in becoming a Trainee Agent. Carver said she was well qualified, but did not offer her the chance to take the agent aptitude test and failed to put her into any agent selection pool. After being rejected by Carver, Muriel told Agency Manager Matt Madison that she wanted to become a State Farm agent, but Madison told her it would be difficult for State Farm to hire a woman because they had no way of protecting women. She contacted Agency Director Don Fullerton, told him she wanted to apply to become a trainee agent, but was not given an agent aptitude test nor permitted to complete an application. She contacted Agency Manager Manny Pirrone, told him of her interest in becoming a State Farm agent, and asked to take the agent aptitude test. Pirrone said he did not have any agent aptitude tests. Later, she received a call from a State Farm Agency Director, who told her that Pirrone would let her take the aptitude test. She took it and passed, but was not offered the opportunity to complete the application process, nor was she put into any agent selection pool.

Still undaunted, Muriel spoke with Agency Director Eugene Miller, who told her that State Farm would not hire her because she did not have a college degree, had not demonstrated an ability to run her own business, and was unwilling to relocate. She replied that many State Farm agents did not have college degrees, that she had demonstrated she could run a State Farm agency, and that State Farm never had offered her a job to relocate to. Miller acknowledged that many State Farm agents did not have college degrees, but claimed it was a new requirement.

Despairing of ever having an opportunity to complete an application, let alone become a State Farm Trainee Agent, Muriel applied to Farmers Insurance Company and was appointed a Farmers sales agent. Since her appointment, she consistently had been one of the top-selling Farmers' agents in the Long Beach area.

I explained to Muriel and Bob that I wanted to file a class action lawsuit against State Farm, which meant that Muriel, as a "class representative," would represent not only her interests, but also the interests of past, present and future women who had been, who continued to be, or who would in the future be interested in becoming State Farm sales agents. As a class representative, she could not settle the case just for herself and that any settlement would have to include remedies for the class of women, not just herself or Daisy. I told her, "I will not settle this case, nor accept any offer of attorneys' fees, until adequate remedies for discrimination against women as a class are obtained. I need your promise that you will not seek to settle your claims unless the class you represent also obtains fair and adequate relief. Can you make that commitment?" "Guy, I don't want anything for myself. I just want to make sure that State Farm never treats another woman like they treated me," said Muriel. I asked Bob how they felt about that, and he responded, "I'm 100% behind Muriel. They didn't treat her fairly and I agree she should do something about it." This would have been a pretty good response from anyone, but I thought it was quite a progressive stance from a Republican couple from Orange County!

Before filing suit, I tried to use the EEOC administrative process to obtain more information about State Farm. The EEOC complied by sending a list of questions to State Farm, but the information provided by State Farm in response was not particularly useful. State Farm took the position that trainee agents were "independent agents," not employees of the company, and therefore that State Farm was not obligated to provide information about the composition of the State Farm salesforce. This response at least identified one defense I was certain to face—that the agents were not "employees" covered by Title VII. I wasn't very worried about this defense, as what I had heard from Daisy and Muriel made it clear that State Farm agency managers and directors completely controlled the recruitment, selection, appointment and training of trainee agents, State Farm provided a monthly subsidy to trainee agents, the agents were permitted to sell only State Farm products, and State Farm retained the right to terminate agents. Thus, it wasn't possible to become an "independent" State Farm agent unless State Farm decided to select, appoint, train and subsidize a person. This complete control over the access to these sales positions would be sufficient to bring the complaints of Daisy, Muriel and the class of women they would seek to represent within Title VII and its prohibition of employment discrimination based on gender.

The EEOC issued Notices of Right to Sue to Daisy on March 2, 1979 and to Muriel on April 29, 1979. On June 1, 1979, I filed a class action lawsuit against State Farm (*Kraszewski v. State Farm General Insurance Company, et al.*) in the United States District Court for the Northern District of California (San Francisco), alleging a pattern and practice of sex discrimination in the recruitment, selection and appointment of State Farm trainee agents in California from 1974, continuing to the present. Along with the lawsuit, I issued a press release to major California newspapers and the news wire services for the purpose of publicizing the lawsuit and, hopefully, notifying women who had experienced discrimination by State Farm about the lawsuit. I was particularly interested in obtaining additional witnesses to State Farm's employment discrimination and in finding a plaintiff to represent State Farm's Central California Region. Muriel had experienced discrimination in State Farm's Southern California Region and Daisy in the Northern California Region, but to avoid the argument that Muriel and Daisy could not represent women in the Central California Region, I might need a woman who had had experiences similar to Muriel and Daisy's somewhere in Central California.

My press release attracted pretty good coverage from the newspapers, and the next day I received a call from a woman named Wilda Tipton, who said she had read an article about the State Farm case in the local edition of the *Los Angeles Times*. She had been employed as a State Farm agency secretary, office manager, and solicitor in the Oxnard–Ventura area for thirteen years, and she told a story of discrimination that was almost identical to Muriel's experiences. The location of the discrimination was within State Farm's Central California and I felt confident the scope of the class would be determined to cover all of California. I immediately filed an EEOC charge of discrimination for Wilda, and intervened her into the lawsuit when the EEOC issued a Notice of Right to Sue for her.

The case was assigned to United States District Judge Charles B. Renfrew, the same federal judge who had presided over my first

Title VII case against Trans International Airlines. Within a month of filing the lawsuit, Judge Renfrew scheduled a Status Conference. I appeared, and Paul J. Laveroni, of Cooley, Godward, Huddleston, Castro & Tatum—a large San Francisco corporate defense firm—appeared on behalf of State Farm. After attorney introductions, Judge Renfrew said, "Mr. Laveroni, I have read the Complaint in this case. I am not prejudging the merits, but if the facts the plaintiffs have alleged are true, and State Farm has hired as few women agents as plaintiffs claim, your client has a serious problem. Now, I got to know Mr. Saperstein in another Title VII case and I know him to be a very reasonable person. I suggest you meet with him as soon as possible and begin to explore the possibility of settling this case."

I was exhilarated at the Judge's comments, both for the personal recommendation and his alertness to the salient facts of the case, but, most importantly, for the strong suggestion that the facts warranted settlement. I thought Laveroni would have to report the Judge's comments to State Farm, and that State Farm would have to reconsider the factual pattern of discrimination that so impressed Renfrew and seriously consider settlement, just as Prudential had considered settlement early. In the hallway outside Judge Renfrew's courtroom, I told Paul that I could see already that the State Farm agency managers predominantly were hiring their friends and relatives as agents, many of whom lacked good credentials for the job. "This may be a great system for the agency managers, because they can hire their friends and sons, but it's a bad personnel system for State Farm. This is a highly attractive job and State Farm should have a competitive hiring system open to all, including women and minorities, that would produce a more highly qualified, and diverse, salesforce. Protecting the agent position as a white-male club for friends and relatives of the agency managers is not in State Farm's interest. Opening this job up to a wider range of a people is a win-win solution for State Farm and my clients." I thought this reasoning was transparently logical and that I was being immensely persuasive. Little did I realize, as I stood talking with Laveroni, that serious settlement discussions would not even begin for eight years, that my law firm would expend nearly 600,000 hours prosecuting the claims of the women, and that it would take thirteen years to resolve the case!

RATHER THAN WAIT FOR TIME-CONSUMING DISCOVERY disputes to be resolved by the Court, I began to notice depositions of State Farm agents and agency managers in an effort to gain a better understanding of the trainee agent job, the qualifications for it, and how agents were hired. Despite some attempted obstruction by defense attorneys, the State Farm witnesses were surprisingly candid and a picture of the job and the hiring process began to emerge clearly.

The position of "trainee agent" was the entry-level sales position at State Farm. During the two-year training period, the trainee agent was a direct employee of State Farm, was trained by State Farm agency managers and received a "stipulated monthly payment," which was a subsidy to support the agent while the agent was getting started. After two years, the trainee agent became a "career agent." The career agent ceased to be an employee and became a "captive" agent, permitted to sell only State Farm products, controlled, rewarded, disciplined, and terminated by State Farm agency managers. The career agents were independent only in the sense that they would set up their own offices and manage their own office expenses.

The qualifications for the job were minimal or non-existent, depending on the agency manager, and were arbitrarily and inconsistently applied. Despite having told Muriel, Daisy and Wilda that a college degree was required, there were, in fact, no minimum education requirements. State Farm had hired many trainee agents without even a high school degree and at least one agent with only an eighth grade education. Similarly, there were no experience requirements. In fact, State Farm preferred to hire agents with no prior insurance sales experience; State Farm wanted to hire agents without pre-established bad habits selling insurance and train them "the State Farm way." There was no minimum investment required; one agent testified that you could start up a State Farm agency with only "a pencil, reverse directory and telephone."

State Farm was, and is, the largest seller of casualty insurance in the world. This was due to many factors, which certainly included the fact that it had good products to sell, provided good service, and had effective television and print advertising. Unlike many insurance companies who had hired unlimited numbers of agents on the theory that the agents can at least sell to their friends and relatives, State Farm limited the number, and protected the geographical areas, of its agents. Thus, its agents, on average, were the most highly compensated in the industry. In 1980, new trainee agents in California netted approximately $17,000 in their first year and $29,000 in their second; career agents netted approximately $80,000, after deducting expenses (approximately $150,000 in current dollars). I thought this was pretty good for a job in which a person could be his or her own boss, have flexible hours of work, or even, as I was learning, work very little. I saw no reason why the job would not be at least equally attractive to women as it had been to men. Indeed, I was fast becoming aware of a pool of women like Muriel, Daisy and Wilda—State Farm agency office managers, secretaries and solicitors—who often were doing much of the work of agents, but at far lower levels of compensation. Like Muriel, Daisy and Wilda, I expected that many of these women had been asking themselves, "Why can't I be an agent and make $80,000 a year?" State Farm itself characterized the agent job as "The Golden Opportunity." Why was this "Golden Opportunity" only open to men?

Although I was obtaining useful information from talking to my three plaintiffs and other women who had had similar negative experiences with State Farm, as well as deposing a few State Farm agents and managers, it was necessary to obtain documents directly from State Farm and obtain their formal responses to a serious of questions ("interrogatories") about the State Farm agent position and why it was a near-exclusive domain for men.

To obtain such information, I submitted a series of interrogatories and requests for documents seeking, among other things, records of all women who had expressed interest in becoming trainee agents, personnel files for the agents State Farm had hired (in order to develop an understanding of the type of qualifications the male agents had when hired), company descriptions of the agent position, recruitment policies and practices, the hiring process, advertisements depicting agents (on the theory that pictures of a company's employees convey a powerful message about the kind of employees that company hires, encouraging people who fit the pictures to apply and discouraging others), earnings information for agents, agency training materials, and all computer-based personnel information about State Farm agents and employees in operations positions. State Farm objected to nearly all discovery I requested, frequently contending that it had no obligation to produce discovery until plaintiffs provided "credible evidence" to support the allegations underlying the discovery requests. United States District Judge Thelton E. Henderson, who took over the case when Judge Renfrew became Deputy Attorney General in the U.S. Department of Justice under President Carter, later would characterize State Farm's objections as "recognizable as an absurdity to anyone even passingly familiar with the American discovery process." Nevertheless, State Farm's absurd objections were having the effect intended—delaying discovery, forcing me to expend large amounts of time and money seeking orders compelling discovery, and delaying trial.

State Farm's obstructionist tactics forced us to file many motions to compel production of discovery and to obtain nine pretrial Court orders compelling discovery. Consequently, the beginning of trial was delayed significantly due to defendant's discovery stonewalling. Judge Henderson characterized pretrial discovery as "unusually protracted and dispute-ridden."

It is unfortunate, but true, that large corporations, when faced with civil rights complaints prosecuted by relatively small and undercapitalized plaintiff law firms, attempt to obstruct and delay discovery, and make litigation as expensive and protracted as possible, thereby subjecting plaintiff's counsel to extreme cash-flow pressures. Unlike defense counsel, who are paid in full on a monthly basis for their time expenditures and expenses, plaintiff's attorneys in large-scale civil rights cases cannot rely on their clients to pay attorneys' fees and expenses—which often run into the millions—and must wait to the end of the case, after they have prevailed, to file a motion for an award of reasonable attorneys' fees and costs. Defendants can delay receipt of fees even longer (often 2–3 more years) by appealing any decision on the merits of the case and/or the attorneys' fees award. In the meantime, of course, the plaintiff attorney must continue to pay salaries, rent, expenses of litigation, etc., as well as his or her living expenses. When the case is large, the "cash-flow" problems can become insurmountable, forcing an early settlement on disadvantageous terms, or worse, dismissal of the case and bankruptcy for the attorney.

While not a great film, *Civil Action* accurately portrayed these economic realities. While my firm and I managed to survive this type of economic warfare—in my case, by repeatedly refinancing our house and borrowing from every source of credit I could find—many attorneys I know did not. One, Rick Seymour, who certainly is one of the country's best Title VII class action attorneys, went bankrupt while winning thirteen Title VII cases in a row! Although he ultimately would be paid in those cases, his private law practice was demolished by the negative cash flow caused by defense delay tactics, and he was forced to abandon private practice and take a job with a foundation, where his salary would be paid on a regular basis. Indeed, when I began my Title VII class action practice in 1972, I knew many attorneys in the Bay Area who were prosecuting employment class actions. Ten years later, nearly all had disappeared from Title VII class litigation, beaten by adverse cash flow. They found refuge in more secure, and regularly paid, areas of legal practice. State Farm had a gigantic economic edge on me. They were trying to wear me out and starve me out.

In late 1980, I filed a motion to certify the class pursuant to

Rule 23 of the Federal Rules of Civil Procedure. I defined the class as:

> All female applicants and deterred applicants who, at any time since July 5, 1974, have been, are, or will be denied recruitment, selection and/or hire as trainee agents by defendant companies within the State of California.

The definition was ambitious in that it included both actual job applicants and "deterred" applicants. While "deterred applicant" classes were relatively rare, the experiences of both Muriel and Wilda fit that description perfectly. In fact, State Farm so successfully discouraged their attempts to apply that they never were permitted even to file applications. Failure to include deterred applicants within the scope of the case would vastly limit the impact of the case, and reward State Farm for keeping women from applying.

The class certification motion was heard on January 19, 1981, and on September 9, 1981, Judge Henderson issued his decision provisionally certifying the class requested, including deterred applicants, finding that all requirements of Rule 23 were met. The numerosity requirement (a class action may be maintained only if "the class is so numerous that joinder of all members is impracticable") was met by showing that 369 women had applied, but not been hired, for the agent position during the relevant time period; in addition, an unknown number of women had been discouraged from applying, such as Muriel and Wilda. State Farm argued that "common questions" did not exist because hiring decisions were made individually by agency managers in different parts of the state and under diverse circumstances, but Judge Henderson found that the allegations of systematic discrimination in recruitment, hiring and training, coupled with a centralized decision-making process that required approval by regional vice presidents for any trainee agent to be hired, were sufficient to raise "common questions" under Rule 23. The "typicality" requirement was met by the three individual plaintiffs raising claims that were "sufficiently parallel" to the claims raised on behalf of the proposed class. The plaintiffs were adequate representatives of the class (Rule 23 requires that "the representative parties will fairly and adequately protect the interests of the class") because (1) "plaintiffs' counsel had the necessary expertise," and (2) there was no evidence "which would suggest the presence of collusion," and (3) the interests of the named plaintiffs were not antagonistic to the interests of the proposed class. Lastly, the lawsuit sought declaratory and injunctive relief as a remedy for present and future unlawful discrimination, making certification under Rule 23(b)(2) appropriate; indeed, the Advisory Committee Notes to Rule 23 acknowledge that race and sex discrimination cases are the prototypical (b)(2) class actions.

The class certification order was important, indeed pivotal, but like any pretrial certification order, it was only provisional. All elements of Rule 23 would be challenged by State Farm and would need to be proven at trial, now scheduled to begin in March 1982.

Discovery proved to be so contentious, and State Farm caused so many delays in producing information in response to our requests, that we decided to file a motion for a discovery plan, pursuant to new rule 26(f) of the Federal Rules of Civil Procedure. Rule 26(f) permitted the framing of discovery requests in a more organized and comprehensive manner than individual interrogatories and requests for documents, and offered the potential of greater court involvement and supervision of discovery. Judge Henderson, recognizing the obstinacy of State Farm, as well as the impending trial date, issued a comprehensive discovery order which included discovery of all records of applications and AIB tests and a schedule of monthly court hearings monitoring the progress of discovery.

Unlike most state courts, the federal courts require the filing of extensive and complete Pre-Trial Statements by each party. These Statements are intended to include the identification of all witnesses the parties intend to call, as well as all documents to be introduced as evidence. The Court reviews the parties' statements and issues a binding Pre-Trial order, which governs the conduct of the trial. This Order, among other things, includes rulings regarding permitted testimony and witnesses and the admissibility of evidence. Submitting witnesses and evidence at trial that was not previously set forth in the Pre-Trial Statement, and permitted by the Pre-Trial order, is very restricted and most often limited only to witnesses and evidence that rebuts evidence that could not reasonably have been anticipated.

In compliance with the Federal Rules, we submitted a Pre-Trial Statement that identified over fifty witnesses and hundreds of documents we intended to introduce, but State Farm, true to form, continued to try to hide the ball by identifying only six witnesses and fewer than a dozen documents. We were forced to bring a motion to compel State Farm's compliance with the Federal Rules, and Judge Henderson, after a Court hearing on the motion, ordered State Farm to identify all the witnesses it intended to call, and documents it intended to introduce, at trial, warning State Farm in the process that "anything not disclosed will not be admitted." This Order prompted Laveroni to move for a trial continuance, arguing that the disclosures the Court had ordered would require a substantial amount of time, and maintaining the existing trial date would cause State Farm substantial prejudice. I vigorously protested, concluding my remarks by looking directly at Laveroni, and referring to Laveroni's persistent pattern of non-disclosure told the Court, "We shouldn't listen to him complain about a headache when he's spent the last two years jamming a pencil up his nose." Sometime later, Judge Henderson's court reporter confided in me, "Since you made that comment, we've really been looking forward to this trial!" Time for trial was estimated to be four months. Our trial team would consist of me, my partner Jeff Brand, associate Ruby Udell, and our paralegal, Ruth McCreight.

A week before trial, Paul Laveroni, State Farm's lead counsel, made a settlement offer: a total payment of $225,000 for all claims of the three plaintiffs and the class, reasonable attorneys' fees and costs, and State Farm's agreement to hire 20% female agents for three years. I considered the offer to be a joke, and told him so. The monetary value of *each* plaintiff and *each* class member's claims exceeded $225,000 and three years of hiring women agents at a 20% rate would barely dent the male-dominated salesforce. I demanded $10 million, as pled in the original complaint, plus 50% female hires for eight years. I knew that would be the end of pretrial settlement negotiations, and it was.

The trial began in March 31, 1982, with me making the opening statement for plaintiffs. I began by thanking the Court for taking control of discovery and holding monthly pretrial discovery hearings, without which trial could not have begun anytime in the foreseeable future. I explained the experiences each of the plaintiffs had had trying to become State Farm agents, explained why the State Farm agent job was so desirable and why women, as well as men, were attracted to it, explained State Farm's near-complete lack of objective standards and qualifications for the job, the arbitrary and inconsistent application of diverse hiring criteria by State Farm agency managers, State Farm's heavy reliance on nepotism and cronyism in recruiting and hiring new agents, its dismal track record hiring female agents and the resulting overwhelmingly male salesforce, which, even after substantial increases in hiring women following the filing of discrimination charges by Muriel, Daisy and Wilda, remained 96.5% male, and the system of lies and misrepresentations that had discouraged women from even completing the application process. I spoke for an hour and a half.

Paul Laveroni got up, extolled the virtues of State Farm as the world's most successful insurance company, and contended women were not interested in becoming agents, which was why State Farm had been unable to hire women. Drawing upon his Italian heritage, he concluded that, "In Italy, we have a saying: 'does it stick to the wall?' By this we mean, anyone can try to make spaghetti, but it isn't ready to eat, it isn't spaghetti, until you can throw it against the wall and it sticks. As we will see in this trial, plaintiffs' case doesn't stick."

I thought Paul's speech was very entertaining. Paul is about 6' 3", very athletic and fit, handsome in a United States Marine sort of way (in fact, at the time, he was a Colonel in the Marines Reserve), articulate, funny, charismatic, and easy to listen to. His opening statement was like a lot of the legal briefs he had written in the case: clear, forceful, witty, and even persuasive—until you started looking for the evidence and/or caselaw to support the argument, which usually was completely lacking. After fighting—and winning—innumerable discovery battles with Paul, and reading his many rationalizations for not complying with the Federal Rules, I began to realize that he wrote what he wanted to believe, but what he wanted to believe most often was not supported by the facts or law. His writing was passionate and readable, but the core of the argument was missing. Such was his opening statement. We laughed at the spaghetti metaphor, never doubting that we had the facts that not only stick to the wall but would stick State Farm itself to the wall.

Most employment discrimination trials begin with the plaintiffs telling their individual stories, followed by corroborating witnesses and class members with similar tales. In a case of this magnitude, this would have taken a month. During this time, I surmised that Judge Henderson would be thinking, "I know State Farm's female hiring statistics are not good, but I wonder what its explanation will be."

I was so confident of proving the case, I decided, instead, to begin the trial by calling State Farm witnesses—Regional Vice Presidents, Agency Directors, Agency Managers, and agents—and forcing them to explain, on cross-examination, why the State Farm agent job had been maintained as an exclusive men's club. In the middle of the third week of trial, the court reporter, Wanda Harris, told me at a break, "We all were wondering why you would start the case with State Farm managers as witnesses. After listening to them for two weeks, now we understand!" I didn't ask Wanda who she was speaking for, but I assumed she was referring to the court clerk and two law clerks who were sitting through most of the trial, and I hoped her comments included Judge Henderson as well!

Under cross-examination, State Farm's managers were shooting holes through the company's defenses with their testimony long before Laveroni would begin to call his own defense witnesses. Contrary to Laveroni's opening statement claim that the agent job was risky and unattractive to women, Regional Vice President Don Raker testified that a career as a State Farm agent was a "golden opportunity" that offered high income, independence and a feeling of service to the community as some of the benefits. State Farm agents and agency managers testified that State Farm was the best of all insurance companies to work for because of the superiority of the products, strong support of agents by the company, excellent claims service, strong advertising, high income, bonus rewards, flexible hours, control over one's life, and opportunities to travel. We called as witnesses a few of the female agents State Farm had hired recently, and, although trying their best not to harm State Farm's defenses, all testified that they saw no reason why the job would appeal less to women than to men.

State Farm had contended that the qualifications for the agent job were high and the company had selected only the most qualified people available, but witness after witness undermined that contention. State Farm's Regional Vice Presidents, Deputy Regional Vice Presidents, Agency Directors and Agency Managers all testified that there were no objective qualifications for the trainee agent job. They all agreed that there were no minimal education requirements. One State Farm Agency Manager, Roy Solk, testified that an individual need not have more than an 8th grade education to become a State Farm agent. In fact, as one of our exhibits showed, only 46.7% of the State Farm agents hired since 1970 had bachelor degrees.

The testimony of the State Farm managers was consistent and unchallenged that no particular prior work experience was required and that State Farm agents had come from a diverse job background. This was confirmed and highlighted by a plaintiffs' exhibit which showed, based on State Farm's personnel records, that agents had engaged in 113 different occupations immediately prior to their hire, including such unrelated jobs as barber, beer distributor, and grocery clerk.

Rather than specific education or prior job experience, State Farm managers relied on a bewildering, and often inconsistent, array of subjective criteria to recruit, select and hire trainee agents. Ask ten State Farm agency managers what they were looking for and you would get ten different answers. These included, "motivation," "desire," "stability," "financial strength," "a pattern of success," "intelligence," "leadership," "initiative," the ability to make "extremely sensitive and subtle judgments," the ability to withstand "a demanding career," the ability to make "extremely difficult judgments," "organizational activities," "age, marital status, sport or hobby, income, number of children and occupation of friends," "the type and amount of insurance owned," "references," "work history," "ability to learn," "ability to meet people easily and relate well to them," "ability to plan well and establish realistic goals," "desire to work hard," "aptitude for insurance sales," "interest in high income," "enthusiasm," "proficiency in using the telephone," "positive attitude," "competitive attitude," "willingness to sell to friends," "direct contact with customers in previous jobs," "willingness to work at night or weekends," "willingness to work independently," "grades in school," "educational history," "active social life," "physical activity," "thoughtful and realistic about future," "perseverance," "good judgment," "integrity," "intellectual capability," "occupationally disturbed," "some education," "neatness," "sincerity," "inquisitiveness," "interest," "creativity," "stick-to-it-tiveness," "ambition," "energetic and active," "tolerant," "reliable," "a person that you like and respect," "the kind of person you would buy insurance from," someone who "relates well with the interviewer," etc.

The reliance on such wide-open, highly subjective, selection criteria really was a non-system that permitted the State Farm managers consciously and unconsciously to apply untested biases, prejudices and assumptions, resulting in the hire of their friends, relatives and acquaintances. These subjective hiring criteria were utilized by State Farm managers, directors and vice presidents who were, until shortly before trial, 100% male (141/141 male). I suspected there also was a strong tendency among managers to hire new agents that looked like some agent they knew who was successful; since the State Farm agents were nearly 100% male, the "model" of the successful State Farm agent was a man and the gender of the sales force perpetually replicated itself—to the exclusion of women.

The result of this system was indisputable: in 1976, the year Muriel filed EEOC charges, State Farm had 1,594 active agents in California; 1,588 (99.6%) were men. By contrast, in State Farm's non-sales jobs ("operations"), which generally were lower-paid clerical and technical jobs, 63.5% (2,151 of 3,385 employees) were women. State Farm really was two different companies: the female-dominated, low-paid support staff, and the nearly all-male, high-income sales staff.

State Farm's use and misuse of highly subjective hiring criteria as well as blatant discouragement or rejection of women were illustrated at trial by the testimony of sixteen women who had tried to become State Farm agents (in addition to the testimony of Muriel, Daisy and Wilda.)

Dorothy Dillard, a long-time State Farm agency secretary and office manager, testified that her Agency Manager told her, "I don't hire women, and, in any case, being an agent is too difficult for women because of the long hours and hard work." Besides, he wouldn't want to "take a good secretary away from an agent."

Sarah Cline, another State Farm office manager, expressed her interest in becoming a State Farm agent to six State Farm managers and directors. Agency Director Eugene Miller told her that there was an "unwritten law in the region" that State Farm would not hire a female because of a fear that women would be raped and wouldn't want the responsibilities of the job anyway. Miller falsely told Cline that she had to have a college degree and be married to become a State Farm agent. "I am married," said Cline. "OK, then you have to be single," replied Miller. Still undeterred, Cline talked to another State Farm Agency Manager, who told her a college degree was required. She went back to school, completed forty-seven college units in one year, and got her degree. She returned, degree in hand, and spoke with four State Farm Agency Managers and was told falsely that "no openings" existed. She gave up on State Farm, applied at Farmers Insurance Group and became a successful sales agent for Farmers.

Deborah McCamish, who had been employed in a State Farm regional office and several State Farm agencies, told five State Farm managers and agents she wanted to apply to become a State Farm agent. She falsely was told a Bachelor of Arts degree and "a large financial commitment" were required. She never was given the aptitude test (AIB), nor told how to file an application. She, too, left and became a successful Farmer's agent.

Esther Molina, who then was running a State Farm agency office in a Hispanic neighborhood near Fresno for an agent who did not speak Spanish, inquired about becoming a State Farm agent herself, but was told she had to have a college degree, would have to make a substantial financial investment, and would have to go back East for six weeks of training—all lies. She also was told that "it was difficult for women to become agents because business people did not respond to women as they do to men." She, too, was never told about the aptitude test nor given an application.

Barbara Bryley, another State Farm agency office manager, was told by Agency Manager Robert Carver that "State Farm did not hire females and that to become a trainee agent either a college degree or five years work experience was necessary." During his trial testimony, Agency Manager Carver conceded that Bryley's agent, Dick Sandberg, threatened to sue "everyone in sight" if Bryley was made an agent. One more State Farm agent who didn't want to lose his meal ticket! He lost her anyway; disgusted with State Farm, Bryley left to become a successful agent with Farmer's Insurance.

Mary Lou Hollander, while working in a State Farm agency, was told by the agent that "you do everything I do." Nevertheless, when she sought to become a State Farm agent, Agency Manager Ed Casselman told her that a woman seeking a trainee agent position would be "swimming against the stream" because State Farm had a policy not to hire women.

When Sharon Barnes contacted a State Farm Agency Manager, she was told that State Farm did not hire women agents and that if she took the aptitude test, she should not use the name Sharon and suggested she rename herself "Sam" or "Seymour." When she took the aptitude test, she used the name "S. McGee" to hide her sex. Nevertheless, on passing the test, she was told by Agency Manager Vance Basler that the agent job was not suitable for women because it was not appropriate for women to knock on doors. I asked Basler if he had any idea how many women worked as social workers, knocking on doors in many of the worst neighborhoods in America.

Judith Napier testified that she went to State Farm's Southern California Regional office looking for a sales position. She was told that State Farm was looking only for male "newly graduated law students." Andrea Pardue also sought a sales position at the Southern California Regional Office, but was asked to take a typing test and told to apply for a clerical job. Neither was permitted to take the sales aptitude test or fill out an application for sales.

While the door to agency was being shut in the faces of these women, and many more who did not testify at trial, State Farm was rolling out the agency red carpet for male relatives. In fact, it was State Farm's written policy that encouraged the hire of "sons and sons-in-law, brothers, brothers-in-law, and other close relatives of State Farm agents." The State Farm policy memo noted that many State Farm agents were related to other State Farm agents, "the principal categories being brothers, brothers-in-law, and fathers and sons." The pro-nepotism policy statement concluded that "our purpose [is] to foster such relationships; we want more sons and relatives of our agents in the agency force." It was not until November 1977 that State Farm revised this policy to include "daughters." The impact of the policy and practice of male nepotism was profound. From 1970–81, 370 of the male State Farm agents in California had relatives employed at State Farm. Nepotism at State Farm ran from the highest State Farm position in California (Regional Vice President) down to trainee agents. Regional Vice President Roger

Tompkins—one of the nastiest witnesses State Farm presented—
was the son of a member of the Board of Directors of State Farm
Life Insurance Company who had been employed by State Farm
for forty-one years. Roger's brother also was a State Farm Regional
Vice President and his nephew was a State Farm field claims adjuster.

Deputy Regional Vice President Ray Wehde approved the appointment of his son, "Billy," as an agent in Monterey. Ray's twin
brother also was a State Farm Regional Vice President and his
brother-in-law was a State Farm agent. Ray's appointment of his
son as a State Farm agent was an especially strong example of how
the hiring process was manipulated to favor relatives.

Billy Wehde did not present even a hint of the "success pattern"
State Farm claimed it looked for in hiring new agents. He had left
four colleges, he had never held a job for more than six months,
and the jobs he had held prior to his appointment as a State Farm
agent were not compelling, to say the least—grocery bagger, bar
waiter, underwriting clerk, manual laborer. He had never lived in
Monterey, the site of the office given to him, had no contacts there,
and wasn't even living in California when his dad solicited him to
become a State Farm agent. He had almost no assets (as I recall, his
only real asset was a muscle car his dad had given him) and he was
in debt, despite borrowing heavily from his dad throughout his
college and work years. In no way was he as qualified for an agent
position as any of the women who testified about their arbitrary
rejections by State Farm, yet he was handed a plum agency. Nepotism was certainly alive and well at State Farm!

Perhaps it is unfair to pick on Billy, as there were so many State
Farm nepotees like Billy. Randy Fueger, son of a State Farm agent,
was hired as a trainee agent despite failing the aptitude test; his
only visible qualification was his prior experience as a secretary in
his father's office—the type of experience, of course, that didn't
seem to help any of the women agency secretaries become agents.
Despite his thin resume, Randy rejected the first State Farm agency
offered to him because it was in an area he did not want and State

Farm accommodated him by creating a special agency for him.

Agency Manager Richard Curtis testified that he had approved the hire of Glen Johnson, son of a State Farm agent, William Cortland Lancaster, son-in-law of a State Farm agent, and Larry Pirrone, son of a State Farm Agency Manager and nephew of another State Farm Agency Manager. At the time of his hire, William Cortland Lancaster had only $1,000 in the bank, had no college degree, no permanency in either residency or job experience and was, in the words of State Farm Agency Manager Matt Madsen, "the weakest candidate I had ever presented to Mr. Curtis."

State Farm's well-known preference for male nepotism in hiring agents not only closed off a large number of agent positions to women, it also broadcast a message to women that they were not wanted. Hearing that message, many women would not even bother trying to apply and face rejection—like the women who testified at trial.

PROVING THAT STATE FARM HAD HIRED few woman agents was the easiest part of the trial. We simply introduced the company's records into evidence. But proving that, absent discrimination, more should have been hired was a far more complicated task. In employment discrimination cases where access to the application process is not restricted, one need only compare the percentage of qualified women or minorities who applied for a particular job with the percentage hired, to measure the disparity that could have been the result of discrimination. But in the State Farm case, the "applicant flow" of women had been reduced by the unwillingness of many State Farm managers to permit women to begin the application process by taking the aptitude test (AIB) or completing an application ("Confidential Personal History Form"), by State Farm's reputation as a company that did not hire women agents, by product ads that portrayed its salesforce as all-male, and by nepotism and cronyism. Thus, the actual flow of agent applicants was not an accurate measure of the number, or percentage, of women who were available for hire as State Farm agents, absent gender discrimination, and a surrogate measure of "labor market availability" had to be developed. This was not only the most difficult part of the case, but also the most important, since the measure of labor market availability not only would help determine State Farm's legal liability for discrimination to the class of women, it also would heavily influence the ultimate remedy we sought—a hiring order that would greatly increase the hiring of female agents.

To handle this most important of tasks, I hired Professor John H. Pencavel, Chairman of the Economics Department at Stanford University, and a leading authority on labor economics, including the supply and availability of labor. I hired John in a number of employment discrimination cases, and he was one of the most interesting expert witnesses I ever had the pleasure of working with.

John was a challenge; he was quite conservative and often seemed to be enjoy himself most when he disagreed with me or challenged my most cherished social or political values. Whenever he thought he had scored a good debater's point with me, I would get a "Aha, I've got you with that one!" followed by a roar of laughter. One day, sitting with John at an outdoor terrace at Stanford having lunch, he introduced me to Thomas Sowell, the famous opponent of affirmative action, and encouraged Sowell to tell me what was wrong with affirmative action. Then John piled on, trying to convince me that hiring orders could distort the labor market. "Of course," I replied, "but where discrimination has distorted the flow of labor, some corrective measures are required to bring the market back to rational distribution of labor resources." But no matter what John's political leanings were, they never interfered with his scientific discipline and labor market analyses, which were superb.

John was incredibly smart and quick-thinking, and, having been born and raised in England, his British accent further enhanced the confidence and erudition he projected. Of course, qualities like these often come with some arrogance, and the only real challenge presenting John as a trial witness was keeping the appearance of arrogance under control. John's State Farm trial testimony explaining his estimation of the labor market availability of women for the trainee agent job was flawless—clear, concise, well-reasoned, and persuasive.

Professor Pencavel presented a written report and testimony analyzing the availability of women for hire and training as State Farm agents in California. In forming his estimate of the availability of qualified women, he relied on population and labor market data from the "General Social and Economic Characteristics" and "Detailed Characteristics" of the U. S. Census of Population, California, Current Population Surveys, The California Statistical Abstract prepared by the California Employment Development Department, State Farm agent earnings, and personnel data, and the qualifications and characteristics of State Farm agents. He considered a number of different concepts of relative female availability to insure a reliable estimate—one that is not "sensitive to the particular criteria chosen"—and concluded that the percentage of women that had been available for the trainee agent job was "between 35 and 45 percent with a central tendency of 40%."

In arriving at these estimates, Professor Pencavel began with very broad concepts of labor availability, which he subsequently amended and refined in a manner consistent with State Farm's actual hiring practices. He factored into his analysis levels of education by men and women, occupations, and salary. Relying on extensive studies showing that the supply and availability of labor depends on the terms of the job, and that the most obvious factor influencing interest in a particular job is the salary, he assumed that individuals would gravitate towards those jobs that pay more. In fact, this assumption is supported by many studies which show that even small changes in the earnings of a particular type of job will significantly change interest in that job. Thus, it is reasonable to expect, for example, that college-educated women who are underemployed and underpaid in other jobs, as well as the female secretaries, solicitors and office managers in State Farm agency offices, will be interested in State Farm agent jobs that pay $100,000 after a few years, and that male executives already earning high incomes will be less interested in becoming insurance agents.

Professor Pencavel also testified that the characteristics State Farm claimed to be most significant in the hire and success of a State Farm agent did not screen out women disproportionately to men; in other words, the characteristics and qualities State Farm was looking for were found equally in women as well as men. These factors included, for example, good health, technical ability and intelligence, willingness to be trained for two years, to take a state licensing test, to commute or travel on the job, to exercise initiative, meet and talk to prospective clients about insurance, not be a convicted felon, etc. Likewise, there was no basis to conclude that women lacked the subjective characteristics that State Farm managers emphasized anymore than men (i.e., factors such as "integrity," "intellectual capability," "ability to manage time," "ability to handle rejection," "desire to increase income," etc.). Professor Pencavel did not testify that these qualities would be found in every woman, but only that there was no reason to believe that men had these qualities and characteristics in greater proportion than women.

On cross-examination, Professor Pencavel toyed with Laveroni, showing mastery of the subject matter but perhaps too much disdain for Paul's intellectual limitations. I didn't want him to create any sympathy for Laveroni in Judge Henderson's mind, but, I must say, I sat at plaintiffs' counsel table completely on cruise control knowing Pencavel needed no help from me, and enjoying watching him run circles around Paul. As soon as the cross-examination was over, the Court took a recess. John came over to me and, referring to Laveroni, said, "He's worse than an undergraduate!"

After presenting plaintiffs' case for two months, we ended with the testimony of Muriel Kraszewski, Wilda Tipton and Daisy Jackson. Each testified on behalf of themselves by telling the details of how State Farm had treated them when they attempted to become State Farm agents, and also as examples of how women, in general, had been treated by State Farm.

Muriel explained that she had sought to apply for an agent job with eight State Farm sales managers, yet never was seriously considered, put in a selection pool, or offered a position, despite meeting all the stated requirements for the job. She had worked in State Farm agency offices for nearly twelve years as an agency secretary, solicitor and office manager, had successfully performed nearly all the State Farm agent functions, including selling, had a net worth of $104,000 and was willing to invest in an agency if any investment was required (it rarely was), had taken college-level insurance courses, and had extensive contacts in the community. She understood that a State Farm trainee agent received a Specified Monthly Payment, but that there was some "risk" that such payments might not fully cover office overhead and return an immediate profit, and was willing to accept any such risk. In fact, she became an agent for Farmers Insurance despite the greater risk that she would have to pay back her monthly subsidy to Farmers if she failed as a Farmers agent (State Farm required no pay back for unsuccessful trainee agents). After her numerous attempts to become a State Farm agent were rebuffed, Muriel became a Farmers agent and frequently had been one of their top three agents in the Long Beach region.

Muriel's husband, Bob, testified that he fully supported Muriel's efforts to become a State Farm agent. When Laveroni tried to challenge this in his cross-examination, Bob smiled and said, "I'd have to be pretty dumb not to want my wife to make $100,000 a year, Mr. Laveroni. I'm not that dumb."

We further established that shortly after State Farm Agency Manager Bob Carver told Muriel he had no agent positions open, he hired a male agent and that Agency Manager Lon Matz hired four male agents during the period he claimed he had no openings.

Wilda Tipton testified that she had worked in State Farm agency offices for nearly fifteen years as a secretary, office manager, and solicitor selling all lines of insurance. Her agent, William Bremmer, confirmed that she solicited business in and outside of the office and that her work was "excellent." Wilda talked to a State Farm

Agency Manager as early as 1969 about becoming an agent and was told, "it is not possible." Five years later, she applied again to Agency Manager Hicks, who misinformed her that a two-year college degree was required to become a State Farm trainee agent. She returned to school, completed 50 college units, and obtained her degree. Nevertheless, Hicks appointed six new agents in the Oxnard–Ventura area without ever considering Wilda for any of the open positions. His last male hire, Steve Abrahams, was only 26 years old, had no prior sales experience and was terminated within a year for "poor performance."

After Hicks refused to consider Wilda, and hired Abrahams, Wilda and her husband, Otis, met with Hicks and Agency Director Vern Gallagher. Gallagher explained that Bremmer, the agent Wilda worked for, feared losing her and opposed her appointment as an agent and he had no openings anyway. Gallagher's statement that no openings existed proved to be untrue, as a male, Terry Lutz, was soon appointed to an open position in Oxnard. Gallagher referred Wilda to Agency Manager Robert Larkin, who then was hiring agents in Simi Valley, a rapidly growing area nearby. Larkin asked Wilda, in front of her husband, if she would be willing to relocate to Simi Valley and work nights, if necessary. She said she would. Nevertheless, Larkin told Wilda that his agents were men and working nights would present a problem for her, concluding, "Women can't handle this position." Following this meeting, Larkin did not return any of her calls. At this point, she testified she called me after reading in the *Los Angeles Times* that I had filed a lawsuit against State Farm.

Her husband Otis, the former Chief of Police of the City of Oxnard, corroborated Wilda's account of the meeting with Larkin, and Larkin's statement that "women can't handle" the job.

Daisy Jackson's testimony was the most prolonged of the three named plaintiffs, due to the fact that her claims were based not only on several rejections of her applications, but also on the unequal terms of her appointment and her discriminatory termination. In the end, her story was fully corroborated—even by State Farm managers—and her case was perhaps the most compelling example of unfair and unequal treatment presented during the four-month class action trial.

After telling the plaintiffs' stories, we rested our case-in-chief. It had taken two months of trial time. It now was State Farm's turn to answer the charges and the extensive evidence of a pattern and practice of discrimination against women.

STATE FARM BEGAN ITS DEFENSE by attempting to prove a series of highly dubious propositions: That the trainee agent position was not really a "job" (and, thus, not covered by Title VII), that it was just an "opportunity" to become an independent agent, that it was not a particularly attractive opportunity due to the requirements of the position, the amount of money each new agent needed to invest in the agency and the risk of failure. Because of these, and other, negative features of the position, women had not been interested and available for the position—thus, it should not be surprising that 93.1% of the agents hired in the twelve years preceding trial were men. Furthermore, State Farm had been highly selective in its hiring of trainee agents and had hired only the "most qualified" [men] available.

The contention that the trainee agent position was not a "job" within the meaning of Title VII was, both factually and legally, completely absurd. The only possible way for someone to become a State Farm Career Agent was to be hired as a trainee agent for two years. During this two years, State Farm paid a negotiated salary (the "Stipulated Monthly Payment"), and controlled all aspects of the new agent's training, office location, and sales performance. Trainee agents represented only State Farm Insurance Companies in the sale of insurance and were compensated directly by State Farm for sales that exceed the monthly salary. Moreover, the only path to advancement in sales management jobs at State Farm was by first becoming a trainee agent. The position was the "entry level" sales job because prior insurance sales experience was not required—indeed, it was discouraged—and was the first rung in the

State Farm sales division ladder. Even State Farm management witnesses were forced to admit these facts.

State Farm managers and agents attempted to portray the trainee agent job as undesirable to many by emphasizing—indeed, exaggerating—the need to invest in the agency, the risk of failure and the necessity that a prospective trainee agent be financially secure before taking on the risks of agency. To support this claim, State Farm called as witnesses seven of its female agents, among others.

Phyllis Frank testified that her trainee agent period had been financially precarious and she had earned little money during two years of training. A review of her office financial statements, however, revealed she had been writing off as an "office expense" a large and expensive collection of decorative porcelain. On cross-examination, she was forced to admit the obvious—a porcelain plate collection was not an essential "expense" for a trainee agent, and that without this "expense," her bottom-line profitability as a trainee agent had been good. A more candid defense witness, State Farm agent Jeanne Triby Sullivan, testified that the only expenses that needed to be incurred to become a trainee agent were "a pencil, telephone and a reverse directory." Moreover, other female agents who testified on behalf of State Farm admitted that their financial resources were very limited before becoming trainee agents. At the time of her hire, Career Agent Linda Leaming was working as a secretary to support five children and a totally disabled husband. Career Agent Carol Newland admitted that at the time of her hire, she was living "hand to mouth," and Linda Moore described herself as "a classic case of failure," in that, prior to her appointment as a trainee agent, she had no college degree, no friends or contacts in California, and no stable employment. Nevertheless, despite meager financial resources, all of these women became successful State Farm agents and Linda Moore became State Farm's first female Agency Manager in the United States (shortly before trial!). Likewise, many of the male agents who became successful State Farm agents had little or no money available at the time they became trainee agents. After this collection of admissions, it was implausible to contend that a high net worth or substantial available cash was necessary to succeed as a trainee agent.

Despite attempting to portray the trainee agent position as a risky venture, State Farm managers were forced to admit that the failure rate of State Farm trainees was the lowest in the insurance industry, that State Farm had the lowest turnover of agents in the industry, and that State Farm agents had the highest average earnings in the industry. Indeed, during the course of four months of trial, State Farm failed to produce a single witness who declined a trainee agent position due to perceived "risk" or a single example of failure due to lack of adequate capitalization.

State Farm's attempts to portray the trainee agent job as risky and unattractive were greatly impeded by its own documents. State Farm's recruiting brochure, "What's Your Career Worth? Half Your Life," described the agent position as providing "a future and career that few other fields could offer." The brochure promised a chance for advancement, high income potential, security, and a feeling of "contributing to the welfare of others." State Farm's Career Presentation, used in recruiting trainee agents, described the trainee agent position in glowing terms without a negative comment. It promised the opportunity for "increased income each year," "security," "complete training and aggressive promotional backup," "job satisfaction," "financial assistance to provide a financial floor of stable income," "no financing is required," and the overall effort required to become an agent was simply described: "It's easy."

Presented with these documents, State Farm officials conceded the attractiveness of the job. Regional Vice President Donald Raker, for example, testified that a career as a State Farm agent was a "golden opportunity," and admitted that the high income, the independence, and the feeling of service to the community were great job benefits.

THE MOST SERIOUS DEFENSE PRESENTED BY STATE FARM concerned the issue of the "availability" of women for the trainee-agent position.

Rather than look at various categories of female participation in the labor force, as Professor Pencavel had done, State Farm sought to have "availability" measured only by the proportion of women who had taken the aptitude test (AIB) at State Farm. This proportion, 14.6%, was far below the 35–45% Professor Pencavel had testified was the appropriate measure of female availability for the job. Ironically, even State Farm's experts conceded that the disparity between 14.6% availability and the 6.9% hiring of women was "statistically significant" (a statistician's term meaning a probability of less than 1 chance in 100). Measurement of State Farm's female hiring agent using any of the availability criteria Professor Pencavel used resulted in even more powerful conclusions that chance could not explain the disparities (one chance in a billion-plus) and that sex discrimination was the likely explanation why so few women had been hired. Defeating State Farm's availability theory, and getting the Court to accept plaintiffs' theories of availability thus was crucially important not only to establish classwide liability, but also to the attainment of a strong remedial Court order increasing the hiring of women.

State Farm presented three experts on these issues: Professor Richard Singleton, an experienced and accomplished econometrician from the Stanford Research Institute who had testified in many Title VII cases and was considered the leading defense witness on availability issues; Elizabeth Milrod, Ph.D., an economist, and Dr. Wayne W. Sorenson, who was trained as an economist and statistician and who was head of State Farm's Research Department. Of the three, Singleton was the most formidable and dangerous, as he had the background, knowledge and experience in the field of labor economics to most effectively challenge Professor Pencavel; he also was the most experienced witnesses. I had deposed him four times prior to trial and he had managed to elude many of my efforts to pin him down on details and had provided, instead, frustratingly ambiguous answers. His evasiveness, however, would serve him less well at trial than it had in pretrial depositions.

The first witness to be called by State Farm on the availability issues, however, was a research assistant from State Farm's Research Department, whose testimony was intended to lay the foundation for some of the statistics about AIB test-takers that Sorenson, Milrod and Singleton later would be testifying about. Before the research assistant was very deep into his testimony, however, he referred to a new exhibit State Farm intended to introduce into trial—one not previously identified in the Pre-Trial Order. I was stunned that State Farm would try to introduce a new exhibit, one not previously disclosed, as Judge Henderson had issued a tough Pre-Trial Order that I thought forced the disclosure of all exhibits intended to be used at trial and made the exceptions for so-called "rebuttal" evidence very narrow. As I listened further, I became even more incredulous, as the witness was testifying about a compilation of women who had signed "Declaration of Understanding" forms. I had been seeking such information for over a year and had been told by State Farm in open court and in signed responses to discovery requests that such information did not exist.

I jumped out of my chair demanding that the Court permit me to review the new exhibit and "voir dire" the witness to determine where this data had come from before the exhibit was introduced into evidence. Judge Henderson, who had been through a dozen pretrial discovery fights in the case, and who instantly recognized the significance of this new data, gave me permission to do so. I noticed he was leaning forward, sitting on the edge of his seat, as I began to unravel the story that would lead to the largest award of sanctions for discovery abuse in the history of the federal courts.

I quickly reviewed State Farm's new exhibit, which contained summaries of information and counts of individuals who had signed Declaration of Understanding Forms and taken the AIB test. I knew instantly that these summaries had to be based on actual Declaration of Understanding forms and AIB test cards, which State Farm previously had claimed did not exist. The witness, who appeared to have no knowledge of our prior discovery requests, and

State Farm's false responses, readily explained that the exhibit was compiled from AIB cards and Declaration of Understanding forms, and from a special subset of the general computer personnel file E.GSS.APHDATA, which contained information *by name* of women who had taken the AIB test. By suppressing this information and denying me access to the names of the female test-takers prior to trial, State Farm had seriously restricted my ability to contact the women who had applied for trainee agent positions, but were not hired. This group likely would have some of the most extensive, and compelling, stories of discrimination to tell. Further, State Farm's delay in producing this information would cause prejudice to the rights of these women to participate in the trial and to file their own claims of discrimination, as some would have relocated in the interim and would not be found.

I was incredulous that State Farm—and/or Paul Laveroni—would have lied about the existence of these important documents and the computerized data, and then tried to use the same documents and data affirmatively! What chutzpah! What stupidity! It's one thing to lie and say something doesn't exist, but then to turn around and try to use the same information that they claimed didn't exist on State Farm's behalf astonished me. How dumb did they think I was? Did they think that I, or the Court, would miss this transparent deception?

As Laveroni made his feeble and absurd argument that this exhibit was admissible into evidence, but that plaintiffs had no right even to review the underlying documents, Judge Henderson interrupted him, and with obvious anger and indignation, told Laveroni, "Mr. Laveroni, I hope you have twenty cents in your pocket, because I want you to turn around, walk through those doors, go to the nearest phone to call your client, and have those documents in this courtroom today by 2 p.m. And, I will deal with you later!" With that, he stormed off the bench.

We sat there for a moment stunned in silence. I turned to Paul and said, "I don't know why you pull stunts like this. It makes you and your client look like shit." At that, Jerry Reynolds, State Farm's

Assistant General Counsel, who had attended all court hearings and every day of trial without ever talking to me, stood up and reassured me that, "State Farm is very happy with the way Paul is representing us." "That couldn't possibly be true," I replied.

At 2 p.m., we all returned to the courtroom, where Laveroni explained that the documents and computer data were at State Farm's national headquarters in Bloomfield, Illinois and that they would be delivered to me and the Court early next morning. With that, Judge Henderson turned to me and asked, "What do you want me to do to remediate this? Do you want a trial continuance?"

I consulted with Jeff and Ruby. On the one hand, our pretrial discovery and preparation had been seriously damaged by being denied access to this group of women. On the other hand, the trial was going extraordinarily well for our side. If the trial were continued for more than a short time, we might have trouble getting back on Judge Henderson's trial calendar for perhaps another year. We didn't want to lose another year, or the trial momentum we had established, so we requested a one-week trial continuance to permit us to undertake some limited discovery.

We did our best to track down some of the women whose names were revealed to us in the Declaration of Understanding forms and computer data, and took depositions about the test-taking process, then returned to Court a week later to continue the trial. Wayne W. Sorenson, State Farm's statistical expert took the stand and introduced State Farm's "test-taker" flow analyses, which showed less significant disparities in hiring women agents than comparisons with census-based data, but which even he conceded showed "statistically significant" disparities. Moreover, his testimony was impeached by State Farm documents that did not support his definition of an "applicant" as a person who took the AIB test. State Farm's recruiting brochures, Agent Selection Guides, and the testimony of State Farm agency management personnel either did not define an applicant as someone taking the AIB or rejected the term "applicant" altogether. State Farm's Regional Vice President Don Raker, for example, testified that, "the term applicant is not appropriate... very few apply... State Farm recruits trainee agents, searches them out, digs them up."

Furthermore, statistics that only counted AIB test-takers as "available" and interested in becoming State Farm agents ignored the extensive pre-screening that occurred before the AIB test ever was given, as well as extensive evidence, including admissions by State Farm managers that some State Farm agency managers refused to hire women agents; such managers were hardly likely to recruit women or administer an aptitude test to them. Agency Manager Warren Buckingham admitted that in thirty-two years of hiring agents for State Farm, he never had recruited a woman. Deputy Regional Vice President Ray Wehde had authored a memo we obtained in discovery which admitted that "some agency managers refuse to hire women agents," and Agency Manager Linda Moore testified, "there probably are agency managers who won't hire women." When I asked her what State Farm intended to do about such managers, she said she "hoped" that these managers would either "die or retire." Assuming we won the class trial, I was confident that Judge Henderson would figure out a faster and more effective remedy than death and retirement. And measuring the availability and interest of women only by the number of women taking the aptitude test ignored the impact of "word-of-mouth" recruitment by the all-male sales managers, the failure to post or advertise trainee agent openings, the effect of State Farm's agent image in the company's advertisements and brochures, State Farm's heavy reliance on male-only nepotism in recruiting agents, and State Farm's well-known reputation as a company that would not hire female agents.

State Farm then brought on experts Elizabeth Milrod and Richard Singleton to criticize and attempt to undermine Professor Pencavel's analyses and conclusions regarding the interest and availability of women for the trainee agent job. They claimed that Pencavel's analyses were invalid because he assumed that the personal qualities sought by State Farm in its trainee agents were universal throughout the population. But Pencavel made no such assumption. He did not assume these qualities were present in everyone, but only that there was no reason to believe that men have these qualities in greater proportion than women. Singleton and Milrod not only failed to present any evidence to support a contrary assumption, but Milrod even reinforced Pencavel's assumption! Elizabeth Milrod testified that she knew of no difference between men and women in the following characteristics and abilities:

—ability to manage time
—drive and energy
—financial ability to become trainee agents
—ability to learn and retain material
—ability to meet and relate to people
—ability to plan well and establish realistic goals
—aptitude for insurance sales and potential to perform the duties of a trainee agent
—interest in high income, security, and the satisfaction of working as a private businessperson
—ability to complete assignments in a timely manner
—ability to maintain a strong ego and handle rejection
—desire to increase income each year
—desire to advance rapidly within a career
—desire for the security of a career in trainee agency which includes selling highly regarded products, receiving personal help in getting started, and having the benefit of an aggressive promotional support system.
—the desire to receive satisfaction by contributing to the welfare of others
—the desire for recognition in the community
—the ability to sell insurance

State Farm criticized Professor Pencavel's educational and occupational refinements of his availability analyses, but failed to provide evidence supporting the criticisms. Milrod claimed that women constituted a minority of persons with "big ticket" or commission sales experience, but admitted that "big ticket" or commission sales experience was not required and Regional Vice President Roger Tompkins had testified that State Farm preferred to hire trainee agents *without* prior sales experience. Likewise, Milrod's criticism that Professor Pencavel's analyses included women with retail sales experience, which she contended was dissimilar to selling insurance, was totally negated by the fact that State Farm's own documents stated that individuals in retail sales jobs were "an excellent source of trainee agent candidates."

The defense experts criticized Professor Pencavel for including part-time and unemployed workers, but this criticism ignored the fact that many State Farm agents were hired while working part time or even unemployed. Their criticism that Professor Pencavel's conclusions were contradicted by the supposed small percentage of women with entrepreneurial experience was impeached by the fact that entrepreneurial experience was not a requirement for hire, and few of the male trainee agents hired had prior entrepreneurial experience. Furthermore, the factual basis of this criticism was incorrect, as 40.2% of the self-employed sales workers in California were women—a workforce participation figure directly in line with Professor Pencavel's conclusions.

Dr. Singleton criticized Professor Pencavel for using broad labor force categories to arrive at his availability conclusion, stating that more "refined" categories were necessary. But neither Singleton nor Milrod identified any "refined" categories that they thought more accurately measured the availability of women for the trainee agent position. And when confronted with the sources for the recruitment of trainee agents recommended in State Farm's Agency Manager recruitment materials and asked whether the list sounded like a "wide net," Dr. Singleton conceded it "sounds pretty broad."

None of State Farm's experts had even dented Pencavel's analyses. John had anticipated the relevant issues, done the appropriate research, and his conclusions shone even more brightly after State Farm's experts had tried to impugn them. I felt Judge Henderson—and any appellate court that might review the case—would have no difficulty accepting Pencavel's conclusions and measuring State Farm's dismal record of hiring women agents against the far greater numbers of women who would have pursue the trainee agent position if State Farm had offered equal employment opportunities to women.

State Farm agency managers testified that few women had been interested in the trainee agent jobs they had available, but on cross-examination it became apparent the lack of "interested" women was the product of male-oriented recruitment. Agency Manager Gerald Eastabroook, for example, testified that five of six trainee agents he hired had been recruited in the locker room of the Newport Beach Athletic Club—some in the showers. I asked him, "How many women did you recruit in that shower?" Agency Manager Warren Buckingham admitted that in thirty-two years of hiring trainee agents, he had never recruited a woman.

Deputy Regional Vice President Ray Wehde tried to explain the lack of female agents at State Farm as "like the situation with the Vietnamese. They weren't available for a long time, but now we're hiring Vietnamese agents." We asked him, "When did the Boat Women arrive in California?" When presented with a memo he wrote which acknowledged the lack of female hiring, Wehde admitted that, "We haven't done enough to sell the career to women."

State Farm presented the testimony of six female agents—all but one recently hired—to explain how well they had been treated by State Farm. But the testimony backfired, as each readily admitted that once they were presented with an opportunity to become a trainee agent, each jumped at it. None saw any reason why an agency career was any less attractive to women than to men. These women also contradicted State Farm's suggestion that family childrearing responsibilities impaired the availability of women to become agents, as nearly all of State Farm's female agents had family responsibilities, which had not interfered with their careers as agents. In fact, being their own boss and having flexible hours made the job more "family friendly" than most careers. Moreover, as we pointed out in our cross-examinations of State Farm witnesses, lower-paid female agency office managers, secretaries and solicitors had children too, yet worked full time.

At the conclusion of State Farm's defense case, it was clear to me that State Farm had no coherent explanation for its underhiring of women agents and had presented no coherent defense. I hoped Judge Henderson had seen the evidence the same way I had.

The parties presented closing arguments summarizing the evidence and testimony introduced over the course of four months of trial. In my summation, I referred back to Laveroni's opening statement metaphor about cooking spaghetti, I handed the Court and Laveroni packages of high-quality uncooked Italian spaghetti and told the Court that we had carefully tested the same spaghetti, thrown it against the wall, and it stuck—just as had the evidence we presented at trial. I thought the Court—maybe even Paul—appreciated the sense of humor, but there was no question which side was walking out of the trial with confidence.

Jeff and I had been working twelve to sixteen hour days for four months—putting on our witnesses during the day, then meeting with witnesses and preparing them for testimony the next day, or preparing cross-examination of State Farm's witnesses. I looked at myself in the mirror. My face was pasty-white and my eyes had black rings around them. I wondered who this guy was—he looked ten years older than me. But, despite looking terrible, I felt wonderful, completely energized, ready to go more rounds with State Farm.

I need not have worried. Many more rounds with State Farm were waiting.

8

The Battle with State Farm
Continues

*"To stake all one's life on a single moment, to risk everything on one
throw, whether the stake be power or pleasure, I care not—there is no
weakness in that. There is a horrible, a terrible courage."*

—Oscar Wilde

SHORTLY AFTER CONCLUSION of the class trial, the Court notified
the parties that it had appointed Professor Mary Kay Kane,
former Dean of Hastings School of Law, as a Special Master.
She was charged with investigating the facts, writing a report, and
making recommendations regarding the possible imposition of
sanctions for State Farm's withholding and late production of discovery. I greeted the notice with mixed emotions. On the one hand,
it was good to see that Judge Henderson was taking the discovery
abuses seriously; on the other hand, I did not know Professor Kane
and she was described to me by other attorneys as "rather conservative." I hoped her brand of conservatism did not include defer-
ence to large insurance companies and corporate defense firms.

Professor Kane requested legal briefs on the discovery abuse
issue by both sides and, after all were submitted, issued a lengthy
report to the Court, which the Court served on the parties. My fears
of her "conservatism" proved groundless. She took the Federal Rules
of Civil Procedure, and the obligation to reasonably and fully comply with federal discovery rules, seriously; her findings and recommendations included tough sanctions against State Farm. Judge

Henderson gave the parties the opportunity to respond in writing to Professor Kane's report, then issued his own Order.

The Court held that plaintiffs' prior discovery requests, and two pretrial Court Orders "should have resulted in defendant's timely production to plaintiffs of the AIB cards and Declarations of Understanding." Further, "[d]efendants through their counsel failed to make a good faith effort" to produce these documents, resulting in "substantial actual prejudice" to plaintiffs. Likewise, State Farm's failure to produce a special subset of the general computer file which contained the names of female and minority AIB test-takers violated two Court Orders compelling discovery and "caused plaintiffs substantial actual prejudice by seriously undercutting plaintiffs' ability and efforts to identify and locate other class members." Instead of producing this important information in a timely manner, "defendants through their counsel blithely maintained that no computerized records of AIB test-takers by name existed," wrote the Court.

Defendants' failure to produce the AIB cards and Declarations of Understanding, in violation of two Court Orders, "constituted flagrant bad faith and callous disregard for their responsibilities both to plaintiffs and to this Court." This amounted to civil contempt of Court "which might have warranted a finding of criminal contempt:"

> Defendants and their counsel in this case evidently decided to take a "sporting chance" by ignoring legitimate discovery requests and violating Court Orders: if the abuse went uncaught and plaintiffs prevailed, defendants figured to reap substantial benefits in unpaid claims by their successful frustration of plaintiffs' attorneys' attempts to locate class members; and even if the abuse was caught, defendants figured to get off fairly lightly if plaintiffs prevailed on the merits, since this is a civil rights action in which plaintiffs would receive attorneys' fees anyway, and to get off extremely lightly if defendants prevailed on the merits, since there would be little other than attorneys' fees for which plaintiffs could be compensated. Under these circumstances, the Court has labored long in attempting to devise sanctions which

would deter defendants and their attorneys from taking such a sporting chance in the future...

Court Order, June 9, 1983

As a remedy for defendants, and their attorneys' discovery abuses, the Court ordered defendants to pay $250,000 to class members located after the ordinary period for the payments of claims has elapsed, provided that the Court enter judgment against State Farm in the case, $50,000 to plaintiffs to be used to locate missing class members, $5,000 to compensate for the harm caused by the failure to produce gross and net compensation data, reasonable attorneys' fees and costs in the amount of $131,939.75 for work expended in obtaining four pretrial discovery orders and briefing the sanctions issues to the Special Master and the Court, and $2,918.67 to compensate the Special Master—a total of $439,858.42. Of that amount, the Court ordered Paul Laveroni's law firm to pay $93,469.88. I believe this was the largest monetary sanction for discovery abuse a United States federal court ever had awarded, and the amount was paid in full by State Farm and its attorneys, with no appeal to the Court of Appeals.

The discovery sanctions order was widely reported in the legal media and I soon received calls from two past presidents of the California State Bar Association urging me to file a complaint against Paul Laveroni seeking his disbarment. But I had no interest in relitigating the discovery abuse issues in another forum; I preferred to spend my time prosecuting my case. And, despite Paul's obstinacy in discovery, I enjoyed his pugnacity and sense of humor and was not interested in ruining him. I knew his firm would face a monetary sanction far greater than $93,469.88, as it was only a matter of time before Paul would get fired and be replaced by another law firm. As events would turn out, this ultimately would cost Laveroni's law firm more than $100 million in future billings in the case.

At the same time the discovery sanctions issues were being litigated, the plaintiffs and State Farm each submitted lengthy "Proposed Findings of Fact and Conclusions of Law," summarizing the parties' respective versions of the facts, evidence, and legal conclusions to be drawn from the evidence. Our proposal ran over 200 pages. Now, it was up to Judge Henderson to sift through the facts and law, as well as the extensive notes he had taken throughout the trial, and render a decision. I hoped it would be soon, as I was anxious to move on to the remedies phase of the case and I also hoped to be paid for the seven years I had been working on the case. But I could only sit and wait for the class trial decision.

NOT LONG AFTER SUBMITTING THE PROPOSED Findings and Conclusions, I received a call from an attorney who introduced himself as "Tom Powers, from Steptoe & Johnson." He explained that he had been hired by State Farm "to try to settle the *Kraszewski* case" and a meeting was set up in San Francisco a week later. In the interim, I did some reference checking on Powers. His reputation was impeccable: he had litigated many important Title VII cases, including several he had argued in the United States Supreme Court, he was considered a man of honor and intelligence, and several people I spoke with referred to him as "the Dean of the employment defense bar." Steptoe & Johnson was a major Washington D.C. law firm, and Tom was the Managing Partner, which confirmed the respect his peers had for him, as well as suggest that he was someone who could resolve problems and settle cases. I long ago had despaired of Paul Laveroni understanding the depth of the legal hole his client was in, and I was ecstatic that State Farm would seek the advice of an employment expert like Powers.

Jeff and I met Powers in a conference room at Laveroni's office. Sitting at the end of the conference table were Laveroni and Jerry Reynolds, Assistant State Farm General Counsel. Jerry had sat through every court hearing and every day of trial, but had spoken to me only once, when he defended Paul when his discovery abuse had been exposed. At all other times he ignored me. I would come into the courtroom in the morning and say, "Good Morning" to Jerry. He never responded, so I made a point of saying "Hello" or "Good Morning" every day. I knew it made him uncomfortable.

But this day, he said "Good Morning" to me and even shook my hand! Was I about to enter an era of civil relations with State Farm?

Powers was tall, angular, and courtly. He sat across the table from me and said he would like to understand my analysis of the case. I began a long explanation of the evidence we had presented at trial, emphasizing the labor availability analyses and the statistical proofs of discrimination, supporting my evidence with case authorities, when appropriate. Whenever I thought a point important enough to repeat, Tom would gently interrupt to say, "I understand the point." After an hour or so, I realized no repetition was required; Tom understood the significance of what I was saying the first time. His questions were intelligent and pertinent. Despite his low-key demeanor, it was obvious I was in the presence of someone who knew a lot about Title VII—probably more than I knew. After presenting my case, I said as courteously as I could, "The trial did not go well for State Farm." Tom quickly responded, "That is my understanding, also." I looked to Jerry Reynolds and asked him, "Do you disagree with that assessment?" Jerry firmly said, "No." We agreed to meet again the next day. Jeff and I walked out of the building and, referring to Powers, I said, "I loved his style and demeanor. What class!" Clearly, Tom Powers was someone who deserved his reputation.

We returned the next day and discussed the case for another full morning. After lunch, Tom asked, "What will it take to settle this case?" I replied, "Ten years of hiring women at 50% of sales agent hires in California, $22.5 million in back pay, plus reasonable attorneys' fees." Tom thanked me for presenting my interpretation of the evidence, promised to speak with State Farm and get back to me. I immediately regretted making a $22.5 million demand. I knew the case would be worth much more once I obtained a class liability verdict from the Court.

A week later, I got a call from Tom's law associate, Jane McGrew, seeking additional information about my settlement offer. She was much younger and more hard-edged in her approach than Tom had been. She made it clear she wasn't at all impressed with my case, and certainly wasn't impressed enough to justify what she considered my outlandish settlement offer. She proceeded to outline some of the cases she had worked on, concluding with the comment, "I've defended much worse examples of discrimination than the *Kraszewski* case." I responded, "Jane, that tells me a lot more about you than it does about the *Kraszewski* case." That was the last time I ever heard from her.

Another meeting was arranged with Tom, this time with us meeting at a hotel in San Francisco with Jerry Reynolds, but with Paul Laveroni conspicuously absent—which was a good sign. After mildly emphasizing the risks of litigation and the delays of a possible appeal—all standard fare in settlement discussions—but never once attacking my premise that plaintiffs' evidence was solid, Tom offered a six-year decree at 40% female hiring, $6.5 million in back pay, plus reasonable attorneys' fees. The offer was much improved over State Farm's prior offers—particularly the offer of six years of hiring 40% female agents—but I was relieved. I was afraid he was going to offer me $22.5 million. I was broke, but in my mind my "accounts receivable" ledger was large and growing! I certainly wanted to settle the case and get paid myself, but I was haunted by the thought of settling out too cheap after what State Farm and Laveroni had put me and the women through.

Before much time passed, a contingency I never had counted on arose. Judge Henderson returned from a short fishing vacation in Mexico seriously ill with some exotic virus. I was told he was in Alta Bates Hospital with a very high fever and a virus that his medical doctors were unable to diagnose. I was told his ability to return to the bench—maybe even his life—were in jeopardy.

I was very concerned for Judge Henderson, who is a man whose life I greatly admired. He had grown up poor in South Central Los Angeles—the site of the film *Boyz in the Hood* about the tough life of poverty and gangs. He managed to escape with good grades and football ability, obtaining a football scholarship at the University of California, where he played running back. Years later, I represented a good friend of his, Stan Wilkerson, who had played football with Henderson at the University of California. Stan told me, "Thelton was the hardest hitter on the team, despite his small size." After suffering a career-ending football injury, Henderson worked for good grades and was admitted to Boalt Hall School of Law, going on after graduation to work in the United States Department of Justice, build a successful private law practice, and become a Dean at Stanford Law School. Plus, he played a guitar and tap-danced. He also was a man of the people; often we would see him taking the main elevator downstairs to get a cup of coffee at the snack shop, rather than take the elevator reserved for judges. He was one federal judge who hadn't forgotten his roots and wasn't afraid to mingle with ordinary people, and I greatly respected that. His life was a model for anyone to emulate, but was a tremendously important example of success for young black men. Plus, people who knew him well said he was a very decent and likeable person. So, I was concerned about his health. But I was also concerned about myself and the *Kraszewski* case. If Judge Henderson was unable to return to the bench, the case might have to be re-tried before another judge—causing perhaps years of further delay and more expense, as well as giving State Farm a chance to present a better defense the second time around, perhaps with a better law firm. I was stretched financially about as far as I could go and wasn't sure I could sustain the expense and delay of a second trial. Fortunately, Judge Henderson rallied and made a recovery, but he was not able to return to the bench more than part time for a year. As a consequence, he fell behind in his work and the *Kraszewski* decision was delayed.

I WAS NOT IDLE WHILE WAITING for the *Kraszewski* decision. Among other things, I filed three more class actions against State Farm. The first, *Burkman v. State Farm*, was a California class action for discrimination against women in promotional opportunities in non-sales positions. Before filing the case, I made a courtesy phone call to Tom Powers to tell him I would be filing another class action against State Farm the next day. My motives were a bit more complex than mere courtesy, however. I knew that Cooley Godward would not be hired to defend this case, due to the serious discovery abuses in which they had engaged in the *Kraszewski* case. I knew that when Tom reported to State Farm that I was filing another case, they would ask him to recommend another law firm and that there was a good chance Tom would recommend Bruce Nelson, head of the employment department at Morrison & Foerster, a huge defense firm headquartered in San Francisco. Tom knew Bruce well from ABA Labor and Employment Section activities and Bruce was extremely well respected by his peers, including me. I thought it would be good for me to have Bruce on the other side of the case, as he was both smart and reasonable. Moreover, I anticipated that whoever picked up the defense of the *Burkman* case also would inherit the *Kraszewski* case.

The next day, as planned, I filed the new case. Late that evening, I received a phone call at home from an obviously elated Bruce Nelson, telling me that he would be representing State Farm in the *Burkman* AND *Kraszewski* cases. I said, "Congratulations, but you owe me one. I steered those cases to you by notifying Tom yesterday of the new filing." Bruce was a bit surprised, but very appreciative, and he immediately told me, "I want to get to work immediately on the *Kraszewski* case and see if we can settle it. Let's have lunch." We set up lunch the following week at a restaurant at the Embarcadero overlooking San Francisco Bay and my associate Brad Seligman and I went to meet him.

As soon as we sat down to lunch, Bruce wanted to know, "What will it take to settle the *Kraszewski* case?" I explained our position: Ten years of hiring 50% female agents in California, publication of notice of trainee agent job openings, more outreach and recruitment of women, reasonable attorneys' fees and costs—which I explained could be litigated separately before the Court—and an individualized claim procedure for the claims of class members who had suffered sex discrimination in the recruitment, selection, appointment or hire of trainee agents. My demand for a claim procedure was new, as previously I had demanded a lump-sum amount of class back pay, and Bruce wanted more details.

I explained that I had decided that the individual claims of class members were too large to reduce to a formulaic recovery from a fixed fund and that the size of the individual claims, which I estimated to then be worth $50,000 to $400,000, were large enough to justify a procedure that would ferret out the good claims from the bad and reward the actual victims of State Farm's discrimination. Notice of the claims procedure would be publicized in the media with ads that State Farm would pay for, notices would be posted at all State Farm offices, and individual notices of the right to file claims would be mailed to all past and present female State Farm employees and applicants for employment, regardless of what job they might have applied and/or been hired for. Disputed claims would be heard and decided by special masters the parties would agree to, with my firm representing claimants and Morrison & Foerster ("MoFo"), Bruce's firm, representing State Farm. To streamline the presentation of evidence, we would agree on a schedule of back pay to be paid to winning claimants, with amounts varying according to the year each claimant suffered discrimination. The claim procedure would be co-extensive with the class definition the Court had adopted—meaning both applicants and deterred applicants would be permitted to file claims. All claimants who fit within the class definition would be entitled to the so-called "Teamsters presumption," a presumption that arises from a 1977 United States Supreme court case (*International Brotherhood of Teamsters v. United States*) which presumes that all members of the class were victims of discrimination, but permits the defendant an opportunity to prove that a particular individual did not suffer from the pattern and practice of discrimination that had been proven in the class trial. Thus, the "Teamsters presumption" has the important effect of shifting the burden of proof—which the plaintiff normally carries—to the defendant.

Bruce was very intrigued by the idea of a claims procedure, seeing in it both the basis for settling the case, and, I surmise, the opportunity for him to hire more attorneys and bill more fees. Bruce was a bit of an entrepreneur who had participated in at least one other claims procedure in a Title VII case—albeit a much smaller one—and I think my proposal appealed to this entrepreneurial spirit. In any case, he pursued my claim procedure proposal with great enthusiasm and concluded the lunch by saying, "This has been extremely positive. I think we can work this out and settle the case."

A week later, I got another call at home from Bruce. He said he was at his cabin skiing at Lake Tahoe for a week and wanted me to drive up immediately, stay at his cabin, and begin working on a settlement agreement, which would include a 50% hiring goal and an individualized claim procedure. I was elated at this development but didn't want to appear overanxious, and told him, "Work shouldn't interrupt your vacation. This can wait until you get back next week." A few days later, on a Saturday, I went to my weekly morning of inner-city basketball at Live Oak Park, in Berkeley, and returned home around 1 p.m. feeling fabulous, as I had just played three hours of basketball, which always made me feel great. Plus, I was on the brink of settling the biggest case of my life! As I walked into the house, the phone was ringing. I picked it up and on the phone was Paula Downey, one of Bruce Nelson's associates. "I know you were a friend of Bruce's and I wanted you to be one of the first to know. Bruce was found dead this morning in bed," she said. I was stunned. "What happened?" I asked. "We don't know yet, but Bruce had a serious fall skiing a couple of days ago, hit his head, and the doctors think it might have been a hemorrhage in his brain." I thanked Paula for the courtesy of calling me, then hung up the phone, drained and astonished by the sudden turn of events. Aside from feeling terrible for Bruce and his family, I knew immediately that the settlement Bruce and I had in mind was dependent on Bruce selling it to State Farm. He was charismatic, powerful, and persuasive and I felt confident he could sell the ambitious deal. I had no confidence that anyone else at MoFo could or would promote a settlement on the basis of an individualized claim procedure. My hopes had climbed a mountain with Bruce and now had plummeted into a deep hole.

A week later, I attended Bruce's memorial service. His two girls spoke about what their daddy had meant to them. Listening to them was devastating. Bruce was only 40 years old and in the prime of life when he died. I pondered my own mortality.

After the service, an attorney introduced himself to me as Kirby Wilcox, an employment attorney with Morrison & Foerster. Kirby said MoFo's representation of State Farm was "on hold," while State Farm pondered the effect of Bruce's death on their choice of MoFo. Several weeks later, Kirby told me that State Farm had interviewed several major firms at company headquarters in Bloomington, Illinois about legal representation in the *Kraszewski* and *Burkman* cases, that he represented MoFo in the interview and MoFo had been selected. I asked him what the winning pitch had been, and Kirby told me with a sparkle in his eyes, "You'll love this. I went into the interview and told them, 'I know you hired Bruce Nelson and you don't know me. Compared to Bruce Nelson and Guy Saperstein, I'm a nobody. I don't have the Title VII reputation or experience that Guy has, but I match up well with him in one very important category. I'm as stubborn as he is!'" I congratulated him, although I wondered what State Farm's acceptance of the "stubbornness" pitch portended for the future of the case. I was to find out.

THE JUDGE ASSIGNED to the *Burkman* case was not favorable, as I drew United States District Judge Samuel Conti. Conti had a reputation for being irascible and erratic on the bench and was considered hostile to civil rights cases. Maybe I should have retained Madame Fatima before I filed it! I knew it would be difficult to certify the class in this case (i.e. satisfy the "commonality" or "typicality" requirement of a class action) because, unlike the *Kraszewski* case which involved only one entry-level job, *Burkman* sought to encompass many jobs, with varying job descriptions and qualifications. Without class certification, I would be left with the claims of a handful of individual plaintiffs and the impact of the case would be minimal.

The *Burkman* case was taken over by Ray Wheeler, the new head of MoFo's labor and employment department, and Kirby took control of the *Kraszewski* defense. Ray was a traditional labor lawyer and had little or no Title VII experience; he was smart, but his lack of Title VII experience made him suspicious about much of what I said about Title VII. When this was added to the fact that he demonstrated little sense of humor, my relationship with him became pretty dull.

Ray was smart enough to realize my most serious problem in the *Burkman* case would be certifying the highly diverse class I sought to represent. The Northern District of California Local Rules provided that plaintiffs' motion for class certification had to be filed within six months of serving the complaint on defendants, so, prior to the first status conference with Judge Conti, Ray and I worked out a reasonable schedule for class discovery and the filing of pleadings on the class certification issues that complied with the Local Rules. We appeared before Judge Conti at the status conference and explained the schedule for determining the class issues, which would have plaintiffs filing their motion in October. As I was explaining the proposed schedule, Judge Conti leaned over the bench and asked his calendar clerk, "When is the first available date for trial?" The clerk responded, "October." "OK, we'll set the trial to begin the first week in October," directed Judge Conti. As Ray began to protest that the class certification issues had to be decided before trial could be set, Judge Conti intoned, "Next case." As we walked out of the courtroom, I turned to Ray and said, "Well, I guess this solves my class cert problems!" I knew that Judge Conti's irrational decision to ignore the class certification stage meant that plaintiffs could proceed to trial with their broad-based class allegations intact and that this was exactly what State Farm feared most.

Faced with the prospect of going to trial on broad allegations of discrimination, and the uncertainties inherent in such erratic judicial behavior, State Farm chose to settle the *Burkman* case prior to the October trial date. The settlement was not the strongest ever obtained, as the liability period of the case mostly included the years

following the *Kraszewski* complaint when State Farm was beginning to clean up its act by hiring and promoting more women, but
we did obtain court-enforced goals and timetables for the promotion of women in non-sales jobs and back pay for the named plaintiffs. Judge Conti's erratic behavior had worked in my favor.

Many years later, a local legal newspaper was doing a profile of
Judge Conti and I told them Conti had the reputation among many
attorneys of being "a lunatic." Shortly thereafter, I was at a Christmas
party put on by a friend of mine; the doorbell rang, I opened the
door, and who should be standing there but the "lunatic" himself—
Judge Conti and his wife. Despite my unflattering characterization
of his judicial reputation, we talked for an hour and I found him to
be warm, interesting, very charming, and even a witty person—
totally unlike his public image and reputation. I regretted my comment to the newspaper, and, henceforth, decided I would express
opinions about my own experiences and what I knew first-hand,
not opinions based on "reputation."

THE SECOND CASE I FILED against State Farm while waiting to conclude *Kraszewski* was a discrimination class action in Texas brought
on behalf of women and Hispanics, *Estrada v. State Farm*. Although
I normally tried to stay as far away from the EEOC as possible in
litigating my cases, as I had a low opinion of their litigation ability,
in this case cooperation with the EEOC would be very much to my
benefit, as the EEOC had filed a "Commissioner's Charge" of discrimination that offered the chance of greatly increasing the period of liability—and, thus, the potential amount of back pay—
that would be available in my case. Therefore, I scheduled a visit to
Washington, D.C. to speak with the head of the EEOC, Clarence
Thomas—now Associate Justice of the United States Supreme
Court. Mr. Thomas already had established himself as an arch-en-
emy of class-based remedies, yet that was exactly what I would be
seeking in the *Estrada* case, and I wanted his help. As I sat in the
anteroom to his office, an assistant of his came out to explain, with
great emphasis, that it would be counterproductive for me to dis-

cuss my class remedies and class claim procedure ideas with him and that I needed to stick to safe topics with Chairman Thomas, or risk his vaunted temper. I listened politely, then walked into Chairman Thomas' office and immediately began explaining why class remedies and a class claim procedure would be required in the *Estrada* case. I didn't get much of an argument from him, the meeting was pleasant, and the EEOC later agreed to cooperate.

Years later, shortly after Thomas was nominated to the United States Supreme Court by President Bush, who introduced him as "the most qualified lawyer in America," I was invited to speak at the Mid-Winter Meeting of the Labor and Employment Section of the American Bar Association. I considered this group, which had invited me to speak many times, to be the most important group of employment lawyers in the country, as it included the most experienced Title VII class action defense attorneys with national practices—attorneys like Tom Powers, Steve Tallent, Laurence Ashe, Gary Siniscalco and, before he died, Bruce Nelson. They also made it a point to meet in some of the finest golf and tennis resorts in the country, which also gave me a strong incentive to attend. I walked into a reception in progress the evening before my speech, and I was immediately invited to join a group of about fifteen employment attorneys—nearly all corporate defense attorneys from major law firms—and was asked, "What do you think about Clarence Thomas' nomination?" I said, "I think he is completely unqualified." The defense attorneys nodded their agreement and one of them said, "Do you realize that not a single law firm represented in this room would hire Clarence Thomas?" That was a truly devastating indictment of Thomas. He had spent his legal career practicing employment law, yet his peers in the employment bar—including both plaintiff and defense attorneys—had such a low opinion of him, none would hire him. Yet he was on his way to the United States Supreme Court as "the most qualified lawyer in America," according to President Bush! I considered his appointment to be an insult to every good lawyer in America, and I think everyone in that room did too.

The *Estrada* case would be filed in Houston and I needed to associate local counsel, so I called Steve Susman, of Susman & Godfrey. Steve was, and is, a highly successful attorney who has litigated major antitrust and securities class actions on behalf of plaintiffs, as well as represent important clients such as the Bass family and House Speaker Jim Wright, and often is included in lists of "The Best Trial Lawyers in America." A wall in his Dallas office is full of newspaper and magazine articles extolling his many victories. I told Steve what my case was about and he said he would be happy to meet with me.

I flew to Houston to meet with the potential plaintiffs in the case and Steve. Steve had a spectacular office in a large Houston high-rise and, despite the opulence of the surroundings, I wanted to assure myself that his hourly rate would not undercut mine, which was $350 at the time. So I asked him what his rate was. In a perfect Texas drawl, he told me, "Well, my normal rate is $475 an hour, but if you really want my attention, it's $625." I was curious, so I asked him, "What do your clients get for $625 an hour that they don't get for $475?" "More attention. They get their calls returned sooner. Their files don't sit on the edge of my desk," he offered.

I knew Steve had a fabulous reputation in Texas, as well as nationally, and I tried to interest him in the case by telling him about the facts, as well as explaining that I had a good track record of obtaining "multipliers" of my hourly rate in civil rights applications for attorneys' fees. I ran off a list of 2.0 multipliers I had obtained—a longer list than any civil rights attorney in the country. Steve listened politely and when I was finished, he said, "A two multipler? I prefer those 10 and 20 multipliers." I realized that, no matter how well I had been paid as a civil rights attorney, I was still a neophyte about fees compared to the big class action litigators in other areas of practice. In any case, despite the relatively small fees the *Estrada* case was likely to produce compared to other cases he handled, Steve agreed to associate on the case, and his firm did everything asked of them promptly and effectively from start to finish without a hint of dispute or disagreement.

The case was assigned to United States District Judge David Hittner, a former prosecutor. Hittner was described to me as an abrasive, no-nonsense, law-and-order Republican, but a good lawyer who was not known to be biased against civil rights cases. I found him to be straightforward and confrontational—sometimes bordering on abrasive—but open-minded and fair. He would state his opinions strongly and sometimes argumentatively, but that did not mean he had made up his mind or was closed off to discussion—rather, it was his way of saying, "This is what I think, so if you want to change my mind, you better start talking and it better be good!" I've always loved judges like this, because they expose their thought process and the reasons they might be opposed to what I was seeking. This allowed me to understand what was bothering them about my position—and then to answer their concerns, and, hopefully, alter their positions. The tough judges for me always have been the silent ones, the ones who don't reveal what they are thinking until they've written a decision, and that is too late to interact with them and change their minds.

Judge Hittner provided ample opportunities for interaction. He began the case by telling me at the first status conference, "I heard you did well with your California case against State Farm, but that doesn't mean anything to me because this is a different case," then yelling at my law associate at another hearing and threatening to hold her in contempt for not standing up fast enough as he entered the room, then opening motion and discovery hearings by indicating he did not agree with our claims about the time and geographical scope of the case, yet listening intently to my explanations and ultimately ruling in favor of plaintiffs on important discovery issues.

State Farm was represented by Fulbright & Jaworski, perhaps the most powerful law firm in Texas. Nevertheless, at no time did I feel Judge Hittner "hometowned" us or favored the defense in any way. He went with the best argument, which, on most occasions, we had. The Fulbright lawyers were tough, but fair to deal with, and after they failed in their dispositive motions, they entered into settlement negotiations with us and the EEOC which resulted in an affirmative action hiring and promotion order, $12 million in back pay for the class, to be distributed on a formula basis, and an agreement that plaintiffs were entitled to reimbursement of attorneys' fees and costs. I appeared in Court to argue the fees motion, and with Steve Susman standing alongside me with his $475/$625 hourly rate, Judge Hittner had no trouble awarding my firm its full hourly rates, plus a multiplier for risk and delay.

I was happy to conclude the *Estrada* case, as I was tired of travelling to Houston. Aside from the rigors of travel, Houston was a destination with the worst weather I'd ever seen: one time the wind and dust were blowing so hard that tumbleweeds were flying down the streets in downtown Houston; the next time I visited, rain and sleet fell for two days; the summer was like a blast furnace—so hot pedestrians walked in subterranean, air-conditioned tunnels. And the land was flat as far as the eye could see from the 50th floor of one of Houston's modern—near-empty—high-rise office buildings. But I did manage—with the help of the Fulbright lawyers—to return to California with a beautiful pair of Luchese cowboy boots to remind me of my experiences in Houston and how fortunate I was not to have to live there.

WHILE WAITING FOR THE *KRASZEWSKI* DECISION, I was contacted by two women who complained that they had tried to obtain employment at the Lucky Stores Northern California distribution center in nearby San Leandro. Carol Bockman, an experienced, licensed truck driver, who then was driving large trucks for Safeway Markets, had applied for a truck driving job with Lucky Stores, a large grocery-store chain, only to be told that "a woman's place is on the hood of a truck, not behind the wheel." I never figured out if that meant women were supposed to have sex on the hood or were just hood ornaments, but it definitely meant they weren't going to get hired to drive big trucks. The other woman, Juanita Leonardini, complained that Lucky Stores had refused to hire her as a permanent warehouseman. I asked her what the lifting requirements were and she said, "up to 100 pounds, including large sacks of vegetables and produce." Juanita wasn't very big, so I asked her if she could handle that much weight and she assured me, "I grew up on a farm bucking 100-pound bales of hay. Potato sacks are easy."

I filed charges of discrimination with the EEOC, and asked to see if there were any "like or related" charges against Lucky Stores. Lo and behold, three years earlier, the EEOC had filed a Commissioners' Charge against Lucky Stores in United States District Court in Sacramento. On further checking, the EEOC case had been assigned to U. S. District Judge Raul A. Ramirez, a relatively young Hispanic judge with a reputation as having been a good trial lawyer and a solid state court judge. What his attitude would be in a sex discrimination case involving traditionally "male" jobs was not clear, and I harbored some concern that a "macho" attitude toward heavy physical work might be a problem. Nevertheless, based on his general reputation, I was happy to file my case in Sacramento and file a "related case" motion to have the case assigned to Judge Ramirez.

Before filing the case, however, I called the EEOC and spoke with the attorney handling its case against Lucky Stores. I asked him what evidence they had against Lucky Stores, and he said, "we have statistics showing that very few women have been hired to work in the warehouse, those that do get hired are hired on a temporary basis and never are given enough work to qualify for permanent status. As for truck drivers, they just don't hire women." I asked how many women they had found to be witnesses to Lucky Stores' discrimination and he said, "None." I asked him if Lucky Stores maintained records of applications from women, and he said, "No." I then asked, "Well, how do you intend to prove the case?" "By statistics. Title VII cases permit proof of discrimination by statistics alone," he said. I responded, "That is a very optimistic reading of Title VII caselaw, but even if it was true that statistics alone could prove discrimination, that's a lousy way to present a case. You need live witnesses to tell real stories of actual discrimination in order, in the words of the United States Supreme Court, to 'bring the cold statistics to life'." I was astounded by the EEOC's lackadaisical approach; the case had been on file for three years and they didn't have a single witness. That would not be the way I would proceed with the case.

The day before filing our case, I issued notices to the press that the next day at 9 a.m. my two clients and I would be holding a press conference at the entrance gate to the Lucky Stores Distribution Center to announce a major class action lawsuit. The next morning, Carol, Juanita and I showed up at the gate to hand out packets for the press announcing and explaining the lawsuit. Four of the five local television stations showed up with cameras, and most of the local newspapers were there with journalists and photographers. I made my statement explaining the lawsuit, Carol and Juanita then explained their experiences with Lucky Stores, and we all answered press questions. As this was going on, large trucks were going in and out of the gate and many of the trucks were honking with their loud air horns, some were yelling profanities at us, and a few even flipped us the bird. As soon as Carol and Juanita saw this, they tried to stand in front of the gate and hand copies of our press release to the truck drivers, who responded by trying to run them over, spitting out more profanities and flipping them off. Meanwhile the television cameras were rolling. It was great theater, aided by the fact that Carol and Juanita were very attractive women, as well as being quite courageous dodging the trucks. Blue-collar women! The television stations loved the action and the Lucky Stores story ran as the No. 1 news story that night on the 6 and 11 p.m. news shows of all four stations. As with all my class actions, I had obtained an 800 number for the case, which was prominently displayed in my press release, and several local newspapers published it, along with my name. Over the course of the next few days, 300 women called my office with stories about the discrimination they had experienced at the Lucky Stores distribution center. Since, as a practical matter, I would only be able to call 15–20 women as trial witnesses, my search for anecdotal witnesses was over; one well-done press conference had brought in more factual evidence than the EEOC had obtained in three years.

People often criticized me for my use of the press in his way, but I steadfastly defend this practice. It was never a matter of aggrandizing my name in the press; what was at stake was notice to the class that a case was being litigated on their behalf and, if they wished to influence the result in the case, they needed to step forward. Indeed, a class action, if certified, can conclusively determine the legal rights of absent class members; if they fail to step forward, rights can be lost by inaction. Moreover, there often is no other practical way to obtain evidence. Indeed, in the *Bockman v. Lucky Stores* case, I had been told by the EEOC that records of employment applications were not maintained; if true, this would mean that, without notice through the press, the women who had suffered discrimination when they attempted to be hired at Lucky Stores might never be found. So, using the press in an affirmative way is not only ethical, it often is *required* to litigate class action cases effectively.

The Lucky Stores case was defended by a local Oakland firm, not one of the national mega-firms that we normally faced off against. Lucky Stores' lead counsel, George Barron, was a smart guy—he had been on law review at UCLA School of Law—but he was out of his depth in a Title VII class action. Indeed, at times I wasn't sure he even understood how much was at stake in the class part of the case. Instead of making the defense of the class allegations his priority, he focussed on defeating the individual claims of the two named plaintiffs. Thus, he spent days deposing Carol and Juanita, while assigning a young associate, Jonathan Wong, to the formidable task of deposing my statistical expert, Professor Richard Drogin, and my labor market availability expert, Professor John Pencavel. Jonathan was an inexperienced attorney with no prior experience in a Title VII class action and no knowledge of labor market availability or Title VII statistical proofs. While he was left to flail around trying to take the depositions of the two most important witnesses in plaintiffs' case, George was trying to impeach the individual claims of Carol and Juanita. George was focussing on two individual claims worth less than $50,000 each, while Jonathan was left the task of dealing with class evidence that involved millions of dollars of liability and an affirmative action Court order for class members. I was astounded at the misunderstanding of priorities by the defense and the terrible job they were doing preparing their defense—but I enjoyed every minute of it. I wasn't proud; I was quite happy to let opposing counsel make my job easier!

The jobs at issue in the Lucky Stores cases were truck drivers and warehouse workers, and both jobs required heavy physical labor. I anticipated there would be many disputes about what each job required, and whether women were capable of such work, so instead of relying on conflicting descriptions of the work, I decided to make a film. I obtained a Court order permitting me to film the work done in the distribution center and hired Avi Stachenfeld, a Harvard Law School graduate turned filmmaker who I had gotten to know while playing basketball at a local school. Avi, Carol, Juanita and I showed up at the distribution center and, accompanied by Jonathan Wong, began to film.

There was no real dispute that women were capable of driving trucks—indeed, Carol had a California license to drive large trucks, but the job included hooking up large trailers to the tractor, which meant that a 3,000 pound "dolly" had to be rolled under the front of the trailer and attached before hooking up the trailer with the tractor. We began by having Carol demonstrate, on camera, how this was done. She made it look easy, so I decided to try it myself. It wasn't easy. The ground was not perfectly level, and pushing 3,000 pounds even slightly uphill required all the strength I had. So the camera filmed Carol handling this heavy task nimbly, and me—presumably the stronger male—struggling. No objections from Jonathan.

Next we went into the warehouse, filmed the layout, then filmed specific job tasks that required either heavy lifting or placing items high overhead (which, arguably, might require workers to be a certain minimum height). With Juanita as the model and guide, she explained each of the jobs and proceeded to perform them. There were large bags of different types of vegetables weighing up to eighty pounds each and Juanita handled them easily—just like she had handled bales of hay; when I tried the same task, I did less well. The heaviest task required walking up and down about ten steps carrying five-gallon buckets of honey which weighed eighty–ninety pounds. Again, Juanita handled it easily, while I looked like someone who was better suited to white-collar work.

Lucky Stores had maintained that women, in general, were too short to place items on the top shelves of storage racks and that use of stepstools took too much time. We brought an inexpensive stepstool—the kind with wheels that collapse when a person stands on the stool—and easily demonstrated how quickly they could be used; indeed, the stool made the task easier and probably would prevent injuries, as the top shelf was a stretch even for someone 5' 10" tall.

The last set of jobs we filmed were the meat-packing and deli jobs. Here, employment discrimination in action could not possibly have been shown more graphically. There were two production lines—one for packaging cut meat, the other for packaging other delicatessen items, such as cheese. The tasks appeared to be identical, yet the meat packaging was done by men, the deli packaging by women. And—no surprise—the meat packagers (male) were paid significantly more than the deli packagers (female). In addition, all the supervisors were men. We had our film and I felt confident the film would be more persuasive than anything anyone would say about the nature of the jobs.

Shortly before the trial was scheduled to begin, I received a long letter from Juanita (with a copy sent to the Court) informing me that she had become a born-again Christian, had learned that God's place for women was at home serving her man, not working at any warehouse, and that her equal employment lawsuit was the work of the Devil and had to be dismissed. Juanita always had been a little unstable, but we liked her and she sure could handle the heavy work at the Lucky Stores warehouse. She was tough. One day, she took me out to a ranch outside of Livermore to show me how she could "buck bales" of hay with the cowboys. Sure enough, she could grab a huge bale of hay, weighing roughly 100 pounds, and throw it up on a truck, often over her head. She said it was all technique, but I didn't want to try it! Another time she showed up with her fourth husband (Juanita was only 24 at the time) and asked me to help solve his employment problems with his foreman. On talking to the poor lad, I realized that whatever problems he was having at work were the proximate result of his painful love for Juanita and her wandering eye. A week later, she showed up in the office with an older man who was wearing a flashy shirt open down the front to his navel, exposing several pounds of gold chains to match his gold bracelets, gold rings, gold eyeglasses and gold shoe adornments. "Juanita and Mr. Las Vegas are here to see you," ad-libbed my secretary in announcing them. We liked to think of her as "colorful" and "entertaining," but the Christian schtick was over the edge. I wrote back to her, explaining as nicely as I could that my mother had been a Sunday School teacher, that I had grown up in a Christian church and that God believed in fairness for everyone—even women. "If women want to work in a warehouse they should have the right to do so if they can competently do the work. Furthermore, I have been working on your case for three years without pay and I don't want you to screw it up with anti-feminist, right-wing Christian bullshit," as I tactfully put it. More to the point, the case had been certified as a class action, I now represented a large class of women who were interested in equal employment opportunities at Lucky Stores, and I had no intention of dismissing the case. I decided not to call Juanita as a witness and hoped the defense would not be smart enough to call her.

The next bit of great pretrial news came from my bank, which informed me that the firm's line of credit, which had been extended to $600,000, was tapped out and would not be extended further. Moreover, repayment, in full, was due in six weeks. I surveyed my other sources of credit: my parents and Jeanine's parents—maxed out; the Jewish Federation loan program—maxed out; Consumers Cooperative Credit Union—maxed out; my house—no more equity left; credit cards—beyond all limits. My statistician had just sent me a bill for $58,000—for one month's work—and now we were about to start trial, which would cost me far more than that in expert witness expenses alone. But most of those bills would not be due until after trial, so technically I was still solvent!

With that as the financial backdrop, two days before trial George called up and offered $1 million to settle the case, along with a Court-enforced agreement to hire significant numbers of women in warehouse and truck driving jobs, and $1 million in attorneys' fees. I went down the hall to talk to Brad Seligman, who would try the case with me. I presented the offer to Brad. He asked, "What do you want to do?" I said, "Let's go to trial." Brad said, "Right on!" I called George back to thank him for the offer, but told him it was rejected.

Brad and I set up shop in a nice garden motel in a low-rent section of Sacramento over the weekend, and trial began on Monday. We would try the case with a fine young EEOC attorney, Fritz Wollett, as our case had been consolidated with the EEOC case. Brad had done a great amount of work preparing the Lucky Stores case for trial and desperately wanted to do something he never had done before—make an opening statement in a major trial. He had earned it and I gave it to him. Furthermore, he had clerked for the Chief Judge in the Eastern District, Lawrence K. Karlton, and knew our judge, Raul Ramirez. Raul knew Brad was smart and I knew he would listen to Brad intently.

Brad gave an excellent, hour-long opening, covering all the issues and outlining what we would prove. I could see Judge Ramirez was taking notes. Then George Barron stood up, unveiled two large aerial photos of the Lucky Stores Distribution Center and explained—painstakingly slowly—where in the photo different tasks were performed. We had no idea why he was wasting time in an opening statement on such trivia—indeed, trivia that was uncontested and would play no part in the trial. It simply made no difference to the issues that would be contested at trial where the meat department was located, where vegetables were loaded, where the frozen goods were stored, etc. It was the most boring, inconsequential and irrelevant opening I ever had heard.

We began putting on evidence the next morning. I wanted to begin by showing our film, as the film—more clearly than words could describe—showed the kind of work that was at issue in the case, and, as a bonus, showed my two plaintiffs doing the work competently and easily. I would have to lay the foundation to introduce the film with the filmmaker, so I told Avi that he would be the first witness, that trial began at 9:30 a.m. and he had to be on time. At 9:30 a.m., Judge Ramirez was on the bench, I was at the podium ready to begin, the film was loaded and ready to roll, but Avi was missing. There were a few evidentiary matters unrelated to the film to resolve, so Judge Ramirez took the time to raise these issues, but I remained nervous about Avi, as my next witness was not showing up until the afternoon. At 9:45 a.m., the doors in the back of the courtroom swung open, and in walked Avi wearing a white linen suit that looked like he had slept in it for the last two weeks—the *auteur* filmmaker! Avi took the stand, made his apologies for being late, then explained through my direct examination how the film was made. We rolled the film for its two-hour length, with Avi and me providing commentary and no objections were made by the defense to my comments about the film or even to the parts of the film showing me doing some of the tasks poorly, in comparison with the women. Judge Ramirez asked intelligent questions about the job tasks throughout the showing of the film. It was clear that he had the picture and any fears I may have had about his latent or active male chauvinism dissipated.

We called as our next witness Lucky Stores' warehouse manager. Brad cross-examined him for most of a day and systematically demolished him. The next day, I took the next witness, Lucky Stores' Labor Relations Manager. I had taken his deposition, where he had done fairly well trying to explain the lack of female hiring, and expected him to be the most difficult and important defense witness we would face; he was a smart guy and he knew his subject.

I had prepared for my cross-examination in advance of trial, but I stayed up late the night before in the motel going over and revising my attack, while Brad and Fritz, who would have the day off while I worked over the Labor Relations guy, went into town to have a few drinks and hear some music.

The cross-examination began and the witness did pretty well, but after about two hours, he made a few mistakes by deviating from his prior deposition testimony. Each time, I would impeach him with his inconsistent prior testimony. The subject matter of these impeachments was not hugely important, but I noticed the witness was getting rattled and not showing the confidence he had begun with. We broke for lunch, but I stayed in the courtroom, reviewing his deposition transcript and sharpening my examination while Brad brought me back a sandwich from the federal cafeteria.

After lunch, we began where we had left off and the witness continued to disintegrate, as I caught him in one testimonial inconsistency after another, until I realized he wasn't presenting any defense to my questions—he was letting me lead him into any admission I wanted him to make. I couldn't believe what was happening; it was way beyond any expectations I had when I began the cross-examination and almost too good to be true. As he was making another damaging admission, I turned around and looked at plaintiffs' counsel table. Brad and Fritz were laughing so hard they were doubled over, with their heads between their knees under the table! He was giving away the whole case. After this, and Brad's work on the warehouse manager, I didn't know what was left of Lucky Stores' defenses. The Court adjourned for the day.

I had noticed that a well-dressed man who I didn't know had been sitting in the courtroom for the past two days. When Court adjourned, I walked back to him, introduced myself, and asked him what his interest in this case was. He introduced himself as an experienced Assistant United States Attorney and said he never had seen a civil rights case or class action trial before, and wanted to observe one for a few days. As I was speaking with him, Bob Woods, a senior partner in George Barron's law firm and a member of the

Board of Directors of Lucky Stores, who had been watching the last two days of trial, walked up and stood beside me as I spoke with the Assistant United States Attorney. "What do you think of the trial?" I asked the United States Attorney. "You've completely destroyed them," he said. I turned to Bob and asked, "What do you think?" "I cannot disagree with that assessment," he replied.

I thought to myself, "Well, if that's your assessment—and it certainly is mine—why aren't we settling the case," but Bob already was ahead of me. Bob had not come over to talk to me with the intention of passing on congratulations. He wanted to stop the trial and settle the case. I told him we would not stop he trial, but that we were available to discuss settlement immediately. We agreed to meet after dinner at a local law office.

Brad, Fritz and I met with Bob, George and Jonathan. Bob clearly was in charge of the negotiations for Lucky Stores; George said little. We made our demands: female hiring rates of 30% in the warehouse jobs and 10% for truck-drivers, a full-time monitor to oversee the warehouse operations to be selected by plaintiffs and paid for by Lucky Stores, $3 million in back pay for the women, plus reasonable attorneys' fees and costs. By the end of the evening, I could see the money was not going to be the problem, but the female hiring rates—which were higher than ever previously established for heavy-lifting and truck-driving jobs, and the presence of a monitor selected by us, was not going to be easy to sell to Lucky Stores. Bob again asked for more time, and the postponement of trial. We wanted to help Bob, who appeared to be an effective and persuasive problem-solver, and his request for some time certainly was not unreasonable, but we said no; we wanted to keep the pressure on them until the minute all issues were settled. Brad, Fritz and I went out for a few drinks, laughed ourselves silly remembering the events of the day, then dragged ourselves to bed.

We returned to Court the next morning a little bleary-eyed, but still exhilarated about the events of the day before. George Barron took the podium as we were about to call another witness and announced to the Court that, "The parties are very close to settlement of the case and it would be counterproductive to continue the trial. We need time to talk to our clients and work out details with the plaintiffs." I told the Court I disagreed with that assessment: "We have had some encouraging discussions with Lucky Stores, but nothing has been agreed to. Until agreement on at least core issues has been reached, the trial should continue and we have our witnesses ready, your Honor." Judge Ramirez, who had done some amateur boxing and was a very street-savvy guy, knew exactly what was going on: We had Lucky Stores on the ropes, and wanted to deliver the knockout punch before we handed them an agreement to sign. "Since plaintiffs have their morning witness here, and he has come from out of town, we will take testimony in the morning and recess for the day at noon. Since this is Friday, that will give you Friday afternoon, Saturday and Sunday to settle the case. George, if you really think the case is close to settlement, that is enough time. If it is not settled, trial will resume Monday morning. The parties are to notify my chambers Sunday night whether or not the case has settled," ruled the Judge. He had given both sides what they wanted: To Lucky Stores he gave time to settle the case; to plaintiffs, he kept the pressure of trial on the defendant.

We worked all weekend, finally settling the major issues late Sunday night. We got everything we sought. Lucky Stores agreed to the adoption of factual findings of evidence submitted in trial by plaintiffs and highly adverse to Lucky Stores' prior positions in the litigation, such as the following: "There is no evidence that men have greater success at passing Lucky's pre-employment tests than men"; "a variety of unweighted subjective criteria are utilized by Lucky's during the hiring process"; Lucky Stores' practice of not forwarding applications from women that did not specify a position "has had a disparate impact upon female applicants, which is not justified by business necessity"; "Prior to 1984, no female was employed as a blue-collar worker in the bakery or garage, or was a permanent full-time truckdriver"; "For the period 1975–1983, there were no women hired into the garage department, no women hired as boxpersons, bakery production workers, shippers, pasteurizers, pallet repair workers, permanent hostlers, meatcutters or engineers"; "For the 1975–83 period, there were approximately 3,600 work opportunities in class positions, of which only 16 (0.44%) were women"; "For the 1980–84 period, there was a substantial applicant flow of women interested in class positions, consisting of approximately 2,000 female applications, the majority of which were not forwarded to plant managers"; "Using either applicant flow or labor market availability data, substantial, statistically significant disparities between Lucky Stores' hiring rates and these data are observed resulting in standard deviations of over 10 to nearly 24"; and "Sex is not a bona fide occupational qualification for any class job, and business necessity does not require the hiring of males only for any job." I have never seen—before or since—a defendant in a Title VII settlement admit to such facts.

We obtained an injunction prohibiting future discrimination, an agreement by Lucky Stores that it would abandon use of any height requirement and the requirement of a Class I driving license for hostler jobs, an agreement to adopt and enforce an anti-sexual harassment policy, new recruitment and application procedures, including the hiring of a personnel recruiter "whose primary function shall be to recruit qualified women for class positions," notification of job openings to a list of women's' organizations, newspaper publication of job openings, and, most importantly, goals and timetables for the hiring of women into class jobs. These hiring goals ranged from 10% for truck drivers and engineers to 30% for warehouse jobs—including heavy-lifting jobs. These hiring goals were imposed for ten years. Both the goals themselves and the ten-year length of the decree were the highest ever obtained in a Title VII decree for such non-traditional and heavy-lifting jobs. The requirements imposed on Lucky Stores would be monitored by class counsel and by a full-time monitor, selected by the EEOC, paid by Lucky Stores, and approved by the parties, who would be on-site inspecting conditions in the distribution center, empowered to investigate any claim of harassment or disparate treatment by women.

In addition to the injunctive (i.e., prospective) relief, class members would be paid $3 million through a claim procedure administered by class counsel, with disputes resolved by three female arbitrators, and be entitled to seek instatement with retroactive seniority. In any instatement proceeding, once the claimant established a minimal prima facie case for instatement, Lucky Stores had to disprove the claimant's case by "clear and convincing evidence." This was the first time ever, to my knowledge, that a defendant in a Title VII claim procedure had been saddled with this higher burden of proof. It was my intention to make State Farm the second to share that distinction.

We concluded the drafting late at night, and after Brad and I had finished congratulating each other, I sat at home after everyone had gone to sleep feeling thrilled with the achievement. But the Saperstein household, and the law firm, still were broke. The Consent Decree provided that plaintiffs were the "prevailing parties" entitled to attorneys' fees and costs, but didn't state how much. That important issue was left to Judge Ramirez to decide. Once the Judge made his decision and issued his award, Lucky Stores could appeal to the Court of Appeals, but the Consent Decree required Lucky Stores to pay 75% of the award to us during the pendency of any appeal.

After notice to the class and final Court approval of the Consent Decree, Lucky Stores offered $1 million, which approximately was the value of our time at our normal hourly rates. We countered with a demand for $2 million, arguing that a reasonable fee must take into account the risk of loss, the delay in obtaining payment, and the exceptional hiring quotas obtained. Settlement of the fees issues was not forthcoming, so both sides filed lengthy briefs, supported by testimony of attorneys regarding hourly rates, risks of litigation, results obtained, etc., and I argued the motion before Judge Ramirez. After an hour-and-a-half hearing, Judge Ramirez ordered Lucky Stores to pay us $1.75 million—$1 million for the normal hourly rates and a 1.75 multiplier to reflect exceptional results and excellent work by plaintiffs' counsel.

A few days later, I got a call from Bob Woods about the fee award. He said that Lucky Stores wanted to get a second opinion about appealing the fee award. He knew I was an expert in attorneys' fees law, and asked if I would recommend someone for him to talk to. I always got a special pleasure when my opponents asked me for advice; it indicated I had earned a level of trust from the opponent. But it presented me with a dilemma. Should I recommend a bad attorney, who might do a lousy job litigating the fees issues for Lucky Stores, but who also might give Lucky Stores a lousy opinion about settling the fees issues, or should I recommend an excellent attorney who might later turn into a formidable foe? I decided to take the higher road, and told Bob, "I'll give you the name of the toughest lawyer I've ever had to face in a fees litigation. He's also the best employment lawyer I've litigated against— Gil Diekmann."

Three weeks later, Jeanine and I rented a little cabin in the Sierras and took off for a few days by ourselves. Late one afternoon, I called Gil from a phone booth and asked him what he intended to do about Judge Ramirez' fees award. It was winter and the weather in the mountains was cold. We spoke for an hour, with Gil critiquing those parts of the award that he thought he might be successful in attacking on appeal. We ended the conversation with me agreeing to take a 3% discount in the award, and Lucky Stores agreeing to pay the remainder immediately. I hung up the phone, shivering in the 30° temperature, but warm in the knowledge that I could repay my creditors. It had taken fourteen years, but for the first time, the firm was out of debt and profitable! Jeanine and I popped open a bottle of champagne and went out for a wonderful dinner. It felt especially good knowing I would be able to pay the credit card bill when it arrived at home.

NOT ALL OUR EMPLOYMENT CLASS ACTIONS turned out so well. Brad successfully prosecuted a discrimination case against Furnishings 2000, a large retail furniture store chain. We had invested tens of thousands of dollars and thousands of hours of time proving the claims of discrimination by the time the company agreed to hire more women and minorities. We then turned to the subject of attorneys' fees and costs. Defense counsel, with a straight face, said his client was near insolvency and offered us "300 Naugahyde couches" in settlement of our fees claim. I thought to myself, "We have hundreds of thousands of dollars in fees and costs invested in this case and we're supposed to accept 300 Naugahyde couches in full payment?" Nevertheless, I went to a Furnishings 2000 store to look at their couches, returning to tell Brad, "It's a bunch of junk." We rejected the offer, but we should have taken it. Two months later, Furnishings 2000 declared bankruptcy and we got nothing for our efforts.

9

The State Farm
Claim Procedure War

"When they boo you, you got to make 'em pay."
—Satchel Paige

JUDGE HENDERSON WAS SLOW to recover from his illness—but, fortunately, he did recover. He was off the bench for nearly six months, then returned on a part-time basis for a year. As a result, it was not until more than two years after the conclusion of the *Kraszewski* trial that I received a phone call from his law clerk informing me that a decision had been made and an opinion written. He said he would put it in the mail, but I interrupted to say I'd send someone to pick it up immediately. I didn't want to wait a day longer.

The decision arrived in a sealed envelope. I quietly went into my office to read it. It was heavy. I opened it and looked at the last page to see how long it was, but made certain not to look at the text; the last page was numbered "192." I had a long read. I was tempted to jump to the last section to see if we had won, but decided, instead, to read it beginning to end. I was confident we had won, but I didn't want to jinx ourselves by peeking at the conclusions. A foolish superstition, perhaps, but I was willing to endure and even enjoy the suspense.

The decision began with a recitation of who the parties were and the jurisdictional facts, and then discussed the trainee agent position, where the first hint that the decision was going my way came: The Court found the position to be "entry-level," with few pre-requisites. The decision's description of the characteristics of the job tracked the evidence: "a golden opportunity" for substantial earnings, independence, and security. Undisputed in the evidence, and accepted as true by the Court, were the demographics of the State Farm workforce: 154 male and 1 female Agency Managers; 1,782 male agents, 65 women; and 1,276 male trainee agents hired, 94 women (nearly all of them after Muriel Kraszewski had filed her charges of sex discrimination). Professor Pencavel's Analysis of Relative Availability Report, and his trial testimony, were extensively surveyed—and accepted as establishing an accurate measure of the availability of women for the sales job. The Court noted the extensive admissions by State Farm managers that confirmed Pencavel's assumptions and conclusions, noting that, while State Farm's experts had made criticisms of Pencavel's analyses, their criticism was undermined by the managers' admissions and also not supported by contrary availability data. The Court specifically noted that State Farm's explanations of why it had not hired more women agents were not supported by credible facts and that the extensive testimony by women who had experienced blatant discrimination had not been rebutted.

Comparing Professor Pencavel's availability estimates with State Farm's hiring of agents, the Court found disparities that went far beyond the legal standard of "statistical significance." The United States Supreme Court previously had held that 2 to 3 "standard deviations" (roughly 5 chances in 100 to 1 chance in 1,000) established a presumption of discrimination. In *Kraszewski*, the statistical disparities ranged from 1 chance in 10 to the 69 power (i.e., 1 chance in 10 with 69 zeros after the ten) to 1 chance in 10 to the 911 power (i.e., 10 with 911 zeros)! In other words, there was almost no chance that State Farm's hiring pattern of agents could have resulted in such an imbalance of men and women by chance, or absent discrimination. The statistical proofs were as strong as any I've ever seen in a Title VII case and were the civil rights equivalent of DNA testing. State Farm's "applicant flow" theory of availability was rejected, due to the overwhelming evidence that State Farm had depressed the number of female applicants by its active discouragement of women. Instead, when compared to Pencavel's estimate of the labor market availability of women, the low percentage of AIB test-takers was evidence of the effectiveness of State Farm's deterrence of women, the Court found.

The Court concluded that State Farm's underhiring of women agents was the result of State Farm's failure to advertise agent positions, the reliance on word-of-mouth recruitment by a nearly all-male managerial workforce, the active deterrence of women, the use of recruiting brochures and product advertisements that depicted only men as agents, State Farm's reputation for not hiring female agents, nepotism that overwhelmingly favored males, and the arbitrary and disparate application of subjective hiring criteria. The Court found these practices common to the class, confirmed its prior certification of the class, and held that State Farm was liable for discrimination against the class, as well as for its discrimination against Muriel, Daisy and Wilda. The victory was complete and total—as broad as the allegations pled in the complaint. I was exhilarated, but perhaps even more important than my immediate exhilaration, I realized that the decision was so well supported by the trial facts that it would be almost bulletproof on appeal.

State Farm's analysis apparently was the same, as shortly before the thirty-day appeal period ran out, Kirby Wilcox informed me that no appeal would be taken. The class victory would stand; I now could pursue class remedies for the women, as well as obtain payment for ten years of work on the case.

I put together an application for payment of reasonable attorneys' fees and costs for nearly ten years of work—a total of $5.25 million, including a 2.25 upward adjustment (multiplier) for the risk of loss, delay in payment of fees, superior legal work, and excellent results—and filed the petition, supported by numerous prominent members of the bar, including even corporate defense attorneys. It was the best and most comprehensive fee application I ever had prepared—more than 300 pages, including affidavits and exhibits—but, then again, it also was the biggest fee I ever had sought. Long before State Farm's response was due, Kirby called with a proposal to settle the fees and costs issue. He asked me to cut $10,000 off the request—less than a 0.002% discount. State Farm obviously had no interest in a fight about what I was worth! I took this as a compliment, accepted the offer and State Farm made payment immediately. It represented the highest hourly rates, largest upward adjustment, and largest total fee ever obtained by a civil rights attorney. However large, I knew most of it would be reinvested in my continuing battle in the *Kraszewski* case—which was far from over—our other class actions against State Farm, and our developing litigation against large grocery and restaurant chains for their race and sex discrimination.

The settlement of the fees issues led me to think we might also be able to settle the remedies issues. My optimism was ill-founded, however. Instead of continuing discussions, State Farm filed a preemptive strike—a motion to establish a fixed fund of $13.1 million and impose it on the class as "full make whole relief." It was a bold, but cynical, move. Back pay for the class amounted to hundreds of millions of dollars, by any measure. Establishing a $13.1 million fund would not only underpay the victims of class discrimination that had been judicially determined, under State Farm's proposal the money would be paid out on a formulaic basis. No attempt would be made to locate and determine which women actually had suffered discrimination by State Farm. I characterized State Farm's proposal as the "Put-The-Money-On-A-Stump-And-Run" remedy.

There were no United States Supreme Court or Ninth Circuit precedents invalidating damage funds in favor of individual claim hearings, but Supreme Court cases had strongly affirmed that the principal objectives of Title VII are "to eliminate the vestiges of employment discrimination and to make persons whole for injuries suffered due to such discrimination." The Supreme Court, in

Albemarle Paper Co. v. Moody, the seminal case in the field, directed that "the injured party is to be placed, as near as may be, in the situation he would have occupied if the wrong had not been committed." The trial courts were directed to "make possible the fashioning [of] the most complete relief possible." I thought it was clear that applying these core principles to the *Kraszewski* case meant that hearings should be conducted to identify actual victims and, when found, they should be paid the full value of the back pay each had lost as the result of State Farm's employment discrimination— not be paid four or five cents on the dollar, as State Farm's fund proposal would do. Indeed, in this case, it would be a denial of due process to deny actual victims the right to collect the full value of back pay and, instead, impose a limited fund on them.

We filed lengthy responsive pleadings to State Farm's motion, and the motion was heard by Judge Henderson on June 18, 1986. State Farm sought two major rulings from Judge Henderson: (1) an order rejecting individualized hearings for class members in favor of imposing a $13.1 million fund on the class; and (2) an order limiting the claims class members could file to only 214 trainee agent jobs filled by men, on the premise that 214 constituted the "shortfall" between the Court's finding of 40% female availability and the number of female agents State Farm actually hired.

Kirby Wilcox, arguing on behalf of State Farm, relied mainly on a series of false and misleading statements about the likely nature of an individualized claim procedure and the value of potential claims. He claimed that the $13.1 million fund State Farm proposed to create to pay all claims constituted "the full measure of State Farm's back pay liability" and characterized my contention that the case was worth hundreds of millions as "a complete fabrication" having "no basis in Title VII precedent, logic or fact." He argued that an individualized claim procedure would, at a minimum, "produce a process spanning 7,000 consecutive days—more than nineteen years." I responded to such misrepresentations by showing the value of individual claims and identifying the number of positions filled by men—which numbered over 1,000. The math was not hugely complicated; potential claims were then worth more than $200 million, a figure that could rise to $500 million if State Farm continued to delay payments of back pay to class members. Wilcox's estimate of "nineteen years" was based on the absurd assumption that only one attorney would defend claims, and it assumed that no claims would settle. On average, more than 90% of all civil cases settle and a procedure like this, where claims would be similar, was likely to produce an even higher rate of settlements than normal. I said 2–3 years was a more likely estimate of time. Further, no matter how long individualized claim hearings might take, imposing a limited fund on claimants would deny due process and eviscerate Title VII's mandate of "make whole" relief. As for State Farm's argument that only 214 jobs could be contested in a claims procedure, I argued that the breadth and intensity of State Farm's deterrence of women made it difficult to know how many women would have applied and been hired in a discrimination-free environment. Moreover, even if State Farm had hired 40% women agents, that fact would not bar any individual woman from claiming she suffered discrimination, as the Supreme Court had rejected the so-called "bottom-line" defense (i.e., rejected the notion that if a company's "bottom-line" employment of women or minorities reflected parity with labor market availability, individual women or minorities would be barred from filing suit).

A month later, Judge Henderson issued his decision on the remedies issues presented by State Farm's motion. Relying on the Title VII cases we had emphasized, he held that "the goal at the remedy stage of Title VII is 'to make victims of unlawful employment discrimination whole…'" While individualized hearings may not be required when individual hearings would strain judicial resources "beyond feasible limits," or result in a "quagmire of hypothetical judgments," individualized hearings are the *preferred* method of determining damages in Title VII cases, citing *International Brotherhood of Teamsters v. United States*. The Court dismissed State Farm's argument that individual hearings would take 19 years:

> On the basis of the record before the Court, defendants'
> bogeymen of nineteen years is not credible. Rather, plaintiffs'
> projection that the claims procedure would take only 2–3
> years appears far more reasonable, both in light of the facts of
> this case and of the Court's past experience with litigation of
> this nature.

This case would not require complex and hypothetical individual determinations, as it involved only one entry-level job—not "complex and speculative career patterns." "Moreover, plaintiffs have agreed to the use of stipulated average earnings in order to make the back pay calculation simple," wrote the Court. Lastly, "and perhaps most importantly," wrote the Court, "where large sums of money are at stake, the presumption in favor of individualized hearings would appear to be critical. In this case, unlike in the cases cited by defendants, individual class members are alleging entitlement to very large back pay awards as full compensation for their injuries." Based on the assumption that approximately 1,000 claims would be filed in the case, the Court ordered individualized hearings to proceed; if, however, "many more" than 1,000 claims establish a prima facie case of discrimination, the Court indicated it would reconsider its order on the basis that individual hearings could be "unwieldy." Although leaving the door open for "reconsideration" of this order was a perfectly reasonable thing for Judge Henderson to have done, State Farm later seized on this possibility as a lifeboat to escape the effects of individualized hearings and attempted to prolong and sabotage the efficient processing of claims in an effort to show that the individualized hearing process had become "unwieldy"—but that's getting ahead of the story.

Judge Henderson made two other rulings that were critically important to the claims procedure that would follow. First, he held that once claimants demonstrate that they applied or were deterred from applying for agent positions, State Farm must bear the "heavy burden" of showing by "clear and convincing evidence that even absent discrimination the woman would not have been hired. Second, the Court rejected State Farm's claim that its liability should be limited to only 214 positions, based on the Court's estimate of labor force availability. Such a cap on liability would violate Supreme Court precedents which reject a "bottom-line" defense, as well as the principle that victims of discrimination cannot be determined to have been wronged simply because women had been hired to other positions. The Court ended its decision by encouraging the parties to negotiate "the specific details that will govern the Stage II proceedings."

State Farm had completely lost its motion to limit liability. Worse for State Farm, the Court had ruled on two issues—the burden of proof and the number of positions it would be liable for in a Stage II procedure—that would dramatically, and adversely, affect the amount of money it would ultimately pay to claimants. It was an audacious attempt by MoFo to seize the offensive, and it completely backfired.

At this point, I expected State Farm to want to negotiate settlement of the case. The die had been cast: State Farm would not be able to cap its liability at a low figure and would have to face claims from 1,000+ claimants. It didn't take a rocket scientist to calculate that these claims potentially were worth hundreds of millions of dollars. Indeed, I could calculate State Farm's back pay exposure with a hand-held calculator. But State Farm stuck to its ridiculous $13.1 million offer.

I immediately began work on a motion for injunctive relief, filed it, and a hearing was scheduled. Prior to that hearing, Wilcox contacted me and expressed an interest in negotiating all remedies issues. I suggested we begin with the injunctive issues, as I expected the money issues would be more intractable. I worked diligently with Kirby and Erica Grubb, representing State Farm, and after many meetings a "Consent Decree Regarding Injunctive Relief" was agreed to.

State Farm agreed that, for ten years, 50% of the agents it hired in California would be women. Since State Farm had greatly increased the hire of women agents after the *Kraszewski* lawsuit was filed, we really were getting eighteen years of guaranteed high levels of female hiring, and the 50% rate was as high as I have ever seen in any Title VII case. I was confident that hiring this many women agents would change the culture of the company and that returning to the pre-*Kraszewski* good-old-boy system of hiring would not be possible. Since these jobs were so highly compensated, the monetary value of the sales jobs women would obtain under this decree would be worth billions of dollars in increased future income to women. Moreover, the increased female hiring in California would force State Farm to increase its hire of female agents throughout the United States, as it would not be possible to maintain a modern hiring system in California and an archaic system elsewhere—not to mention the fact that State Farm did not want me filing more *Kraszewski*-type lawsuits in other states.

In addition to greatly increasing the hiring of female agents, the Decree created three new positions, one in each region, of Recruitment Administrators. The function of these Recruitment Administrators, all of whom had to be women and whose selection was subject to my approval, was to "work with and train Agency Managers and other responsible individuals in recruiting and retaining qualified female Trainee Agents." Objective minimum qualifications were created for trainee agents and trainee agent vacancies were publicized and posted generally, and made available to applicants for agent positions. Training programs were developed to promote the recruitment and hire of women agents, and the training of female trainee agents was to be monitored by the Recruitment Administrators. Recruitment Administrators were required to make regular recruitment visits to colleges and universities with large female enrollments, and to community organizations with female outreach programs in an effort to locate potential female trainee agents. State Farm agreed to advertise the trainee agent position in newspapers, magazines and trade journals, to feature female agents as role models in the ads, and to declare State Farm's interest in hiring female agents. State Farm was required to file detailed reports with me and the Court describing its recruitment, training, and hiring activities. Plaintiffs were provided with discovery rights if State Farm failed to meet any hiring requirements and female trainee agent applicants were provided rights to have any complaints of sex discrimination investigated by the Recruitment Administrators and reviewed by Class Counsel and the State Farm Regional Vice Presidents. Class Counsel was entitled to payment of attorneys' fees by State Farm for time spent administering, monitoring, enforcing and defending the Decree.

The Injunctive Consent Decree included everything I had hoped for. But now the difficult work would begin on the back pay issues. State Farm would have to negotiate on my turf—as I had won the class liability trial and the right to individualized hearings—but I knew each concept, principle, sentence, word and comma in a claim procedure decree would be contested in negotiations with Kirby. Kirby's weakness as an attorney was his inability to understand the big picture; his strengths were his attention to detail and his tenacity. We would be negotiating a lot of details and I didn't expect it to be easy.

Since the three individual plaintiffs, Muriel Kraszewski, Daisy Jackson and Wilda Tipton, had proven their individual claims during the class liability trial, I demanded immediate settlement of their claims. During a period of nearly twelve years, Muriel, Daisy and Wilda never once had asked me what their claims were worth or what they might get out of the lawsuit; their focus was completely on changing State Farm for the benefit of women in the future who would want to become State Farm agents. I called Muriel first and asked her, "What do you want to settle your case?" She replied, "The only thing I want is for you to get paid, because you have worked so hard on this case, and for you to make sure that State Farm never treats other women like they treated me." I said, "Thank you very much for that sentiment, but what do you want for yourself?" Muriel replied, "If I get ten cents, that will be enough." "If you get $421,000, will that be better?" I asked. "Oh, that will be fine, too," said Muriel. Daisy and Wilda also received $421,000—the full value of their back pay claims. In addition, these three women are permanently enshrined in my personal Hall of Fame for being perfect plaintiffs,

witnesses, and clients, and for always putting the cause of changing State Farm's employment practices above their individual interests. No lawyer ever could have finer clients.

I negotiated with State Farm for a year about the terms of the
claim procedure, fighting over every issue, word and comma, and
emerged with a 105-page "Consent Decree Regarding Monetary
Relief, Instatement Relief, and Notice," backed by 200+ pages of
exhibits. It was the most complex agreement I ever had seen in a
civil rights case; it literally established a mini-court system for the
processing and adjudication of 1,000+ expected highly valuable
claims.

The Monetary Decree appointed eight special masters to administer the claims procedure. At the top, as Chief Special Master,
was former United States District Court Judge Charles B. Renfrew,
who, ironically, was the federal judge initially assigned to the
Kraszewski case. As Chief Special Master, Judge Renfrew was authorized to decide appeals from decisions of the Discovery and
Motion Special Master, Kathy Kelly, and appeals from decisions of
the five Hearing Special Masters. I wanted someone of Judge
Renfrew's stature to head the procedure, in anticipation that State
Farm would file a motion for reconsideration of Judge Henderson's
order that the case proceed on an individual hearings basis and
take an appeal to the Circuit Court of Appeals for the Ninth Circuit. If any appeal reached the Court of Appeals, I wanted them to
think, "Despite whatever State Farm says about the hearing procedure, Charlie Renfrew is running it and we have a lot of confidence
in him." Although Judge Renfrew perhaps was not as liberal as other
special masters I could have chosen, I knew he would run the claims
procedure fairly and efficiently; more importantly, the esteem with
which he was held by the legal and judicial community would be
my insurance policy against State Farm's motion for reconsideration.

For the crucially important position of Discovery and Motion
Special Master, we appointed Kathy Kelly, a labor arbitrator and
professor at law. She had worked as a special master in our Lucky

Stores case and we had found her to be a tough, smart, no-nonsense judge; most important, she rendered decisions promptly. With 1,000+ claims at issue and defense counsel with an unlimited budget, we anticipated a lot of motions. If the Motion Special Master could not decide issues quickly, the procedure would become buried in paper, claimants would not obtain relief, and State Farm would have laid the foundation for a return to its formula-relief proposal. As events would develop, hundreds of motions were filed by State Farm and us in front of Special Master Kelly and she was put under enormous pressure to decide issues and keep the claims procedure moving forward.

Douglas Young, a well-respected litigator from a big San Francisco firm was given authority as "Attorneys' Fees and Costs Multiplier Special Master" to decide a specific fees issue, and five "Hearing Special Masters"—all experienced labor arbitrators, including four women—were designated to hear claims. Later in the procedure, three Settlement Special Masters were added—a total of eleven special masters, including two former United States District Court Judges and two former California Supreme Court Justices. It was a distinguished, and expensive, group, and State Farm had to pay for all of them.

The Monetary Decree identified 1,093 specific trainee agent positions that were filled by men during the period of classwide discrimination against women. Pursuant to Judge Henderson's order, women could claim that discrimination occurred in the filling of all those positions. However, the Decree provided that there could be no more than one successful claimant per position and that my firm, acting as Class Counsel, could represent only one claimant per vacancy. Claimants could establish a prima facie case of entitlement to damages by showing as of the time of her application or deterrence that:

1. She applied, or was deterred from applying for a trainee agent position filled by a man;
2. She was not offered a trainee agent position;
3. If she failed to take the California insurance sales licensing

examination, she did so because of a State Farm policy or practice that caused her to believe her application for a trainee agency position would be rejected;

4. She was in good health;
5. She was an insurable driver;
6. She was at least 21 years old;
7. She had access to adequate financial resources to invest in an insurance agency (an amount which ranged from $1,500 in 1974 to $7,000 in 1987);
8. If she was an applicant or deterred applicant after April 19, 1978, she could pass State Farm's aptitude test;
9. She has taken and passed the California insurance sales licensing examination before filing a final claim; and,
10. She applied or was deterred 60 to 420 days before the position she challenges was filled.

State Farm could rebut a claim of discrimination by proving, by clear and convincing evidence:

1. There was no vacancy available;
2. A female filled the vacancy;
3. The claimant was less qualified than the man selected; and,
4. The claimant was rejected for another sexually non-discriminatory reason.

State Farm was required to pay for all costs of the claim procedure, including costs of all special masters, formal discovery, including all depositions, travel, meals and lodging for all claimants and their attorneys to depositions and hearings, sixteen toll-free telephone lines for Class Counsel to communicate with claimants, as well as attorneys' fees, travel and costs for its own witnesses and attorneys. I knew this amount would be substantial and would grow exponentially the longer the claim procedure lasted.

State Farm was also required to pay Class Counsel our attorneys' fees and expenses for all work performed through the end of the period set aside for evaluating claims, for all law and motion work related to the Motion for Reconsideration that State Farm was expected to file, and for legal work related to any appeals or collateral attacks on the Monetary Decree. All other legal work—specifically, work preparing and litigating Final Claims, claim hearings, and motions to modify or interpret the Decree—were to be paid by State Farm on a prevailing party basis, meaning we had to win to get paid. To compensate for the risk of losing and the delay in receiving payment, the Decree permitted a 1.35 multiplier, meaning that our hourly rates in prevailing cases would be 1.35 times our regular rates.

I knew that the shifting of many costs and fees to State Farm that normally are borne by plaintiffs would be a huge advantage in the ultimate resolution of the claims procedure in our favor. To my great surprise, it took years for State Farm and their attorneys to understand the underlying economics of the claim procedure and the financial and legal disadvantages they operated under. Their basic misunderstanding of the economics of the deal delayed the final resolution of the case, but, in the end, greatly enhanced the total recovery for the women.

In an effort to streamline evidentiary requirements and facilitate resolution of claims, we agreed on a class formula for the determination of back pay. This formula took into account, among other things, the year in which the discrimination had occurred, the average earnings of State Farm agents, the average interim earnings of women, and interest on back pay. For 1974 claimants, such as Muriel, Daisy and Wilda, the amount of back pay was $421,000 when the Monetary Decree was signed. For claimants who had suffered discrimination more recently, it was much less. For all claimants, the amounts of back pay awards would increase over time to reflect the accumulation of interest at 10%, and, possibly, the continuation of back pay to the dates of individual judgments or settlements—an issue I was unable to settle with State Farm.

In negotiations, Wilcox contended that the accrual of back pay should stop when the Injunctive Decree was approved, on the theory that, by committing to hire 50% female agents, sex discrimination had stopped and back pay for claimants should stop. My response was, "Apples and oranges. The Injunctive Decree's hiring goals will benefit women now and in the future who want to become State Farm agents, but will do little or nothing for the women who suffered discrimination many years earlier. These women have gone on to other careers and few can turn back the clock to reapply as trainee agents. Back pay for these women should accrue until the date they receive payment for past discrimination or the date State Farm offers to hire them to a specific agent position." This was a really big-ticket issue. As a matter of law, I considered the issue a slam-dunk for us, as prior United States Supreme Court and Court of Appeals cases had favored the continuation of back pay. Nevertheless, MoFo refused to settle this issue, so we agreed to disagree and let Judge Henderson decide the issue, subject to an appeal to the Court of Appeals for the Ninth Circuit. We agreed that resolution of this issue would not delay the claim procedure, which would go forward.

To begin the claim procedure, three notices were mailed to every female employee and applicant for employment since 1974, regardless of what jobs they had been employed in or applied for— a total of 70,000 women. For letters that came back in the mail as undeliverable, tracing through the U. S. Postal Service and Internal Revenue Service tracing procedures were used. Also, $300,000 of the money awarded to plaintiffs as discovery sanctions was permitted to be used for additional tracing using sophisticated computerized databases. Notices were posted in all State Farm offices and all agents' offices, and notices were published in newspapers throughout California. State Farm was required to pay for all mailing, tracing and notices.

In addition to the mailed and published notices, the announcement of the State Farm settlement received front-page news coverage throughout the United States, including the front page of the *New York Times*, where I was quoted as estimating the amount State Farm would pay out as between $100 and $300 million, and Kirby Wilcox stated the amount would be "far less than $100 million." The *New York Times* was kind enough to include our 800 number for obtaining claim information in their news article. In addition, Muriel and I were interviewed on "Good Morning America" by Joan Lunden. Muriel herself was a one-woman publicity machine; her winning personality, and the compelling story she told, led to articles about the State Farm case in national magazines and local newspapers—all of which helped notify women who had experienced discrimination by State Farm that a claims procedure was now available.

The barrage of media attention was not without its humorous side. Near the end of the day of the announced Monetary Consent Decree, I received a call from *The Recorder*, the leading legal newspaper in Northern California. The reporter asked me what the case was worth, and I told him, as I had been telling reporters throughout the day, "Claimants will recover between $100 and $300 million." The reporter said that Kirby Wilcox said that estimate was hogwash and that we would be lucky to recover the $13 million State Farm had offered previously. Tired of hearing Kirby continue to make that claim, I told the *Recorder* reporter, "Tell Kirby that I have the following proposition for him and State Farm: If I fail to recover at least $100 million for claimants, my firm will forfeit all attorneys' fees. However, if I recover more than $100 million, State Farm will agree to double our fees."

When I came into the office the next morning, my partner Chuck Farnsworth was reading a copy of the morning's *Recorder*. He looked up as I walked in and asked, "Did you really offer to bet our fees double-or-nothing with State Farm? Without talking to your partners?" I said, "Yes, but don't worry. We will recover more than $100 million, and, besides, Kirby and State Farm will never take the bet!"

Anticipating that the vast amount of publicity we generated would lead to the filing of many more claims than available positions, the Monetary Decree provided for the filing of an Initial Claim Form and a Final Claim Form. The Initial Claim Form was a short document that solicited basic information. Approximately 6,400 Initial Claim Forms were filed, but 80% of these claimants had not taken or passed the insurance aptitude exam or the California insurance sales licensing exam, which were prerequisites for becoming a State Farm sales agent in California and for obtaining relief under the Monetary Decree. So aptitude insurance exams had to be arranged for nearly 5,000 women. To facilitate the taking and passing of the State insurance exams, we provided exam training materials to claimants and arranged with the California Department of Insurance for examinations to be given four times in twelve locations throughout California. Fees and expenses for the exams and training materials were paid by State Farm. Many of the Initial Claimants chose not to take the state licensing examination or failed to pass it.

The Monetary Decree established a 270-day Hold Period for testing and for the investigation and evaluation of Initial Claim Forms, followed by the filing of Final Claim Forms challenging the hiring of male agents. All formal discovery was suspended during the Hold Period and State Farm was required to produce the personnel files of the 1,093 male agents it had hired during the liability period and all documents and information State Farm and its agents had regarding any of the 6,400 initial claimants. During the Hold Period, we reviewed and evaluated each of the 1,093 personnel files of the male agents hired, and gave each male agent a numerical ranking of the anticipated strength of the evidence State Farm would offer in claiming that the female claimant would not have been hired because the male hired possessed superior qualifications. We applied the same ranking system to the women claimants who passed the exams and provided information to support the filing of a Final Claim. After interviewing the claimants, we revised our rankings to reflect personal characteristics of the claimants that were not revealed in claim forms and documents.

Following the evaluations of the male agents selected and the women claimants, we had to match claimants to male selections, since discrimination could not be proved in the abstract, only in connection with a specific job vacancy and a specific male hire. Since a large percentage of the claims were from women who had been deterred from applying, and deterrence had been widespread and extensive, the terms of the Monetary Decree permitted women to identify a time period when they would have applied but for deterrence, and specify where they would have been willing to take a trainee agent job. Some women said "anywhere in California," or "anywhere in Southern California." The expanse of the time frame and locations permitted us great flexibility in matching claimants to positions, which was highly favorable to the class of claimants, as it permitted us to maximize the number of Final Claims, but it became an incredibly complex and difficult job. We wanted to match claimants and men in a way that would both maximize the number of Final Claims women would file and the number of claims the women had a reasonable chance of winning. Thus, we wanted to challenge positions at times and places where it was plausible to believe the women would have been hired, absent discrimination, and also to match strong claims with strong male hires and our weak claims against weak male hires. Since State Farm had the burden of proof under the terms of the Decree, claimants ranked "7" should beat men ranked "7", or lower, and women ranked "2" should beat men ranked 2 or lower. Of course, this assumed our rankings were accurate, and that the Hearing Special Masters would agree with our assessment of the women claimants and male hires and that evidence obtained in formal discovery would not fundamentally alter the assessments! Obviously, many facts would be disclosed in formal discovery that would change the complexion of a case, but at the matching stage, we could only do our best with the information we had.

In the end, we filed 982 Final Claims, challenging 982 male hires. This number, which represented 90% of the total number of male hires, was a bit of a stretch, as we had difficulty finding claimants for the early years of liability (1974–77), and the quality of the early claims was lower than the more recent claims. This was not because women didn't suffer discrimination in the early years, but rather the effect of the passage of time. The claims in the early years were almost entirely claims of deterrence, where there was no record of an application for a trainee agent position. Moreover, the early claimants often had no documentation corroborating their interest in a State Farm sales job. This was understandable, as few people maintain files of correspondence going back 10–15 years, but it made the job of proving the claimant's interest more difficult. Lastly, the early claims suffered from clouded memories, particularly regarding specific dates, names of persons contacted, and the like. This, too, is understandable when dealing with events 10–15 years earlier, but we anticipated that claims based on faded memories and lack of documentation would face some skepticism from the Hearing Special Masters. Nevertheless, we wanted to file as many early claims as possible, as we knew—indeed, we had proven in the class liability trial—that discrimination against women had occurred in those years, and because the claims for the early years were the most valuable of claims. So, we decided to err on the side of being aggressive, and filed as many for the early years as possible.

Under the terms of the Monetary Decree, we could represent only one claimant for each male hire and only one claimant could win a claim hearing. Consequently, we sent letters to approximately 300 potential claimants informing them that we would not prosecute their claims because we thought their claim was weak or defective for one reason or another. We further informed these women that our assessments were not final and that each of them had the right to file and prosecute a Final Claim with their own attorney. Claims were potentially quite valuable ($400,000 to $700,000 each); we were prosecuting them on a contingent-fee basis and knew that private lawyers outside our firm also would consider taking them on a contingent-fee basis. In the end, approximately fifty claimants we had rejected filed Final Claims with private attorneys or in *pro per* (on their own).

We immediately filed notices for the taking of 1,116 depositions of challenged male agents and State Farm managers who had been responsible for their hire, and State Farm noticed depositions of our 982 claimants. Depositions began and continued at the rate of approximately five per day.

The amount of work required of our office to get women tested, review and rank 1,093 male agent personnel files, review initial claim forms, review documents about claimants provided by State Farm and the claimants themselves, interview claimants and file nearly a thousand Final Claims within 270 days was staggering, and my office staff had to expand to meet the workload. I would retain overall management responsibility over the *Kraszewski* case, but I needed someone to manage the daily operation of the claim procedure. For this task, I hired David Pesonen. David had graduated from Boalt one year ahead of me and was chosen valedictorian of his class. Prior to going to law school he had organized and led the first successful fight in the nation to stop construction of a nuclear power plant and has been called "the father of the antinuclear movement." After law school, he became a trial lawyer in Charles Garry's law firm, trying many cases, and winning an $8 million trial verdict in a libel case—then the largest libel verdict in history. He became Director of the California State Department of Forestry under Governor Jerry Brown, a Superior Court Judge, and General Manager of the East Bay Regional Park District. He combined two needed skills for the job—extensive trial experience and experience managing people and projects.

We expanded our offices in Oakland, hiring seven attorneys, seven paralegals, and support staff to handle the expected workload. In anticipation that a large number of claimants would come from Southern California, we opened up an office in West Los Angeles, sub-leasing space from the Center for Law in the Public Interest, and staffed this office with three attorneys and three paralegals. As the claim procedure went forward, and became a war, we realized we had significantly underestimated the workload and began to add additional staff. At the height of the claim procedure, our firm had grown to 44 attorneys and 165 total employees. Our opponents, Morrison & Foerster, ultimately utilized 144 attorneys and ran up over $100 million in fees defending State Farm. Nothing like this had ever been seen in a civil rights case; only antitrust and large product liability class actions rivaled *Kraszewski* in scope and cost, and most of those cases were presented by groups of law firms, not one small or medium-size firm.

ALTHOUGH THE SHIFTING OF COSTS from plaintiffs to State Farm was a great strategic advantage to us, we had a problem State Farm didn't have. The Monetary Decree provided that plaintiffs' attorneys' fees and costs were to be determined by Judge Henderson. But after an acrimonious fight with State Farm over fees, Judge Henderson appointed a Special Master to conduct hearings regarding our fees applications and make recommendations to him. For this job, Henderson appointed his close friend, William Bennett Turner. I have no doubt the Judge thought he was doing us a favor by appointing Turner, but it proved to be an unfortunate choice for us.

Turner was an inappropriate choice because he had interests adverse to my firm and attitudes about attorneys' fees in civil rights cases that failed to match the magnitude of the tasks we were undertaking in this case. When I began practicing civil rights law in the Bay Area, Bill Turner was the king of civil rights lawyers, owing to his work with the NAACP Legal Defense Fund and his prosecution of many civil rights cases. He had an excellent reputation and I have no reason to believe he didn't deserve every bit of it. But as I rose in the ranks of civil rights litigators, I began to compete with Bill for attention, cases, and law associates. I recall competing against Turner for a very hot law associate prospect, Elizabeth LaPorte. Elizabeth had the highest academic qualifications and had clerked for one of our favorite federal judges, Marilyn Hall Patel, who gave her a rave recommendation; plus, Liz had been spectacularly impressive in her interviews with us. She was offered jobs by several firms—probably by every firm she interviewed with—and her choice boiled down to two, Turner's firm or mine. In trying to convince her to take my offer, I never said anything negative about Turner, but instead emphasized my firm's achievements and the cases we then were filing. Liz, however, chose to work with Bill, explaining to me essentially that my firm was on the ascendancy, but Bill Turner had the bigger reputation. I was disappointed, and thought she had made a mistake, but I understood that Bill's reputation was a lure. As time went on, however, my firm grew in reputation and the importance of the cases it was prosecuting, while Bill's shrank. Soon, I was attracting more attention and recruiting the best law associates, as well as paying them more than smaller firms like Turner's.

Many lawyers from small firms, like Turner, do not understand the logistics and finances of large-scale litigation. This problem became particularly aggravated for me in the *Kraszewski* claim procedure. No one in the history of the Title VII litigation ever had obtained more than $35 million in a case (a much larger case against United Airlines), and Turner did not believe or understand that hundreds of millions of dollars were at issue in our case. Turner, with the experience of running a very small firm (successfully), also did not understand how much staff was necessary to prosecute nearly 1,000 claims. As a consequence, he reviewed our staffing requirements and fee claims suspiciously and did something no other judge ever had done—cut our fees requests, which impaired out ability to hire staff to process claims.

In contrast to Turner, the Chief Special Master, Charles B. Renfew, had come from a mega-firm, Pillsbury, Madison & Sutro, and then was General Counsel to Chevron, where he managed large-scale litigation. His attitude was, "State Farm is paying for it. Hire enough staff to get the job done on time." Thus, at the same time Turner was impairing our ability to hire more staff by cutting our fees requests, Renfrew criticized us—properly, in my opinion—for seeking an extension of the Hold Period (which he reluctantly granted). Renfrew understood the magnitude of what we were trying to accomplish, Turner did not.

Having our fees requests reduced was particularly aggravating because we knew our opponent, MoFo, was using twice as much staff and charging higher hourly rates. To prove this, I filed discovery requests, seeking to obtain evidence of MoFo's billings. There is a great amount of legal support for such discovery and every court previously had provided such discovery to me in contested fees disputes. The reason is obvious: attorneys on both sides review the same documents, depose the same witnesses, appear at the same hearings, write the same number of briefs, and normally should be expected to expend roughly the same amount of time. Thus, where the defense attorneys are found spending twice as much time as the plaintiffs' attorneys working on the same case, complaints that plaintiffs' counsel are spending too much time on the case are not taken very seriously. In such discovery in previous cases, *never once* had my firm expended more time litigating a case than our opponents and I was 100% confident that discovery in the *Kraszewski* case would show the same thing—indeed, I expected it to confirm that we were twice as efficient as MoFo.

Incredibly, Turner denied the discovery—the only judge ever to do so in any of my cases. After an appeal to Judge Henderson, and Henderson's indication that some discovery would be appropriate, Turner made the even more incredible ruling that State Farm would be required to produce the requested discovery to him— but not to us. Thus, we were denied the right to review the defense bills and impeach their claims that we were overstaffing and over-billing the case, and Turner was able selectively to use evidence from MoFo's billings.

Turner's fundamental misunderstanding of the claim procedure was well-illustrated by his comment in the *American Lawyer* magazine that, "The fees on both sides dwarfed the amount paid to the claimants, at least in the early stages." The "early stages" he was referring to was the Hold Period, a period of investigation and evaluation that *preceded* the filing and litigation of formal claims. It never was contemplated that *any* money would be paid out to claimants until claim hearings began, but Turner misunderstood even this most obvious feature of the procedure.

Despite the constraints on staffing caused by Turner's fees orders, our firm continued to expand due to the burgeoning workload of the claim procedure as we completed the Hold Period and began the claims hearings. This was an incredibly difficult period for us, as we not only had to get ready to try four to five cases a month, while conducting discovery on more than 900 other cases, we also wanted to anticipate legal and interpretive issues that likely would arise in many hearings and obtain comprehensive rulings from Law and Motion Special Master Kelly in advance of the claim hearings.

In negotiating the Monetary Consent Decree, I had demanded, and obtained, a procedure for "Comprehensive Issue Resolution," which provided the right to file motions "to resolve any procedural or substantive issues pertaining to the conduct of all or any portion of the Claim Hearings." This right permitted the Discovery and Motion Special Master, Kathy Kelly, to make broad rulings which minimalized the danger of inconsistent and/or incorrect legal and interpretive decisions by the Hearing Special Masters. It also saved us the time and expense of having to litigate the same issues over and over again, which would have given MoFo, with their vastly greater amount of staff and resources, an advantage.

As soon as the Hold Period ended, Barry Goldstein, an extremely knowledgeable and experienced Title VII attorney I had hired from the NAACP Legal Defense Fund, worked night and day with me drafting a broad Comprehensive Issue Motion Concerning Legal Standards for Application of the Order and Burden of Proof, which attempted to anticipate, and obtain rulings, on all core issues of proof that we thought would arise in the Claim Hearings. It was the broadest motion I have ever filed and writing it required every bit of knowledge and experience Barry and I had accumulated over our combined thirty-five years of Title VII experience, and it had to be prepared under great time pressure. Our ability to strategize the legal issues that would arise in the Claim Hearings permitted us to cover a lot of subjects and write quickly. Barry's work with me on many State Farm comprehensive issue motions gave us an edge on State Farm throughout the claim procedure, no matter how many attorneys MoFo threw at us.

We filed our big motion making thirty proposals for comprehensive rulings, and Kathy Kelly heard oral argument on it over the course of three days. The oral argument went well for us, with

Barry and I operating like a tag-team in responding to objections and arguments made by MoFo regarding our thirty proposed orders. We expected a good order from Kelly, and we got it a month later when she issued a 48-page decision that largely supported our legal positions.

State Farm's first objection was to Kelly's jurisdiction over the issues we had raised. State Farm's strategy was to try to take as many issues as possible back to Judge Henderson in an effort to pile work on him—a very busy federal judge—in the hope that he would become tired of managing the claim procedure, find it unmanageable, and rule in State Farm's favor when they filed a motion for reconsideration of the Judge's Order that Stage II should be conducted as an open-end individualized claim procedure. This motion for reconsideration was their great hope that damages could be contained and plaintiffs forced to accept a low lump-sum payment of claims. Our strategy was to keep as many issues as possible in front of the special masters, not because we did not like Judge Henderson, but because we knew he had already expended a gigantic amount of time on this case in the Stage I proceedings, he maintained a regular caseload of 400–600 cases, and putting him in the position of having to make many decisions regarding the conduct of the claim procedure would be placing an unfair burden on him that could result in a decision to forego individual damage determinations in favor of a lump-sum class payment. Furthermore, being a busy federal judge, it would be difficult for Henderson to make decisions about management of the claim procedure with the speed necessary to keep the procedure moving efficiently. This, of course, was the seminal idea behind the Monetary Decree's appointment of eight special masters to conduct the claim procedure and leave only a limited number of issues for Court decision.

Due to the importance of the question whether Kelly had jurisdiction over our motion, as well as the consequences to the efficient conduct of the claim procedure if she declined jurisdiction, Kelly first considered her role in making comprehensive rulings involving "interpretations" of the Decree. She held that while the

Decree granted authority to the Court over matters of interpretation and implementation of the claim procedure, that authority was to be exercised only where authority to interpret the Decree and implement the claim procedure was not "otherwise specifically provided in the Decree." She then noted that authority to "interpret" the Decree was specifically granted to all the special masters. Further, the Decree expressly gave Kelly the authority to resolve all comprehensive issue motions, which our motion clearly was. On that basis, State Farm's objection to her jurisdiction was rejected.

Kelly next considered the thirty comprehensive orders we had proposed, discussing the arguments put forth by both sides in support of differing interpretations of the Decree's burden of proof requirements. Including the jurisdiction issue, Special Master Kelly accepted the interpretations advanced by plaintiffs for twenty-four of the issues, rejected two of our proposed orders, and rendered split decisions on five of the orders—an 85% win for us. Barry and I were elated, particularly with her acceptance of jurisdiction over comprehensive issues, the speed with which she ruled on such a lengthy and complicated motion, and, of course, the acceptance on most issues of the interpretations we had advanced. Had she denied jurisdiction and passed the issues on to Judge Henderson, the claim procedure would have floundered, State Farm would have delayed the resolution of the case even further, and a motion for reconsideration might have been granted, resulting in an inadequate lump sum payment to the class—State Farm's real objective. My rejoicing was short-lived, however, as the claims hearings had begun and we were having a tough time.

THE MONETARY DECREE PROVIDED that the claim hearings would be scheduled according to the dates of the hires of the male agents the claimants challenged, with the earliest hires going first. This was entirely appropriate, as the women claiming they suffered discrimination by State Farm in 1974 had waited a long time for justice and deserved to have their claims heard first. While this was fair, the sequencing of claim hearings, with the 1974 claims going first, presented great problems for us.

As shown in the class liability trial, in 1974 State Farm not only was not hiring female agents, its deterrence of women was so extensive that few women even sought to apply, and almost none submitted written applications or began the appointment process. So, it was no surprise that nearly all our 1974 claimants were "deterred applicants," meaning they had been discouraged by State Farm policies and practices of discrimination from applying. There were no written employment applications to support claims of deterrence and State Farm maintained no records of women who had expressed interest in agency positions. Since few people maintain records of employment contacts going back many years, few claimants had copies of letters inquiring about State Farm agency work, or notes about who at State Farm they had talked to about applying. In short, the early claimants had little or no documents or other forms of objective evidence corroborating their interest in becoming State Farm agents, and had to rely instead on their memories and the memories of friends and relatives. With claims being worth over $500,000 each at that point, the special masters understandably had some reluctance to believe everything the claimants said without corroboration.

Secondly, there was no way a special master could compromise a claim, the way juries often do. Juries faced with a weak liability case, but real damages, frequently compromise by voting in favor of a verdict for plaintiffs, but then reduce the damage award. The *Kraszewski* special masters did not have this option: every successful claimant got $500,000+, not a penny less. This all-or-nothing feature of the procedure, coupled with the lack of objective evidence and the historic amounts of these civil rights claims, encouraged close scrutiny of claims by the special masters—in some cases, more scrutiny than I wanted.

Claim No. 1, which I tried with Fritz Wollet, who I had hired away from the EEOC, presented an example of such proof problems. Christine Johnson, a very attractive and professional black woman originally from Tyler, Texas with a Masters degree in education, was Claim No. 1. She challenged the appointment of Greg Caves, who was appointed in Fresno in September 1974. Due to the fact that there normally was a substantial delay between applying for a trainee agent position, completing "precontract" work, and being appointed, the Monetary Decree required that any applicant needed to prove she had applied at least sixty days before the challenged appointment. And since the liability period for the class did not begin until July 5, 1974, this meant Chris Johnston had to prove that her application was filed between July 5th and 9th, 1974. She claimed she filed an application by mail within that narrow time period, but had no copy or record of the letter. State Farm claimed it never received a letter application from her.

I called Chris as the first witness. She explained how she had worked her way through Fresno City College and Fresno State, working as a sales clerk at Sears and J. C. Penney, selling Avon products and subscriptions to *Ebony* magazine and working for Head Start, obtaining a B.A. in Social Work and Psychology and a Masters in Education. Following graduation, she had worked as a social worker and job developer for the Fresno County School's Head Start program, then as a manager in the Fresno County School District. In 1969, she became an Assistant Professor at Fresno State, teaching psychology. In addition to her full-time job at Fresno State, she taught part-time evening, weekend and summer classes through Fresno State and the Fresno Model Cities Program, and worked as a consultant to the City of Fresno on an affirmative action program. She was active in the community through her college sorority, faculty governance, professional associations such as the American Association of University Women and the Business and Professional Women, and was an active member of the NAACP, the National Council of Negro Women, and her church, and had received an award from the City of Fresno for "Outstanding Participation in Community Services." Her testimony showed her to be intelligent, articulate, charming, socially active, and ambitious—all qualities that State Farm extolled when they hired men.

In filing out her Personal History From, Chris attempted to fill out the form as if it were July 1974, when she applied, as was required. Not surprisingly, due to the passage of time, some of the information she provided from memory was incomplete and incorrect.

Chris testified that in 1974 she contacted the Fresno State Placement Office and was told that a State Farm recruiter would be interviewing on campus. She scheduled an interview and met with a white male she described as blond, slim, of medium height, in his mid-thirties; she did not recall his name. She expressed interest in selling insurance, but the recruiter showed no interest in her and terminated the interview after ten minutes, handing her a packet of information about State Farm, which included a form to fill out and mail back. She was discouraged by the way she had been treated, but she held on to the packet and several weeks later, at a family barbecue held to celebrate "Juneteenth" (June 19th, the date slaves were emancipated in Texas), she talked about her interview with her brother, Elgie, and a family friend, John Whitfield—both of whom worked for Allstate Insurance. Both men encouraged her to submit an application to State Farm, which she did several weeks later, indicating an interest in a sales position. In response, she received a second form in the mail requesting background information and a list of references. She attended a family barbecue to celebrate July 4th, talked to some of the references, then completed the form and mailed it to an address in Southern California a day or two after July 4th.

After not hearing from State Farm, she sought help from Dr. Felton Burns at Fresno State, who located a State Farm agent in Fresno for Ms. Johnson to talk to. From the agent office, she obtained a number in southern California to call, but was unable to obtain any information about the status of her application despite several phone calls. She discontinued her pursuit of State Farm and took a job with another company.

Her recitation of events was corroborated by Dr. Felton Burns, Elgie, John Whitfield, and Roslyn Bessard. Dr. Burns recalled talking to Ms. Johnson about her job search, said he had recommended that she contact State Farm, and recalled her saying that she did not get the job with State Farm, but was unsure of the exact date, placing it somewhere toward the end of the 1974 academic year, which would be May or June. Her brother Elgie recalled conversations with Chris about her interview with State Farm, but lacked details of the events. Her former sister-in-law, Roslyn Bessard, recalled attending the July 4th party in 1974, recalled Chris saying she had applied for work with an insurance company, but thought she was seeking managerial work. She fixed the date of the party as occurring shortly after her husband had graduated from Fresno State and they both had moved to the San Francisco Bay Area, because they had to travel back to Fresno for the party. This was good corroboration of the date and Chris' interest and application for insurance work, but on cross-examination she thought the job applied for was in management, and she was not sure the company was State Farm.

John Whitfield recalled talking to Chris about the possibility of working for Allstate, his employer, but he advised her to pursue a job with State Farm, as State Farm had the most professional operation, its agents worked out of their own offices rather than a booth in a store, and State Farm sold multiple insurance lines. He also testified that he told Chris that Allstate was sensitive to nepotism issues, which would be a concern because her brother Elgie was an Allstate claims representative in Fresno.

On cross-examination, Chris had trouble remembering some important details and events surrounding her application with State Farm. She was unable to identify with certainty the references she submitted to State Farm, and provided some inconsistent testimony on this issue. Although she testified to her clear recollection of the dates and events of her July application, she had a less than clear recollection of other dates in 1974; she could place the date when she learned of the State Farm job opportunity only within a six-month period and the date of her interview only within a four-month period, leaving open at least the possibility, if not the inference, that the precision of her recollection of the application date should be doubted. She did not retain a copy of the job application, which State Farm suggested was unlikely for someone who had been a professional job developer, and provided descriptions of the application document that were inconsistent in minor, but notable ways. Chris admitted, on cross examination, that information she had submitted in her personal history form was not correct: her form stated a 1969–1974 income of $2,300 to $2,700 a month and a net worth of $35,000, but subpoenaed documents from her 1971 divorce showed a family income of $1,500. Her form claimed a $7,000 savings account, but her credit union records showed the account was not opened until 1988. Her memory of job applications to other employers in 1974 was foggy, again casting doubt on the clarity of her memory of her experience with State Farm. She also demonstrated an imperfect memory about more recent events, such as her 1985–88 employment history. And it was revealed that she had shaded the truth about her education history and her involvement in a prior litigation. None of these memory lapses and incomplete answers, taken separately, was serious, but the cumulative effect of a pattern of missing details and recollections was harmful to the credibility of her claim that she was certain her application was submitted sometime between July 5–9, 1974—a necessary predicate to her claim. I watched as State Farm's attorney, Linda Shostak, systematically cross-examined Chris on the inconsistencies and gaps in her memory, angry that Chris, who I liked and believed very much, would have her credibility damaged, but respectful of Linda's excellent trial skills.

The most serious problem with Chris Johnson's story, however, was her insistence that the recruiter she talked to in Fresno was from State Farm's Southern California office, and that she had mailed her forms to State Farm at a Southern California address. As explained by State Farm witnesses, this was highly unlikely, as Fresno was part of State Farm's Northern California region and any job recruiters normally would be from Northern, not Southern California. Likewise, the Fresno State Farm agent office she contacted would have referred her to the Northern California Regional Office, not Southern California, as Chris claimed.

The trial lasted seven days and was followed by the submission of post-trial briefs by both sides, summing up the evidence. Shortly thereafter, Hearing Special Master Armon Barsamian rendered a 49-page written decision. Chris Johnson, Claimant No. 1, had lost her claim.

I assigned the most experienced trial lawyers I had to the first group of claims—Barry Goldstein, Brad Seligman, Dave Pesonen, Susan Guberman-Garcia, Fritz Wollet, and myself. We lost the first five claim hearings and seven of the first eight. Fortunately, we settled four claims, including one for Sarah Cline, one of my best witnesses at the class liability trial, for the full value of the claim, $586,068, so we were able to recover fees on five of the first twelve claims. However, we had to do better, both to survive as a law firm and to meet my publicly-announced prediction that we would recover $100 to $300 million in the claim procedure.

The *esprit de corps* among my staff of attorneys, paralegals, case clerks, and support personnel had been strong, but doubt and demoralization began to appear. At our weekly staff meetings, which I presided over, I tried to explain that the special problems we were having with the early claims would not continue and that things would turn around. I felt my role was floating between quarterback and cheerleader.

Now, if MoFo had been smart, at this point they would have approached me with a global settlement offer. We were down; the trend of results was running against us and in MoFo's favor. They should have realized that, due to the large transaction costs, and the value of claims, a settlement of claims was inevitable and that this would be the best time for State Farm. They should have used the first group of cases, and our average recovery rate, as the basis for settling all remaining claims. But instead of offering to negotiate a full settlement, they became even more arrogant and belligerent in dealing with us—"the Saps," as they called us.

We hung together and kept going; five trials were scheduled

each month, and we had a lot of work to do. We proposed the addition of three Settlement Special Masters and the use of settlement conferences. Two former California Supreme Court Justices, Joseph Grodin and Cruz Reynoso, and a former United States District Judge, Raul A. Ramirez, were selected and the settlement conferences began to produce more settlements. MoFo continued to add staff to the defense team; we counted an astounding 144 attorneys who worked on the defense! Frequently, they had four to six attorneys at claims hearings, while we had one or two. They were outraged that I took a picture of one of the claim hearings showing six MoFo attorneys aligned against one of my attorneys, Susan Guberman-Garcia, and attached the photo to our attorneys' fees applications when Susan won the hearing. Nevertheless, despite the fact that MoFo was using two to three times the number of attorneys and paralegals that we were using, the fees Special Master, Bill Turner, continued to reduce our fees. At one settlement conference, Judge Ramirez asked me, "Who are you guys fighting, the Red Army?" We couldn't keep up with the "Red Army" (MoFo). We expanded to 44 attorneys and 165 employees, but I could not afford to expand further. I needed to send a message to State Farm and MoFo that they could not push us into the sea. I sent a letter to a half-dozen small plaintiff employment firms asking them each to handle a few claims on a contingent fee basis. Everyone I talked to agreed to help. We developed a manual to aid them in understanding the claim issues and held training courses for the law firms and their attorneys.

In the next twenty claims, we won seven, lost seven, and settled six, thereby getting paid for work on thirteen of the claims. With the automatic 1.35 multiplier for risk and delay, we were recovering 88% of our normal hourly rates. At this rate of recovery, plus the guaranteed fees State Farm had to pay us for certain motion work, we could litigate claims forever; State Farm could not bankrupt us.

Our recovery rate improved. In the next ten claims, we won two trials, lost one, and settled seven. Then, we won six straight, and nine out of ten trials, while settling fifteen claims—thus obtaining recoveries for twenty-four of twenty-five claimants and fees for ourselves. As each verdict arrived at our office, shouts went up and down the hall as everyone poured out of their offices to congratulate the winning trial team. We were on a roll. State Farm was crazy to continue, but, instead of seeking mediation or settlement, MoFo got nastier—even going so far as filing a motion with the Court challenging our fee agreements with the claimants as unfair and unethical, seeking to portray themselves as the protectors of the claimants. Their real purpose, of course, was quite the opposite: by limiting our fees, they hoped to starve us and weaken our representation of the claimants. There was nothing illegal or unethical about our retainer agreements—indeed, I charged the claimants below-market fees—and the Court completely rejected State Farm's absurd motion.

The news for State Farm was even bleaker than their diminishing trial results. The Monetary Decree had failed to resolve an important money issue—the date that back pay for claimants would terminate. I considered this issue to be a clear winner for plaintiffs, but MoFo continued to delude itself and State Farm in thinking they had a real chance on the issues.

Following briefing and a hearing on the back pay issue, Judge Henderson ruled in an extremely thorough decision that back pay liability continued until the date each individual claimant obtained a judgment or settled her case. This made perfect—and obvious—sense, as the claimant had obtained no remedy, and continued to suffer the loss of pay, until the date of judgment in her favor, or settlement of her claim. In his decision, Judge Henderson deducted one year's back pay from each claimant's potential award, although neither State Farm nor I had suggested this. The reason for the deduction was that the judge did not want State Farm to bear the increased liability attributable to the delay caused by his illness.

I would have lived with the one-year deduction in order to resolve the termination date issue once and for all, but State Farm appealed the liability termination order to the Court of Appeals for the Ninth Circuit, so I cross-appealed the one-year back pay deduction. I argued the appeal for the plaintiffs, with the EEOC supporting our position as Amicus Curiae. State Farm contended that sex discrimination ended with the District Court's approval of the Consent Decree Regarding Injunctive Relief. From that point forward, Kirby argued, State Farm was obligated to appoint women to at least 50% of its trainee agent positions. Thus, since discrimination against women as a class had ended, back pay should not continue to accrue in favor of individual claimants. In response, I argued that the 50% hiring requirement, as well as other provisions of the Injunctive Decree, had ended discrimination against women as a class, but no individual claimant was entitled to any remedy under the Injunctive Decree until she obtained an individual judgment or settlement of her claims. The approval of the classwide injunction, therefore, could not operate as a termination of back-pay claims. I also contended that justice required that the costs of any delay in the judicial proceedings—even increased costs occasioned by a judge's illness—are to be born by the wrongdoer, not the victims of discrimination. On August 31, 1990, nearly eight months after the claim procedure had begun, the Court of Appeals ruled that Judge Henderson was correct in holding that back pay continued to accrue for each claimant until the date that claimant obtained an individual judgment or settlement and was not cut off as the date of the Injunctive Decree. The Court of Appeals stated:

> [T]he principal objectives of Title VII are to eliminate the vestiges of employment discrimination and to make persons whole for injuries suffered due to such discrimination. The Court directed that "[t]he injured party is to be placed, as near as may be, in the situation he would have occupied if the wrong had not been committed." Since *Albemarle*, the Supreme Court and lower courts have, as a matter of course, awarded back pay relief to plaintiffs, and, also as a matter of course, have granted that back pay until the date of judgment. Such relief has uniformly been viewed as necessary to put the victim in the place he would have been—to make him whole.

This was the Court of Appeals' polite way of saying State Farm's litigation of this issue was pretty dumb.

On our cross-appeal of the one-year deduction of back pay, the Court of Appeals reversed Judge Henderson. Citing a United States Supreme Court case which had been decided under the National Labor Relations Act (on which the remedy provisions of Title VII were modeled), the Court of Appeals held:

> In reducing each individual's back pay award by one year to avoid "penalizing" State Farm for the court's delay, the district court impermissibly shifted the burden of the delay to the wronged employees. Accordingly, we reverse that portion of the court's order.

It was one of the few errors Judge Henderson made in this lengthy and complicated case.

The practical effect of continuing back pay to the dates of individual judgments or settlements was huge; if the claim procedure was allowed to run its course, the continued accrual of back pay would double the women's total recovery. This should have been no surprise to State Farm, as, in the words of the Court of Appeals, continuation of back pay to the date of individual judgments/settlements was required by Supreme Court and Court of Appeals precedents and was awarded by the lower courts "as a matter of course." State Farm should have factored this into their calculations and tried to settle the case in 1986, when Judge Henderson ruled that an individual claim procedure approach would be followed, in 1988, when the terms of the Monetary Decree were agreed to, and certainly by 1989, when we filed 982 Final Claims. At any of those points, the monetary value of the case could have been computed with at least ballpark precision and a reasonable offer made to plaintiffs. But all I heard from Kirby was silence.

Following the Court of Appeals panel decision, Kirby, in an act of desperation, sought review by the entire Court of Appeals, but failed to obtain even one vote from the appellate judges in favor of State Farm's petition, then filed a petition for *certiorari* with the United States Supreme Court, seeking to reverse the Court of Appeals. Five months later, on April 1, 1991, the Supreme Court denied State Farm's petition, again without even a single justice voting in favor of State Farm's petition.

I heard nothing from State Farm about the back pay decision, and continued to prepare claims for trial, as eight to twelve claim trials now were being scheduled each month, and to supervise the representation of all claimants. Six weeks passed, and late on a Friday afternoon I received a call from MoFo senior partner Bob Raven, who announced, "I have been asked by State Farm to initiate settlement negotiations with you as soon as possible. I'm willing to meet with you tonight, tomorrow morning, at any time over the weekend, including early in the morning or late at night. You just tell me when you're available." The tone of his voice was pure desperation, and I loved it. After ignoring my settlement solicitations and not making a single offer for six years—while the value of the claim procedure skyrocketed—now they had to talk to me immediately! I responded, "I'm going out with my wife tonight and tomorrow night, and Saturday and Sunday mornings I coach a soccer team. I think Sunday evening probably would be OK, if Barry is available."

Having Bob Raven call like this sent us a signal that State Farm was serious and desperate. Bob was the President of the American Bar Association and MoFo's biggest name partner. A tall, handsome man with white hair, he was generally well liked and well respected within the bar. I knew him from the years he had spent on the ABA's Judiciary Committee, where he had helped to stop the approval of some particularly unqualified candidates President Reagan had nominated to federal judgeships. And he had done a favor for my wife: on the way to an ABA National Convention, where I was scheduled to speak, Jeanine and I ran into Bob on the plane. Jeanine complained about the ABA's practice of giving the wives name tags labeled, "Mrs. Guy Saperstein." She told Bob, "We have our own identities and the labels should reflect our real names." Bob promised to do something about it, and he did; at the next ABA National Convention, all the spouses—men and women— had labels reflecting their real names. He was a true corporate liberal.

Barry and I met with Bob and a group of MoFo attorneys, including Kirby, at a high-end hotel in San Francisco. After the normal pleasantries, Bob got down to business, explaining that he had great respect for the work we had done representing the women in the case, that State Farm was very serious about settling the case, and that now was the time to put differences behind us, make peace and settle the case on a global basis. I asked him what he meant by "global basis," and he said "all claims." I said that was not possible; there were about twenty-five claimants that we had rejected who now were being represented by their own counsel. I could not represent those claimants, nor could I assure him or State Farm that those claimants would want to settle their claims. I added that, in our opinion, those claims generally were less meritorious than the claims we represented and that I would expect those claims to settle on the same, or lesser, basis as the approximately 850 claimants I represented, but that in no case would I speak for those women nor permit the settlement of my approximately 850 remaining claims to be predicated on the settlement of claims I did not represent. I added that "global settlement" could not mean settlement by 100% of my clients either. Some number of claimants would not want to settle and would have to be provided a right to opt out of any "global" settlement. He asked me how many I thought might opt out and I said, "The number of potential opt-outs will be determined by the richness of the settlement offers. At your 1985 offer of $13.1 million, the number of opt-outs would be 100%. As the offer increases, so will my and the claimants' enthusiasm increase. Which brings us to the reason we are here. If you have an offer to make, we'd like to hear it."

Bob looked at Kirby, then turned to me and said, "$66,887,562." Kirby began to explain the basis of the offer, but I interrupted him: "Kirby, I don't need to know how you arrived at that number because it is wholly inadequate. Your offer represents approximately $80,000 per claim, when we are recovering, on average, more than $200,000 per claim. It is not an offer I would recommend to the claimants and without my recommendation, they won't take it."

Bob, visibly agitated now, said "$67 million is a lot of money, more than ever paid out in a civil rights case. I'm shocked and disappointed at your response." I said, "I'm sorry to disappoint you, but I've been disappointed for twelve years that State Farm and your firm have failed to evaluate this case properly and make an appropriate offer. You've delayed and rolled the dice, and, in the meantime, the price has gone up." Bob: "What is the price?" "Barry and I will get back to you on that," I said.

Three weeks later, we met with them a second time and presented our demand for $251.5 million. Bob's disappointment turned to fury over our ingratitude. The meeting ended abruptly, with no plans for subsequent meetings.

State Farm did not respond to our demand. Instead, MoFo filed a Motion for Order of Reference seeking the appointment of a settlement judge. I had no objection to that motion and proposed in our response that the Court appoint either former United States District Judge Raul A. Ramirez or United States District Judge Eugene F. Lynch as the settlement judge. Proposing Judge Ramirez, the Lucky Stores judge who had resigned his federal judgeship and now was working for Orrick, Herrington & Sutcliffe, a large corporate defense firm, was somewhat predictable. As a United States District Judge, he had had an excellent reputation as a settlement judge, owing to his quick intelligence and forceful, no-nonsense approach; and as a *Kraszewski* Settlement Master, he had become familiar with the case. And we had done well in front of him in our first Lucky Stores class action. He was Hispanic and was known as a liberal judge in civil rights cases. Most civil rights attorneys would have promoted a judge like Judge Ramirez for this role.

Proposing Judge Lynch was an unconventional choice for plaintiffs in a civil rights case. Judge Lynch was a Republican, appointed by President Reagan, no less. He was considered a "conservative" judge, not known for any particular knowledge about or preference for civil rights causes or cases. I knew MoFo would jump at my proposal of Lynch, and they did, phoning me promptly to inform me of their concurrence in my recommendation—their haste prompted perhaps by their concern that Judge Henderson might assign one of the more liberal District Court Judges to the case.

I think that Judge Henderson may have appointed a more liberal settlement judge to the case had I not proposed a judge that I knew State Farm would be happy with, but I was more interested in getting the job done than party labels. Judge Lynch had treated me fairly in my age discrimination case before him, I liked him and I was willing to trust my intuition about him. He had a great reputation among lawyers as a settlement judge who knew how to get at the heart of the matter and push both sides. He was not ideological about particular causes or labels; he was a judge who had a reputation of being fair in all types of cases. He was not known for long, intellectual written decisions, but he had a quick mind and did the homework necessary to understand issues. And, because he would have the confidence of MoFo and State Farm, I knew that whatever Lynch recommended would carry great weight with State Farm. In short, he had the ability to settle the case. I hoped my intuition that he would see the dispute more like I saw it than how MoFo would present it was accurate. With both sides in agreement, Judge Henderson appointed Judge Lynch and a settlement conference was scheduled for the afternoon of September 17, 1991.

Prior to the settlement conference, I submitted a Settlement Conference Statement explaining the long history of the case, the results of the back pay litigation, and the current status of the individual claim procedure. I included a brief chart of the history of all settlement offers by State Farm:

1982:	$ 225,000 (pre-trial)
	$ 1,000,000 (during trial)
1983:	$ 3,000,000 (post-trial)
1984:	$ 6,500,000 (pre-verdict)
1985:	$13,100,000 (post-verdict)
1991:	$66,887,562 (claim procedure)

Time and hundreds of thousands of hours of work clearly were working in our favor!

The main purpose of my Statement was to do an economic

analysis that would show Judge Lynch how foolish continued litigation was for State Farm. Indeed, under any rational cost-benefit analysis, State Farm had to settle the case now. I explained that we had gotten off to a tough start with the 1974 claims, but that the 1975 and 1976 claimants were doing significantly better. The 1974 claimants had won only 6 of 17 claims (35.3%), but the 1975–76 claimants had won 14 of 25 trials (56.0%), mostly the result of our ability to be more selective in choosing claimants for years after 1974 because more Initial Claims were filed for later years; I expected this trend to continue and strengthen. Overall, claimants had prevailed by settlement or trial verdict at a 76.7% rate, and the average recovery, including trial losses and dismissals, was $219,132 per claim, not including our awards of attorneys' fees, which were averaging an additional $170,000 per claim. Most significantly, for the 1974 claimants, the average recovery (including trial losses) was $183,509, but for the 1975–76 claimants, the average recovery increased to $232,431. This reflected our increasing success in claim trials and the increasing value of individual claims. Thus, whereas the first claim hearing win for a 1974 claimant was worth $580,068, a year later 1974 winning claims were worth more than $750,000 each—the effect of our win in the Court of Appeals on the back pay termination issue, and the addition of interest. Furthermore, the value of future claims would increase at an even greater rate.

Taking the total average recovery of $219,132 per claim, I projected the total present value of the 821 remaining claims at $179.9 million. However, assuming claimants continued to recover at the same rates, due to the ever-increasing value of claims, if State Farm let the claim procedure run its course claimants would recover $406.7 million, which, reduced to present value, would be worth $328.9 million.

In addition to the escalating value of claims, State Farm had to consider the impact of costs and attorneys' fees. Unlike ordinary litigation, where each side bears its own fees and costs, under the Monetary Decree State Farm was required to pay for nearly everything. Assuming claimants would continue to prevail at the same rates and that the volume of law and motion work would stay the same, I projected additional attorneys' fees of $178.8 million for my firm if the procedure ran its course. Since MoFo had twice as many attorneys and staff defending the case, I conservatively projected future defense fees at $268.2 million, and the future expenses of travel, discovery and special masters at $40.5 million—a total projected transaction cost of $487.5 million. Only by settling the case now could State Farm avoid these enormous transaction costs and the increasing value of the claims.

For settlement purposes, I discounted the potential value of claims by our historic recovery rate, by present value, and, of course, by projected costs and fees that would not be incurred if there was a settlement, and demanded $250.3 million for 821 remaining claimants. I knew I would settle the case for less—indeed, I set my target at $150 million with a 90% approval requirement—but this demand was high enough to give me negotiating room, yet reasonable enough not to antagonize Lynch or drive State Farm away from negotiations.

I had submitted similar arguments and projections to MoFo and State Farm before, in the hope that they would recognize the folly of continuing to litigate claims and the logic of settlement, but had gotten no response until Raven had called, and his response significantly undervalued the seriousness of the trap State Farm was in. Now, I hoped the same projections and arguments would have a greater impact on Judge Lynch than they had had on MoFo and State Farm.

The day after filing the Settlement Conference Statement, we appeared in Judge Lynch's courtroom. The MoFo attorneys sat at the defense table, Barry, myself, and Richard Drogin, our statistician, sat at the plaintiff table. Judge Lynch came in without his judicial robe, and sat in the jury box on the floor level—same as the attorneys. He announced that he had read the materials submitted by each side, but wanted to give each side an opportunity to explain its position.

I began and spoke for about forty-five minutes, explaining much of what had been put in our Settlement Conference Statement and permitting Judge Lynch to ask questions. He asked many questions, and as I sat down, I was convinced he understood the financial points I was trying to make. Then it was Kirby's turn to explain State Farm's position. But instead of responding to my presentation, he launched into a personal attack on me. His thesis was that I had refused to settle the case on a formula basis and was "churning" the claim procedure for attorneys' fees. He seemed to be most offended by the fact that my firm was being paid by State Farm on a non-contingent basis for certain legal work, most notably the law and motion work. He was visibly upset that plaintiff attorneys would be paid for some work on a straight hourly basis, win, lose or draw. Obviously, in his mind such favorable payment terms should be reserved for defense attorneys, not shared with lowly plaintiffs' counsel. Missing in his presentation, of course, was any mention of the fact that he had made an absurdly low offer of $13.1 million in 1985, told Judge Henderson that this was the "full value" of the case, then had sat on that offer for six years while the value of claims skyrocketed. Also missing was any mention of MoFo's fees, which were approximately double ours.

Judge Lynch listened to Kirby fulminate for about ten minutes, then said quietly, "Well, you know what you have to do, don't you?" Clueless, Kirby inquired, "No. What should I do?" "Take it away from him!" said Lynch. "But, how do I do that?" said Kirby. "You settle the case!" Lynch thundered. Kirby inquired, "How do I do that?" "Guy is recovering over $200,000 per case and has approximately 800 cases left. You pay him $160 to 170 million," instructed Judge Lynch. I looked over to the State Farm table when Lynch said this. The blood had drained from their faces: they were in shock.

In proposing Judge Lynch as the settlement judge, I had hoped he would get to the core of the matter and provide some direction to the floundering defense team. He had taken less than an hour to do so! I was thrilled by the Judge's perspicacity, and tickled watching the obvious distress at the defense table. MoFo asked to take a break, and they went out in the hall to talk, returning a half hour later.

Judge Lynch returned to the courtroom and Kirby announced that he had a proposal to make, but that he wanted to make it privately to the Judge in chambers. Judge Lynch asked if I minded, and I said, "No." The MoFo lawyers followed Judge Lynch into his chambers, and all emerged a half hour later. Judge Lynch turned to me and said, with the MoFo lawyers listening: "They seem to have this idea that the claimants really want to settle their claims and get paid, and that if they could present their $67 million offer directly to the claimants, the case would be over. What do you say? Do you want to call their bluff?" "Absolutely," I responded. "Then, fine, let's write a notice to claimants right now," said Judge Lynch, whereupon he and I began to compose a letter to claimants that would explain that State Farm had made a total settlement offer of $67 million, that their individual claim would be worth approximately $80,000, that my firm recommended against accepting the offer, but they could accept it nonetheless, simply by indicating their approval.

At this point, MoFo again asked to talk to the Judge in chambers—privately. Again, they all went into chambers, emerging again a few minutes later. Judge Lynch announced, "I guess they don't want to do that, after all." As he spoke, I saw the gleam in his eyes and sensed that Judge Lynch, a sagacious observer of human behavior, had enjoyed watching me call State Farm's bluff as much as I had. The Judge had shown how astute he was in understanding the core issues, and MoFo had acted like a bunch of buffoons. Never had I seen a group of attorneys sacrifice their credibility so quickly.

The day after our settlement conference, I began trial in Claim 162, which lasted six days. The trial went well and we won the claim. Following that, my wife and I left for southeastern Utah for a week horsepacking and hiking in Grand Gulch, one of the great red rock canyons filled with Anasazi ruins and artifacts. On my return, we met again with Judge Lynch. This time, Bob Raven spoke on behalf of State Farm and he again vigorously defended State Farm's $67 million settlement offer as "more than reasonable and fair." I responded that $67 million might have been acceptable after the class liability trial verdict was rendered in 1985, but now we were engaged in a claim procedure where our success, and the substantial transaction costs State Farm had agreed to bear, compelled a much higher settlement. "State Farm is checkmated. If it doesn't settle this case now, it will continue to face claims with ever-increasing value and incur huge transaction costs, which, by the way, have been greatly increased by MoFo's scorched-earth defense tactics. State Farm has to negotiate on the basis of current realities if it wants to settle the case," I responded.

I don't know if it was the fact that Raven was negotiating in an environment where he had to play the weaker hand, or my somewhat gratuitous (but accurate) comment about MoFo's litigation tactics that set him off, but whatever I said caused Raven to go completely bonkers: "Your demands are excessive by any measure. I was involved in Dalkon Shield litigation, and many of the Dalkon Shield plaintiffs, some of whom were injured more than your clients, got only $500 each. Your clients should be happy with recoveries like that!" The comment was so preposterous that Judge Lynch interrupted Raven's rant to inform him that, "Guy's clients are recovering at the rate of more than $200,000 per claim. I don't want to hear any more about Dalkon Shield cases or $500 settlements!" I think it is the only time I detected anger in Judge Lynch's voice, and his comment was so powerful I didn't have to say a word.

As if this weren't enough to sink Raven deep into a hole, he later had another emotional outburst directed at me in front of Judge Lynch which began, "We are sick and tired of having you, Guy Saperstein, dictate terms of the settlement," and then segued into an attack on something he alleged I had said at a hearing before Chief Special Master Renfrew, which, he alleged, proved my bad faith. I told Raven his facts about the Renfrew hearing were completely wrong, but that he didn't have to accept my version of what had happened. There was a phone in the courtroom, and I said, "Let's call Renfrew right now and you can ask him what happened." Raven responded, "I don't have to call Renfrew. I believe what my associates tell me. I don't have to call Renfew or anyone else," and then stomped out of the courtroom. Raven never returned to another negotiating session.

Bob Raven was gone, but we continued to negotiate. In addition to the amount of money that would be paid to the remaining claimants, State Farm was concerned about the number of claimants who would accept settlement offers. State Farm wanted a "global" settlement that settled as many claims as possible; it didn't want to pay out a substantial sum, then find out that 400 claimants continued to litigate claims. State Farm also was concerned that we, as Class Counsel, would "cherry pick" the best claims—tell the claimants with the best cases to not settle their claims, and, instead, settle only the weakest claims. This, Kirby argued, would leave State Farm in the worst position of all—paying substantial amounts to settle the worst claims, while remaining open to the claimants with the best claims seeking full value through continued litigation.

I told them that State Farm had a legitimate concern, but that they were overestimating the problem. It was not possible to fully evaluate the merits of a claim until formal discovery had been completed. Thus, while formal discovery was in the process of being completed for the claims that were coming to trial, there still were 800+ claims for which discovery was incomplete. For those, we would only be able to give tentative and incomplete advice about the wisdom of rejecting settlement offers in favor of continued litigation. Second, if the settlement offers were substantial enough, the strong tendency among claimants would be to accept them. We already had seen this in the first 150 claims; whenever State Farm made significant settlement offers, the women wanted to take them—sometimes even over our contrary advice. Indeed, due to the willingness of claimants to accept settlement offers when they were substantial, we had found ourselves in the position of trying our bad cases (where small or no settlement offers had been made by State Farm) and settling many cases where the probability of winning claim hearings was high. Thus, I felt confident that if the settlement offers were substantial, the probability of a high percentage of acceptances would be good. Furthermore, the probability of settlements would increase greatly if we, as a general matter, recommended settlement. That would not, of course, prohibit us from recommending rejection even of a substantial settlement offer, where enough formal discovery had been completed to enable us to say with assurance, "Reject the settlement offer because we feel confident you will win the claim." Lastly, I told MoFo I could never agree to settle all 821 remaining claims, but I would agree that the "global" settlement could be voided unless a certain percentage of claimants—State Farm sought 100% but I suggested 85%—accepted the settlements. After much negotiation, State Farm and I agreed that the threshold would be set at 87.5%—that is, individual settlements would be "voidable" unless at least 87.5% of all remaining claimants, i.e., 718 of 821 claimants, accepted the settlement offers.

I felt very confident that threshold could be achieved. Moreover, even if only 600 claimants accepted offers, State Farm would be unlikely to void the acceptances, as it still would be in State Farm's interest to settle 600 cases even if it couldn't achieve its ultimate objective of settling all claims. However, to encourage settlements I suggested that State Farm sweeten the pot by making "incentive payments" to each claimant based on the total number of acceptances. These "incentive payments" would begin if 91% of the claimants accepted offers and would increase as the total number of acceptances approached 100%. I told MoFo that it was in State Farm's interest to settle as many claims as possible, and a settlement of 800 claims was worth more than settling 700 claims. They agreed to the concept, but the total value of the settlement remained in dispute.

Privately, I told Judge Lynch that we would come off of our $250 million demand and would settle the remaining claims for an amount consistent with the recoveries we had obtained in litigating the first 150 claims. Judge Lynch accurately had figured out this was $160–170 million. To MoFo, after repeatedly presenting them with their downside scenario, I agreed that some discounts in claim values were appropriate. First, ten of our claimants had been hired as State Farm trainee agents after being subjected to discrimination at an earlier date. For these women, back pay was cut off as of the date of their hire, and their claims were worth less than unhired claimants, whose back pay continued to accrue. Second, claim values would be discounted to reflect "present value," since settling claimants would be paid now, not in the future. Third, we would discount the total potential value of claims to reflect the pattern of settlements and trial wins/losses we were obtaining in litigating claims. And, fourth, since the burden of proof on State Farm's defenses would change under the Monetary Decree for all claims that arose after February 14, 1983, we would slightly discount post-February 14, 1983 claims. MoFo thus had all the signals it needed to understand the remaining claims could be settled for $160–$170 million, but they wouldn't make the deal, preferring, instead, to periodically threaten to make unilateral offers to claimants—a bluff they had tried once before and which now we just laughed at.

While we were stalemated in this fashion, a somewhat fortuitous event intervened. A year earlier, using some of the information we had obtained in the *Kraszewski* case, we had filed a nationwide age discrimination case against State Farm, claiming discrimination on the basis of age in the hire of trainee agent's with several middle-aged men and women in the American Association of Retired Persons as the plaintiffs. The *Pines v. State Farm* case was filed in Orange County, California, and the case was assigned to United States District Judge Alicemarie H. Stotler. Judge Stotler was a 40-ish, surprisingly attractive, Republican judge who was described to me by local attorneys as "a very solid lawyer, intellectually curious, very fair, conducts a good hearing, asks intelligent questions, not a Republican ideologue." We felt very comfortable with that description and she turned out to be exactly as described—a federal judge in the best sense of the word.

MoFo represented State Farm in the *Pines* case and State Farm assigned its chief labor counsel, Dale Bock, to monitor the case. A crucially important hearing was scheduled in the *Pines* case. The issue was whether the Court would facilitate notice to potential plaintiffs about how to "opt-in" to the case. This was necessary because the Age Discrimination in Employment Act (ADEA) does not permit a true class action where a few plaintiffs can represent a class of individuals with similar claims who are not before the Court. Instead, the ADEA requires individuals who are "similarly situated" to "opt-in" to the action by filing written consents to become plaintiffs. We sought to have the Court facilitate opt-in procedures by ordering State Farm to produce nationwide information about agent applicants 45+ years old, including names and addresses of these potential plaintiffs, so we could provide notice to them that a "collective" action alleging age discrimination by State Farm was being conducted and providing them a right to join the action. Without such discovery and notice, the action would be limited to our plaintiffs and would have no real impact on State Farm. To be entitled to such Court "facilitation," we had to show that State Farm had a common, centralized policy or practice of age discrimination in hiring agents, that our plaintiffs were "similarly situated" to other 45+ year olds who had been denied hire, and that State Farm's hiring of persons 45+ years old deviated significantly from the available pool of 45+ year olds who would be interested in a State Farm trainee agent position.

Barry and I argued the motion for plaintiffs and presented evidence of State Farm's written policies encouraging the hiring of trainee agents in the "25 to 45 year old" age range, labor market statistics which showed the availability of workers 45 and older for this kind of job, and affidavits from 69 witnesses providing evidence and examples of State Farm's age discrimination in hiring agents.

MoFo countered in a fashion we had learned to expect in the *Kraszewski* case—they filed a motion for sanctions against Barry and two of our associate attorneys, alleging they had submitted false affidavits, in MoFo's words, "dishonestly." In fact, we had withdrawn the affidavits as soon as the declarants had testified inconsistently at depositions, and we did not rely on the tainted declarations (which were only three of sixty-nine submitted) in our motion for Court facilitation.

At the hearing, Judge Stotler demonstrated little interest in MoFo's sanctions motion—and later denied it entirely—but showed great intellectual curiosity in our motion for Court facilitation, the history and background of the Age Discrimination in Employment Act, the labor statistics used to support our motion, and the pattern evidence, and asked probing, intelligent questions throughout the hearing. It was an absolute pleasure for Barry and me to work before a judge who was so well prepared and asked so many good questions, and we enjoyed the opportunity to put so much of our own knowledge and experience on display in responding to her inquiries. We clearly out-argued the MoFo lawyers and we felt confident the result would be good.

After the hearing, State Farm's chief labor counsel, Dale Bock, who had been watching the hearing, approached me. Heretofore, he had been very stand-offish and only minimally civil. However, on this occasion, he shook my hand warmly and said, with the look of great surprise on his face, "You know you and Barry are very good lawyers." I wanted to respond, "Of course, what did you expect?" but I kept my response to a simple, "Thank you for the compliment." Later, as I got to know Dale a little better, I realized what had happened: MoFo had demonized us as cunning, unprincipled devils to State Farm, but now, in person, Bock saw that we were smart, principled, and reasonable—even in front of a Republican judge—and that it was State Farm's own lawyers who had chosen the low road with a stupid sanctions motion and a less-than-stellar performance in arguing the merits of the main motion. Perhaps State Farm should not have so much confidence in what MoFo says, Bock was beginning to think.

I have no doubt Bock's reports back to State Farm about his observations of our and MoFo's behavior proved instrumental in forging peace with State Farm. After Judge Stotler granted our motion for Court Facilitation and ordered State Farm to produce discovery of names and addresses of individuals 45 years and older who had been denied hire as trainee agents, and ordered nationwide notice of the right to opt in to our case, we negotiated the largest monetary settlement in the history of the Age Discrimination in Employment Act with State Farm.

Even more significantly, the stalemate in the *Kraszewski* negotiations broke, and State Farm agreed to settle the remaining claims for $160 million—the amount I had told Judge Lynch would do the job and the amount he had told State Farm they would need to reach at the first settlement conference. Each claimant who accepted State Farm's offers would receive between $151,200 and $283,543— all-time record amounts in a civil rights case. With the amounts previously recovered in claim hearings, and the attorneys' fees obtained for claim procedure work and winning the class liability trail, the total recovery was $250 million—then the all-time record in a civil rights case. (This amount would be exceeded ten years later in a case against a large government agency, *Hartman v. Albright.* The attorneys who prosecuted *Albright* subsequently gave credit to me and the *Kraszewski v. State Farm* case for our path-breaking work in the class claims procedure.) After working on the case for over fifteen years, and having the firm expend nearly 600,000 hours prosecuting the case, closure was at hand. We thanked Judge Lynch for his wise counsel, shook hands with the MoFo attorneys, then walked straight to Judge Henderson's chambers. I wanted him to be the first to know the case was settling and to thank him for the tremendous amount of time and effort he had devoted to the case— without which the great hiring order and the historic monetary recovery would not have been achieved. The smile we got from Henderson when we told him the case had settled was gigantic, and he said, "This is the best Christmas present I could possibly get!" He was as happy as I was that the case was over and that he wouldn't have to face me and Kirby snarling at each other again! Then Barry and I walked straight to a nearby restaurant, where we knocked down two bottles of champagne, replayed some of the battles we had had with MoFo in the case, and enjoyed a good dinner.

ALTHOUGH THE CASE HAD "SETTLED," formal settlement would not actually occur until at least 87.5% of the claimants accepted individual offers. Notices were sent to each claimant explaining the offers and the process of acceptance or rejection, and hundreds of claimants called for advice. Thereafter, the agreements began to arrive at the office; in the end, more than 99% of the offers were accepted and every claimant received a bonus payment of $16,200. The handful of claimants who did not accept the "global" settlement offers subsequently settled their claims, or, in the case of two claimants, took their cases to trial and won.

Once the 87.5% settlement threshold had been met, State Farm checks, which required my signature, began arriving at my office at the rate of about 100 per day. I would begin each day signing checks and dispensing $15–20 million. I felt like Santa Claus, although the money was no gift—it had been hard-earned!

One morning I received a letter from one of the settling claimants, and she said she was extremely happy to be receiving such a large settlement, but she felt she owed something to the women who had litigated but had lost their claim hearings before the global settlement was achieved. She said, "These women helped till the ground for the rest of us. They helped make the class settlement possible. I think a fund should be established for them, and I will begin it by contributing $10,000 from my settlement to share with them." This $10,000 became the genesis of the "Kraszewski Appreciation Fund," which collected over $400,000 from winning claimants to pay losing claimants more than $10,000 each. I've never heard of this happening in a class case of any type, and it was a marvelous testament to the generosity and sense of community these women shared.

The historic monetary recovery was, of course, tremendously satisfying. But State Farm's response to the settlement also was remarkable. When the settlement was announced to the press, instead of issuing the usual corporate disclaimers ("We admit no wrongdoing. We settled simply to avoid continued litigation costs," etc.), State Farm stepped up to the plate and took responsibility, telling the press, "It is clear the Court found us guilty...we clearly weren't doing the job…and we acknowledge that." "We were interested in getting this over and getting money to the truly injured." "We're very pleased this has finally come to an end… It's certainly not a proud period in our history." And, my favorite: "We were like Robert Duran in the ring with Sugar Ray Leonard, and we said, 'No mas'." I had been a very mediocre boxer in intramural boxing competitions in college, and I relished State Farm putting me in the same class as Sugar Ray!

More important than the corporate *mea culpa* was the action State Farm took to implement fair employment practices. State Farm changed its recruitment and training procedures for women, expanded its outreach to the "women's market," exceeded the 50% female hiring requirements set by the Injunctive Decree, and generally provided women the opportunity to be successful State Farm sales agents that they never had when Muriel Kraszewski and Daisy Jackson commenced the class action lawsuit.

After monitoring State Farm's performance under the Injunctive Decree for several years, I called Dale Bock to pass on my congratulations to State Farm for exceeding the 50% female hiring requirement each year. "State Farm has done more than what was required, their performance has been exemplary, but tell me, what do they think about the changes? Is it something they feel was forced down their throats and resent, or do they accept the changes?" I asked. Dale didn't have to answer, of course, but he said, "As far as we're concerned, you're the guy who brought us into the 20th century of personnel practices. We now are hiring better quality agents than ever before and the women are selling as well, or better, than the men." I asked, "Is this your opinion alone, or do others feel this way?" "I speak for the Board and the company. We have the best sales force we've ever had and you are the main reason," he said. For me, the fact that women agents are being hired on a fair basis and enjoy equal employment and opportunities at State Farm, and the fact that State Farm accepted these changes into the company culture as a better way of doing business—not just something imposed by a Court—is a more important result than the $250 million we recovered.

The case gathered great attention from the media, including a front-page profile of me in the *Wall Street Journal* ("Doing Well: A Law Firm Shows Civil Rights Can Be a Lucrative Business"), *Business Week* ("The Swat Team of Bias Litigation"), the *Oakland Tribune* ("Doing Good and Well"), the *San Francisco Business Times* ("The Lawyers Businesses Fear Most"), and my inclusion in the *National Law Journal's* list of "The 100 Most Influential Lawyers in America"—the first time a private civil rights attorney ever had been included in this exclusive list. But the *American Lawyer*, a glossy national magazine read primarily by corporate attorneys, published a very long article about the case ("Runaway Train") that omitted many salient parts of the story, accepted MoFo's misrepresentations without seeking corroboration, focused on personalities, and attacked me for making too much money from the case, ignoring, of course, the fact that defense counsel had billed more than double my fees, despite suffering the biggest loss in civil rights history.

I wrote a fifteen-page letter to the magazine, which to its credit, was published almost in its entirety. The article had tried to fix responsibility on me for not settling the case earlier, but ignored the actual settlement history of the case. I pointed out that, despite the magazine's claim that MoFo was hired in 1985 specifically to settle the case, MoFo had made only one settlement proposal, its $13.1 million offer in 1985, which Kirby told Judge Henderson represented State Farm's "full back pay liability," and characterized my representation that the case was worth hundreds of millions as "a complete fabrication" having "no basis in Title VII precedent or logic or fact." Compared to the ultimate recovery of $250 million, Kirby's comments were foolish, to put it kindly, but the *American Lawyer* ignored the discrepancies between Kirby's claims and the actual results, preferring to attack "the greedy plaintiffs' lawyers."

Two years before the case settled, MoFo's litigation department had proposed that a $60 million settlement offer be included in State Farm's Motion for Reconsideration, but Wilcox rejected it. This crucial piece of settlement history was confirmed by the author of the *American Lawyer* article, but was omitted from the published story. Revealing this, of course, would have shown that even as late as 1990, MoFo was low-balling the value of the case, but even this low-ball amount was too high for Wilcox and/or State Farm to offer. In light of the $250 million recovery, a competent news magazine would have asked MoFo to explain the decision not to offer $60 million in 1990, but *American Lawyer* omitted this information as well.

The article had MoFo criticizing me for filing too many motions, and it accepted MoFo's uncorroborated claim that many were frivolous, filed primarily for the purpose of charging attorneys' fees to State Farm. Missing in the article was the fact that Class Counsel was *not once* assessed sanctions for bringing or defending a motion unnecessarily, while State Farm and its attorneys were assessed sanctions worth nearly $2 million—perhaps a federal court record.

The underlying premise of MoFo's complaints about Class Counsel being paid for motion work was that if lawyers are paid on an hourly, non-contingent, basis, they churn work. However, if that premise is correct, what conclusion should be drawn from the fact that MoFo was guaranteed payment for all work—win, lose or draw, necessary or unnecessary?

It long has fascinated me how corporate defense counsel believe almost religiously that they have been put on earth with the mission to charge and collect fees, but that it is "hypocritical" for plaintiffs' attorneys to be paid—particularly civil rights attorneys. The psychological satisfaction of prosecuting civil rights is supposed to be reward enough—as though I were supposed to pay 44 attorneys and 165 employees, plus associated overhead and litigation costs, fight the largest insurance company in the world, and prosecute the biggest civil rights case in history with psychological satisfaction alone.

I asked the *American Lawyer* to look at the numbers and ask the question they had avoided: How much were the lawyers on each side paid and what did their clients receive in return?

Based on what several Cooley, Godward and MoFo attorneys

confided in me, and what the *American Lawyer* was able to confirm, State Farm spent approximately $145 million in attorneys' fees—$110 million for defense fees and $35 million to Class Counsel (we also recovered $30 million from claimants pursuant to their contingent fee agreements). What did State Farm get for its $110 million defense fees and what did the claimants get for the $30 million they paid?

It is easy to compute the recovery to the class. They obtained the strongest injunctive relief ever ordered in an employment discrimination case—a hiring order which required the hire of 50% female agents for ten years (plus five years of accelerated female hiring that State Farm undertook before the injunction was entered). Since the agent jobs are so valuable (net earnings of more than $100,000 per year), this relief alone has returned in excess of $1 billion to the direct beneficiaries of the *Kraszewski* Decree and billions more indirectly to beneficiaries of increased female hiring by State Farm in states other than California, and in other jobs. In addition, the *Kraszewski* claimants obtained a *net* recovery of $185 million in damages—an amount that is more than five times greater than the largest prior recovery in a civil rights case and 1,412% greater than State Farm's original $13.1 million claims offer. Over 96% of all claimants received recoveries that averaged over $200,000 each—an amount more than ten times greater than any previous Title VII class action.

What did State Farm get for its $110 million investment in defense fees? A loss of approximately $300 million more than was necessary! If MoFo had put $100 million on the table (instead of $13.1 million) after State Farm lost the class liability trial, I would have taken it, provided that satisfactory entitlement procedures could have been agreed upon, and if I had rejected $100 million, I have little doubt Judge Henderson would have imposed some type of formula recovery on plaintiffs or figured out how to get us to take it. That would have avoided the eventual $250 million recovery by claimants and Class Counsel, the $110 million in defense fees, and the huge transaction costs of special masters, depositions, travel, lodging, transcripts, etc. which the Decree required State Farm to pay. In other words, if Wilcox had evaluated the monetary liability the same way I had, he could have saved his client approximately $300 million. Instead, he apparently sold State Farm on the idea that my recovery estimate of $100 to $300 million was "a fantasy," and marched his troops forward. It was a very expensive march!

In all, my firm recovered approximately $65 million in attorneys' fees for 16 years of work; this covers nearly 600,000 hours of billable time for attorneys, paralegals, case clerks and word processors—roughly $110 per hour. Few law firms or clients would find this excessive. By contrast, State Farm paid $110 million to defense counsel, who took no risks and were paid regardless of outcome. The fact that the result for State Farm was the biggest monetary and injunctive loss in Title VII history apparently did not diminish MoFo's fees one cent.

Looking back on the case, I do not have any fundamental complaints about how MoFo defended it. Had they offered $100 million after the class liability trial loss, I would have taken it or the Court would have imposed it and our clients would have received far less than they ultimately obtained. Had MoFo offered $60 million in February 1990 (as their Litigation Department recommended)—our low point in the claim hearing procedure—we would have been dealing from a position of weakness. Instead, MoFo stonewalled and gave us time to ride out the 1974 claims and try the 1975–76 claims, which were qualitatively better, and in which we prevailed by settlement or trial win more than 80% of the time. And if MoFo had not tried to bury us with their resources and frustrate our efforts to expedite claim resolution, the transaction costs might not have become so burdensome for State Farm. Indeed, that is one of the wonderful ironies of the *Kraszewski* case: MoFo tried to overwhelm us with their resources, but, instead, due to the fee and cost-shifting mechanisms of the Monetary Decree, made the transaction too expensive for their client to continue.

MoFo presided over the biggest loss—by far—for a defendant

in American civil rights history. State Farm's loss in the *Kraszewski* case was the civil rights equivalent of the sinking of the Titanic. The loss would not have been near this magnitude if MoFo had not hardballed the defense and stonewalled settlement for over six years. I and my clients became richer for it and other companies were shown that employment discrimination can be very expensive.

THE IMPACT OF *KRASZEWSKI* exceeded even the historic relief that was obtained in the case. Although *Kraszewski* was limited to California, State Farm moved quickly to improve its hiring and promotion of women and minorities throughout the United States. The State Farm ads one sees today, which include women and minority agents, reflect a company that is highly diverse and successful.

The *Kraszewski* case was a quantum leap in the cost of discrimination. Previously, the largest recovery in an employment discrimination case had been $36 million on behalf of over 10,000 class members; the $250 million recovered for a class of just 985 claimants raised the stakes for corporate America. If it happened at State Farm, it could happen anywhere minorities or women were excluded from employment opportunities. The case was widely reported in the media and in trade journals and I received over one hundred invitations to speak to groups of corporate attorneys and personnel managers.

One speaking invitation I got came from an unlikely source—the State Farm Agents Association, an organization that represented the nearly all-male State Farm agents. Out of curiosity, I went to Santa Fe to speak at their national convention. As I was being introduced, I received a standing ovation! I was bewildered—why were they applauding me so enthusiastically? In any case, I gave my speech describing the *Kraszewski* case, then said I would take questions. The first man who stood up explained that State Farm had instituted new rules for recruiting and selecting new agents that were making it hard for his son to get hired; he had promised his son that he would be able to take over his agency, which previously had been the norm at State Farm, and now his son was being asked to compete for the job. How unfair! "Maybe you guys don't really understand who I am," I said. "I'm the guy who broke up the system of nepotism and cronyism and forced State Farm to adopt modern professional recruitment and hiring procedures. I'm the guy that has made it hard for you to pass on your agencies to your sons. That's the bad news. The good news is that your daughters now are eligible to become State Farm agents!" After answering questions, I received another standing ovation, and at lunch afterwards with their Executive Committee, they offered to hire me as their General Counsel! I thanked them, but explained that such a job would be a conflict of interest with my continuing representation of the women in monitoring the Injunctive Consent Decree. Apparently, they considered me something of a hero for standing up to their Goliath and winning. They respected that because they had their own issues with State Farm, mostly regarding the career agent contract, and knew what a formidable opponent State Farm could be. I thanked them for the job offer, but had to laugh to myself about it as I left their meeting.

While there were lessons for corporate America in the *Kraszewski* case, there also were lessons for me. I saw that large companies often do things that are not in their own best interests, yet rigidly defend their unproductive practices. It never was in State Farm's true interest to allow their agency managers to hire agents mostly on a friendship or family basis. Cronyism and nepotism restrict the market for good employees, as they favor friends and relatives, while erecting barriers to highly qualified candidates who do not have close family and friendship relationships. The State Farm agent job was, and is, highly desirable, as it offered exactly what State Farm brochures said—high pay, independence, and good working conditions representing the world's most successful insurance company. State Farm long ago should have opened up competition for the job so that the most qualified candidates could be recruited and hired. That was in State Farm's interest. By contrast, what State Farm defended so vigorously in *Kraszewski* was not its legitimate interest in hiring the best qualified agents, but instead the interests of the agency managers in hiring their own friends and relatives. Sure, it was nice for State Farm managers like Ray Wehde to be able to hire his college dropout, grocery bagger son for a plum State Farm agency, but it never was in the company's interest to allow him to do so. Hiring agents like Ray's son meant that more highly-qualified applicants—applicants with real "success patterns"—would not be considered. I explained this many times to State Farm's lawyers, but the explanation did not seem to register until the Court had made extensive findings of discrimination and the company was facing hundreds of millions in costs and damages.

It also was not in State Farm's interest to exclude women from insurance sales. Men in this country are still the predominant wage earners, and women are in a more economically precarious position than men. The untimely death of a male wage earner without insurance has a far greater economic impact on the family than the death of the mother. Thus, it is women who have a greater interest in buying life insurance than men, and women agents have a better chance of understanding the need for life insurance and selling it. The same is true for other types of catastrophic loses that can impact families and for which casualty insurance provides protection. It was in State Farm's interest to tap this "women's market" by aggressively hiring female agents; it was not in State Farm's interest to perpetuate an all-male, father-son-friend sales force, or spend hundreds of millions defending the wrong system.

I have been asked often, "If employment discrimination is irrational and not in the interest of employers, won't discrimination just stop?" If the world were run purely by logic, the answer would be "yes." But companies like State Farm often are guided by inertia, not logic. They have been conducting their business a certain way for a long time, and have felt they were successful. "Why change?" "Why rethink old practices?" And, "Why let some smart-ass lawyer from Oakland tell us how to run our company?" That's the attitude I have faced so often. Perhaps there should be a better way, but sometimes these companies just need to be hit over the head with a big mallet to get their attention.

I also was amazed at State Farm and its attorneys' inability to do a rational analysis of the value of claims, or do a cost-benefit analysis regarding the value of continuing to litigate claims for so many years. I had no trouble estimating damages, computing transactional costs for State Farm, or determining that the damages and costs would sink State Farm and force a favorable result for plaintiffs. The calculations were simple enough for me to do on a hand-held calculator. The one thing I expected from an insurance company was the ability to evaluate and cost out risks. Why was State Farm's calculations—as represented by its ridiculously low offers prior to 1991—so far off base? Why was a smart guy like Kirby Wilcox unable to understand that my 1988 estimate of damages was accurate, not a "fantasy"?

And I also saw, again, how the interests of defense lawyers can diverge from the interests of the client. Attorneys do not like to bring bad news to clients, for fear of losing their business and their own fees. Throwing gasoline on the raging fire—which MoFo did on a regular basis—profited MoFo, which was billing State Farm $3 to 4 million *per month* at the height of the claim procedure, but wasn't in the interest of State Farm. Although the *Kraszewski* case was perhaps the most egregious example of this in a Title VII case, I have seen the same thing in other areas of litigation and never have understood why companies permit it to happen. Maybe these companies should be using big mallets on their own lawyers!

10

More Battles with Racism, Sexism, and Kirbyism

> *"We are all pilgrims on the same journey...*
> *but some pilgrims have better road maps."*
> —Nelson De Mille

WHILE I WAS BUSY with the *Kraszewski* case, our firm continued to prosecute two major employment discrimination cases—one which would result in the largest recovery ever in a race discrimination case, and the other would become the second $100+ million sex discrimination case.

The race case, *Haynes v. Shoney's Restaurants*, came to me as a by-product of my interest in hiring Barry Goldstein away from his job at the NAACP Legal Defense Fund. Barry had worked for LDF since graduating from Columbia School of Law in 1970 and was running their Washington D.C. office. He had a considerable reputation, and I had met him at American Bar Association conferences, where he and I often were invited to speak. In 1986, when I was preparing the attorneys' fee application in the *Bockman v. Lucky Stores* case, I hired Barry as an expert witness for the purpose of preparing an affidavit evaluating and commenting on the results we had obtained in the case. Timing was short and Barry was forced to do the work while on vacation with his family in Maine, relying on a local law library for research. Despite the logistical handicaps, Barry produced a sixty-page affidavit that was close to encyclopedic in its references to other achievements in Title VII consent decrees, and, by the way, placed the *Bockman* achievements at or near the top in several categories. I was enormously impressed with the quality of his scholarship, and after the *Bockman* application was completed, decided I would try to hire Barry away from Washington, D.C.

It was not hard convincing Barry that he should join our firm. He knew we were litigating some of the biggest civil rights cases in America, that we had an excellent reputation, and that we had sufficient capital to persevere to the end of long cases. I assured Barry that at our firm he would be backed up by a staff of smart young attorneys and paralegals and would be able to operate as a true "lead counsel." I also offered him an income many times his income at the NAACP Legal Defense Fund.

Barry had one major condition on joining our firm. The NAACP and a private lawyer in Florida, Tommy Warren, had recently investigated a Title VII class action in Tallahassee against Shoney's Restaurants. The NAACP had invested several hundred thousand dollars in funding expenses of the case, but their continued funding of the case was uncertain. Barry wanted assurances from me that the firm would take the case—and fund it. The scope of the case was huge—hundreds of Shoney's restaurants spread out over twenty-three states—and Shoney's already had shown that the battle would be bitter and protracted. I knew the expenses, alone, that our firm would have to advance could be millions and that the case was venued in a conservative forum, Pensacola, Florida.

I met with Tommy and he explained that race discrimination started at the top of Shoney's. Shoney's CEO, and major shareholder, was Ray Danner, who often voiced his support of the Ku Klux Klan, encouraged Shoney executives to donate to the Klan, and reputedly was a major supporter of the Klan himself. Witnesses had told Tommy that Danner regularly brought up the subject of race at corporate meetings, insisting that the Klan was right about the separation of the races and telling his subordinates that the number of blacks in management and customer-contact positions at Shoney's should be kept as low as possible. As a consequence, out of 441

Shoney employees at the supervisory or supervisory-trainee level, only 7 were black (1.6%), only one of 68 division directors was black, and 75% of all black Shoney employees held jobs in three low-paid jobs with no customer-contact—bus person/dishwasher, prep person, and breakfast bar attendant.

I was scheduled to give a speech at the American Bar Association's Labor and Employment Section Meeting at Amelia Island, near Jacksonville, Florida, so I asked Tommy if he would take me to see a Shoney's Restaurant in operation. Tommy picked Barry and me up for lunch and on the drive to the restaurant told me what to expect: "We'll be greeted by a hostess, who will be white. Near the cash register will be a man in a white shirt. He will be the manager and he will be white. The waitresses will all be white. The young men who will bus the tables will be black. And, hidden from view, the kitchen workers will be nearly all black."

Tommy, Barry and I sat down for lunch at the Fernandina Beach Shoney's. The script unfolded exactly as Tommy had predicted. As we waited to be served, Tommy told me that Ray Danner liked to make on-site visits to the restaurants to see if they were "too black." On those days, the black employees were told to stay in the kitchen. On one of Danner's unannounced visits to a Shoney's Restaurant, a black employee was locked in the freezer to keep her out of Danner's sight.

I listened to Tommy's stories, while surveying the scene before me, then asked Tommy, "What kind of attorneys' fees do the federal courts award civil rights attorneys down here?" Tommy said, "About $125 at the top end." This was less than half what we normally obtained in California for young associate attorneys! I asked about the judge, we were likely to get, United States District Judge Roger Vinson. Tommy said he was a conservative Republican, appointed by Ronald Reagan, but not a racist and considered by most lawyers to be fair in his decision-making. I thought about the egregious nature of the discrimination, the segregation of blacks into low-paid, dead-end jobs, and the enthusiasm of Tommy and Barry for the case. I also pondered the legal risks of prosecuting a civil rights case in the Eleventh Circuit, the most conservative venue in America for civil rights cases, the huge amount of money I might have to advance to prosecute the case, and the very low attorneys' fees we were likely to recover for a civil rights case in the South, if it was successful. I didn't ponder long. I turned to Tommy and Barry and said, "Our firm is a civil rights law firm. We shouldn't be afraid of doing a race case in the South." I figured I would use the money I was making in the State Farm claim procedure to fund the Shoney's case!

With that condition met, Barry joined our law firm and, shortly thereafter, Tommy and Barry filed the Complaint in Pensacola, Florida and drew Judge Vinson. Ironically, when Barry left the NAACP Legal Defense Fund and joined our firm, the Washington D.C. *Legal Times* wrote a story about his decision titled, "Bad Timing," referring to the slew of adverse civil rights decisions that were coming from the Republican-dominated United States Supreme Court and making civil rights litigation even more difficult and risky. Despite these unfavorable trends, our firm continued to win cases and Barry played a major role in the firm's successes in the 1990s.

IT WOULD BE A TREMENDOUS UNDERSTATEMENT to describe Tommy Warren as merely "colorful." Tommy had achieved celebrity-rogue status long before he became an attorney, and the circumstances of his becoming a lawyer only enhanced this further.

"Touchdown Tommy" quarterbacked his high school football team, Coral Gables High, to the state championship, becoming All-City, All-State, All-South and All-American in the process. He was offered football and/or baseball scholarships by fifty-three universities before he accepted a football/baseball scholarship from Florida State University. Quick to capitalize on his stature, before accepting the FSU scholarship he negotiated a written agreement that he would be excused from spring football practice so he could play baseball. On the FSU freshman baseball team he led the team in hitting.

On the FSU football team, Tommy became both leader and rebel—a leader because of his athletic talent, his ability to read defenses, and his charisma, a rebel because he chafed at the authoritarianism and isolation of college football. By his senior year, Tommy became a leader of the "Dissension" group of players and was appointed the team's representative to negotiate with the coaching staff about the brutality of spring football practice and NCAA rules that FSU appeared to be violating. In his first year of law school, he publicly exposed the brutal and illegal aspects of spring practice to the local press, which led to the NCAA imposing severe sanctions on the FSU football program.

Despite his critique of the football program, and a number of serious injuries, Tommy excelled at quarterback, leading FSU to five straight wins in 1970 before being injured. Dan Henning, the FSU offensive coordinator, and later an NFL head coach, told a reporter, "Those five games are the most efficient I've ever seen by any quarterback. I would be willing to stack that five-game span against any in the history of any FSU quarterback."

During Tommy's junior year, FSU recruited its first black player, Calvin Patterson. Patterson did well his freshman year, but had difficulty handling the pressure of being the first and only black on the team. Tommy asked the coaching staff to make the younger player his roommate. Through Patterson, Tommy began to understand the pressures and problems a black man faced trying to succeed in a white world. Tommy also began to see the similarity of authoritarianism in football with the oppression of racism and U.S. militarism in Vietnam. Following graduation, Tommy worked on a voter registration project, and then in the Governor's office, where he persuaded then-Governor Asker to integrate the Florida Highway Patrol. This led to his decision to go to law school and become a civil rights attorney.

Soon after graduating FSU Law School and passing the bar, Tommy and his older brother, John, were on board a shrimp boat 700 miles south of the United States that was stopped and boarded by a U.S. Coast Guard cutter. A search of the boat turned up $41,500 in U.S. currency, 46,800 Colombian pesos, a trash compactor, a couple of hundred plastic garbage bags, and a yellow legal pad with the names of Colombia contacts and lists of equipment to be used to load and package marijuana. The skipper of the boat told the Coast Guard that the workers had promised him $10,000 to take them to Colombia to pick up a load of marijuana.

Tommy spent the next six years of his life challenging the Nixon Administration's drug interdiction program and the admissibility of the evidence seized by the Coast Guard, but, in the end, he and his brother served 4½ months in federal prison. While defending, and appealing his criminal prosecution, Tommy worked as a paralegal on Title VII discrimination cases with attorney Kent Spriggs. By the time of his release from prison, he had seven years of productive legal work in the Florida legal community, and, aided by thirty-five letters of support, including one from a former president of the American Bar Association and another from one of the agents who had investigated the case against him, Tommy was reinstated to the Florida bar.

Before our firm became involved, the Shoney's lawyers were quick to tell us that Tommy was a drug runner and convicted felon. At various stages in the prosecution of the case against Shoney's— most notably when Shoney's challenged the "adequacy" of plaintiffs' counsel at the class certification hearing—Shoney's lawyers reminded the judge of Tommy's past. This stratagem didn't seem to work with Judge Vinson and it certainly didn't intimidate us. We loved Tommy for who he was and recognized he had paid a heavy price for his mistake.

More importantly, Tommy was proving to be the most awesome investigator of facts I've ever seen. He was coming up with testimony and affidavits in support of plaintiffs' contentions that ranged from black applicants for employment at Shoney's, white managers who had been pressured to effectuate Shoney's racial discrimination, and even high officials in Shoney's management, who confirmed that the discrimination originated at the top. The collection of facts was so overwhelming that, less than three months after the Complaint was filed, Tommy proposed that plaintiffs file a motion for summary judgment. Tommy argued that the evidence was so strong, we needed to show it to Judge Vinson as soon as possible so that he would know how serious the case was, and show Shoney's, as well, how much evidence it was facing. Barry and I thought it was an extremely bold move, but after lengthy discussions between us, and also discussions with Tommy, we decided to do it. At a minimum, the extensive evidence of discrimination that would be a part of plaintiffs' summary judgment motion would buttress plaintiffs' motion for class certification, which already had been filed. This was the only time I've ever seen plaintiffs in a Title VII class action file a motion for summary judgment, let alone file one so early in the prosecution of an action.

In less than a month, Barry and Tommy put together a summary judgment motion that was based on "voluminous and compelling direct evidence that Shoney's, Danner, and RIC acted in a viciously racist manner." This evidence included testimony from more than two dozen white former Shoney managers and supervisors in thirteen states, and affidavits from fifty current and former black Shoney's employees from every division in the company. Plaintiffs' brief stated, "The plaintiffs' proof establishes a paradigm of discrimination. Blacks may enter some doors to work in restaurants located in black areas or in the kitchens of other restaurants, but as to other doors, such as those leading to positions dealing directly with the public or leading to managerial positions, the Defendants, in effect, have erected signs reading 'Whites only'."

Shortly after the summary-judgment motion was filed, Tommy received a phone call from Shoney's general counsel, "If you were trying to get our attention, it worked," he said. Shoney's wanted to begin settlement discussions. Then Barry received calls from Jim Neal and Steve Tallent, both indicating they had been brought into the case to equitably resolve the issues. These calls were significant in that they indicated that Butch Powell, a hardball litigator who had been managing the defense and leading the personal attacks on Tommy would no longer be calling the shots and that two litigators with national reputations would take a more independent look at the case. Barry had known Steve Tallent from ABA activities, and I knew him from my case against Prudential Insurance Company, where he had shown himself to be an honorable and innovative attorney, and Jim Neal, the former Watergate prosecutor, had represented many major high-profit clients and had a fine reputation for his skills as a trial attorney and his integrity in negotiations.

Neal and Tallent wanted something from us—a litigation moratorium. Barry and Tommy were reluctant to agree to a moratorium, and I concurred. Plaintiffs had the momentum in the litigation—a moratorium would give Shoney's a chance to catch up—and we couldn't be sure that Neal and Tallent would continue to speak for the company. Indeed, there was chaos and disagreement on the defense side—which we didn't know about at the time—but which could result in the return to a stonewall defense posture. So, as the price for agreeing to a moratorium, Barry and Tommy demanded that Shoney's turn over all of the company's computerized employment records, which would be critical in proving class liability as well as analyzing damages for settlement negotiations, and that Shoney's pay the substantial expenses of evaluating this mass of data. On this basis, the parties agreed on a three-month moratorium for settlement negotiations. We immediately turned the computerized information over to our statistical firm, Drogin & Kakigi, who began to analyze the data and report back to us on a near-daily basis.

As soon as the information was fully analyzed, Barry, Tommy and I met with Jim Neal, Steve Tallent and Butch Powell in our Oakland office. Barry and I had met Steve many times before, and, as usual, he was charming and knowledgeable, always trending toward the ironic. Jim Neal, who we were meeting for the first time, looked the role of a former United States prosecutor—robust, fit, perhaps a former linebacker. He was, of course, preceded by his major-league reputation, and, like many who have become bigger and more successful than even they thought might happen, tried to show us he still was a regular guy. This didn't stop him from dropping names of some of his famous clients or telling a few attorney "war stories," but we liked him and enjoyed the stories. We figured he might be important to selling any deal we might make to Shoney's managements, but that Steve Tallent would provide the real Title VII expertise on the defense side. Butch Powell sat quietly in the background, a dark, brooding presence. I figured he was just hoping the settlement discussions would blow apart so his scorched-earth defense tactics would be vindicated.

Barry took the lead in analyzing the data, showing how it supported plaintiffs' pending motion for class certification and provided ample evidence, along with our anecdotal testimony, to support a class liability verdict for plaintiffs. He set forward the affirmative action plan that would be needed to remedy past racial discrimination and integrate blacks into all levels of the company, then explained our analysis of damages. Our monetary demand: $400 million! I have no doubt this was substantially more than they expected us to demand and I suspect they didn't think we were serious. Indeed, in the twenty-five years since Title VII was passed, the largest Title VII recovery had been $36 million in a sex case against United Airlines; no one had come close to recovering even $100 million. In any case, they expressed shock at the number, claimed that Shoney's was in dire financial circumstances, then made plans for another settlement meeting. There was, in fact, some merit to Shoney's claims it was cash-poor and in debt. The company recently had recapitalized itself, borrowing to buy back $140 million of Ray Danner's stock. Ray Danner was a named defendant who personally had orchestrated much of the discrimination plaintiffs complained about, so it was natural for us to expect that he would contribute a substantial sum of his own money to any settlement. As time went on, Shoney's itself would seek Danner's contribution to a settlement.

Two more meetings were held before Shoney's made a counteroffer, which actually consisted of two options: (1) $32 million, or (2) franchise rights for Shoney's restaurants in the State of California. We were disappointed with the money option and inclined to laugh off the franchise offer, but I suggested we at least explore what the franchise rights might be worth. Barry and Tommy agreed and we called a professional money manager I knew, Roger Engemann, and explained our situation. Roger flew up from Los Angeles to talk about it further, then suggested that we engage a respected Wall Street portfolio manager to analyze the offer, which we did. In the end, Tommy, Barry and I decided that we were civil right lawyers, and that we didn't want the damages payments to our clients to be dependent on our abilities as restaurant entrepreneurs. As far as taking the franchise offer, and then selling it to a third party, we concluded this was too problematic to satisfy the "fair, adequate and reasonable" standard of settlement of a class action. The exercise had been interesting, but we had no choice but to return to the bargaining table, or litigation.

In the middle of the litigation moratorium, a new player entered the picture—Len Roberts, the new Shoney's CEO. Len immediately conducted his own investigation of plaintiffs' allegations, and, as he was later to admit to Steve Watkins, author of the excellent book about the Shoney's case, *The Black O*, Roberts concluded, "Much of plaintiffs' record is truthful." He scheduled a meeting with Tommy, Barry and me in Oakland to respond to our counteroffer of $250 million in addition to a court-enforced affirmative action plan and monitoring of the company by plaintiffs' counsel to ensure compliance.

Roberts arrived in our Oakland office with Steve Tallent for two days of settlement negotiations. Rather than rely on his very knowledgeable attorney, Roberts tried to charm us with his own life story and his professed commitment to solving the past discrimination problems at Shoney's. He had no objections to a court-enforced injunction that would end race discrimination at Shoney's nor to goals and timetables that would increase the employment of blacks at all levels of the company. He said, "The company should do that anyway." But he couldn't grasp "the money thing." Any large financial settlement would "bankrupt Shoney's." "Why do we want to do that?" he asked. We responded that we had reviewed Shoney's present and projected profitability, that the money could be paid out over a period of time, and Shoney's could afford what we were asking for. With that, the first day ended without us hearing a monetary counteroffer from Roberts or Tallent.

The next morning began with a little contrived drama. Steve Tallent arrived in our offices alone and announced that Len Roberts was downstairs sitting in a taxi and would soon come upstairs to make Shoney's "last offer," which amount Steve claimed even he didn't know. Roberts arrived shortly thereafter, sat down and offered $20 million. This was $12 million less than Shoney's first offer of $32 million! We were stunned at the implausibility of the offer, as Shoney's faced hundreds of millions in potential liability to thousands of blacks who were subjected to Shoney's discrimination, plus punitive damages for the egregiously willful nature of the racial discrimination. Indeed, the Watkins' book reveals that, at the time, Tallent had told Roberts that liability to the Shoney's class could be as high as $400 million and Jim Neal had recommended that Shoney's offer $100 million to settle the case. Nevertheless, Roberts seemed deeply offended that we didn't accept his promises to end racial discrimination at Shoney's as satisfaction of all plaintiffs' demands. I believe he simply failed to analyze Shoney's monetary liability for past acts of discrimination separate from Shoney's future obligations to clean up its act. In any case, the meeting ended with Roberts making direct threats: "If you continue to be unreasonable about money, I will make this a personal battle between you and me. We will spend more and more money on litigation and this fight is going to get nastier and bloodier. I'm not going to let Shoney's commit suicide because of some San Francisco law firm." The meeting ended before I even could inform him he was in Oakland, not San Francisco.

Len Roberts had responded with his emotions, not his intellect, but the decision not to settle the case at this point was not clearly irrational. We still faced the daunting task of trying to certify a company-wide class in front of a Reagan-appointed judge in

Pensacola, Florida. Classes as large as the one plaintiffs were seeking were rare in Title VII cases; if we failed to certify a class, the case would be worth very little, and, if the class certified was smaller than what we were seeking, the case would be worth less, perhaps much less. Consequently, for whatever reason, good or bad, we returned to litigation. Butch Powell was reinstated as lead counsel with instructions to get tough, and the more rational Steve Tallent and Jim Neal receded into the background.

TOMMY AND BARRY WENT BACK to the litigation war with a changed legal landscape. One of the adverse United States Supreme Court decisions the Republican majority handed down on a 5-4 vote was *Patterson v. McLean Credit Union*, which reinterpreted 42 U.S.C. § 1981, one of the post-Civil War statutes intended to end racial discrimination. For many years, § 1981 had been broadly interpreted to apply to racial discrimination in hiring, promotion, termination, and harassment, and § 1981 was an attractive statute in race cases because, unlike Title VII which provided only for the recovery of back pay, § 1981 allowed for punitive damages and jury trials. The Supreme Court's reinterpretation of the law limited § 1981 only to race discrimination in the formation of contracts. For the Shoney's plaintiffs, this meant that claims for discrimination in hiring could still give rise to a claim for punitive damages, but that all other claims—for discrimination in promotion and termination, as well as racial harassment on the job, were not protected by § 1981. In short, the effect of *Patterson* on the Shoney's case was to reduce the amount of potential liability Shoney's faced.

Tommy, Barry and a half dozen younger attorneys restarted the litigation engine and worked to acquire more evidence against Shoney's and Ray Danner. Plaintiffs' evidence ultimately filled over 200 boxes of records, implicating 210 Shoney's managers and supervisors in racially discriminating behavior, generating scores of statistical analyses of Shoney's hiring, promotion and termination patterns, and deposing hundreds of witnesses with specific allegations of Shoney's race discrimination, including twenty-three white former Shoney's managers. In response, Shoney's provided testimony from its officers and managers that discrimination had not occurred and statistical evidence attempting to explain that whatever underrepresentation of blacks in certain jobs existed at Shoney's was the result of societal discrimination, not unlawful job discrimination by Shoney's.

On this record, in January 1991, the first hearing on plaintiffs' motion for class certification was held, with Barry arguing the class issues and Tommy responding to issues raised by individual plaintiffs. After a long hearing, Judge Vinson announced that he had decided to grant "conditional" certification of the class, provided that plaintiffs amend the complaint to add additional named plaintiffs to adequately represent all class issues, but also indicating that the class claims under § 1981 could be restricted: "The evidence that's been filed in this case is somewhat overwhelming and I think the plaintiffs have certainly established just about all the prerequisites you probably need to in many respects with regard to the liability issue." Despite this strong—albeit, preliminary—endorsement of the strength of plaintiffs' case, Shoney's continued to litigate the case aggressively.

A two-day rehearing of the class certification issues was held in November 1991, with Judge Vinson giving plaintiffs seven hours to present witnesses and/or provide argument. Plaintiffs put on a couple of witnesses, but chose to take most of the time for argument of the legal issues, based on the voluminous factual record that had been submitted. It was the longest legal argument Barry ever made. He highlighted the best of the factual declarations, explained plaintiffs' statistical analyses, then critiqued the misassumptions and fallacious conclusions of Shoney's statistical expert. I didn't attend the hearing, but I have every reason to believe the reports I got that he was excellent. Indeed, at the conclusion of the hearing, Judge Vinson reaffirmed his intention to certify the class, set a firm discovery cut-off date, and an early trial date. The Judge still had not ruled, however, on the exact class definition, plaintiffs' and defendants' cross-motions for summary judgment, or the applicability of new provisions contained in the recently-passed Civil Rights Act of 1991. Meanwhile, the parties waited for trial to begin.

In the interim, settlement discussion recommenced, first with another absurd $20 million offer from Len Roberts, followed by an offer for $65 million—both rejected. Then, on June 2, 1992, Judge Vinson issued his formal class certification order. He certified one of the largest classes in Title VII history—90% of what plaintiffs' had sought—and rejected Ray Danner's motion for summary judgment. Plaintiffs, as expected, due to the *Patterson* case, lost most of their § 1981 class claims, but those claims were certified under Title VII. Shoney's had lost a crucial battle, and now faced trial before a judge who previously had characterized plaintiffs' evidence of Shoney's racial discrimination as "somewhat overwhelming." A few months later, a minor defendant settled out for slightly less than $1 million, and then Shoney's agreed to pay $132.5 million, including $22.5 million in attorneys' fees and costs, in addition to implementing strong affirmative action program for blacks—the largest monetary settlement of a race discrimination case in United States history. Of the $132.5 million, Ray Danner paid $67 million, certainly an all-time record penalty for a corporate officer in a civil rights case.

Nearly 21,000 claimants ultimately received $105 million from this settlement. Perhaps even more important, Shoney's quickly and effectively took measures to dramatically increase the employment of blacks at all levels of the company, as well as black ownership of Shoney's franchises. It was an historic victory on all levels.

The partnership of our firm with Tommy Warren did not end with the Shoney's case. Two years later, our firm collaborated with Tommy on another major case arising in Florida—a gender-discrimination action against Publix, a large grocery chain. The case settled in 1997 for $81.5 million.

DURING THE PROSECUTION of our sex discrimination case at the Lucky Stores warehouse distribution center, we began receiving complaints of gender discrimination at Lucky's retail stores. As soon as Brad Seligman and I concluded the trial of the warehouse case, and settled it, Brad, now a partner, took up the prosecution of the Lucky Stores retail stores case (*Stender v. Lucky Stores*).

To a great extent, the patterns of gender discrimination in the retail stores mirrored the discrimination we had found in the distribution center. Women were channeled into the lower-paying jobs in the delicatessen, bakery and general merchandise departments, while men were hired into the better-paying jobs in the grocery and produce departments. The female jobs paid $5 to $6 per hour less than the male jobs and offered fewer opportunities for promotion. There were no women district managers, only 4 female merchandisers out of 28, only 10 female store managers out of 160 stores, and only 12 female assistant store managers out of a total of 164. And although 34% of Lucky Stores salesforce was female, only 3% held management positions.

Once again we were matched up with Morrison & Foerster, again with Kirby Wilcox as lead attorney for the defense. The judge assigned to the case was United States District Judge Marilyn Hall Patel, who I first had met as a Municipal Court Judge in Oakland. We liked the match up and the judge very much!

During formal discovery, we found out that shortly after we had concluded our warehouse case, Lucky Stores had hired Russell Specter, a former EEOC attorney, to conduct affirmative action workshops for Lucky Stores Northern California store managers. Handwritten notes of the store managers taken at these sessions revealed some Archie Bunker-type observations about women in the workplace: "women cry more"; "customers might object to seeing a woman in management"; "women do not want the promotions"; "conflict for men to have a woman as boss"; "hard to change old habits, still see the 'success model' as a white male"; "women should be stronger"; "women are considered the weak sex"; "women don't have the drive to get ahead"; "women are not the breadwinners"; "customers might object to seeing a woman in management," etc. In one exercise, Specter had managers close their eyes and visualize a "successful manager." Most visualized a white male. In addition to making these comments, many of the managers admitted that Lucky Stores needed to do a better job of promoting women.

Predictably, Kirby claimed these comments were not properly discoverable, were inadmissible as privileged "attorney–client" communications, were inadmissible under the so-called "critical self-analysis" privilege, and, in any case, were meaningless because they reflected social stereotypes, not the declarants' own feelings. Judge Patel disagreed, holding that the notes were discoverable, and later ruled that the attorney-client privilege did not bar their admissibility into evidence because Specter had been hired to conduct "sensitivity" training sessions, not operate as an attorney, and that the store managers were not Specter's "clients" in any case. The alleged "critical self-analysis privilege" was not a recognized legal "privilege" and nearly all courts had rejected it. Nevertheless, it raised an interesting policy issue—Lucky Stores had chosen to conduct its training sessions for the purpose of improving the status of women in its workforce, and trial use of damaging admissions obtained in such sessions might have the effect of discouraging companies from conducting such training. But Judge Patel, in line with prevailing authorities on this issue, apparently decided that the probative value of the comments outweighed the policy reasons that MoFo claimed would be imperiled by admitting such evidence.

Kirby's spin on this direct evidence of discriminatory attitudes by Lucky Stores managers was that the notes showed nothing of the sort; the notes were merely the result of Lucky Stores attempt to elicit stereotypes so they could be corrected. This explanation, of course, failed to answer the obvious question: Why did the Lucky Stores managers have those stereotypical attitudes, and did they reflect Lucky Stores' behavior?

It was rare to obtain this type of direct evidence of discriminatory intent, and, coupled with statistics showing significant gender imbalances in the workforce, gave us an extremely strong case.

Nevertheless, Kirby made no serious settlement offers and the case went to trial. The trial lasted ten weeks. Kirby characterized the gender imbalances in the workforce as merely "an appearance" of discrimination and claimed that the statistical imbalances were the result of free choice—women were not interested in promotions or better-paying jobs. Relying on application forms, Wilcox contended women "aren't equally interested in all these opportunities." Of course, as in the State Farm case, jobs listed in an application form reflect more than an applicant's interest; they also reflect what kinds of jobs women and minorities are hired into, what they see in the existing workforce, and how men are encouraged to seek specific jobs while women are steered in different directions.

As the trial was about to begin, MoFo hired a public relations firm to spin its version of the case to the legal press and the spinners did a good job. Throughout most of the trial, if you read the legal press, you would have thought our firm was highly unreasonable and that Lucky Stores was winning the case. The press accounts aggravated us, but we knew Lucky Stores was getting shellacked in trial. The local legal newspaper, *The Recorder*, was particularly receptive to the Lucky/MoFo point of view; we suspected it might have something to do with the fact that MoFo did legal work for them. In any case, we didn't really understand what MoFo was trying to accomplish with a PR campaign; it wasn't a jury trial, so jurors were not going to be influenced by reading newspapers. Were they trying to influence or intimidate Judge Patel? If so, they really had picked the wrong target, as Judge Patel wasn't going to be intimidated by anyone.

A year after the class trial concluded, Judge Patel issued a 193-page decision. The decision firmly rejected Lucky Stores' fanciful "lack-of-interest" defense and concluded:

> "Sex discrimination was the standard operating procedure at Lucky with respect to placement, promotion, movement to full-time positions and the allocation of additional hours."

The Court ruled that Lucky Stores had failed to collect accurate information about job applicants and apply consistent criteria to personnel, resulting in "ambiguous and subjective" placement, promotion and training practices that led to workplace segregation.

Following the decision on class liability, Judge Patel established a schedule for determining appropriate remedies. Brad and Kirby agreed on a 110-page comprehensive affirmative action plan to eliminate future discrimination and increase the employment of women at all levels, but the parties were far apart in valuating damages—we estimated damages to the class at $155 million, Kirby at $3 million to $6 million. As Yogi Berra once said, "It's déjà vu all over again!"

While the class remedies issues were still pending, MoFo took an absolutely extraordinary and inexplicable step. They filed a massive motion with the Court of Appeals for the Ninth Circuit seeking to have Judge Patel disqualified from further involvement in the case, citing numerous alleged trial errors MoFo claimed she had made. Even if the allegations had been true—which they were not—the appropriate remedy would have been to appeal the class liability decision after the remedies had been determined, not seek disqualification of a judge who had been handling the case for five years. We perceived the motion as an act of desperation, if not madness.

Apparently the Court of Appeals saw MoFo's disqualification motion much the way we did, because instead of considering the merits of MoFo's motion, the Court of Appeals issued an order requiring the MoFo attorneys to appear and show cause why they should not be sanctioned for filing a "frivolous petition" and "vexatiously and unreasonably increasing the cost of litigation." This became front-page news throughout the legal community, as it was a rare event when a major corporate law firm was ordered to show cause why it should not be sanctioned or accused of "frivolous," "vexatious," and "unreasonable" litigation tactics by a federal court of appeals.

Recognizing that Kirby and his crew could not defend themselves, MoFo was forced to hire an outside attorney, John P. Frank, a partner of Phoenix's Lewis & Roca, who had served as counsel to Anita Hill during the Clarence Thomas confirmation hearings, and bring in their own senior partner, Bob Raven. At the Court of Appeals hearing, Mr. Frank contended that the MoFo lawyers should be "applauded" for raising the issues they raised in their 100-page attack on Judge Patel, not penalized: "We're genuinely puzzled as to why we're here," Frank told the Court. Showing clear disdain for Frank's presentation, Chief Judge Browning interrupted him, telling him the only argument of interest to the Court was whether the petition was filed in good faith. The message from Chief Judge Browning was unmistakable: "Your clients filed an incredibly stupid motion, and the only way they're going to escape sanctions is by showing that they thought the motion had merit." All Brad had to do was sit at plaintiffs' counsel table and keep from smiling. Afterwards, responding to MoFo's contentions that Judge Patel's rulings had placed heavy burdens on Lucky Stores, Brad said, "The cross they say they are carrying is of MoFo's own making." The comment by Brad—who always had a fine touch with the press—was exactly on point and far more elegant than my comment under similar circumstances about Paul Laveroni.

Two weeks later, the Court of Appeals issued a one-page ruling, stating,

> [T]he court admonishes counsel for submitting to the court a petition for mandamus which the court regards as an entirely inappropriate attempt to circumvent the regular appellate process and for including in that petition a request for reassignment of the action which the court regards as a wholly unjustified reflection upon the trial judge.

With that as background, MoFo now had to return to that very "trial judge" to face a determination of class damages.

Lucky Stores' in-house labor counsel, Hank Raucci, had other ideas. Raucci asked Steve Stemerman, an attorney for Lucky Stores' unions, to set up a meeting with Brad. "Raucci thought that perhaps a fresh, different approach to the settlement talks might be more fruitful," Stemerman said. Within days of the Court of Appeals admonishment of MoFo, Brad and Raucci met. They liked each other immediately; both were smart and direct. They built trust quickly. Brad began negotiations with a $125 million demand; Raucci began at $20 million, then moved up. Within weeks, they had agreed in principle to a $107 million settlement—contingent on Lucky Stores securing a reasonable amount of coverage from its insurance carrier; $60 million would pay damage claims, Lucky Stores would spend $20 million on affirmative action programs for women, Lucky Stores would hold another $13 million in a contingency fund for the class in case Lucky Stores failed to meet the employment goals set out in the injunctive decree, and $13.75 million would be paid for attorneys' fees and costs. After a series of private arbitrations between Lucky Stores and its insurance carrier, which Brad attended and participated in, an agreement was reached between Lucky Stores and the insurance company and the $107 million deal was finalized, publicized, and the class damages were distributed.

Afterwards, Wilcox, who never had offered more than $11 million to settle the case, and who had to suffer the embarrassment of having it publicly disclosed that he had been shut out of settlement negotiations, accused Brad of being intransigent, obstinate and unreasonable in making "stratospheric" money demands. Brad responded by noting that MoFo never had offered more than $11 million and that he was "quite satisfied with the second largest sex discrimination settlement in history." As for me, reading Kirby's public accusations of Brad's unreasonableness, and remembering how he never had offered me more than $13.1 million in the State Farm case, until his quantum leap to $250 million, I just had to laugh and wonder, "When are his clients going to figure him out?"

11

Denny's Slams African-Americans and Shocks America

"It is possible to believe that all the past is but the beginning of a beginning, and all that is and has been is but the twilight of the dawn."

—H. G. Wells

LOCATED IN FORTY-NINE STATES, with 1,500 restaurants conveniently placed on major thoroughfares and near freeway exits, open 24 hours a day, with a "Grand Slam" breakfast costing $1.99, plus a free meal on your birthday as their way of saying, "Thank you for coming to Denny's." A great program, but it wasn't working for African-Americans.

A group of eighteen African-American teenagers—all members of an NAACP youth group—had just attended a college forum sponsored by Tuskegee University. They were well-dressed and hungry and went to the Denny's Restaurant on Blossom Hill Road in San Jose for a meal. A Denny's manager greeted them, but refused to seat them unless each person paid in advance of ordering their food. One of the teenagers, Kristina Ridgeway, a high school senior, approached a group of white teenagers she knew and asked them if they had been asked to pay a cover charge or prepay for their food. They had not. Looking around, she noticed nine other white and Latino teenagers and learned that they also had not been asked to pay a cover charge or pay in advance. Kristina and her friends realized they were being asked to pay in advance because

Denny's suspected—based only on their skin color—that they might walk out without paying. "Here I was getting ready for college, planning to be an attorney, and Denny's saw me as a criminal who's going to eat and run," said Kristina. When Kristina got home, she explained what had happened to her father, William. Mr. Ridgeway got in his car and drove directly to Denny's, but his questions were not treated seriously. They asked him, "Do you want a free meal?" "I wanted answers and they thought they could buy me for eggs and sausage," said Mr. Ridgeway.

It was Rachel Thompson's thirteenth birthday and she said she wanted to go to dinner at Denny's. Her parents, Danny and Susan Thompson, and her two brothers, Jason and Danny, Jr., drove to a Denny's just north of San Francisco. When it came time to order, Mrs. Thompson told the waitress it was Rachel's birthday, which entitled Rachel to Denny's free "Birthday Meal," and presented the waitress with Rachel's baptismal certificate as proof of her date of birth. The waitress consulted with the manager and refused to honor Denny's birthday meal promotional offer.

Two African-American women, Meling Harrision and Catrana Law, were eating at another Denny's in San Jose with a friend of East Indian ancestry, Navjot Nijjar. The Denny's manager ejected them, telling the three women, "There are too many of you here." After being ejected, the women decided to go to another Denny's to test Denny's behavior. They observed white patrons being admitted, seated, and served. Ms. Nijjar, the lightest-skinned of the three, went inside and asked a Denny's manager if she could use the restroom. The manager said yes, but when he saw she was with two African-American women, he told her to leave the restaurant.

Demetrece and Michael Maxwell, a veteran San Francisco police officer, flew to San Diego to watch Ms. Maxwell's brother play a football game for California State University, San Diego. After the game, they went to Denny's and were told they would have to pay for their food before they would be seated. Ms. Maxwell asked three white customers if they had been required to pay for their food in advance, and they said they had not. Similar experiences by African-Americans were reported in other Denny's restaurants in California.

The sign at the Tully Road Denny's in San Jose says clearly, "Open 24 Hours." But Ray Norton, a white Denny's employee, watched in amazement one night when young African-American customers stepped out of their cars in the Denny's parking lot only to see Denny's employees rush to the front door to close and lock it. Only after they left were the doors unlocked and opened. "I couldn't believe it," said Norton. "I said to the manager, 'This is ludicrous. How can you be doing this?' But I was told this was how the game was played." Later, at regular district meetings, Norton was told that "A-A's"—the in-house code for African-Americans—were a problem because they were boisterous, left small tips, and left without paying. "We were told to take whatever measures we could to keep A-A's to a minimum. You could seat white customers ahead of A-A's. You could put A-A's in the rear and stall on serving them. You could ask A-A's to pay before eating. Or, if you really wanted to get the job done, you could lock them out," said Norton. Denny's called this "blackout" and the purpose was to discourage African-Americans from coming to Denny's.

One of my new partners, Mari Mayeda, presented me with these compelling stories of racial discrimination, but I had to ask myself and her several questions: How widespread was this discrimination? Were these stories, strong as they were, just isolated examples of what Denny's was sure to claim was just bad service, not racial discrimination, or were they representative of a pattern and practice of discrimination that would support a viable class action against Denny's? And even if a class could be established, what would the individual claims be worth? After all, this wasn't discrimination in employment, where the loss of a job opportunity could be worth hundreds of thousands of dollars in lost wages. Although humiliating and unfair, how would a judge or a jury value a claim of denial of service, particularly in light of the availability of other restaurants? And assuming we were successful in establishing a class and winning a class liability trial, how would we handle large numbers of claims, where the value of each claim might be relatively small? We had spent hundreds of thousands of hours prosecuting claims in the *Kraszewski* case, would we be forced to invest a huge amount of resources prosecuting claims that might be worth just a few thousand dollars each?

On the other hand, I said to myself, if this kind of behavior wasn't stopped and made an example of, might other restaurants be encouraged to treat black customers the same way? And what about hotels, motels, theatres, bus stations—in other words, all other types of public accommodations? How could we call ourselves a civil rights firm if we only prosecuted cases with large individual damages? It seemed clear that we had a responsibility to do the case and I authorized Mari, who would be lead counsel in the case, to proceed.

Mari, working with the Public Interest Law Firm of San Jose, which originally had referred the case to our office, proceeded to investigate the claims. They not only located and identified more African-Americans who had had similar experiences with Denny's, they also located several former Denny's employees who confirmed that Denny's treated black customers differently than white patrons. Thus, on the basis of complaints by thirty-two individuals, and confirmation by Denny's employees, we filed a statewide class action in United States District Court in San Jose, and held simultaneous news conferences in San Francisco, Los Angeles, San Diego, and Sacramento. Speaking at a news conference in San Francisco, Mari stated, "This is Jim Crow discrimination. It is reminiscent of segregated lunch counters in the Deep South of the 1950s. It is appalling that African-Americans are being subjected to such offensive treatment in California family restaurants in the 1990s."

From the moment the case was filed, it took on a life of its own. The publicity generated by the media coverage of our press conferences started the phones ringing on our toll-free (800) Denny's hotline with hundreds of complaints of race discrimination against black Denny's patrons. The media ran story after story about the case, and Jay Leno, Dave Letterman, and other television and radio comedians seemed to have a new joke every day about Denny's racism: "Come to Denny's for that old-fashioned service. The kind you used to get in Birmingham, Alabama in 1960," Leno joked.

Wounded by the public comments and criticism, Denny's took out full-page ads in *USA Today* and other newspapers. The ads, titled "An Open Letter to Denny's Customers and Communities," stated:

> As you may know, allegations of discriminatory behavior have been made against a very small number of Denny's restaurants in California... And, while we take such allegations very seriously and are committed to fully investigating and addressing every single charge, we vigorously deny any pattern of discriminatory behavior at our restaurants.

Denny's chairman, Jerry Richardson, told the press, "I won't sit idly and let these things be said about us... I don't think we package all the positive things we do. We assume people knew already, which is a mistake. We've got to tell the world all the good things we do." Richardson said he had met with "black leaders" since the lawsuit was filed, and added that he didn't think the California lawsuit would derail his bid for a new National Football League franchise.

Then, bad as the situation was for Denny's, it got much worse. Six black Secret Service agents in Annapolis, Maryland to protect President Clinton for an appearance at the United States Naval Academy were refused breakfast service at an Annapolis Denny's. They ordered breakfast, and when it didn't arrive, reordered several more times. After an hour, they left without being served. A group of white Secret Service agents sitting nearby was served promptly. These were not hip-hop blacks in baggy pants that Denny's might claim looked like they would leave without paying; they were distinguished-looking men dressed in Secret Service uniforms and ties. The story was a legal and public relations nightmare for Denny's, and the incident was doubly embarrassing, as it occurred on the same day that Denny's settled a separate bias complaint in California with the Department of Justice promising equal treatment to customers of all races. Speaking for the President, White House Communications Director George Stephanopoulos said, "Obviously a court will have to make the final determination of what happened, but…discrimination against black Secret Service agents would be a serious problem." Shortly thereafter, Denny's fired the manager of the Annapolis restaurant. On national TV, Dan Rather said, "These agents put their lives on the line every day, but they can't get served at Denny's."

A week after the Annapolis incident, Denny's announced it had made a deal with the NAACP to hire and promote more minorities, to promote ownership and management of Denny's restaurants by minorities, to find a black person to serve on the board as TW Services, Denny's parent company, and to find minority investors for Chairman Richardson's proposed NFL team. However, neither the NAACP agreement nor Denny's agreement with the United States Department of Justice provided compensation for the actual victims of Denny's discrimination. That task was left to private litigation.

Despite the fact that Denny's had been hit with a succession of prominent and embarrassing claims of racial discrimination, their attorneys took an aggressive posture in litigation, filing a motion to dismiss our case on several grounds, including the claim that our case was moot because of Denny's agreement with the Department of Justice—regardless of the fact that this agreement provided no monetary compensation for the victims of Denny's discrimination—and that, in any case, our case could not proceed as a class action as the nature of the discrimination was individualized, not class-based.

To counter Denny's legal assertions, we filed fifty-four declarations by customers and former employees, each testifying to incidents of race discrimination at Denny's. One of the declarations was from the wife of a black United States District Judge, Kenneth M. Hoyt of Houston. Veola Hoyt testified that she and her husband had attended a judicial conference in San Francisco, then had decided to drive north to visit the redwoods in Northern California. They arrived in Yreka late at night, and went to Denny's, the only restaurant in town open at that hour. Despite being well dressed, they were forced to wait an inordinate amount of time to be served—although the restaurant was near-empty—and were treated rudely and served cold food. Despite the great power that federal judges exercise, Judge Hoyt, recalling the incident, said, "A kind of helplessness came over me."

Faced with this evidence, United States District Judge James Ware wasted little time in rejecting Denny's motions to dismiss our case and strike out class action allegations, thus permitting our case to proceed as a class action for damages. Our office was receiving calls on a daily basis from all over the country with complaints of racial discrimination by Denny's, while Jay Leno, David Letterman, and Arsenio Hall continued their jokes each night about Denny's on national television. (Jay Leno: "Denny's is offering a new sandwich called the Discriminator. It's a hamburger, and you order it, then they don't serve it to you.") Denny's business had fallen off 10% in the previous quarter, and now Judge Ware had rejected the only legal motions that could have gotten Denny's out of trouble quickly. No case of ours had ever struck such a responsive chord with the public; people—justifiably—just couldn't believe this kind of stuff was happening in the 1990s. Denny's had little choice but to try to settle the case, and soon.

Shortly thereafter, I got a call from Tom Pfister, Denny's lead defense counsel. Tom wanted to fly up from Los Angeles and meet with us as soon as possible about settling. I told him I would have to gather together the other attorneys from around the country who had lawsuits against Denny's on file, including the Lawyer's Committee for Civil Rights in Washington, D.C.— but I was sure we could meet the following week. The morning of our meeting with Denny's, the attorneys all met in my office and discussed strategy. My partner, Barry, insisted we should be courteous and respectful, listen to what they had to say and not respond until we all had a chance to caucus and discuss their offer.

Tom Pfister showed up with the President of Denny's and began to present Denny's offer, as we sat and listened in our conference room. He explained what corrective action Denny's was willing to undertake, and, in some cases, had already undertaken. Much of that already was required under the agreement with the United States Department of Justice and we had no quarrel with the requirements of that agreement, except that it didn't go far enough. Then Tom addressed the damage issues, explaining that Denny's would donate $3 million to various civil rights groups. As I listened to Tom—a lawyer I genuinely liked and respected—I began to boil with anger. Denny's was in a desperate situation that required they settle and stop the bleeding, yet that was the extent of their absurd offer. I interrupted Tom before he finished, demanding, "Is that it? Is that all the money you're offering?" Tom said it was. So I said, "OK, I've heard enough," and walked out of the room, with the other attorneys following.

We went back into my office and went around the table for comments. I waited for everyone else to voice their opinion before I spoke: "It's a promising start"; "They seem sincere"; "This is not the end of negotiations, it is only the beginning"; "We'll be able to move them from their $3 million," etc. Then, I spoke:

> "This is total bullshit. Denny's is being demolished in the press and on national television, their earnings are way down, and we have a fabulous lawsuit—yet they haven't offered a dime of damages to victims of their discrimination. Maybe they can get away with that with the Department of Justice and the NAACP, but they can't with me. They are going to take remedial action to make sure this kind of behavior stops in the future, but they also are going to pay damages—a lot of damages. In fact, we're going to go back into the conference room and tell them that if they want settlement discussions with us to continue, they have to put $20 million on the table by tomorrow morning. That $20 million would be entirely for damages, to be paid to victims of their discrimination. And

> $20 million is only a down payment; $20 million will not
> settle this case, it will only allow Denny's to continue talking
> to us about settlement."

I looked around the room. People were stunned at my reaction and my demand, including Barry. Everyone in the room who
spoke counseled a more conciliatory reaction, expressing fears that
my tough line would scare them away and kill settlement before it
really got started. We went back into the conference room and I
spoke for the plaintiffs:

> "Tom, Denny's has to take remedial action no matter what. It
> is required under the Department of Justice decree and
> Denny's has to do it anyway, because it can't continue to incur
> the public humiliation and increased damage liability that
> each new incident of discrimination brings. I have no doubt
> we can work with you on that and get agreement, provided
> that any remedial agreement is backed up by a strong
> program of monitoring Denny's future behavior.

> The main issue that divides us, however, is money. You
> indicated Denny's is willing to donate $3 million to various
> civil rights groups. That is fine, but as far as I'm concerned,
> that is your client's charity. It has nothing to do with our
> lawsuit. We are not seeking charity, we are seeking damages
> for Denny's reprehensible behavior. You can give $3 million
> away to any group or groups you want, but you will get no
> credit from us for that. Frankly, I was astonished and angered
> at your money offer, as it bore no relation to the seriousness
> of our lawsuit. Your offer left me with the feeling that time
> spent in settlement negotiations with Denny's is time wasted.
> Therefore, I am going to tell you what Denny's has to do to
> maintain credibility with me. By 10 a.m. tomorrow morning,
> Denny's has to offer a *minimum* of $20 million to settle
> damage claims of the class. That $20 million offer which
> Denny's is going to make tomorrow morning will NOT settle
> this case. It is only Denny's down payment—a tangible
> expression of good faith that will allow Denny's to continue
> these discussions. In the end, Denny's will have to pay far more
> than $20 million to settle this case."

Tom and his cohort left the room. We went back to my office. The mood was heavy gloom. No one said a word in support of what I had done; several attorneys quietly voiced negative opinions: "We overplayed our hand"; "They won't be back"; "It'll be a long time before we have settlement discussions again in this case." I responded, "We broke them today. Just watch."

I walked into the office the next morning around 9 a.m. Tom Pfister was sitting in our reception area, waiting for me. Tom, a former USC basketball player, and still trim and athletic, rose to his full height of about 6' 3", shook my hand, and said, "You've got your $20 million."

Negotiations continued and Denny's agreed to pay $54.4 million, of which our California case received $34.8 million. It was the largest monetary settlement in a public accommodations case in American history. Equally important, Denny's agreed to the toughest monitoring program I've ever seen in a civil rights case. This included establishment of a monitoring office under plaintiffs' control which was empowered to investigate complaints of discrimination at Denny's restaurants and to make hundreds of unannounced "tests" of equal service for blacks, generally using sets of white and black "customers" in the same restaurants at the same time to determine if the black customers were receiving equal treatment. The monitoring office was run by a monitor I interviewed and selected, supported by a staff of investigators and testers—all paid for by Denny's—and by all accounts the monitor did a fabulous job.

Each of our thirty-nine plaintiffs received $25,000, and the rest of the money damages was distributed on a formula basis. Each black person who had experienced discrimination at Denny's needed to fill out a claim form describing the discriminatory incident and identifying the location and approximate date of the incident. The claim forms were not difficult to understand or fill out, but for anyone who needed help, our firm, as Class Counsel, provided free help in filling out and filing the claim forms (paid for by Denny's).

Despite the fact that legal services were free to claimants, a few weeks after notices of the claim procedure were broadcast on radio and television throughout California, and large newspaper ads were published providing information about how to obtain and file claim forms, as well as our (800) Denny's number for anyone needing help, we heard that "claims shops" were cropping up in black sections of Los Angeles, San Francisco and San Jose. Several of the claims shops were being operated by Melvin Belli's law firm! These shops were charging $10 to $30, plus one-fifth to one-third of the claim recoveries, for filling out forms that most people easily could fill out by themselves and for services we provided to all class members for free. The shops were inducing people to hire them with misrepresentations that legal help was required to fill out claim forms, that their help would result in higher recoveries, failing to inform clients that the settlement agreement provided them with free legal representation. People were getting ripped off—paying unnecessary fees—and we decided we had to stop the claims shops and protect the class.

We filed a motion with Judge Ware to enjoin the claims shops from misrepresenting the claim procedure and overstating what their assistance could accomplish. The great Mel Belli, King of Torts, appeared in court to try to defend the indefensible—charging an exorbitant fee for providing virtually no service. It was sad to see—this once-great lawyer, now approaching 90, who once was perhaps America's greatest lawyer, winning many million-dollar-plus verdicts on behalf of injured individuals, and authoring a ten-volume set of books on personal injury litigation, who I watched in Denver twenty-five years earlier give a great closing argument in a medical malpractice case, now reduced to hustling fees off the streets by overstating what his firm could accomplish. Judge Ware, showing sympathy for the mostly low-income African-Americans who had agreed to give up a substantial portion of their recoveries for the minimal service of being assisted in filling out a short claim form, and showing little sympathy for Belli and his firm, ordered Belli to continue to provide assistance to the approximately 2,000 claimants his firm had signed up, but to waive all fees. It was perfect justice: the Belli firm had set out to make a disproportionately high fee for providing little real help, but ended up providing services for free—which, of course, is exactly what the settlement agreement provided for claimants.

AFTER THE CASE WAS CONCLUDED, the most profound comments on the whole experience came from the parents of two of the children who had started the case after being denied service in San Jose. Reginald Braddock, Rodney's father and a Lockheed software engineer for twenty-one years, who had himself been arrested in 1961 trying to buy a hamburger at a whites-only lunch counter in Ocala, Florida, said: "I had gotten complacent in my life, and this woke me up. We didn't complete the job thirty years ago, and I realize now it's going to take more than my lifetime to complete it." And William Ridgeway, Kristina's father and a marketing executive at IBM for twenty-seven years, said: "Will there be a time when we can stop reliving the past and get on with the rest of our lives? I think back on the occasions I used to go to Denny's and sit there and justify the slow service as, well, the waitress is busy. Now, if I got into any restaurant, I have to wonder, am I being subjected to slow service because of what I look like? That's some of the baggage I carry. You try to shake it."

Denny's, too, learned a profound lesson—racial discrimination is socially irresponsible and can be very expensive—and took substantial measures to make amends, in addition to paying out over $54 million. Its parent company, Advantica Restaurants Group, now has three African-Americans and one Hispanic American on its eleven-member Board of Directors, 47 percent of its employees are minorities, 35 percent of Denny's franchisees are minority-owned, and, in 1999, $110 million of its supplier contracts went to minority-owned firms. In 2000,

Fortune magazine selected Advantica Number 1 on its list of "The 50 Best Companies for Minorities."

12

Moving On

"The universe is change, life is understanding."
—Marcus Aurelius

S SOON AS our settlements with State Farm, Shoney's, and Lucky Stores were announced to the press, many of our other defendants showed new interest in settling their cases with us. It seemed like the prospect of paying $100 to $250 million to a group of women and another $20 to $100+ million to defense attorneys provided concrete motivation to settle cases before things went too far. So we began negotiating our cases with a number of grocery chains we had under suit.

Most of the impetus for settlement seemed to come from the companies themselves, not their litigation counsel. It seemed like a second lesson from the State Farm case had been learned, at least by some—be wary of your own lawyers. Some of the differences between outside litigation firms and their clients led to real comedy.

In one of our grocery-store chain cases, Safeway Stores had agreed to settle the case, but their outside litigation attorneys didn't seem like they wanted to let go of the case, and kept haggling over details for weeks. We both agreed in principle that there would be goals and timetables for the advancement of women, but we weren't making much progress toward agreement on what the specific goals and timetables should be. We had been arguing over the interest and availability of women to become managers in the various departments of a grocery store with no resolutions. This type of dispute normally is decided by reference to labor market availability data, and the internal population of women at the company employed in so-called "feeder" jobs (jobs from which the management positions normally are filled). But, one morning, the lead litigation attorney for Safeway arrived at our offices for a negotiation session, and, departing from conventional analysis of such issues, said, "Guy, you know how liberal my wife is and you know how much she supports women's causes. Well, this morning at breakfast, I was talking to her about these jobs and she agreed with me that women don't want more responsibility and wouldn't be interested in those promotions. So, we just don't think the number of female managers should be set very high." I did know his wife—a well-respected partner in a major corporate defense firm. Was I supposed to accept her as the unbiased, controlling authority on labor market availability? Did he expect me to accept his wife's opinion over what my clients told me they really wanted, and in contravention of traditional labor-availability analyses? Should I even take his stupid argument seriously?

I replied, "What a coincidence! I had an almost identical conversation this morning with my wife, Jeanine. I explained the differences in pay and responsibilities between the cashier and clerk jobs and the department manager and assistant manger positions and I asked her whether she thought women would be interested in the management positions. You know what she said? She said women definitely would be interested and there should be a high number of female managers at Safeway." Then, I turned to my law associate, Jack Lee, and said, "Jack, have you ever discussed this issue with Debbie?" Jack, on cue, replied, "Yes, I have, and Debbie definitely agrees that women want those jobs."

At this point, Safeway's General Counsel, Mike Ross, jumped up and said, "Guy, could we talk alone in your office?" I said fine, and Mike and I walked into my office, leaving his litigation lawyers outside. Once the door was closed, he said, "I have to apologize for that ridiculous argument my lawyers just made. It was embarrassing." I said, "No apologies are necessary. I've heard a lot of dumb arguments from corporate litigators."

Then Mike said, "I'm getting really disgusted with how slow these negotiations are moving. Is there some way you and I can settle this case?" I replied, "Absolutely, there are just a finite number of issues left to resolve. I am willing to listen to what you need, and if you listen to what I need, and we both make some compromises, we can settle it right now." Mike said, "Fine, let's try to do that." We spoke for two hours and wrapped up all issues in the case, including attorneys' fees—an issue defense attorneys typically like to drag out forever—before Mike had to leave to catch a plane. As we shook hands in the reception area, he turned to his lawyers sitting nearby and said, "Guy will explain the deal to you. Get it written up," then left for the airport. His lawyers, having already been banished to the reception area while Mike and I negotiated the case to conclusion, then had to suffer the added indignity of having me tell them what the deal was.

This incident highlighted feelings I had been developing about litigation: I was getting tired of the time-wasting behavior many corporate litigation attorneys were putting me through. The aggressively ingenious ways big-firm litigation attorneys have figured out to obfuscate issues and delay resolution of cases had made me a rich man by greatly increasing the time we had to spend and the attorneys' fees our firm ultimately received. But I was beginning to ask myself, "Do I really want to spend the rest of my life locked in rooms with these kinds of people?"

As time went on, I became increasingly impatient with the delay tactics and the unimaginative, but often effective, devices corporate litigators employed to frustrate resolution of the underlying issues. I began yelling at defense counsel, hanging up phones on them, and my letters got nastier. I definitely was not becoming a nicer person! I was beginning to think twenty-five years fighting

litigation wars in the trenches might be enough. I began to consider leaving the full-time practice of law and adding more non-
law activities to my life. Jeanine had retired five years earlier from
her Montessori teaching, and I saw how much fun she was having
with her charitable activities. I began to ask myself, "What do I want
to do with the rest of my life?"

I flew out to Moab, Utah for a few days by myself at our cabin
at Pack Creek Ranch, and hiked in the deep-red rock canyons each
day. I came back to the cabin one night, loaded several John Coltrane and Miles Davis CD's into the CD changer, sat down and
wrote seven pages—117 items—of things I wanted to do. Only a
few of the items on my list were related to practicing law. Looking
at my list, I realized it was impossible to do that many things in one
lifetime. I also realized I needed to get started soon if I was going
to have a chance to do more than a few of them.

I announced my intentions to Barry and Mari, who were
stunned by the suddenness of my decision, and encouraged me to
take a sabbatical and consider returning. My own lawyer said I was
nuts; I should retain my majority ownership of the firm, take a
couple of years off, and then do as much or as little law as I wanted.
But I knew myself better than that. I knew that if I retained majority ownership of the law firm I would continue to manage the firm,
and my partners would continue to let me manage the firm. The
only way for me to move on in my life would be to give up control
of it.

After a period of negotiation over financial terms, I became
"Of Counsel" to the firm, which continues to use my name; I retained an office at the firm, and agreed to continue as lead counsel
in the firm's mega-case against Lockheed Missiles & Space Co., a
large and complex False Claims Act case involving overbilling in
various satellite surveillance programs, with concomitant claims
by United States intelligence agencies and the United States Department of Justice that discovery must be restricted by national security considerations. That case, which I have been working on for
sixteen years, and which has been to the United States Supreme

Court three times, continues.

One of the items high on my list was spending more time with my two boys, Leon and Jacobus. I had tried to be a good father during my career—and Jeanine says I succeeded—but the demands of an intense career had made me unavailable more times than I wanted. Even though the boys were 19 and 22, and away at college, I wanted to be available to spend time with them. A few weeks after I had formalized my retirement from the law firm, Jacobus presented me with my Christmas present—a handwritten Christmas card inviting me and Leon to hike the 225-mile John Muir Trail together, something I had wanted to do since I was a Boy Scout. The following May, Leon graduated from the USC School of Architecture, and we threw a large graduation party for him. At midnight, after all the guests had left, our family sat at the head table, and I handed Leon his graduation gift—a card which, after offering congratulations, said, "Tell us what you want as a gift." I thought he would ask for some camera equipment or a new car, but instead, he said, "I thought you might do something like this, so I have given it a lot of thought and I know exactly what I want." I asked, "What is that?" "I want to go trekking in Nepal with you," Leon answered. I asked, "Don't you want to go with your girlfriend or Jacobus, instead?" "No. I want to go with you for two reasons: I want to share my passion for photography with you, and when we get back, we're going to do a joint photography show with our photographs. And the second reason I want to go with you is that I've always admired how, wherever we go, you always want to talk to people and find out what they think and what their lives are like. I want to share that with you in Nepal," said Leon.

With these two wonderful invitations, Jacobus and Leon had confirmed that my decision to make other things in my life a higher priority than winning lawsuits was a good decision. Since that time, I trekked to Mt. Everest with Leon, hiked the John Muir Trail with Jacobus (236 miles in 31 days), hiked the Tahoe to Yosemite Trail with my niece, Unmi (180 miles in 21 days), kayaked the Grand Canyon with Jacobus, and traveled extensively with Jeanine and friends. I also sit on boards of nine charitable and political organizations, including the Sierra Club Foundation, the Oregon Shakespeare Festival, and Business Leaders for Sensible Priorities (which seeks to switch federal budget priorities from military spending to health and social programs), assisted Jeanine in her charitable projects in integrative health and inner-city youth, consulted with public interest lawyers throughout the country on litigation matters, and continued to litigate the law firm's case against Lockheed. In addition, I became co-counsel in a large False Claims Act case which seeks to expose the falsification of test results in the National Missile Defense Program. I've also written Op-Ed pieces on various topics, co-produced a feature film, written a book about my adventures hiking the John Muir Trail (to be published Spring 2003), drove Formula 1 race cars, mentored a lot of young men and women in various professions, and continued to play basketball three days a week with the 18–24 year-olds at the neighborhood park.

IN MY MENTORING OF YOUNG PEOPLE, I constantly get asked what lessons I learned along my path that might be helpful to them. The first thing I tell young people is, "Take a chance with your life." The greatest obstacle to achieving dreams is fear. Every year, law schools—and other professional schools—produce tens of thousands of graduates who would like to pursue their ideals to help society in some way, but fear that pursuing ideals is not a realistic career option. Yes, they'd like to fight racial or sex discrimination, fight environmental pollution, help children get health care, but the best-paying, most secure, jobs are working for corporate America, they reason. So they take conventional paths, hire on with the big firms, make a big salary, and think they can still pursue their ideals in their spare time. But the big salaries are predicated on big hours and they find themselves doing unsatisfying work, working weeknights and weekends, with little time for much else in their lives. The money is good, but the price is high and the job satisfaction low. Among lawyers in California, surveys show that more than 50% say if they had to do it over again, they would pursue a different profession; similar levels of job dissatisfaction are found in other professions as well. So, even when "successful" financially, the price paid for making conventional career choices often is very high.

Although most people opt to pursue conventional careers for the security such paths seem to provide, these careers often are not secure at all. The 1980s and 1990s saw many large companies—including IBM, once the safest job choice of all—downsize and lay off hundreds of thousands of workers. Corporate mergers had the same impact on jobs and careers. Dot-com companies flew high in the late 1990s, then hit a wall in 2000. More recently, corporate accounting scandals left tens of thousands of employees without jobs and without pensions. The "smart money" choices often are just not as safe and secure as they seem. Risk and chance can't be removed from the equation, so why not choose to do something you really believe in? Aim high, pursue your ideals, because when you love what you do, you are capable of more than you think. Work hard and persevere, even when you encounter failure, which everyone does at some point. Perseverance and commitment are essential to success. When I coached basketball and soccer, I used to say that when you throw the ball, make a pass, or shoot the ball, do it with purpose and commitment. There is no rubber band attached to the ball. If you take a shot or throw a pass without committing to it, it's not going to work, and you can't pull it back. Halfhearted efforts just don't work. Everyone I know who has been committed to his/her own path, has been successful—financially as well as personally. Not everyone has become multimillionaires, but each one has lived a life of sufficient income to be comfortable, and have fulfilling careers.

HAVE CONFIDENCE IN YOURSELF and your own game plan. The biggest mistake I've seen lawyers make is to overemphasize the problems in their cases. As trial approaches, the weaknesses of their cases loom larger and more important, lawyers lose sight of the strength of their cases, and they begin the process of talking themselves out of trying the case and into settlement—often a poor settlement. They seem to think they should have a flawless case, but the flawless case doesn't exist—at least I've never seen one. Every case has problems and weaknesses.

I didn't obsess about the problems in my cases. I tried to keep in mind why I took the case, the things that moved and motivated me. I felt if I could explain the strengths of my case, the judge or jury wouldn't be very bothered by the weaknesses. They would accept my explanations, or find explanations of their own for the weak links in the evidence. The strengths would dominate the weaknesses.

One of my greatest heroes—John Wooden, former UCLA basketball coach—told me a story that provided perfect corroboration of this attitude. In 1989, I attended a three-day basketball camp taught by John Wooden, who was the greatest basketball coach in history—the coach who set a record that never will be broken in winning ten NCAA national basketball championships in twelve years, including seven in a row. Wooden was not only the greatest basketball coach, he is a tremendously wise man. The camp didn't just carry Wooden's famous name, he was present everyday, all day and into the evenings to provide instruction, tell stories and answer questions. One evening, we were doing a "chalk talk" with Wooden and some of his former UCLA players, and I asked the question, "When you had a big game coming up, like an NCAA championship game, how did you scout the opposition?" "Oh, I didn't scout the opposition," Wooden said, "I wasn't really worried about the other team. I always felt that if my boys played their game well, we would win." Now, John Wooden wasn't saying that he ignored the other team—indeed, he was a master at making adjustments during a game—but his emphasis was on playing to his own team's strengths. A legal case, in my opinion, is exactly the same. The same is true in any career or life choice: know your strengths, play to your strengths, don't obsess or be defeated by your weaknesses.

Wooden said something else that was truly counterintuitive, but that resonated with my own experiences. He said, "I always told my boys, 'the team that makes the most mistakes will win.' " He explained this as follows: "Most coaches teach their players not to make mistakes. They emphasize caution and carefulness. But that makes a team slow, rigid, unimaginative, tight—they're trying too hard not to make mistakes. I didn't want my boys to play like that. I wanted them to be aggressive, take risks, push the tempo of the game. The team playing an aggressive, up-tempo style of basketball will make more mistakes than the slow, cautious team that takes no risks, but my team will control the tempo of the game, use their athleticism, and win." That statement encapsulates so much for me: how to practice law, how to make career choices, how to not fear failure, how to live a satisfying, successful life, and it is equally relevant and powerful outside of basketball and law.

I used to tell my lawyers, "We are aggressive in our selection of cases, but we practice an aggressive style of law. I expect you to make mistakes. I think I made about every mistake a lawyer can make. Just learn from your mistakes, accept responsibility for them, and try not to repeat the same one too many times. Try to make new mistakes!" I wanted to enhance, not undermine, their confidence and willingness to take risks.

I WORKED HARD AS A LAWYER. No successful lawyer doesn't work hard. But I always kept balance in my life. I coached my kids' soccer teams for ten years—three practices a week, plus one or two weekend games. I'd be so busy at the office, meeting my kids across town at 3:30 p.m. would seem impossible, but I would go anyway. I was not only a better person and parent for doing it, I was a better lawyer because of it. Because kids, family, hobbies, and activities provide variety, perspective and balance that we all need, especially lawyers. I tried to eat a healthy diet and exercise every day. Even if I only had time to ride a bike to work, play forty-five minutes of rac-quetball or basketball at a nearby gym, or just pump iron for fif-teen to twenty minutes, it was important to do it. Exercise cleared my head and *created* energy when I returned to my desk. People who try to save time by not exercising or eating well and let their bodies fall apart have less energy, more health problems, more time off work, and live shorter, more stressful, and less productive lives.

Jeanine and I never missed our "date" on Saturday nights no matter how busy we were, even when I was living inside the tunnel of a trial. Because no matter how important our work was, we didn't forget to have fun together. Waiting for the kids to grow up, to pay off the mortgage, to achieve career goals, before taking time to have fun is a prescription for forgetting how to have fun. Life is a jour-ney, and you need to enjoy the journey with family all along the way. As a family, we took at least one weekend trip together every month, rain or shine. Most of our trips were in the outdoors and most cost virtually nothing—backpacking, hiking, canoeing, cross-country skiing. We both needed this concentrated time with the kids, and time outdoors in beautiful environments, but most of all we needed this time for ourselves. We never thought we did enough, but people would constantly tell us, "I don't understand how you have time to take so many trips." You make time. You create bal-ance. And the balance you create in your life helps with everything you do, including your career.

LEARN TO WALK in the other person's shoes. I think this is absolutely the hardest thing for most people to do. It is just too seductive and easy to become so wrapped up in your own point of view that other perspectives and opinions get discounted, ignored, or worse, treated as evil. I saw this powerfully in my law practice. Even though I was prosecuting cases under various civil rights acts that had legiti-mate and well-accepted purposes—and usually had powerful sta-tistics to support the claims of unlawful discrimination—many defense attorneys and their clients treated me as the Great Satan, an arrogant interloper into their company's business. "We've been running this business successfully for fifty years. We're not going to let some plaintiffs' attorney from Oakland tell us what to do," was often their attitude. Legitimate disputes that should have led to early searches for solutions became moral crusades; attitude and self-righteousness took over and negotiated solutions became difficult.

What is required to break through that unproductive cycle is neutrality—the ability to try to look at things from your opponent's perspective, the ability to step back and ask, "Why is he or she acting like that? What is he or she trying to protect? Does he or she have any legitimate interests to preserve?" By looking at disputes from my opponent's perspective, I often found that he or she did have some interests that were legitimate and deserving of respect; I also saw that some legitimate goals he or she had could be accomplished in different ways—ways that could accommodate the interests of my clients. Busting up the network of nepotism and cronyism that exists in so many corporations and opening up employment opportunities to a more diverse group of employees, for example, is a win-win situation. The employer increases competition for its jobs and gets to select from a broader and more qualified selection pool, and women, racial minorities, older persons, and disabled workers get more opportunities to be hired and promoted. And, when you try to understand your opponent's point of view, you create credibility for yourself and disarm opposition to your ideas, for if you are willing to try to understand the opponent they often will be more willing to listen to you.

We see the consequence of people failing to do this all the time. We see politicians stating their opinions in ways that fail to acknowledge, let alone intelligently respond to, their opponent's position; the opponent does the same, and the result is two sides talking past one another, not listening to or talking to each other, not dealing with the real issues that separate them, just endless loud posturing. This makes the disputants feel good and leaves their sense of self-righteousness intact, but with the lack of communication creates intransigence and deadlock. Politicians are enjoying themselves and their implacable attitudes, but nothing gets solved and rancor and alienation increase. As I said, it's not easy to try to look at the world from your opponent's perspective—it's just much more effective.

No MATTER HOW IDEALISTIC a lawyer may be, it is important to understand the business and financial aspects of a legal practice. The same is true for all professions.

When I began private law practice, the public interest bar was full of lawyers who wanted to follow their ideals representing people and causes the legal profession had ignored. Many were excellent lawyers, but most were woefully unprepared to handle the financial aspects of a public interest practice. As time went on, most abandoned their public interest cases and gravitated toward conventional types of law practices, where it was easier to get paid for their time, and where payment was hourly, not contingent on success in their cases. Many of these lawyers had what I call the "legal aid mentality"—the idea that it was inappropriate to demand fees or be paid well for their work. I know the "legal aid mentality" well; I was a legal aid lawyer for two years, and when I began my private practice, I usually charged inadequate fees from my clients, and often apologized for charging anything at all. I sent out the signal that I wasn't serious about getting paid, and many clients took advantage of me by not paying at all. I did trials for 50 cents or less an hour, and greatly undervalued myself in my first Title VII case against Trans International Airlines, as I discussed earlier. As I saw other public interest attorneys fall away from public interest legal fights due to the risk and delay of payment, and the often heavy investment of time and expenses required, I knew that if I wanted to survive doing public interest cases, I would have to learn how to be paid reasonable fees. If I couldn't obtain reasonable fees doing civil rights cases, I knew that I, like other public interest attorneys, would face the prospect of spending a career doing smaller cases that would have less impact. I didn't want that to happen.

So I began to learn from successful antitrust and securities lawyers how to obtain reasonable fees in substantial class action cases. And, I adopted a different attitude about fees. I was beginning to realize I was as good an attorney—and often better—than the defense attorneys I was confronting, and beating. Why should their hourly rates be higher than mine? Paying civil rights lawyers at lesser hourly rates devalued not only their legal work, but the importance of civil rights cases as well. Corporate attorneys were being paid substantial hourly rates for doing private legal work that often was not very important, other than to the client—writing wills, planning estates, drafting contracts, etc. Why should a civil rights attorney doing cases that favorably impact hundreds, and often thousands of people, be paid at lower rates?

I abandoned the "legal aid mentality" and refused to be called a "pro bono" lawyer. "Pro bono" lawyers are lawyers that do volunteer work as an adjunct to their regular law practice; they made money and did an occasional "pro bono" case on a charity basis. This is certainly a worthy thing to do and lawyers who do "pro bono" work are to be commended, but I didn't want to make my living writing wills or doing divorces, then take an occasional public interest case, so long as it didn't take too much of my time and cut too deeply into fee-generating practice. I wanted to do civil rights cases *as a career*. I wanted civil rights cases to represent 100% of my caseload and I wanted to be able to do this as long as I practiced law. And I wanted to be able to hire top-flight lawyers and build a firm that would be financially capable of taking on large class actions against major corporations and not have to fold up cases for lack of funds.

In my fee applications, I began to argue to judges that if they continued to pay civil rights lawyers at lower rates, the civil rights bar eventually would be limited to younger, less-experienced lawyers, or "pro bono" lawyers doing an occasional civil rights case. Neither of these types of lawyers would be able to do large class actions—the young lawyers because they would not have sufficient legal experience or resources, and the "pro bono" lawyers because they would not be willing to commit sufficient time to large cases. I began to set my hourly rate at the same rates the first-line defense firms used for lawyers with comparable experience, supporting my fee requests with affidavits from prominent corporate lawyers testifying to legal marketplace rates and where I stood in that marketplace. Eventually I set my hourly rates higher than the best corporate defense firms on the theory that I had become a class action employment specialist and had more experience in those kind of cases than even the high-priced corporate attorneys. By the early 1990s, I had one of the highest hourly rates in California, yet not a single judge—Republican, Democrat, left-wing, right-wing—ever once cut my hourly rate below what I requested. They accepted me as a good lawyer doing important cases and didn't put me in the category "civil rights lawyer—OK to pay less." They learned to put civil rights lawyers on the same plane as other types of lawyers doing complex cases.

I also argued that lawyers doing public interest cases on a contingent fee basis deserved to be compensated for the risk of losing the case and for the delay in receipt of payment—which often was five years or more. I surveyed lawyers in a wide range of types of legal practices and determined that, in the legal marketplace, lawyers adjusted their fees upward by a factor of at least two when they did work on a contingent basis. I presented this evidence to the judges I was practicing before, who had to rule on my fee requests, and began to obtain a long list of "2.0 multipliers," meaning our regular hourly rates were being doubled when we won.

As I began to become successful in my fee applications, I began to receive criticism from other public interest lawyers. Some of this criticism emanated from jealousy, some from the "legal aid mentality" that thought it was inherently suspicious for public interest attorneys to be well paid, some from people who thought I must be selling out my cases to obtain high fees. I recall one annual luncheon of Equal Rights Advocates—a fine women's public interest law firm I supported—where a prominent African-American female civil rights lawyer openly criticized me for obtaining high fees. I reminded her of a conversation we had had a few months earlier riding back from federal court together on BART (Bay Area Rapid Transit). She told me how difficult prosecuting civil rights class actions had been, the financial strain that had been caused by "cash flow" problems (i.e., not being paid for years) and how the payment she ultimately received for the case was insufficient to compensate her for the years of delayed payment and the anxiety created by the possibility she might lose the case and not get paid at all. "This is my last class action," she had told me, "I'll never do another." Indeed, shortly after this conversation, I accepted a new case representing an African-American manager of the Oakland Convention Center who had been fired, and who should I find representing the defendant but this same lawyer!

So, at the Equal Rights Advocates luncheon, I reminded her of our conversation, and told her: "I never would criticize you for working on the defense side, or abandoning plaintiff class actions. We all have families to support and we do what we have to do. But the reason you are not doing plaintiffs' class actions anymore is because you didn't figure out the financial aspects of a civil rights practice. You didn't get paid adequately for your time and the risk and delay of payment. You have no credibility criticizing someone who has figured those issues out. When the next African-American is subjected to discrimination in the workplace, he or she will have to come to me, not you. That is not because I'm necessarily a better lawyer than you. It will be because I have figured out how to make it economically feasible to continue representing plaintiffs in civil rights cases. And as for your veiled suggestion that I've traded class remedies for high attorneys' fees, I will put my case results up against your results, and anyone else's results, because I know I'm obtaining more complete relief for my clients than you or anyone else. Fees never have been traded for class remedies and demands to be paid substantial fees—demands that have to be approved by federal judges—do not undercut class relief. You need to be tough on both issues." The other lawyers at the table were surprised by the openness of this dispute, but I never backed off my position: public interest lawyers deserve to be paid well, and if they aren't, in the long run, many will find other types of legal work.

Whether I convinced this particular attorney or not, as time went on and my attorneys' fees awards matched the results we were getting for the classes we represented, private and public interest lawyers began to hire me to represent them in their applications for awards of attorneys' fees and costs, and I developed a side practice of doing attorneys' fees litigations for other law firms, nearly always in civil rights, consumer, or environmental cases. I even was hired by several large corporate firms to litigate their fees applications in public interest cases they had taken on a "pro bono" basis. My successes in this area enabled many fine lawyers to continue to represent plaintiffs in public interest cases, as well as encourage more lawyers to do employment, consumer and environmental cases. I never wanted to be the only well-paid public interest lawyer; I always felt that "a rising tide should lift all."

Developing an infrastructure to support our litigation also was vital to our success. We grew from two attorneys and no employees to 44 attorneys and 165 employees, and had to modernize and reinvent the firm at every level of growth, both in terms of hiring qualified support personnel and keeping on the cutting edge of technology. We invested heavily in computers, even when it was difficult to afford them, junking our existing system and totally replacing it with new equipment, more terminals, and more memory every two to three years. I'd argue with Helen Thompson, my office administrator for twelve years, "We haven't even paid off the system we bought 28 months ago, and now you're telling me that system is junk, worthless, and must be replaced?" But Helen did her homework, made her case, and won those arguments every time, convincing me that we could be faster and more efficient with the best technology. Soon every lawyer, paralegal and case clerk had terminals at their desks and at their homes, and we were faster, more efficient, and a better law firm.

DESPITE MY COMPLAINTS ABOUT how corporate litigators sometimes delay and multiply litigation, I encourage people to become lawyers, if they have that interest. Law, particularly trial practice, is an inherently interesting profession. It is interesting because it is about people, and people are interesting. Moreover, a trial lawyer encounters, and must learn to relate to, all types of people. One day, I could be preparing someone with less than a high school education for a deposition; the next day, I might be at Stanford talking to the Chair of the Economics Department about constructing a multiple regression analysis as an exhibit in a class action case, and for the purposes of that case I might have to know as much about regression analyses as the university professor. Likewise, judges and jurors span the range of human experience, and you must learn how to communicate with all types of people effectively to be successful as a trial lawyer.

And law, as an intellectual enterprise, is fascinating and complex. Lawyers are ingenious in constructing new arguments, new analogies, new ways of looking at the same words in the constitution or a statute, and new laws are being enacted by legislatures, and new cases decided by appellate courts, every day. It is challenging just to keep up with so much dynamic change.

I think the most fun I ever had practicing law were those times I was confronted with problems or situations I never had seen before, times I wasn't sure what the issue was or what was expected of me, and the only thing I had to support myself were my wits and accumulated experiences. Learning how to understand, control and dominate, even in strange and unfamiliar situations, was the most fun and challenging part of all. Being a litigator provides many such opportunities and challenges.

I've always said I was *practicing* law, emphasizing the word "practicing," because that is what it is. It is too complex to master completely. We get better with practice, but we never get it perfect. I always wanted to do a case perfectly, but I realized that was impossible. I could get better with practice, but I couldn't be perfect. Litigating a case is too complex to fit all pieces perfectly into the puzzle without making at least a few mistakes. It is, and will remain, a great and challenging profession. For those who like dealing with people, ideas, and challenges as well as having an opportunity to have an impact on society, law is a great choice.

For me and my interests, another great choice would have been journalism. I once co-owned a ski cabin in the Sierras with my original law partner, Chuck Farnsworth. We were driving up to the cabin on an icy, slick road, when a Cadillac ahead of us slid off the road and went down a steep embankment. The car traveled fifty to sixty feet down the hillside, and hung up on a rock overhang, preventing it from going into the river and almost certain death for the driver. We scrambled down to meet the driver climbing out of the car and found him shaken, but unhurt. As soon as he was seated and resting, I asked, "Tell me, what went through your mind the moment you went over the edge and realized you were headed into the river?" I think Chuck wanted to kill me for asking such a harsh and unsympathetic question, but isn't that what people really want to know about someone who's lived through such an experience? When we got home and told the story to Chuck's journalist wife, she said, "That is the mind of a journalist." Law suited me well as a career, but I think I would have enjoyed journalism for many of the same reasons I enjoyed law—the chance to deal with a wide variety of people, to see how people behave under pressure and stress, the chance to influence people.

I was particularly fortunate to have become a lawyer at such a fortuitous time in American history. The Civil Rights Act of 1964 had just been enacted, and made effective on July 2, 1965, providing new and expanded opportunities to prosecute civil rights actions in federal court, and supported by an attorneys' fees provision allowing for awards of fees to prevailing parties. The great career I had would not have been possible without this legislation.

This legislation continues to be available to attorneys interested in prosecuting civil rights actions, and there are many more lawyers doing such cases now than there were when I began in 1969. And the 1970s saw many state and federal laws passed to protect the environment and consumers, most of which provide attorneys' fees provisions similar to the civil rights laws. The opportunities for lawyers to work on behalf of the environment, consumers, and civil rights as litigators are greater today than ever before.

MY LEGAL CAREER WAS SUCCESSFUL beyond my imagination, providing me wealth and satisfaction. I've received awards, been included for many years in the National Law Journal's list of "The 100 Most Influential Lawyers in America," won billions for clients and millions for myself, but, in my mind, my career achievements rank below maintaining a joyous marriage with a marvelous and special woman for thirty-five years, raising two sons, and helping to raise our niece, Unmi.

When I was contemplating retiring from the full-time practice of law, my youngest son, Jacobus, sent me this letter:

Hey Dad,

Your family will support you down either road you choose, but you didn't really need me to tell you that. Remember that talk we had over the phone when you were out in Utah, well I really enjoyed it, I feel so fortunate to have the father that I do, and to have the relationship that we do. I feel so fortunate because I think about how many children don't even know their father or can't talk to them and we can have a two-hour plus talk and have it feel like five minutes. I hold this higher than anything one could possibly have. I could never repay you for this, I only hope to be as good of a father to my son or daughter as you have been to me. Out of all your landmark and much celebrated accomplishments in life, I think raising your two sons has been the greatest of them all!

Love,
Jacobus

Shortly thereafter, I received a birthday card and poem from Leon, my oldest son:

> Dear Dad,
>
> *Attitude is everything ... and you definitely have an attitude! But,
> of course, a positive one...*
>
> I want you to know that I value you as a father.
>
> Not for what you have given us,
>   but that's nice.
> Not for what you have done for us,
>   but that's nice,
> Not for what you have taught us,
>   but that's nice,
> Not for what you have shown us,
>   but that's nice.
> It is that you have done all these
> Not to fulfill your dreams,
> But to help fulfill ours.
>
> *For this I love you always, Leon*

These two letters mean more to me than all my achievements in law.

IN YOUR PURSUIT OF A MEANINGFUL CAREER, never forget your family. Never forget to put balance in your life. Have confidence in yourself, don't let fear dictate your choices, pursue your ideals, and persevere with the choices you make. Follow your heart and your best ideals, and you will have a career, and a life, more satisfying than you ever imagined.

Acknowledgments

Growing up with a stern and demanding father is never easy for a son, particularly when that son tends toward the independent and rebellious. Writing this book has helped me better understand the positive side of the lessons I learned from my father, and how those lessons were integral to my success.

My mother was an angel and from her I learned compassion for the underdog and the joy of living every day. I doubt I ever would have become a civil rights lawyer without the example her life provided, or enjoyed life so much.

It is perhaps expecting more than one is entitled to live a life adorned by two angels, but my wife, Jeanine, is my second angel. It is no wonder why she and my mother were so in love with each other. The only question is why they loved me so much. Jeanine shared and supported all the risks I took in my career and I could not have been successful without that support.

Our two sons, Leon and Jacobus, and our adopted niece, Unmi, who Jeanine and I helped raise, provided me a constant source of balance and joy during my legal career. They still do.

I thank my sister, Tina, for suffering my teasing, but, more importantly, showing me that girls can be better than boys in many things.

A handful of teachers saw potential in me, despite all evidence to the contrary, and challenged me to use my brain. Foremost among them is Jacobus tenBroek, my Political Science professor at Cal, who changed the direction my life was heading. His influence on me was so powerful we named our second son in his honor. Gladys Howell, my junior high school math teacher, Alice Dawson, my fifth grade teacher, and Mrs. Case, my second grade teacher, demanded more from me than any of my teachers. I needed more like them.

I am grateful to those classmates who helped me survive law school: Paul Harris, Barbara Rhine, Eric Seitz, Brian Sax, Tom Wilson, Ted Akulian, Steve Bingham, George Mason, and David Pesonen. Without their humor and commiseration, it is likely that one of those times I said, "This is total bullshit," would have found me packing up and leaving.

It is not possible for any one attorney to have prosecuted the large class actions described in this book; each case, and each success, was the product of the work of many fine attorneys, paralegals, case clerks, and support staff. I especially want to acknowledge former law partners: Charles E. Farnsworth, whose sense-of-humor and willingness to tackle any kind of case helped sustain the firm through the early lean years; Jeff Brand, who conducted the State Farm class action trial with me; Barry Goldstein, whose assistance in the State Farm claim procedure was so valuable; and, Brad Seligman, whose brilliance and pugnacity was a constant source of enjoyment.

Helen Thompson, my office administrator, played a special role in my law firm's success. She forced it to modernize computer systems, which helped equalize combat with large corporations. For twelve years, she also provided the kind of loyalty and dedication that money cannot buy.

I am grateful for the chance to have met and litigated against some of the best employment lawyers in the country—Tom Powers, Gil Diekmann, Larry Currey, Bruce Nelson and Steve Tallent. Each demonstrated in their legal practices that not all corporate defense attorneys need be thugs and bullies and that it was possible to represent employers with intelligence and integrity.

I also am grateful for the opportunity to have worked before many fine judges. My personal Judges Hall of Fame includes the Honorable Charles B. Renfrew, the Honorable Thelton E. Henderson, the Honorable Marilyn Hall Patel, the Honorable Eugene F. Lynch, the Honorable Michael Ballachey, and the Honorable Daniel Weinstein—each a great public servant and an interesting person.

This book was conceived at an Oakland Athletics baseball game, when Jane Anne Staw, a very fine author, after years of listening to me tell stories about my cases, demanded that I show up at her office the following Saturday promptly at 10 a.m. "to start taping those stories." Her prodding me to write made this book happen and her criticisms and edits made it a better read. I thank Jane Anne for her help, her friendship, and for allowing me to help mentor her very talented son, Jonah.